World Intellectual Property Indicators 2023

WIPO
WORLD
INTELLECTUAL PROPERTY
ORGANIZATION

Suggested citation: World Intellectual Property Organization (WIPO) (2023). *World Intellectual Property Indicators 2023.* Geneva: WIPO. DOI: 10.34667/tind.48541

First published 2023

World Intellectual Property Organization
34, chemin des Colombettes, P.O. Box 18
CH-1211 Geneva 20, Switzerland

wipo.int

ISBN: 978-92-805-3546-4 (Print)
ISBN: 978-92-805- 3547-1 (Online)
ISSN: 2709-5193 (Print)
ISSN: 2709-5207 (Online)

Cover: WIPO

WIPO Publication No. 941EN/23

Contents

Foreword 4
Acknowledgments 6
Further information 6
Key numbers 7

Patents 8
Highlights 9
Patent statistics 22

Trademarks 65
Highlights 66
Trademark statistics 76

Industrial designs 108
Highlights 109
Industrial design statistics 117

Plant varieties 144
Highlights 145
Plant variety statistics 149

Geographical indications 159
Highlights 160

Creative economy 167
Highlights 168
Creative economy statistics 173

Additional information 184
Data description 185
IP systems at a glance 188
Glossary 193
Abbreviations 201
Annexes 202

Foreword

© Emmanuel Berrod/WIPO

Daren Tang, Director General, World Intellectual Property Organization (WIPO)

This year's *World Intellectual Property Indicators* (WIPI) report reflects the global economic uncertainty that characterized 2022. While countries around the world continued to look toward innovation, creativity, technology, and entrepreneurship, this was set against a global backdrop clouded by rising inflation, a cost-of-living crisis, and tighter monetary supply.

First, the good news. Innovators around the world submitted nearly 3.5 million patent applications last year - a record high. What is notable is the broad geographical base of this growth. Among the top five offices, patent applications at both the IP office of China and the European Patent Office outstripped the global average, with the US returning to growth for the first time since the pandemic. Broaden the lens to the top 20 offices, and we see double-digit increases at the offices of South Africa, India, and Indonesia. For India, this is the sixth year of growth in a row, with patent filings surging by a quarter last year in 2022, the fastest increase since 2005. Notable rises were also recorded at the offices of Algeria, Colombia, Türkiye, and Saudi Arabia.

Trademark filing has returned to a more regular level after a surge of applications linked to the pandemic. Application class counts declined by 14.5 percent last year. But it must be remembered that the overall trend is still one of growth with over 1.5 times more applications filed in 2022 than 2012. We also record a 2.1 percent decline in the number of designs contained in applications. But again, this should be contextualized against a much longer arc of growth, with applications 20 percent above what they were ten years ago.

Beyond the year-to-year figures, the impact of new technologies on IP filings continues as a long-term trend. Even in 2021, when countries around the world were battling the pandemic, patent applications in computer technology grew by 11 percent to around 380,000. This is close to three times the level of 10 years ago, with computing growing faster than any of the other major technology field. Research and technology was found to be the most popular filing sector by applicants seeking trademark protection abroad. All in all, digital technology related IP filings continue to power ahead, despite the backdrop pf global uncertainty.

As governments and businesses navigate this clouded environment, we hope that the insights that stem from the report's rich dataset will serve not only as a robust reference guide, but as a practical tool for strengthening IP systems and supporting innovation and creativity the world over. This is WIPI's true strength, and why we are deeply grateful to Member States and our partners across 150 national and regional IP offices for their continued support of this unique and agenda-setting report on the global IP landscape.

Acknowledgments

World Intellectual Property Indicators 2023 was prepared under the direction of Daren Tang (Director General) in the IP and Innovation Ecosystems Sector led by Marco Aleman (Assistant Director General), and supervised by Carsten Fink (Chief Economist). The report was prepared by Kyle Bergquist, Mosahid Khan, Ryan Lamb, Bruno Le Feuvre and Hao Zhou, all from the Department for Economics and Data Analytics. Peter Button, Yolanda Huerta-Casado and Ariane Besse of the International Union for the Protection of New Varieties of Plants (UPOV) provided comments and suggestions for the plant varieties section. Alexandra Grazioli, Matteo Gragnani and Anouck Jezequel of the Brands and Designs Sector provided comments and suggestions for the geographical indications section. Gratitude is also owed to Enrico Turrin of the Federation of the European Publishers for sharing some of the creative economy data.

Samiah Do Carmo Figueiredo and Jovana Stojanović provided administrative support. Gratitude is also owed to the Information and Digital Outreach Division for the editing and design and to staff in the Printing Plant for their services.

Further information

Online resources

The electronic version of this report and the underlying data can be downloaded at www.wipo.int/ipstats. This webpage also provides a link to the IP Statistics Data Center, offering access to WIPO's statistical data.

Contact information

Statistics and Data Analytics Division
Website: www.wipo.int/ipstats
e-mail: ipstats.mail@wipo.int

Key numbers

IP filing activity by office

Patents	2021	2022	Growth rate (%)	Share of world total (%)
Applications worldwide	**3,400,500**	**3,457,400**	**1.7**	**100.0**
China	1,585,663	1,619,268	2.1	46.8
US	591,473	594,340	0.5	17.2
Japan	289,200	289,530	0.1	8.4
Utility models				
Applications worldwide	**2,924,420**	**3,010,510**	**2.9**	**100.0**
China	2,852,219	2,950,653	3.5	98.0
Germany	10,576	9,469	-10.5	0.3
Russian Federation	9,079	8,521	-6.1	0.3
Trademarks				
Application class counts worldwide	**18,182,300**	**15,543,300**	**-14.5**	**100.0**
China	9,454,735	7,513,504	-20.5	48.3
US	899,499	767,375	-14.7	4.9
India	488,459	500,305	2.4	3.2
Industrial designs				
Application design counts worldwide	**1,513,800**	**1,482,600**	**-2.1**	**100.0**
China	805,710	798,112	-0.9	53.8
EUIPO (EU office)	117,049	109,132	-6.8	7.4
Türkiye	65,924	84,111	27.6	5.7
Plant varieties				
Applications worldwide	**25,200**	**27,260**	**8.2**	**100.0**
China	11,195	13,027	16.4	47.8
Community Plant Variety Office (EU)	3,480	3,193	-8.2	11.7
UK	409	1,702	316.1	6.2

Source: WIPO Statistics Database, August 2023.

Patents

Highlights

In 2022, innovators from around the world submitted a record-breaking 3.46 million patent applications – the highest number of filings ever recorded

In 2022, innovators worldwide filed 3.46 million patent applications, marking a 1.7% increase over 2021 (figure 1.1). Following a 3% decline in 2019, patent applications globally have risen for three consecutive years, with growth rates of 1.5% in 2020, 3.6% in 2021, and 1.7% in 2022. A substantial rise in filings by China, which made 33,605 more applications than it did in 2021, combined with robust contributions from the intellectual property (IP) office of India (15,495 additional applications), South Africa (+3,030) and the European Patent Office (EPO) (+4,832), was the main driver of growth in 2022. The IP offices of Saudi Arabia (+1,858) and the United States Patent and Trademark Office (USPTO) (+2,867) also made notable contributions to overall growth.

Patent applications filed worldwide grew by 1.7% in 2022, marking a third consecutive year of growth

1.1. Patent applications worldwide, 2008–2022

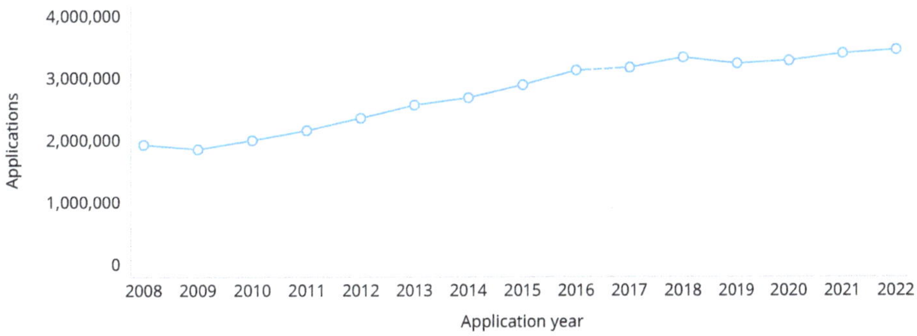

Source: Figure A1.

Worldwide filing of 3.46 million applications comprised 2.41 million resident filings (69.7% of the total) and 1.05 million non-resident filings (30.3%). Since a 2.3% decrease at the peak of the COVID-19 pandemic in 2020, non-resident filings have gron 4.7% in 2021 and 3.1% in 2022. Resident filings, however, only increased by a modest 1.1% in 2022, significantly below the growth rates observed in 2020 (+3.2%) and 2021 (+3.1%).

The long-term trend in global patent applications has consistently been upward. Applications doubled from around 1 million in 1995 to approximately 2 million by 2010, and reached the 3.5 million mark in 2022. It is notable that a substantial surge in resident filings within China has contributed to a significant drop in the global share of non-resident filings, which have decreased from 39.8% in 2008 to 30.3% in 2022 (figure A2).

The IP office of China received 46.8% of global patent applications in 2022

The National Intellectual Property Administration of the People's Republic of China (CNIPA) received 1.6 million patent applications in 2022, up 2.1% on 2021.[1] Since 2015, CNIPA has consistently received over a million applications annually. The USPTO – with 594,340 applications – ranked second, followed by the Japan Patent Office (JPO) (289,530), the Korean Intellectual Property Office (KIPO) (237,633) and the EPO (193,610) (figure 1.2). Together, these top five offices accounted for 84.9% of the world total in 2022, 5.3 percentage points higher than their combined share a decade earlier in 2012. This is entirely due to an unprecedented growth in filings within China. China's share of the world total has risen from 27.7% in 2012 to 46.8% in 2022. In contrast, every other office within the top five has experienced a decrease in share during the same period; for instance, USPTO's share has declined from 23% to 17.2% over the past decade.

The composition and the ranking of the top 10 offices globally remained unchanged between 2021 and 2022. Similarly, the list of IP offices occupying 11th to 20th position has remained the same, albeit with slight differences in the rankings. Notably, in 2022, South Africa, Israel and Indonesia moved up one spot to 17th, 18th and 19th, respectively, while Italy dropped three places to 20th (figure A7). Among top 20 offices, there is a substantial variation in the origin of applications (figure A7). For example, non-resident applicants accounted for nine out of every 10 applications received by the IP offices of Australia; China, Hong Kong SAR; and Mexico. In contrast, only around one in 10 applications received by the IP offices of China, France and Italy was a non-resident application. The resident versus non-resident distribution was more or less even at the EPO, the IP office of India and the USPTO.

Non-resident applicants accounted for 57.5% of total applications filed in the US, but only 9.6% in China

1.2. Patent applications at the top 10 offices, 2022

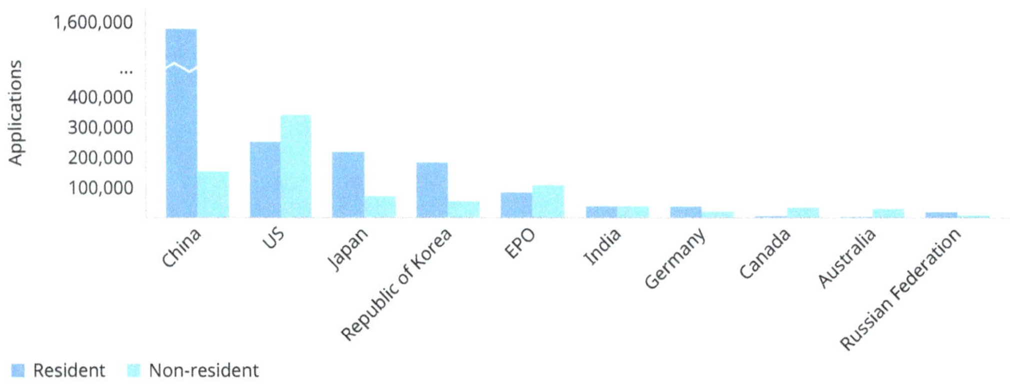

Source: Figure A7.

Among top five offices, China registered strong growth in filings for a third successive year, while the EPO recorded a second straight year of growth. Filings in China grew by 2.1% in 2022, following an increase of 5.9% in 2021 and 6.9% in 2020. The EPO received 2.6% more applications in 2022, compared to a 4.7% growth in 2021. The USPTO (+0.5%) returned to modest growth in 2022 following a decline in the previous two years. Japan's filing level for 2022 is similar to the year before (+0.1%). However, after having experienced four successive years of growth, the Republic of Korea's filings dropped by 0.2% drop in 2022.

A majority of top 20 offices – 13 out of 20 – received a greater number of patent applications in 2022 than in 2021 (figure A8). Among the biggest increases were those at the offices of South

1 Patent applications data refer to invention patents and do not include utility model (UM) applications. UM applications data are reported separately (see figures A53–55). In the United States of America, invention patents are referred to as "utility patents," which should not be confused with utility models.

Africa (+27.6%), India (+25.2%) and Indonesia (+13.3%) – each office reporting double-digit growth. In the cases of Indonesia and South Africa, this marked a second consecutive year of growth, with an increase in non-resident filings driving the overall growth for 2022. India, on the other hand, experienced a sixth straight year of growth, 2022's 25.2% increase being the sharpest since 2005. A substantial increase in resident filings was the main driver of growth overall in 2022.

Seven top 20 offices received fewer applications in 2022 than in 2021, with Italy experiencing a decline of –16.8%, and the Russian Federation (–13.1%) and China, Hong Kong SAR (–8.1%) also reporting significant drops. Australia (–0.4%), France (–0.1%), Germany (–2.3%) and the Republic of Korea (–0.2%) observed a modest decrease in applications in 2022.

Looking beyond the top 20 offices to selected offices of low- and middle-income countries shows that the offices of the Islamic Republic of Iran (8,681), Thailand (8,607), Türkiye (9,119) and Viet Nam (8,707) each received over 8,000 applications in 2022 (figure A9). Algeria (+31.7%) and Colombia (+32.6%) reported the fastest growth in 2022, with a substantial increase in resident filings the main driver of overall growth at both offices. A majority of the selected low- and middle-income country offices reported in figure A10 received more applications in 2022 than in 2021. Non-resident filings were the primary contributor to total growth at all these offices, apart from Algeria, Colombia, the Syrian Arab Republic and Türkiye.

Among the three regional offices, the African Regional Intellectual Property Organization (ARIPO) saw growth of 4.8% and the Eurasian Patent Organization (EAPO) a growth of 2.4% in filings, whereas the African Intellectual Property Organization (OAPI) received 10.3% fewer applications in 2022 compared to a year earlier.

In 2022, offices located in Asia received around 68% of patent applications filed globally, marking an increase of 11.9 percentage points on their share a decade earlier in 2012.

Offices located in Asia received approximately 2.35 million applications in 2022, constituting 67.9% of the world total (figure 1.3). This is to be expected considering that three of the top five offices to have received the most patent applications in 2022 are located in Asia. Over the course of a decade, Asia's share of total applications filed globally has surged from 56.1% in 2012 to 67.9% in 2022. This has been mostly due to robust filing growth in China, which contributed 68.9% of all applications filed within the Asian region during 2022.

Both Europe and North America have seen a significant decline in their shares over the past decade. North America's share has decreased from 24.5% in 2012 to 18.3% in 2022, while Europe's has fallen by 4.4 percentage points down to 10.3% over the same period. The combined share for Africa, Latin America and the Caribbean (LAC) and Oceania stood at 3.5% in 2022, 1.2 percentage points lower than in 2012.

Offices located in Asia received around 68% of patent applications filed worldwide in 2022

1.3. Patent applications by region, 2012 and 2022

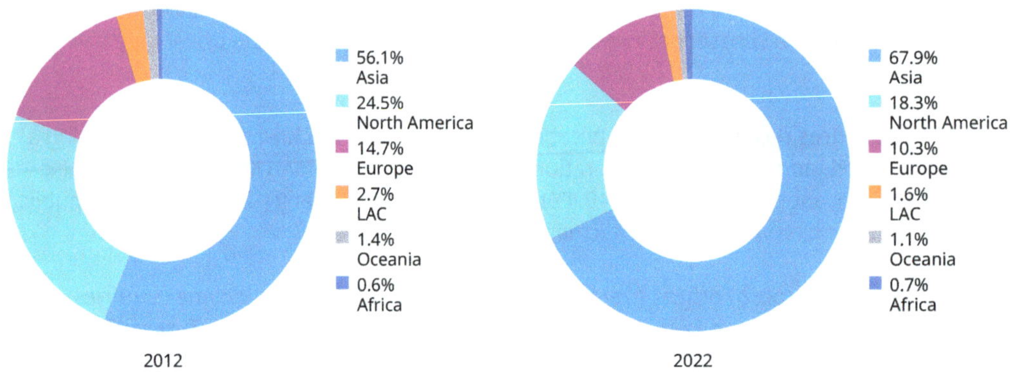

Source: Table A5.

Patent filings since 1883

From 1883 to 1963, the patent office of the United States of America (US) was the world's leading office for patent filings. Application numbers in Japan and the US remained stable until the early 1970s, at which time Japan began to undergo rapid growth – a pattern later observed for the US from the 1980s onward. Among the top five offices, Japan surpassed the US in 1968 and retained top position until 2005. Since the early 2000s, however, the number of applications filed in Japan has followed a downward trend. China surpassed the EPO and the Republic of Korea in 2005, Japan in 2010 and the US in 2011, and now receives the most applications worldwide. There has been a gradual upward trend in the top five offices' combined share of the world total – climbing from 79.6% in 2012 to 84.9% in 2022.

Trend in patent applications for the top five offices, 1883–2022

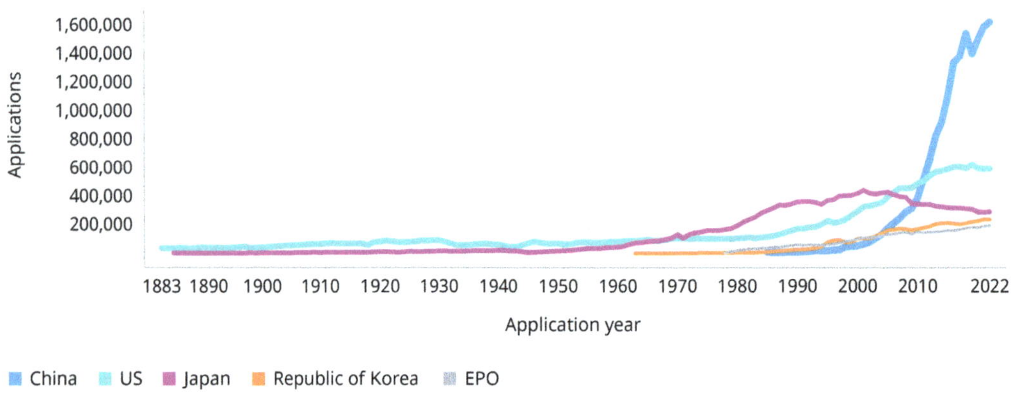

Source: Figure A6.

US applicants accounted for the largest proportion of total non-resident filings made at 14 of the top 20 offices

Applications received by offices from resident and non-resident applicants are referred to as office data, whereas applications filed by applicants at a national or regional office (resident applications) or at a foreign office (applications abroad) are referred to as origin data. Patent statistics based on the origin of residence of the first named applicant are reported in order to complement the picture of patent activity worldwide. Data by origin can be calculated based on either absolute count (an application filed at a regional office is counted once) or equivalent count (an application filed at a regional office is counted multiple times).

In terms of absolute count, applicants from China filed around 1.58 million patent applications worldwide in 2022 (resident plus abroad filings). China was followed by the United States of America (US) (505,539), Japan (405,361), the Republic of Korea (272,315) and Germany (155,896) (figure A17). China (+3.1%), the Republic of Korea (+1.9%) and the US (+1.1%) filed more applications in 2022 than in 2021. In contrast, Germany (–4.8%) and Japan (–1.6%) filed fewer applications in 2022.

In terms of equivalent count, applicants from China filed around 1.59 million equivalent patent applications worldwide in 2022 (resident plus abroad filings). China was followed by the US (515,281), Japan (406,374), the Republic of Korea (272,675) and Germany (157,652) (figure A18). The composition of the top five origins is identical for both absolute and equivalent counts. However, the distribution of resident and abroad filings differs considerably between these five offices. China had by far the lowest share of applications filed abroad, accounting for only 7.7%. In contrast, filings abroad constituted a significant proportion of total applications originating from Germany (60.7%), Japan (46.2%) and the US (51%).

Among top 20 origins, Canada (82.1%), Israel (91.2%) and Switzerland (80.1%) had the largest proportion of total applications filed abroad. Every top 20 origin – presented in figures A17 and A18 – is a high-income country, with the exception of China, India and the Russian Federation. Additionally, a majority of the top 20 origins are European countries. Brazil (6,984) – which has a similar level of filings to Ireland – is the highest ranked origin for the LAC region, while South Africa (2,619) is the top ranked origin for Africa.

Focusing on abroad filings shows US-based applicants filed the most equivalent applications abroad (262,965) in 2022, followed by Japan (187,561), China (121,734), Germany (95,768) and the Republic of Korea (88,927) (figure 1.4). In terms of growth, China (+8.7%), the Republic of Korea (+9.4%) and the US (+6.2%) reported an increase in abroad filings in 2022 compared to 2021, whereas Germany (–4.3%) and Japan (–1.5%) filed fewer such applications over the same period. France (42,145), Switzerland (41,202), the United Kingdom (UK) (37,744), the Kingdom of the Netherlands (24,078) and Sweden (21,344) round out the top 10 rankings for abroad filings.

In 2022, US residents filed over a quarter of a million patent applications abroad

1.4. Patent applications filed abroad by the top 10 origins, 2022

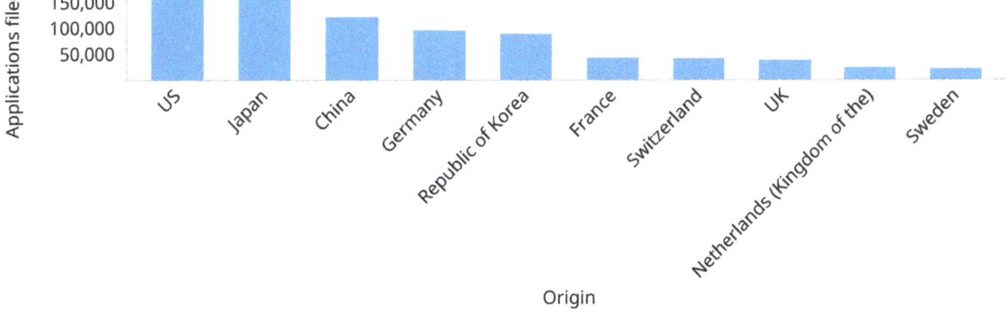

Source: Figure A18.

Analysis of the flow of non-resident applications between origins and offices shows that US applicants accounted for the largest proportion of non-resident filings in 14 of the 20 offices presented in table A19. The proportions ranged from 54.2% at the IP office of Israel to 15.6% at the IP office of Italy. Applicants resident in Japan held the largest non-resident share in four of the 20 offices – namely, China (29.3%), Germany (31.7%), Indonesia (24.5%) and the US (22%). German applicants accounted for 20.6% of all non-resident applications filed in France, while China accounted for 46.7% in South Africa.

Equivalent application count

Applications at regional IP offices are equivalent to multiple applications in countries that are members of the organizations establishing those offices. More particularly, in order to calculate the number of equivalent applications for the African Intellectual Property Organization (OAPI), the Eurasian Patent Organization (EAPO) and the Patent Office of the Cooperation Council for the Arab States of the Gulf (GCC Patent Office), each application needs to be multiplied by the corresponding number of member states. For African Regional Intellectual Property Organization (ARIPO) and the European Patent Office (EPO) data, each application is counted as one application abroad, if the applicant does not reside in a member state, or as one resident application and one application abroad, if the applicant is resident in a member state. The equivalent application concept is used when reporting data by origin.

Republic of Korea residents filed the most patents per GDP and per population in 2022

Variations in patenting activity across countries reflects differences in the size and structure of economies. It is therefore informative to examine resident patent activity with regard to variables such as population, research and development (R&D) spending, and gross domestic product (GDP).

With 7,828 resident patent applications per unit of USD 100 billion GDP, the Republic of Korea continued to be the country filing the most patent applications in 2022 (figure 1.5). Its patent-to-GDP ratio is far above that of second placed China (5,702). Japan (4,200) had the third highest patent-to-GDP ratio, followed by Switzerland (1,645) and Germany (1,374). These five origins have been the top ranking countries since 2018, when the US dropped out of the top five. Finland (1,270), Sweden (1,190), the US (1,170), Denmark (1,054) and the Kingdom of the Netherlands (835) round out the top 10 origins. Among top origins, China has seen a considerable improvement in its resident patent applications-to-GDP ratio, which have increased from 3,812 in 2012 to 5,702 in 2022.

Several countries with a relatively low resident patent application count, including Denmark, Iceland, Luxembourg and Norway, rank among the top 20 origins when resident patent applications are adjusted according to GDP (figure A37). The list of top 20 origins predominantly comprises high-income countries; however, three middle-income countries – China, the Islamic Republic of Iran and the Russian Federation – also feature.

Origins with a high GDP per capita (figure A39) or significant R&D expenditure per capita (figure A40) exhibit correspondingly high levels of resident patent filings per capita.

China's resident patent applications per GDP ratio has increased substantially over the past decade

1.5. Resident patent applications per USD 100 billion GDP for the top 10 origins, 2012 and 2022

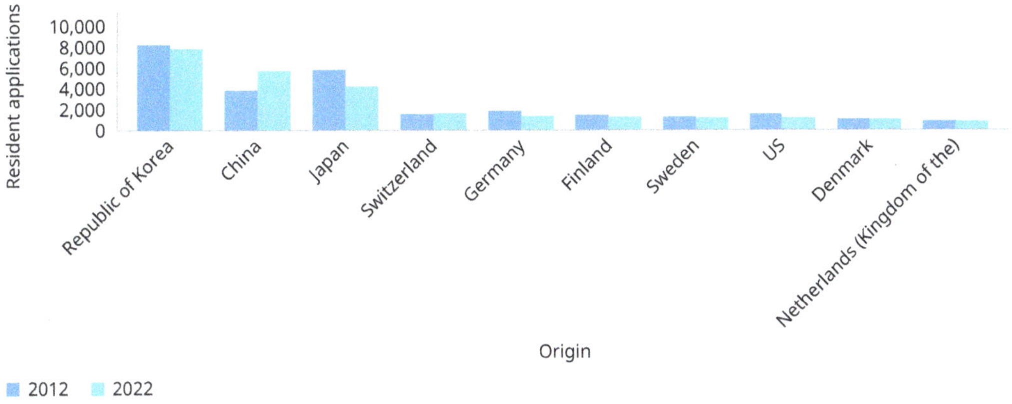

Source: Figure A37.

The profile of resident applications per million population is similar to that adjusted for GDP, but there are subtle differences. The composition of the top 10 origins for resident applications according to GDP and by population is identical, except for slight changes in rank for a few origins. For example, China ranks fourth according to the patent-to-population measure, but occupies second position for patent-to-GDP ratio. The Republic of Korea (3,559) maintains its lead when resident applications are expressed according to population, followed by Japan (1,749) and Switzerland (1,168), ahead of China (1,037) and the US (757) (figure A38).

Patent filings for unique inventions grew by 8.4% in 2020

Patent rights are territorial in nature. In order to protect inventions in several countries, applicants often file patent applications for the same invention in multiple jurisdictions. This being the case, adding patent data from different jurisdictions would inflate the number of new inventions. Patent family data are therefore frequently used in order to eliminate (or at least minimize) double counting. The basic idea behind a patent family is to group together all applications – original and subsequent filings – related to each other via priority filing(s). WIPO has developed indicators for patent families with the aim of capturing the actual number of unique inventions by excluding double counting as far as possible. The drawback of such data is the consequent time lag which can be up to three years.

Patent families worldwide rebounded with 8.4% growth in 2020, following a 7.2% decline the previous year (figure A23). The total number of patent families worldwide amounted to 2.14 million in 2020, double that recorded a decade earlier in 2010 (1 million) (figure 1.6). Applicants from China accounted for more than two-thirds of all patent families (65.2%), followed by Japan (9.1%), the US (8.4%) and the Republic of Korea (7.2%). However, the US (198,947) and Japan (155,059) created by far the most foreign-oriented patent families for the period 2018–2019 (figure A26), which was significantly more than China (81,145), Germany (60,702) or the Republic of Korea (60,503).

Patent filings for unique inventions reached 2.14 million in 2020

1.6. Patent applications and patent families worldwide, 2006–2022

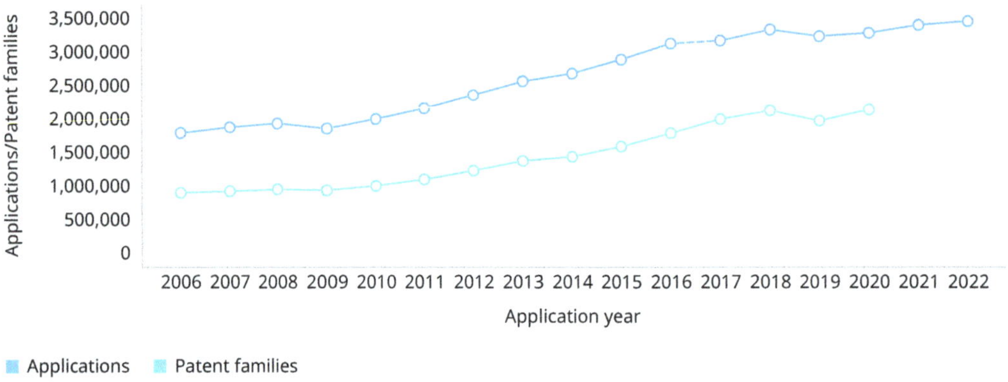

Sources: Figures A1 and A23.

The size of a patent family (indicating the number of offices at which a patent is filed) reflects its geographical coverage. Around 85.5% of patent families created worldwide between 2018 and 2020 were filed at a single office (figure A24). This high percentage is mainly attributable to the filing behavior of Chinese applicants, who mostly filed applications at a single office – 96.9% of patent families from China are single-office families. However, there is a considerable variation among top origins. For example, over half of all patent families originating from France, Italy, the Kingdom of the Netherlands, Sweden and Switzerland covered two or more offices. In contrast, less than 5% of patent families originating from China and the Russian Federation were filed at more than one office.

Origins whose patent families had the widest geographical coverage were Australia (11%), the Kingdom of the Netherlands (11.8%) and Switzerland (18.1%), where more than 10% of patent families covered more than five offices.

Patent families

A patent family is a set of interrelated patent applications filed at one or more offices to protect the same invention. Patent applications in a family are interlinked by one or more of the following: priority claim, Patent Cooperation Treaty (PCT) national phase entry, continuation, continuation-in-part, internal priority, and addition or division. A special subset comprises foreign-oriented patent families – that is, those patent families that have at least one filing office different from the office of the applicant's country of origin. Some foreign-related patent families include only one filing office. This is because applicants may choose to file only at a foreign office. For example, if a Canadian applicant files a patent application directly with the United States Patent and Trademark Office (USPTO) without having previously filed with the patent office of Canada, that patent family will constitute a foreign-oriented patent family with just one office.

In 2021, computer technology was the most frequently featured technology in published patent applications worldwide, comprising 11.1% of the global total

In 2021 – the latest year for which complete data are available owing to the delay between application and publication – computer technology emerged as the most frequently featured technology in published patent applications worldwide, accounting for 11.1% of the world total (table A29). It was followed by electrical machinery (6.4%), measurement (5.8%), medical technology (5.2%) and digital communication (4.9%) These five fields have occupied the top five spots in the ranking since 2012, albeit in varying order. Together, these five fields represented 33.4% of all published applications globally in 2021, 5.3 percentage points higher than their global share a decade earlier in 2011.

Among the top 15 fields of technology, chemical engineering (+11.4%), computer technology (+11%) and IT methods for management (+13.7%) are the three fields to have witnessed double-digit growth between 2011 and 2021. In contrast, audio-visual (+3.2%), pharmaceuticals (+3.2%) and semiconductors (+2.3%) demonstrated the slowest growth rates over the same period.

Among the top 10 origins during the period from 2019 to 2021, China (12.1% of all published applications), the Republic of Korea (8.9%), the UK (8.6%) and the US (12.9%) filed most heavily in computer technology (figure A30). Japan (9.9%) filed mostly in electrical machinery; France (11.3%) and Germany (11.7%) in transport; the Kingdom of the Netherlands (13.2%), the Russian Federation (8.8%) and Switzerland (9.8%) in medical technology.

Among large middle-income countries during the same period, applicants residing in Brazil (8.4% of total published applications) and Malaysia (7.4%) filed most heavily in other special machines; India in computer technology (9.6%); Mexico (12.1%) in pharmaceuticals; and Türkiye (7.5%) in medical technology.

The number of published patent applications related to energy technologies – solar, fuel cell, wind, geothermal and hydro energy – increased from around 29,800 in 2006 to around 46,300 in 2021 (figure A31). Solar energy constituted half (50.9%) of all energy-related applications in 2021, followed by wind energy (19.1%), hydro energy (16.4%), fuel cell technology (12.2%) and geothermal energy (1.4%). China had the largest share of the world total in four of these five fields (figure A32), with fuel cell technology being the one exception for which Japan has the largest share of the global total.

China's patent office granted 14.7% more patents in 2022 than in 2021, marking a third consecutive year of double-digit growth

Offices carry out a formal and substantive examination before deciding whether to issue a patent. The procedure for granting a patent varies between offices. Differences in the numbers of patents granted among offices depend on factors such as examination capacity and procedural delays. For this reason, application data for a given year should not be compared with grant data from the same year.

In 2022, an estimated 1.8 million patents were granted worldwide, up 3.9% on 2021 (figure 1.7). China (798,347) issued the highest number of patents in 2022, followed by the US (323,410), Japan (201,420), the Republic of Korea (135,180) and the EPO (81,086) (figure A13). The ranking of the top five offices has remained unaltered since 2020.

Seven of the top 10 offices granted fewer patents in 2022 compared to 2021 (figure A14). Brazil (–12.4%), Canada (–20.1%) and the EPO (–25.5%) issued considerably fewer patents in 2022 than in 2021, primarily due to a decline in both resident and non-resident grants across offices. The EPO experienced a third consecutive year of grant decline, grants decreasing from 137,782 in 2019 to 81,086 in 2022.

China (+14.7%), Germany (+11.7%) and Japan (+9.2%) are the three offices within the top 10 to have granted more patents in 2022 than in 2021. Both Germany and Japan reported a second successive year of growth, while China recorded its third consecutive year of double-digit growth. A marked increase in patents granted to resident applicants drove overall growth in China and Japan. In Germany's case, both resident and non-resident grants contributed to total growth.

Looking beyond the top 10 offices, the offices of Indonesia (+45.5%), the Kingdom of the Netherlands (+24.3%), Saudi Arabia (+53.7%) and South Africa (+84.5%) recorded substantial growth in 2022, primarily attributable to a strong rise in non-resident grants.

Patents granted worldwide grew by 3.9% in 2022, reaching a total of 1.8 million

1.7. Patent grants worldwide, 2008–2022

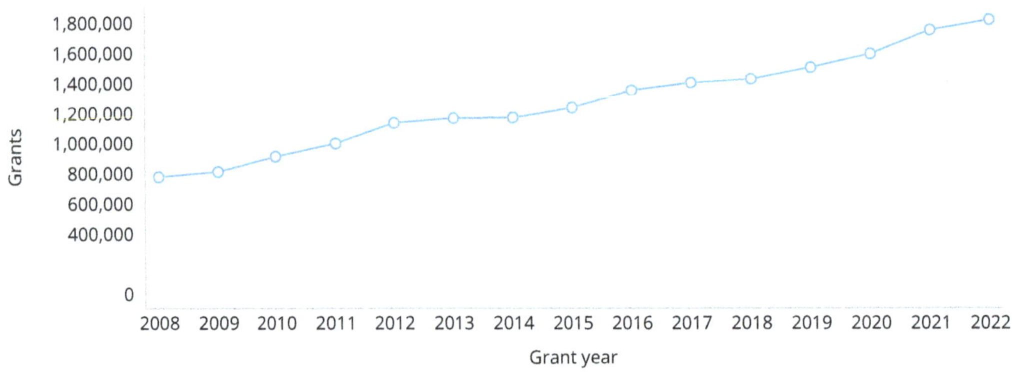

Source: Figure A3.

Asia's share of worldwide patent grants stood at 67.3% in 2022, marking a significant increase of 10.3 percentage points above its global share a decade earlier in 2011. This reflects the fact that three of the top five patent issuing authorities – China, Japan and the Republic of Korea – are located within the region, with China alone accounting for 43.8% of the world total. Offices located in North America accounted 18.7% of patent grants worldwide in 2022, while those in Europe contributed 9.8% to the global total (table A11). The combined share for Africa, LAC, and Oceania amounted to 4.2%. The distribution of patent applications (table A5) and patent grants (table A11) for all six regions exhibit a similar order of magnitude.

In 2022, the highest number of patents in force was in China – accounting for approximately a quarter of the world total

Patent rights generally last for up to 20 years from the date an application is filed. An estimated 17.3 million patents were in force across 137 jurisdictions in 2022. This represents a 4.1% increase on 2021, a growth rate similar to that of the previous year.

In 2022, the highest number of patents in force was in China (4.2 million), followed by the US (3.3 million), Japan (2 million), the Republic of Korea (1.2 million) and Germany (917,232) (figure 1.8). Among the top five jurisdictions, China saw the fastest growth in patents in force in 2022 (+17.1%), closely matching the rate recorded in 2021 (+17.6%). Germany (+4.5%) and the Republic of Korea (+5.3%) also saw strong growth in 2022. Both Japan (+0.4%) and the US (+0.5%) reported more modest increases. Over the past decade, China has recorded an average annual growth rate of 17% compared to Japan's 1.8% and the US's 4%. Beyond the top five offices, Brazil (+25%), India (+16%) and South Africa (+8%) reported notable growth in 2022.

Patents in force in China increased by 17.1% to reach a total of 4.2 million in 2022

1.8. Patents in force at the top 10 offices, 2022

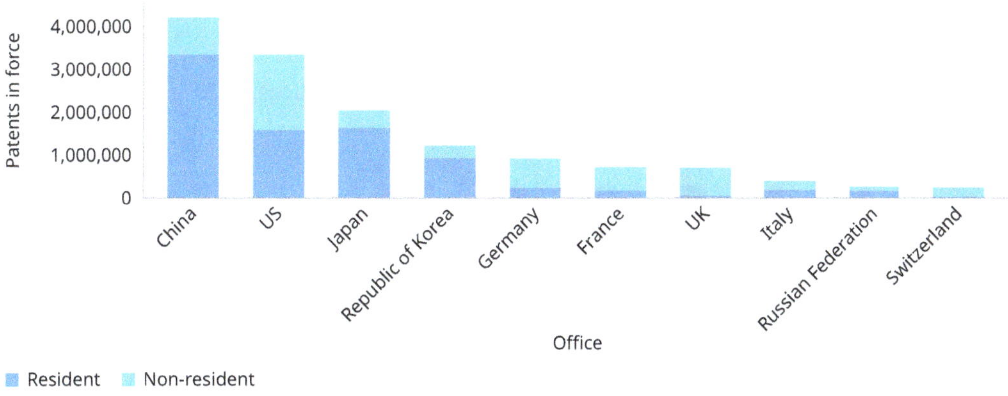

Source: Figure A42.

The source of the patents in force within the top five jurisdictions differs considerably (figure A42). More than half of all patents in force in Germany (73.8%) and the US (52.6%) originated from non-resident applicants, whereas non-resident applicants accounted for a smaller proportion of patents in force in Japan (19.3%), China (20.4%) and the Republic of Korea (23.4%). This trend is somewhat to be expected due to the high share of resident patent grants at the latter three offices (figure A13). Among top 20 offices, non-resident patent holders contributed the bulk of all patents in force at the offices of Luxembourg (99%), Mexico (95.7%), Australia (93.2%) and the UK (92%).

A holder must pay a maintenance/renewal fee in order for a patent to remain valid, and may opt to let a patent lapse before the end of its full term. Among the 87 offices that provided in-force data categorized by year of filing, approximately 39.3% of granted patents remained in force for at least 9 years after the filing date. Additionally, about 17.8% of patents lasted the full 20-year term (figure A44).

Although patents can be maintained for up to 20 years, the average age of patents varies across offices. Among the selected 20 offices reported in figure A45, the average age of patents in force in 2022 ranged from 11.6 years in Brazil down to 6.8 years in Monaco. Patents in force in India (11.4 years), Germany (11 years) and Mexico (11 years) shared a similarly high average age with those in Brazil. When comparing the average age of patents for the 20 offices reported in 2022 compared to 2017, an overall similarity is observed, except for the offices of Brazil and India, both of which saw a decrease in the average age during this period.

Türkiye and the US granted patents for under half of applications processed in 2022

A patent office examines applications and decides whether to grant patent rights. Examination processes differ across offices, which makes cross-country comparisons difficult. Every effort has, however, been made to compile examination outcome data based on common definitions and concepts. In 2022, 87 IP offices shared data on patent examination outcomes – granted, rejected or withdrawn – with WIPO.

Among 10 selected offices, Türkiye and the US granted patents for under half of all applications processed in 2022 (figure 1.9).[2] In contrast, more than three-quarters of applications processed in 2022 resulted in grants at the offices of Australia (78.4%), Japan (75.2%) and the Republic of Korea (72.8%). Rejected applications as a share of the total were highest at the IP offices of China (37.4%) and the US (46.2%). In terms of absolute numbers, China rejected more than

2 Patents granted out of total processed applications data presented should not be interpreted as the "grant rate."

553,000 applications, while the US rejected around 350,000 applications. The proportion of withdrawn or abandoned applications was greatest in Canada (30.6%), India (30.1%) and Türkiye (52%). In terms of absolute numbers, the IP offices of China and the US reported in excess of 129,000 and 85,000 applications as either withdrawn or abandoned, respectively.

China rejected more than 553,000 patent applications in 2022

1.9. Distribution of patent examination outcomes for selected offices, 2022

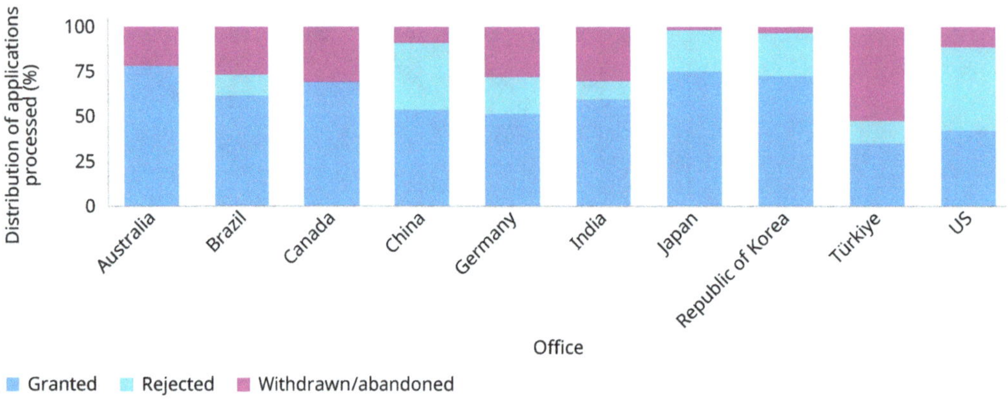

Source: Figure A46.

The stock of pending applications at China's patent office nearly doubled, growing from around 1.3 million in 2021 to approximately 2.6 million in 2022

Patent offices must assess whether the claims presented in applications meet the standards of novelty, non-obviousness and industrial applicability defined in national laws. Processing patents therefore consumes time and resources. The estimated total number of potential applications pending worldwide rose to 6.9 million in 2022, marking a 24.9% increase on the previous year. This estimate is based on data collected from 108 offices. The growth in the stock of pending applications globally is primarily attributable to substantial increases at the offices of China, the EPO and the US.

In 2022, China's pending applications surged to approximately 2.6 million, a notable increase on the 1.3 million recorded in 2021 (figure A47). Following China, the IP office of the US had 1.1 million pending applications, followed by Japan (794,344), the EPO (633,550) and Germany (370,656).

Among the top 20 offices, Australia (+10.4%), China (+94.2%), India (+11%), Malaysia (+16%), New Zealand (+13.9%) and Singapore (+22%) saw a double-digit growth in the stock of applications pending between 2021 and 2022. Conversely, Brazil (–10.9%), Japan (–6.8%), the Russian Federation (–5.7%) and the UK (–5.6%) all managed to considerably reduce the stock of applications pending over the same period. Both Brazil and Japan have reported a year-on-year decrease in their stock of applications pending since 2018.

Where offices have a large proportion of applications pending a request for examination, the scope to reduce the stock of applications pending is somewhat limited, as an office is unable to start the substantial examination process until an applicant has filed a request for examination.

Applications pending

Applications pending is defined as all patent applications, at any stage in the process, awaiting a final decision by a patent office, including those applications for which applicants have not filed a request for examination (where applicable).

Women inventors accounted for no more than 17.1% of all inventors listed in published PCT applications in 2022

In 2022, women constituted 17.1% of all inventors listed in published PCT applications, while men accounted for the remaining 82.9% (figure A33). The proportion of women inventors has increased notably from 10.6% in 2008 to 17.1% in 2022. Moreover, the proportion of women inventors has expanded in every region of the world over the past decade.

About 34.7% of published PCT applications named at least one woman as inventor in 2022, and 95.8% featured at least one man as inventor (figure A34). The share of published PCT applications with at least one woman as inventor has risen from 20.6% in 2008 to 34.7% in 2022, whereas the share of those with at least one man as inventor has decreased over the same period, from 97.6% down to 95.8%.

The gender gap among PCT inventors varies considerably between countries. Of the top 20 origins of published PCT applications, China and Türkiye had the largest proportion of women inventors in 2022 (figure A35). They were the only two origins within the top 20 with nearly one-quarter of women as inventors. In contrast, for Austria and Japan only around one-10th of inventors in published PCT applications were women.

Fields of technology related to the life sciences had comparatively high shares of published PCT applications with women as inventors in 2022. Women represented around 30% of inventors listed in published PCT applications in the fields of biotechnology (30.2%), food chemistry (30.1%) and pharmaceuticals (29.1%) (figure A36). The share of published PCT applications with women inventors was higher in 29 of the 35 fields of technology in 2022 compared to 2021.

Utility model applications worldwide increased by 2.9% in 2022, rebounding from a 2.5% decline the previous year

A utility model (UM) is a special form of patent right granted by a state or jurisdiction to an inventor or the inventor's assignee for a fixed time period. The terms and conditions for granting a UM differ slightly from those for normal patents, including a shorter term of protection and less stringent eligibility requirements.

After experiencing a 2.5% decrease in 2021, filing activity for UMs rebounded in 2022, with a growth rate of 2.9% resulting in a total of 3 million applications (figure A53). Resident applications constituted 99.5% of total filings, with non-resident applications making up the remaining 0.5%. China received 98% of the global total, while the other 82 offices combined accounted for the remaining 2% of UM patent filing.

The IP office of China received 2.95 million applications in 2002, followed by Germany (9,469), the Russian Federation (8,521), Türkiye (5,558) and Japan (4,513) (figure A54). Among the top 10 offices, Indonesia (+25.8%) and Türkiye (+23.8%) were the only two to record double-digit growth in 2002. Both offices also reported double-digit growth the previous year.

Looking at the filing trend over the past decade, Germany, Japan, the Republic of Korea, the Russian Federation and Ukraine underwent a decline in UM filings between 2012 and 2022. For example, applications at the office of the Republic of Korea decreased from 12,424 in 2012 to 3,084 in 2022 (–75.2%), while applications filed at the office of Japan declined from 8,112 to 4,513 (–44.4%) over the same period. In contrast, China has seen an enormous growth in UM patent filings over the same period – applications having increased from 740,290 in 2012 to 2.95 million by 2022. Indonesia, Thailand and Türkiye have also seen an upward trend in UM filing over the same period.

Patent statistics

Patent applications and grants worldwide **24**

A1. Trend in patent applications worldwide, 2008–2022 24
A2. Resident and non-resident patent applications worldwide, 2008–2022 24
A3. Trend in patent grants worldwide, 2008–2022 25
A4. Resident and non-resident patent grants worldwide, 2008–2022 25

Patent applications and grants by office **25**

A5. Patent applications by region, 2012 and 2022 25
A6. Trend in patent applications for the top five offices, 1883–2022 26
A7. Patent applications at the top 20 offices, 2022 26
A8. Contribution of resident and non-resident applications to total growth for the top 20 offices, 2021–2022 26
A9. Patent applications at offices of selected low- and middle-income countries, 2022 27
A10. Contribution of resident and non-resident applications to total growth for offices of selected low- and middle-income countries, 2021–2022 27
A11. Patent grants by region, 2012 and 2022 27
A12. Trend in patent grants for the top five offices, 1883–2022 28
A13. Patent grants for the top 20 offices, 2022 28
A14. Contribution of resident and non-resident grants to total growth for the top 20 offices, 2021–2022 28
A15. Patent grants for offices of selected low- and middle-income countries, 2022 29
A16. Contribution of resident and non-resident grants to total growth for offices of selected low- and middle-income countries, 2021–2022 29

Patent applications and grants by origin **30**

A17. Patent applications for the top 20 origins, 2022 30
A18. Equivalent patent applications for the top 20 origins, 2022 30
A19. Patent applications for the top 20 offices and origins, 2022 31
A20. Flows of non-resident patent applications between the top five origins and the top 10 offices, 2022 32
A21. Patent grants for the top 20 origins, 2022 33
A22. Equivalent patent grants for the top 20 origins, 2022 33

Patent families **34**

A23. Trend in patent families worldwide, 2006–2020 34
A24. Distribution of patent families by number of offices for the top origins, 2018–2020 34
A25. Trend in foreign-oriented patent families worldwide, 2006–2019 35
A26. Foreign-oriented patent families for the top 20 origins, 2018–2019 35
A27. Distribution of technology fields for selected applicants based on patent families, 2018–2020 36
A28. Distribution of technology fields for selected universities and PROs based on patent families, 2018–2020 37

Published patent applications by field of technology **38**

A29. Published patent applications worldwide by field of technology, 2011, 2016 and 2021 38
A30. Distribution of published patent applications by technology field for the top 10 origins, 2019–2021 39
A31. Trend in patent applications in energy-related technologies, 2006–2021 40
A32. Share of patent applications in energy-related technologies for the top five origins, 2019–2021 41

Participation of women inventors in published PCT applications 42
A33. Share of women among listed inventors in PCT applications, 2008–2022 42
A34. Share of PCT applications with at least one woman as inventor and with at least one man as inventor, 2008–2022 42
A35. Share of women among listed inventors and share of PCT applications with at least one woman as inventor for the top 20 origins, 2022 43
A36. Share of PCT patent applications with women inventors by field of technology, 2022 43

Patent applications in relation to GDP and population 44
A37. Resident patent applications per USD 100 billion GDP for the top 20 origins, 2012 and 2022 44
A38. Resident patent applications per million population for the top 20 origins, 2012 and 2022 44
A39. Resident patent applications per capita and GDP per capita, 2018–2022 44
A40. Resident patent applications per capita and R&D expenditure per capita, 2018–2022 45

Patents in force 45
A41. Trend in patents in force worldwide, 2008–2022 45
A42. Patents in force at the top 20 offices, 2022 45
A43. Flow of patents in force between selected origins and offices, 2022 46
A44. Patents in force in 2022 as a percentage of total applications 47
A45. Average age of patents in force at selected offices, 2017 and 2022 47

Patent office procedural data 48
A46. Distribution of patent examination outcomes for selected offices, 2022 48
A47. Potentially pending applications at the top 20 offices, 2022 48
A48. Average pendency times for first office action and final decision at selected offices, 2022 49
A49. Number of patent examiners for selected offices, 2022 49
A50. Average years of experience of patent examiners for selected offices, 2022 49

Patent prosecution highway (PPH) 50
A51. PPH requests by office of first filing and offices of later examination, 2022 50
A52. Flows of PPH requests between offices of first filing and offices of later examination, 2022 51

Utility model applications 52
A53. Trend in utility model applications worldwide, 2008–2022 52
A54. Utility model applications for the top 20 offices, 2022 52
A55. Utility model applications for offices of selected low- and middle-income countries, 2022 52

Microorganisms 53
A56. Trend in microorganism deposits worldwide, 2008–2022 53
A57. Deposits at the top international depositary authorities, 2022 53

Statistical tables 54
A58. Patent applications by office and origin, 2022 54
A59. Patent grants by office and origin, and patents in force, 2022 57
A60. Patent office procedural data, 2022 60
A61. Utility model applications and grants by office and origin, 2022 62

Patent applications and grants worldwide

A1. Trend in patent applications worldwide, 2008-2022

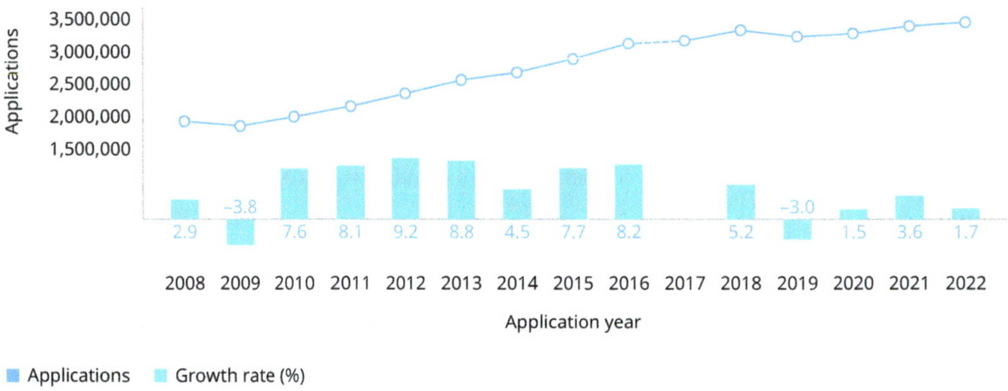

Note: World totals are WIPO estimates using data covering 162 patent offices. These totals include applications filed directly with national and regional offices and applications entering offices through the Patent Cooperation Treaty national phase (where applicable). China's pre-2017 data are not comparable owing to a change in methodology. Due to this break in the data series, and to the large number of filings in China, it is not possible to report an accurate 2017 growth rate at world level (see data description section in Additional information for details).
Source: WIPO Statistics Database, August 2023.

A2. Resident and non-resident patent applications worldwide, 2008-2022

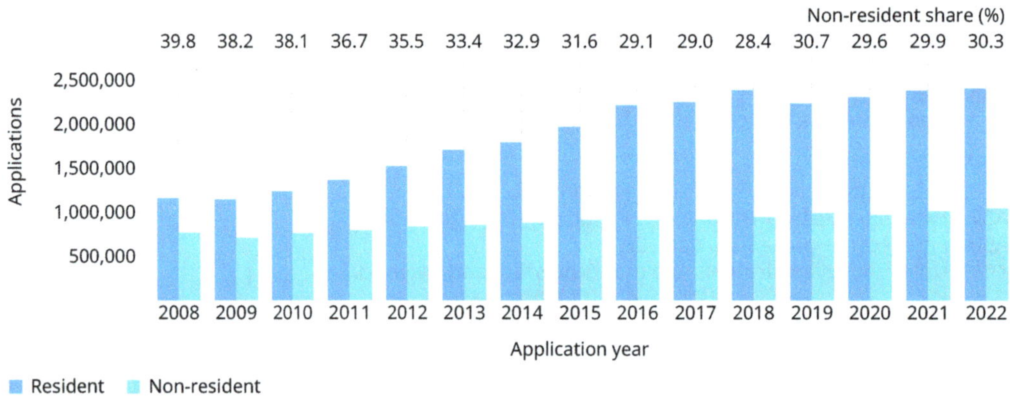

Note: World totals are WIPO estimates using data covering 162 patent offices. These totals include applications filed directly with national and regional offices and applications entering offices through the Patent Cooperation Treaty national phase (where applicable). See glossary for definitions of resident and non-resident.
Source: WIPO Statistics Database, August 2023.

A3. Trend in patent grants worldwide, 2008–2022

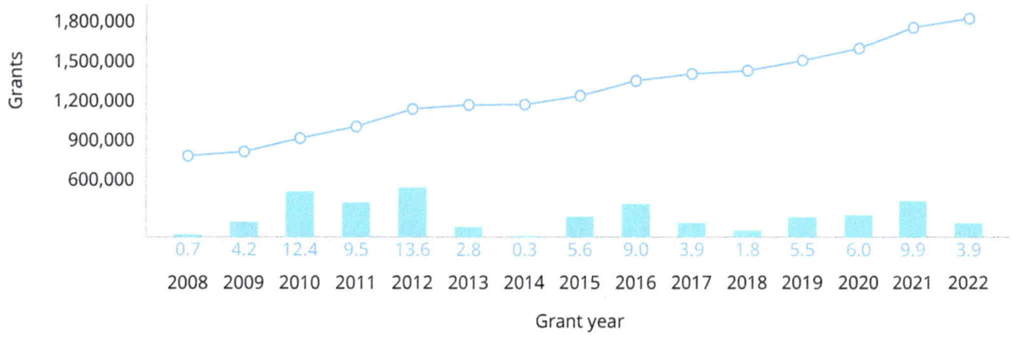

Note: World totals are WIPO estimates using data covering 155 patent offices. These totals include patent grants based on applications filed directly with national and regional offices and patents granted by offices on the basis of the Patent Cooperation Treaty national phase (where applicable).
Source: WIPO Statistics Database, August 2023.

A4. Resident and non-resident patent grants worldwide, 2008–2022

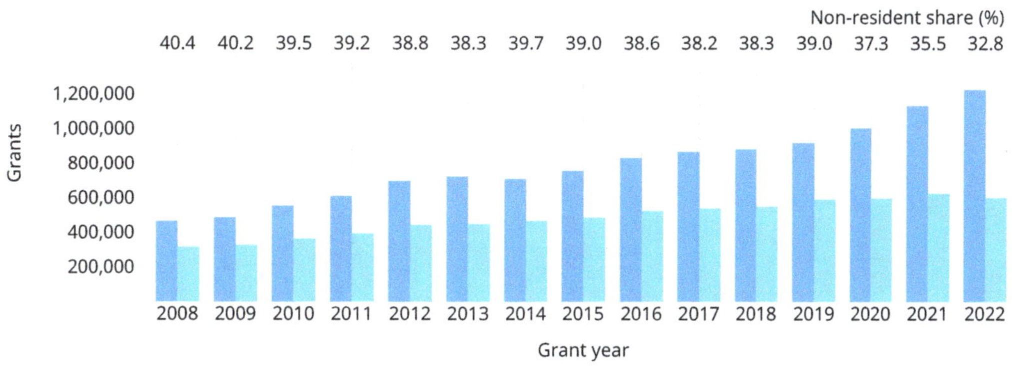

Note: World totals are WIPO estimates using data covering 155 patent offices. These totals include patent grants based on applications filed directly with national and regional offices and patents granted by offices on the basis of the Patent Cooperation Treaty national phase (where applicable). See glossary for definitions of resident and non-resident.
Source: WIPO Statistics Database, August 2023.

Patent applications and grants by office

A5. Patent applications by region, 2012 and 2022

	Number of applications		Resident share (%)		Share of world total (%)		Average growth (%)
Region	**2012**	**2022**	**2012**	**2022**	**2012**	**2022**	**2012–2022**
Africa	14,700	24,300	15.6	19.3	0.6	0.7	5.2
Asia	1,321,300	2,349,200	76.7	82.7	56.1	67.9	5.9
Europe	345,800	355,100	63.2	54.7	14.7	10.3	0.3
Latin America and the Caribbean	63,100	57,000	12.2	13.5	2.7	1.6	–1
North America	578,100	632,400	47.3	40.6	24.5	18.3	0.9
Oceania	33,500	39,400	11.9	6.9	1.4	1.1	1.6
World	**2,356,500**	**3,457,400**	**64.5**	**69.7**	**100.0**	**100.0**	**3.9**

Note: Totals by geographical region are WIPO estimates using data covering 162 offices. Each region includes the following number of offices: Africa (33), Asia (46), Europe (45), Latin America and the Caribbean (31), North America (2) and Oceania (5).
Source: WIPO Statistics Database, August 2023.

A6. Trend in patent applications for the top five offices, 1883–2022

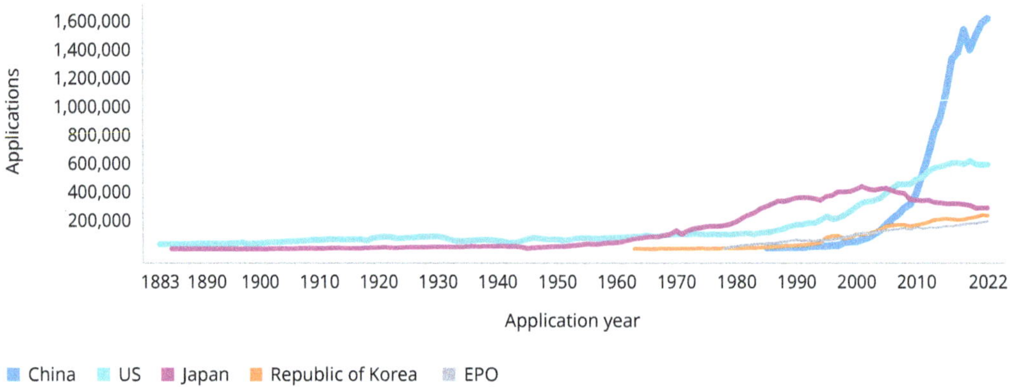

Note: EPO is the European Patent Office. The top five offices were selected based on their 2022 totals.
Source: WIPO Statistics Database, August 2023.

A7. Patent applications at the top 20 offices, 2022

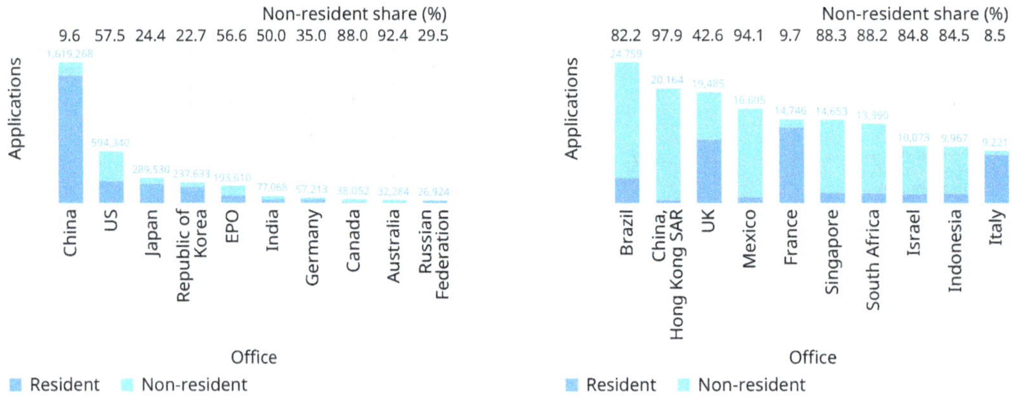

Note: EPO is the European Patent Office. In general, national offices of the EPO member states receive smaller volumes of applications, because applicants may apply via the EPO to seek protection within any EPO member state.
Source: WIPO Statistics Database, August 2023.

A8. Contribution of resident and non-resident applications to total growth for the top 20 offices, 2021–2022

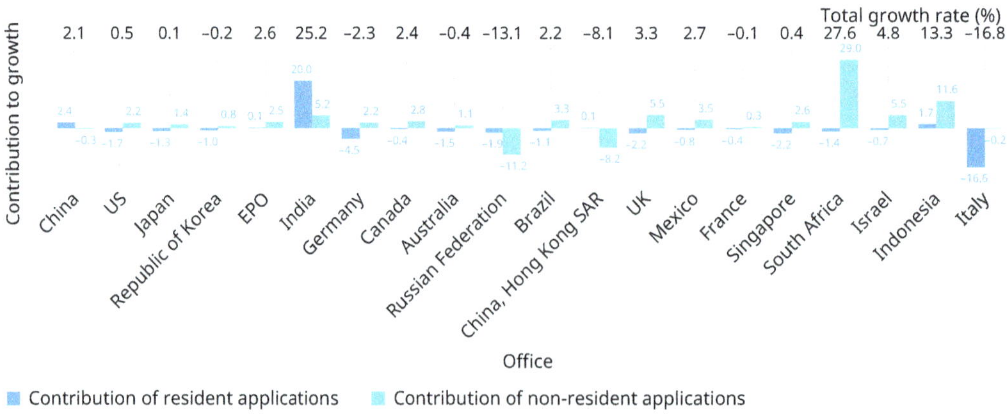

Note: EPO is the European Patent Office. This figure shows the total growth or decrease in applications at each office, broken down by the respective contributions of resident and non-resident applications. For example, applications filed at the IP office of China grew by 2.1%. Growth in resident applications accounted for 2.4 percentage points of this increase, while non-resident applications decreased by 0.3 percentage points.
Source: WIPO Statistics Database, August 2023.

A9. Patent applications at offices of selected low- and middle-income countries, 2022

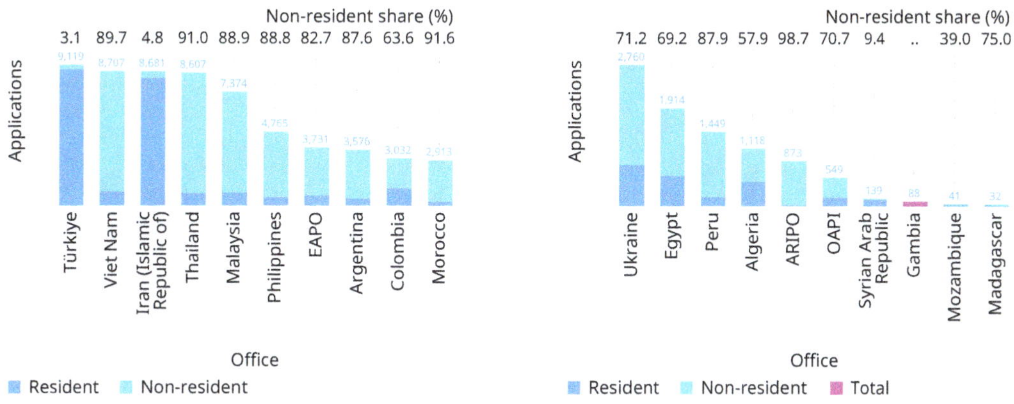

Note: ARIPO is the African Regional Intellectual Property Organization, EAPO is the Eurasian Patent Organization and OAPI is the African Intellectual Property Organization. The selected offices are from different world regions. Where available, data for all offices are presented in table A58.
.. indicates not available.
Source: WIPO Statistics Database, August 2023.

A10. Contribution of resident and non-resident applications to total growth for offices of selected low- and middle-income countries, 2021–2022

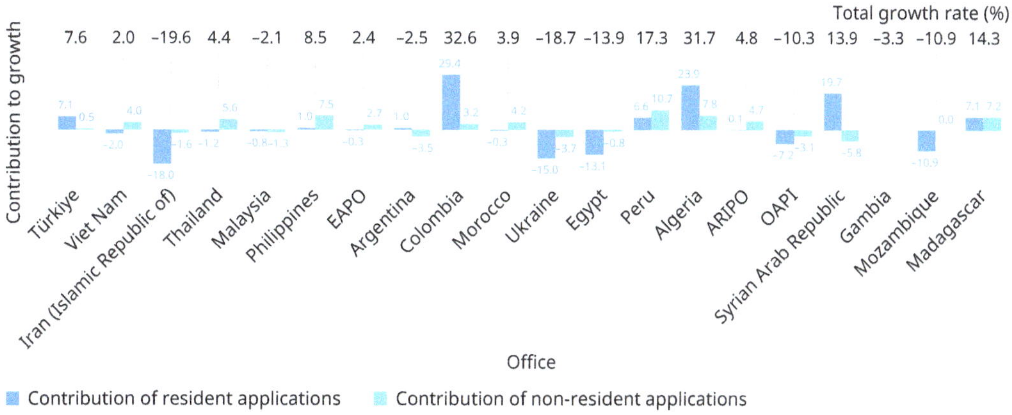

Note: ARIPO is the African Regional Intellectual Property Organization, EAPO is the Eurasian Patent Organization and OAPI is the African Intellectual Property Organization. The selected offices are from different world regions. This figure shows the total growth or decrease in applications at each office, broken down by the respective contributions of resident and non-resident applications. For example, applications filed at the IP office of Türkiye grew by 7.6%. Growth in resident applications accounted for 7.1 percentage points of this increase, while non-resident applications increased by 0.5 percentage points. A resident versus non-resident breakdown is unavailable for Gambia.
Source: WIPO Statistics Database, August 2023.

A11. Patent grants by region, 2012 and 2022

	Number of grants		Resident share (%)		Share of world total (%)		Average growth (%)
Region	**2012**	**2022**	**2012**	**2022**	**2012**	**2022**	**2012-2022**
Africa	10,700	16,200	12.5	8.3	0.9	0.9	4.2
Asia	649,000	1,226,700	72.4	79.3	57.0	67.3	6.6
Europe	159,100	178,700	61.7	56.2	14.0	9.8	1.2
Latin America and the Caribbean	20,200	41,500	5.6	9.1	1.8	2.3	7.5
North America	275,000	341,500	44.9	42.1	24.2	18.7	2.2
Oceania	24,000	18,600	6.9	6.2	2.1	1.0	-2.5
World	**1,138,000**	**1,823,200**	**61.1**	**67.1**	**100.0**	**100.0**	**4.8**

Note: Totals by geographical region are WIPO estimates using data covering 155 offices. Each region includes the following number of offices: Africa (31), Asia (43), Europe (45), Latin America and the Caribbean (29), North America (2) and Oceania (5).
Source: WIPO Statistics Database, August 2023.

A12. Trend in patent grants for the top five offices, 1883–2022

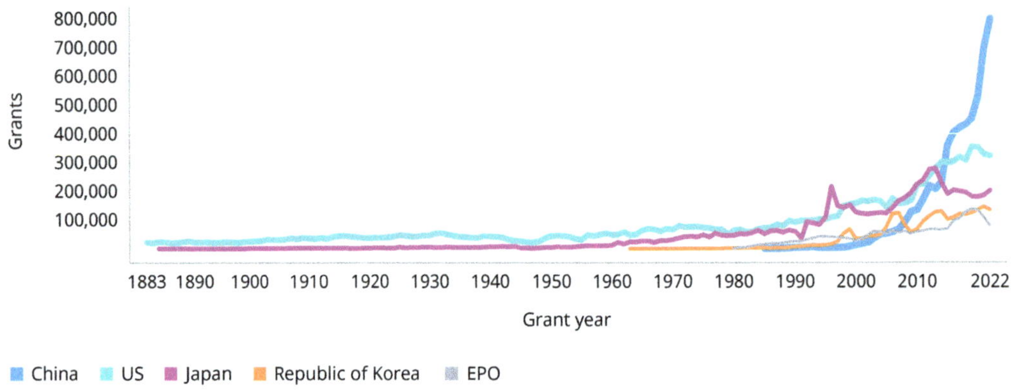

Note: EPO is the European Patent Office. The top five offices were selected based on their 2022 totals.
Source: WIPO Statistics Database, August 2023.

A13. Patent grants for the top 20 offices, 2022

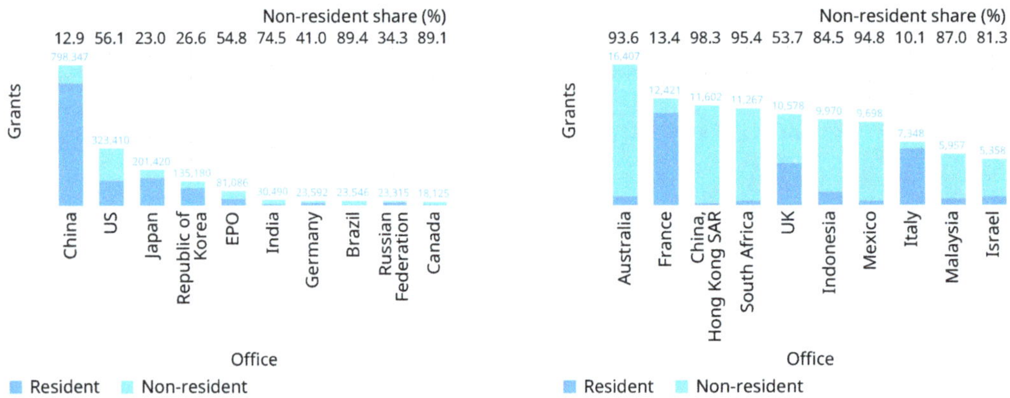

Note: EPO is the European Patent Office. The procedure for issuing patents varies between offices, and differences in the numbers of patents granted among offices depend on factors such as examination capacity and procedural delays. The examination process can take a long time, therefore there is invariably a time lag between application and grant dates. For this reason, data on applications for a given year should not be compared with data on grants for the same year.
Source: WIPO Statistics Database, August 2023.

A14. Contribution of resident and non-resident grants to total growth for the top 20 offices, 2021–2022

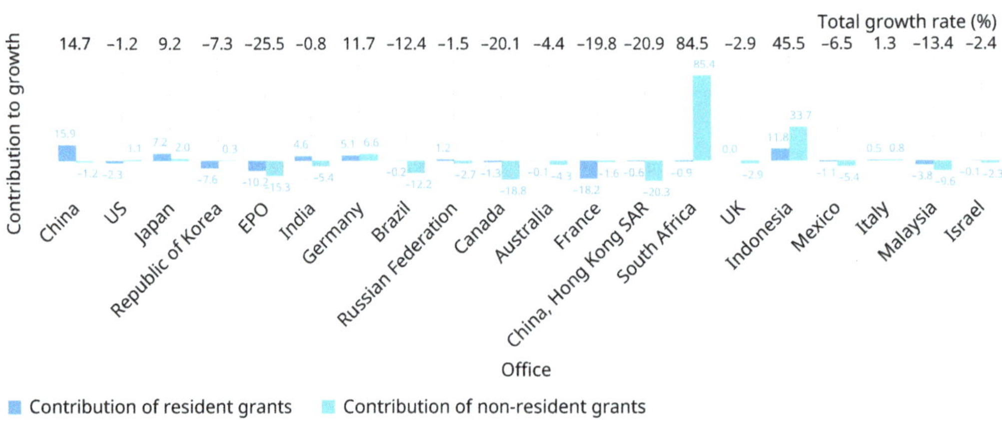

Note: EPO is the European Patent Office. This figure shows the total growth or decrease in grants at each office, broken down by the respective contributions of resident and non-resident grants. For example, the total number of patents granted by the IP office of Japan grew by 9.2%. Growth in resident grants accounted for 7.2 percentage points of this increase, while the remaining 2.0 percentage points came from growth in non-resident grants.
Source: WIPO Statistics Database, August 2023.

A15. Patent grants for offices of selected low- and middle-income countries, 2022

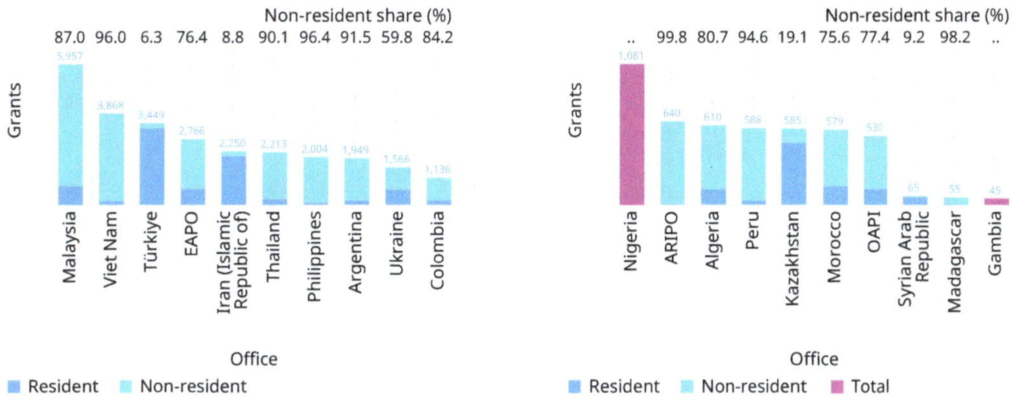

Note: ARIPO is the African Regional Intellectual Property Organization, EAPO is the Eurasian Patent Organization and OAPI is the African Intellectual Property Organization. The selected offices are from different world regions. Where available, data for all offices are presented in table A59.
.. indicates not available.
Source: WIPO Statistics Database, August 2023.

A16. Contribution of resident and non-resident grants to total growth for offices of selected low- and middle-income countries, 2021–2022

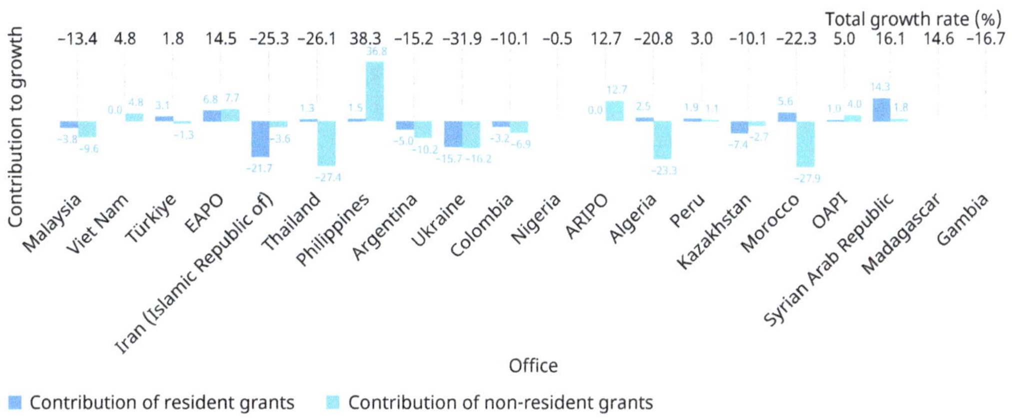

Note: ARIPO is the African Regional Intellectual Property Organization, EAPO is the Eurasian Patent Organization and OAPI is the African Intellectual Property Organization. This figure shows the total growth or decrease in grants at each office, broken down by the respective contributions of resident and non-resident grants. For example, the total number of patents granted by the IP office of the Philippines grew by 38.3%. Growth in non-resident grants accounted for 36.8 percentage point of this increase, while the remaining 1.5 percentage points came from growth in resident grants. A resident versus non-resident breakdown is unavailable for Gambia, Madagascar and Nigeria.
Source: WIPO Statistics Database, August 2023.

Patent applications and grants by origin

A17. Patent applications for the top 20 origins, 2022

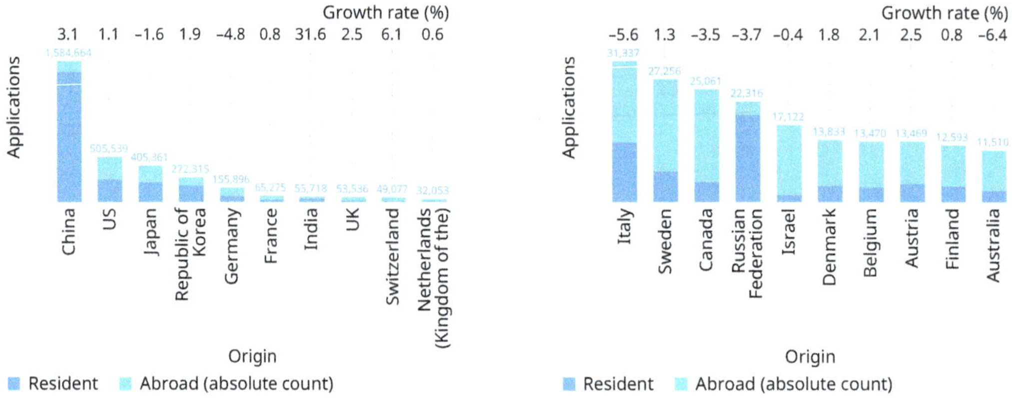

Note: Patent filing activity by origin includes resident applications and applications filed abroad. The origin of a patent application is determined by the residence of the first named applicant. For an absolute count, applications filed at regional offices are counted once, rather than being considered equivalent to multiple applications in the respective member states.
Source: WIPO Statistics Database, August 2023.

A18. Equivalent patent applications for the top 20 origins, 2022

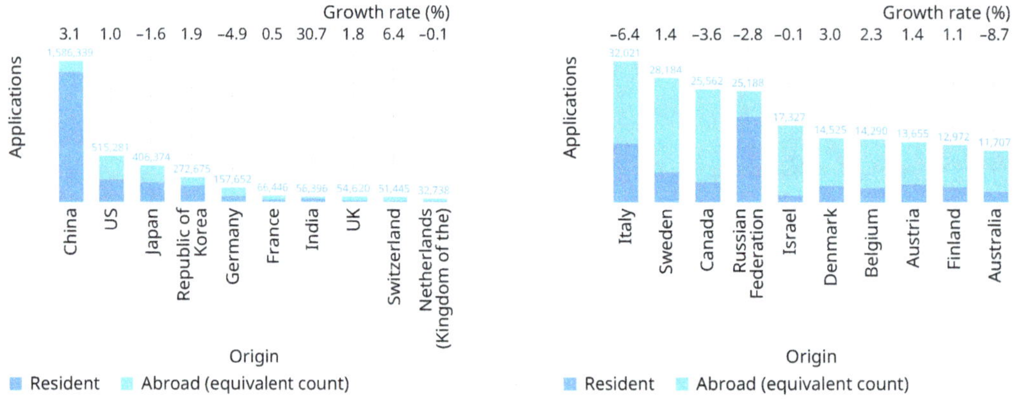

Note: Patent filing activity by origin includes resident applications and applications filed abroad. The origin of a patent application is determined by the residence of the first named applicant. Applications filed at regional offices are considered equivalent to multiple applications in the relevant member states. See glossary for the definition of equivalent application.
Source: WIPO Statistics Database, August 2023.

A19. Patent applications for the top 20 offices and origins, 2022

Origin	Office Australia	Brazil	Canada	China	China, Hong Kong SAR	EPO	France	Germany	India	Indonesia
Australia	2,465	157	515	651	159	1,004	4	9	272	67
Austria	143	224	275	996	99	2,383	9	867	284	46
Belgium	300	269	375	787	190	2,605	53	106	257	54
Canada	740	286	4,564	1,084	355	2,004	9	109	398	49
China	2,117	1,614	1,784	1,464,605	4,261	19,061	153	702	3,914	1,396
Denmark	322	263	344	1,158	151	2,661	7	38	347	84
Finland	230	228	379	906	174	2,139	5	47	544	138
France	816	886	1,481	4,969	382	10,979	13,322	428	1,175	147
Germany	1,333	1,590	1,890	15,218	743	24,685	293	37,199	2,600	341
India	191	208	167	317	42	817	5	41	38,551	255
Israel	413	287	433	1,281	207	1,739	1	97	363	13
Italy	403	569	701	1,844	194	4,869	85	104	530	67
Japan	1,572	1,119	1,252	45,259	1,136	21,577	78	6,339	4,583	2,059
Netherlands (Kingdom of the)	524	525	565	3,224	194	6,799	28	130	975	280
Republic of Korea	890	447	518	18,262	318	10,381	15	1,636	2,817	473
Russian Federation	26	51	59	169	22	197	2	21	103	39
Sweden	488	494	562	2,670	182	5,042	44	360	800	77
Switzerland	1,248	1,292	1,367	4,491	1,082	9,012	145	863	1,381	303
UK	1,488	745	1,601	2,779	708	5,693	47	152	1,130	189
US	14,512	7,748	17,272	43,090	7,375	48,123	169	6,850	14,359	1,844
Others	2,063	5,757	1,948	5,508	2,190	11,840	272	1,115	1,685	2,046
Total	**32,284**	**24,759**	**38,052**	**1,619,268**	**20,164**	**193,610**	**14,746**	**57,213**	**77,068**	**9,967**

Origin	Office Israel	Italy	Japan	Mexico	Republic of Korea	Russian Federation	Singapore	South Africa	UK	US
Australia	70	1	572	109	260	42	197	141	141	3,481
Austria	57	9	446	89	343	133	72	60	16	2,348
Belgium	107	7	564	201	311	114	83	123	84	2,481
Canada	174	6	773	324	533	36	143	131	170	12,184
China	251	64	9,842	834	6,320	1,232	1,588	5,762	863	49,344
Denmark	99	1	510	181	292	72	123	98	57	2,440
Finland	27	1	463	79	232	62	58	99	202	2,385
France	340	58	2,584	454	1,690	390	349	245	74	11,396
Germany	453	114	5,700	1,017	3,697	693	617	475	452	27,693
India	50	5	259	143	134	75	88	615	67	12,396
Israel	1,527	7	906	167	407	81	137	85	70	8,467
Italy	164	8,440	870	278	468	249	107	105	48	5,212
Japan	294	56	218,813	796	13,861	605	1,772	141	526	75,341
Netherlands (Kingdom of the)	226	8	1,852	407	1,128	308	148	162	181	4,388
Republic of Korea	103	6	7,149	336	183,748	532	498	135	276	41,485
Russian Federation	31	1	65	32	62	18,970	20	47	9	899
Sweden	105	43	1,268	285	750	89	118	232	138	5,485
Switzerland	527	108	3,411	774	1,641	721	533	190	429	5,464
UK	411	17	2,390	514	1,447	441	539	272	11,183	13,380
US	4,636	122	26,874	7,668	17,683	1,556	5,086	2,670	3,046	252,316
Others	421	147	4,219	1,917	2,626	523	2,377	2,202	1,453	55,755
Total	**10,073**	**9,221**	**289,530**	**16,605**	**237,633**	**26,924**	**14,653**	**13,990**	**19,485**	**594,340**

Note: EPO is the European Patent Office. Origin data are based on absolute rather than equivalent counts. The top 20 offices and origins are selected based on available 2022 data, broken down by country of origin.
Source: WIPO Statistics Database, August 2023.

A20. Flows of non-resident patent applications between the top five origins and the top 10 offices, 2022

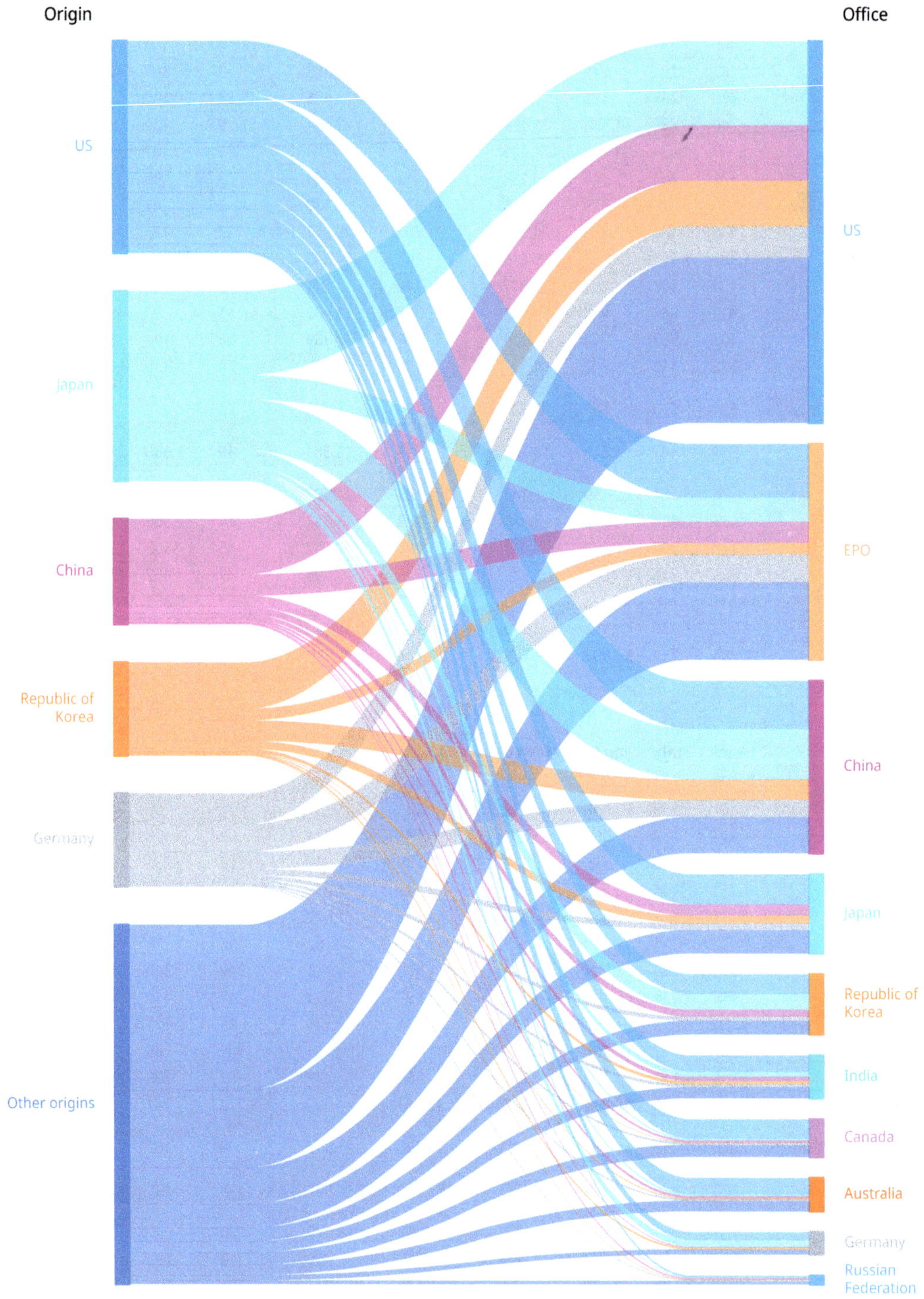

Note: EPO is the European Patent Office. Origin data are based on absolute rather than equivalent counts.
Source: WIPO Statistics Database, August 2023.

A21. Patent grants for the top 20 origins, 2022

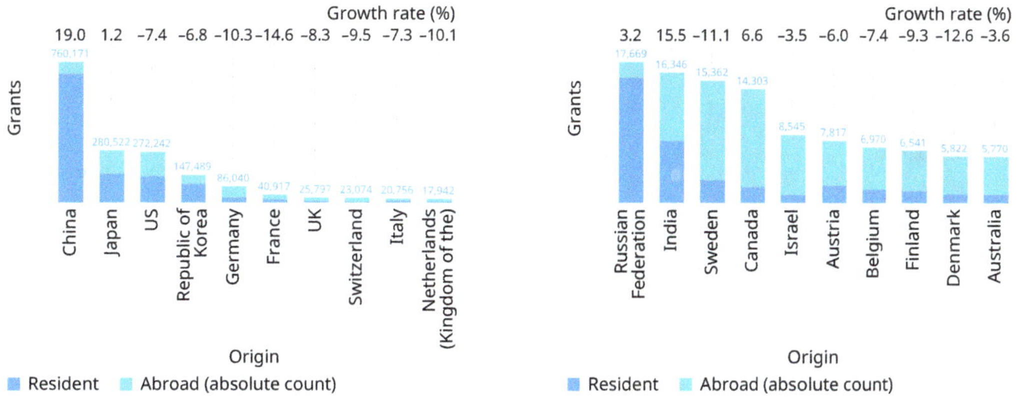

Note: For an absolute count, patent grants issues by regional offices are counted once, rather than being considered equivalent to multiple grants in the respective member states.
Source: WIPO Statistics Database, August 2023.

A22. Equivalent patent grants for the top 20 origins, 2022

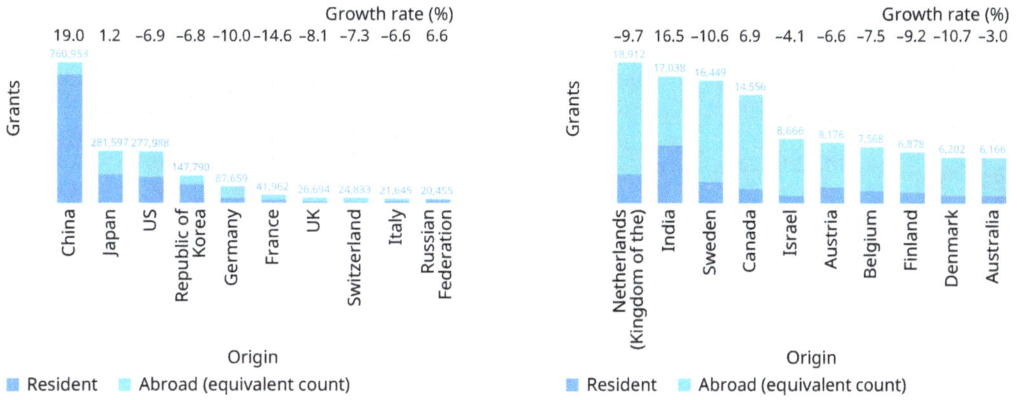

Note: Patent grants issued by regional offices are considered equivalent to multiple grants in the relevant member states. See glossary for the definition of equivalent grant.
Source: WIPO Statistics Database, August 2023.

Patent families

A23. Trend in patent families worldwide, 2006-2020

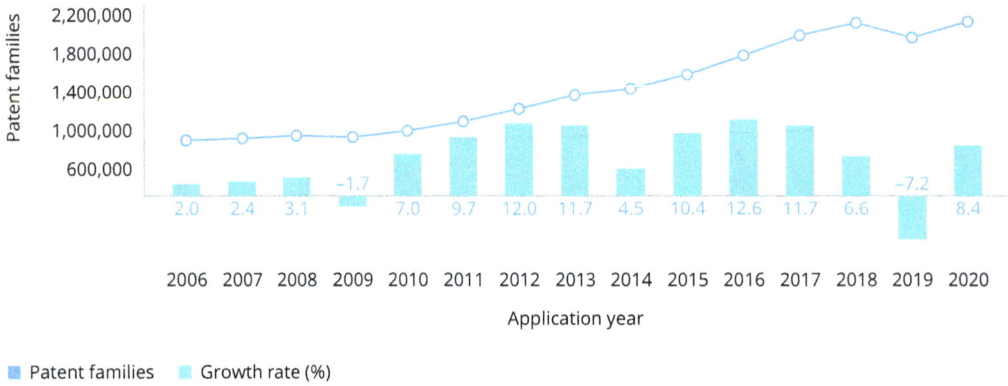

Note: Applicants often file patent applications in multiple jurisdictions therefore some inventions are recorded more than once. To take this into account, WIPO has indicators related to patent families, defined as patent applications interlinked by one or more of the following: priority claim, Patent Cooperation Treaty national phase entry, continuation, continuation-in-part, internal priority, and addition or division. Patent families here include only those families associated with patent applications for inventions and exclude those associated with utility model applications.
Sources: WIPO Statistics Database and EPO PATSTAT database, August 2023.

A24. Distribution of patent families by number of offices for the top origins, 2018-2020

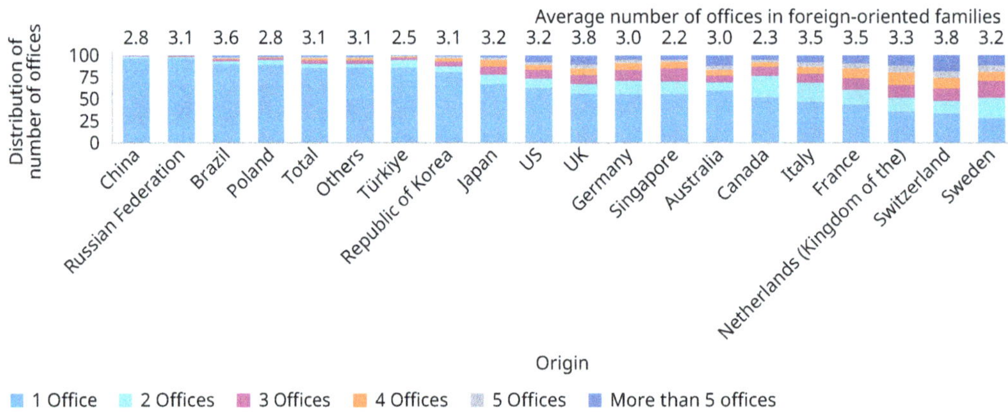

Note: A patent family is defined as patent applications interlinked by one or more of the following: priority claim, Patent Cooperation Treaty national phase entry, continuation, continuation-in-part, internal priority, and addition or division. Patent families here include only those families associated with patent applications for inventions and exclude those associated with utility model applications.
Sources: WIPO Statistics Database and EPO PATSTAT database, August 2023.

A25. Trend in foreign-oriented patent families worldwide, 2006–2019

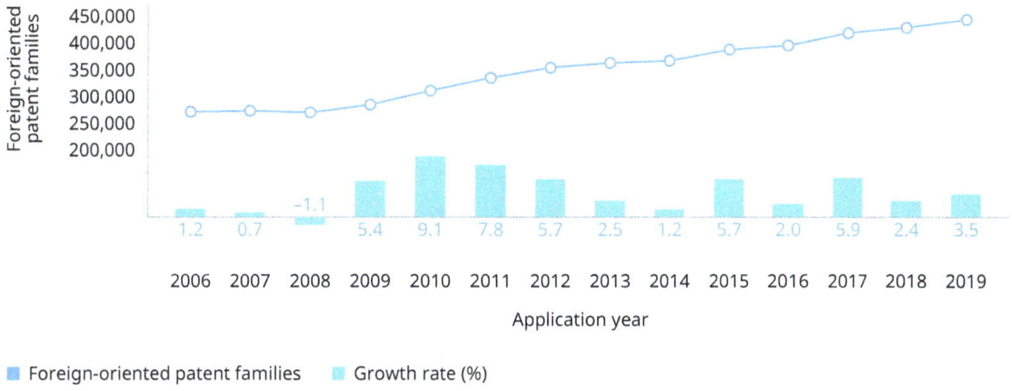

Note: A special subset of patent families comprises foreign-oriented patent families. This includes only patent families that have at least one filing office different from the office of the applicant's country of origin. Some foreign-oriented patent families include only one filing office, because applicants may choose to file directly with a foreign office. For example, if a Canadian applicant files a patent application directly with the United States Patent and Trademark Office (USPTO) without having previously filed with the patent office of Canada, that application and any applications filed subsequently with the USPTO will form a foreign-oriented patent family.
Sources: WIPO Statistics Database and EPO PATSTAT database, August 2023.

A26. Foreign-oriented patent families for the top 20 origins, 2018–2019

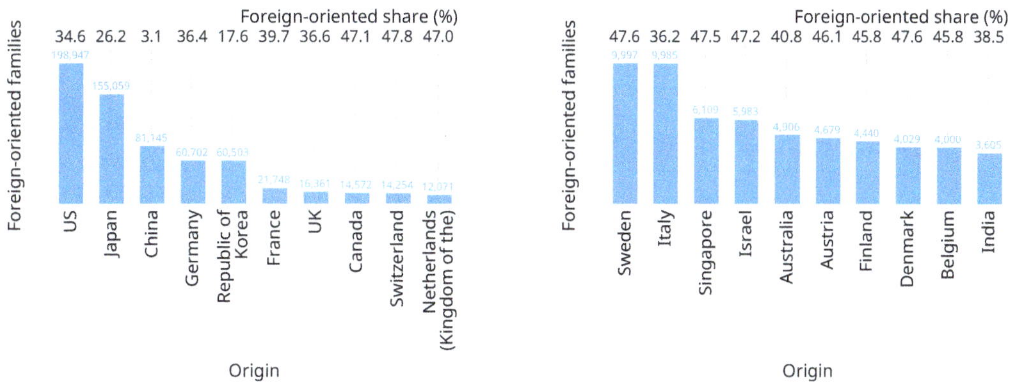

Note: A special subset of patent families comprises foreign-oriented patent families. This includes only patent families that have at least one filing office different from the office of the applicant's country of origin. Some foreign-oriented patent families include only one filing office, because applicants may choose to file directly with a foreign office. For example, if a Canadian applicant files a patent application directly with the United States Patent and Trademark Office (USPTO) without having previously filed with the patent office of Canada, that application and any applications filed subsequently with the USPTO will form a foreign-oriented patent family.
Sources: WIPO Statistics Database and EPO PATSTAT database, August 2023.

A27. Distribution of technology fields for selected applicants based on patent families, 2018–2020

	Applicant									
Field of technology	Canon Inc	Huawei Technologies	Toyota Motor Corp	IBM	Samsung Electronics	LG Electronics Inc	Mitsubishi Electric Corp	China Petroleum & Chemicals	Robert Bosch GmbH	Gree Electric
Electrical machinery, apparatus, energy	3.2	3.0	22.4	1.3	4.3	5.9	20.6	1.1	15.2	9.2
Audio-visual technology	15.8	7.9	1.2	3.4	9.4	8.3	4.2	0.1	1.9	1.9
Telecommunications	6.4	10.7	0.4	3.0	8.0	6.5	3.6	0.1	0.9	1.8
Digital communication	3.1	43.7	1.3	15.9	16.8	30.7	3.2	0.1	2.7	3.3
Basic communication processes	0.2	1.4	0.1	1.0	1.5	0.2	1.4	0.0	0.7	0.5
Computer technology	14.6	21.5	4.1	50.2	23.0	5.6	7.5	3.8	9.0	9.3
IT methods for management	0.7	0.7	3.4	4.7	0.9	0.6	2.1	2.3	0.6	1.5
Semiconductors	2.6	1.6	1.8	9.5	17.8	2.2	6.3	0.0	1.3	0.8
Optics	29.1	2.5	0.2	0.8	3.1	1.1	2.4	0.0	1.6	0.1
Measurement	2.1	2.5	4.6	2.3	3.1	1.7	6.6	11.6	12.3	2.7
Analysis of biological materials	0.1	0.0	0.0	0.2	0.1	0.0	0.0	0.7	0.4	0.1
Control	0.8	1.1	7.0	1.9	0.8	1.8	5.5	0.9	4.6	4.2
Medical technology	2.8	0.6	1.0	2.2	2.0	1.3	0.4	0.0	0.6	0.8
Organic fine chemistry	0.1	0.0	0.0	0.1	0.4	0.0	0.0	11.3	0.1	0.0
Biotechnology	0.1	0.0	0.1	0.1	0.1	0.1	0.0	0.7	0.2	0.0
Pharmaceuticals	0.0	0.0	0.0	0.1	0.0	0.0	0.0	0.0	0.0	0.0
Macromolecular chemistry, polymers	0.4	0.0	0.1	0.1	0.2	0.1	0.1	9.7	0.1	0.1
Food chemistry	0.0	0.0	0.0	0.0	0.0	0.2	0.0	0.0	0.0	0.1
Basic materials chemistry	0.6	0.0	0.2	0.1	0.7	0.2	0.1	15.9	0.1	0.3
Materials, metallurgy	0.2	0.1	1.6	0.1	0.3	0.3	0.3	4.1	0.9	0.1
Surface technology, coating	0.5	0.1	1.1	0.1	0.5	0.3	0.4	0.6	0.7	0.2
Micro-structural and nano-technology	0.1	0.0	0.0	0.2	0.2	0.0	0.0	0.4	1.3	0.0
Chemical engineering	0.3	0.0	0.6	0.2	0.3	0.9	0.4	14.3	0.9	1.3
Environmental technology	0.4	0.0	2.0	0.0	0.3	0.7	0.7	6.3	2.1	1.8
Handling	3.6	0.1	1.3	0.3	0.7	2.5	4.8	0.9	0.9	1.2
Machine tools	0.3	0.0	2.1	0.1	0.3	0.3	1.6	0.4	3.5	0.5
Engines, pumps, turbines	0.0	0.1	8.7	0.1	0.1	3.7	3.3	0.4	8.7	4.6
Textile and paper machines	9.9	0.0	0.1	0.0	0.0	0.1	0.3	1.1	0.1	0.0
Other special machines	1.2	0.1	1.4	0.3	0.3	0.9	0.7	1.5	1.8	0.4
Thermal processes and apparatus	0.0	0.1	0.4	0.2	1.1	7.4	14.2	0.6	1.1	35.7
Mechanical elements	0.4	0.2	6.8	0.1	0.4	1.3	1.0	1.2	5.6	1.9
Transport	0.1	1.2	24.8	0.5	0.4	2.0	4.5	0.2	19.0	1.6
Furniture, games	0.0	0.2	0.4	0.3	0.9	4.1	1.8	0.0	0.3	7.7
Other consumer goods	0.1	0.2	0.1	0.2	1.8	8.1	1.2	0.1	0.2	5.7
Civil engineering	0.0	0.0	0.5	0.1	0.1	0.7	0.4	9.5	0.5	0.4

Note: WIPO's International Patent Classification (IPC) technology concordance table was used to convert IPC symbols into 35 corresponding fields of technology. For an electronic version of the IPC technology concordance table, visit www.wipo.int/ipstats.
Sources: WIPO Statistics Database and EPO PATSTAT database, August 2023.

A28. Distribution of technology fields for selected universities and PROs based on patent families, 2018–2020

Field of technology	Applicant											
	Zhejiang University	Tianjin University	CEA	IFP Energies Nouvelles	Fraunhofer Ges Forschung	DLR	AIST	Tokyo University	Korea Electronics Telecomm	KAIST	University of California	MIT
Electrical machinery, apparatus, energy	6.6	7.0	12.4	4.3	4.8	6.1	8.8	7.5	2.7	5.8	3.4	6.9
Audio-visual technology	1.0	1.1	1.6	0.0	9.3	0.6	0.9	2.5	12.0	2.2	0.7	0.8
Telecommunications	1.3	1.6	1.9	0.0	6.2	3.9	0.4	0.9	7.3	3.9	1.5	2.0
Digital communication	2.0	1.8	2.2	0.0	11.7	2.5	0.5	0.7	23.4	5.6	1.4	1.2
Basic communication processes	0.5	2.0	2.2	0.2	1.5	1.3	0.5	0.4	1.4	1.9	1.1	0.8
Computer technology	17.1	18.3	9.3	1.7	7.1	3.1	2.9	8.1	26.1	21.9	5.9	6.8
IT methods for management	2.4	2.8	0.4	0.3	0.4	1.0	0.9	1.2	4.2	2.7	0.2	0.3
Semiconductors	1.8	1.3	19.1	0.1	4.9	1.1	8.6	2.8	2.8	5.9	3.3	4.0
Optics	1.9	1.2	4.3	0.0	3.7	1.3	2.7	2.1	3.5	3.3	2.7	2.8
Measurement	13.8	16.0	12.6	6.4	11.3	12.1	14.0	10.7	4.6	6.2	5.4	6.8
Analysis of biological materials	1.0	0.6	0.9	1.7	0.8	0.3	2.1	4.8	0.2	1.6	4.2	3.5
Control	2.8	2.3	1.0	0.7	1.4	3.5	0.8	1.7	4.2	1.6	0.5	1.1
Medical technology	4.2	3.3	2.3	1.0	2.6	1.8	3.7	6.4	2.7	5.6	11.8	6.7
Organic fine chemistry	2.5	2.6	0.6	10.7	0.8	0.0	7.3	3.4	0.0	1.0	4.9	2.0
Biotechnology	5.6	3.0	1.2	3.6	1.5	0.1	6.3	12.4	0.1	4.3	19.0	18.2
Pharmaceuticals	3.1	1.3	0.6	0.0	0.8	0.0	1.4	7.9	0.0	2.1	19.7	10.6
Macromolecular chemistry, polymers	2.0	1.8	0.9	1.6	1.9	0.4	2.7	4.8	0.0	1.1	1.1	1.6
Food chemistry	2.4	0.3	0.1	0.2	0.4	0.0	1.0	0.5	0.0	0.4	0.7	0.1
Basic materials chemistry	1.8	2.3	1.4	17.3	1.4	1.1	2.7	1.4	0.1	1.2	1.1	1.1
Materials, metallurgy	2.5	3.6	2.8	4.4	4.7	2.1	10.1	3.3	0.1	2.8	1.6	3.3
Surface technology, coating	1.2	1.8	2.8	0.5	3.1	3.2	4.3	1.6	0.1	2.0	1.3	2.1
Micro-structural and nano-technology	0.7	0.8	2.2	0.0	1.4	0.1	1.6	1.3	0.1	1.2	0.6	1.1
Chemical engineering	3.3	3.6	2.5	22.6	1.9	1.3	6.6	2.4	0.3	4.1	2.7	4.0
Environmental technology	2.7	3.2	1.9	4.9	0.8	0.7	1.6	0.5	0.1	1.3	0.8	1.6
Handling	1.7	1.5	1.0	0.4	1.0	6.7	0.8	1.3	0.8	1.2	0.3	1.3
Machine tools	0.8	1.9	0.9	0.2	3.4	0.6	1.1	1.7	0.1	0.2	0.1	0.8
Engines, pumps, turbines	1.8	1.8	1.6	8.1	1.2	6.3	0.5	1.4	0.1	1.2	0.1	1.1
Textile and paper machines	0.4	0.2	0.3	0.1	0.7	0.7	0.7	0.3	0.1	0.7	0.3	0.6
Other special machines	3.5	2.0	2.2	1.2	4.5	12.2	2.3	1.1	0.3	1.8	1.5	2.5
Thermal processes and apparatus	1.1	1.7	2.8	2.3	1.0	7.3	0.7	0.9	0.1	0.6	0.4	0.7
Mechanical elements	1.4	0.9	1.5	0.9	0.8	4.5	0.8	0.7	0.0	0.9	0.3	1.1
Transport	2.2	1.6	1.4	1.6	1.3	12.5	0.3	1.1	1.8	1.7	0.5	1.6
Furniture, games	0.4	0.4	0.1	0.1	0.2	0.3	0.1	0.3	0.4	0.4	0.2	0.0
Other consumer goods	0.3	0.4	0.4	0.1	0.8	0.9	0.1	0.2	0.2	0.8	0.3	0.1
Civil engineering	2.3	3.9	0.5	2.7	0.7	0.3	0.3	1.4	0.0	0.8	0.2	0.7

Note: PRO means public research organization. A patent family is defined as patent applications interlinked by one or more of the following: priority claim, Patent Cooperation Treaty national phase entry, continuation, continuation-in-part, internal priority, and addition or division. Patent families include only those families associated with patent applications for inventions and exclude those associated with utility model applications. Deutsches Zentrum für Luft- und Raumfahrt E.V. (DLR); Le Commissariat à l'énergie atomique et aux énergies alternatives (CEA); Korea Advanced Institute of Science and Technology (KAIST); National Institute of Advanced Industrial Science and Technology (AIST); and Massachusetts Institute of Technology (MIT).
Sources: WIPO Statistics Database and EPO PATSTAT database, August 2023.

Published patent applications by field of technology

A29. Published patent applications worldwide by field of technology, 2011, 2016 and 2021

Field of technology		Number of published applications			Share of total (%)	Average growth (%)
		2011	2016	2021	2021	2011-2021
Electrical engineering	Electrical machinery, apparatus, energy	125,162	190,881	219,345	6.4	5.8
	Audio-visual technology	74,794	80,653	102,694	3.0	3.2
	Telecommunications	51,153	56,184	57,313	1.7	1.1
	Digital communication	83,341	139,813	169,090	4.9	7.3
	Basic communication processes	15,874	16,509	17,587	0.5	1.0
	Computer technology	134,071	205,037	379,201	11.1	11.0
	IT methods for management	23,970	46,284	86,458	2.5	13.7
	Semiconductors	80,091	83,589	100,927	2.9	2.3
Instruments	Optics	62,104	69,351	74,361	2.2	1.8
	Measurement	78,744	132,066	198,784	5.8	9.7
	Analysis of biological materials	12,160	16,425	20,426	0.6	5.3
	Control	28,472	57,616	81,022	2.4	11.0
	Medical technology	81,957	125,303	177,857	5.2	8.1
Chemistry	Organic fine chemistry	54,375	66,906	65,999	1.9	2.0
	Biotechnology	42,702	58,426	79,392	2.3	6.4
	Pharmaceuticals	73,141	111,690	100,391	2.9	3.2
	Macromolecular chemistry, polymers	29,415	49,069	51,147	1.5	5.7
	Food chemistry	31,603	66,516	44,153	1.3	3.4
	Basic materials chemistry	47,849	84,621	71,481	2.1	4.1
	Materials, metallurgy	40,200	69,110	75,069	2.2	6.4
	Surface technology, coating	33,826	45,310	51,577	1.5	4.3
	Micro-structural and nano-technology	3,609	4,866	5,975	0.2	5.2
	Chemical engineering	39,579	67,133	116,341	3.4	11.4
	Environmental technology	27,103	48,467	67,159	2.0	9.5
Mechanical engineering	Handling	45,460	76,437	106,798	3.1	8.9
	Machine tools	47,120	81,063	119,194	3.5	9.7
	Engines, pumps, turbines	49,867	68,769	60,338	1.8	1.9
	Textile and paper machines	31,274	41,608	45,594	1.3	3.8
	Other special machines	53,103	99,017	126,521	3.7	9.1
	Thermal processes and apparatus	30,936	45,339	54,613	1.6	5.8
	Mechanical elements	47,790	74,859	76,898	2.2	4.9
	Transport	67,406	116,508	142,329	4.2	7.8
Other fields	Furniture, games	42,938	70,571	78,600	2.3	6.2
	Other consumer goods	34,268	53,581	63,428	1.9	6.4
	Civil engineering	59,353	98,443	131,395	3.8	8.3
	Unknown	3,659	5,164	6,469	0.2	5.9
Total		**1,788,469**	**2,723,184**	**3,425,926**	**100.0**	**6.7**

Note: Data refer to published patent applications. There is a minimum delay of 18 months between the application date and the publication date. WIPO's International Patent Classification (IPC) technology concordance table was used to convert IPC symbols into 35 corresponding fields of technology. For an electronic version of the IPC technology concordance table, visit www.wipo.int/ipstats.
Sources: WIPO Statistics Database and EPO PATSTAT database, August 2023.

A30. Distribution of published patent applications by technology field for the top 10 origins, 2019–2021

Field of technology	China	US	Japan	Republic of Korea	Germany	France	UK	Switzerland	Netherlands (Kingdom of the)	Russian Federation
	Origin									
Electrical machinery, apparatus, energy	6.2	4.1	9.9	8.2	9.4	6.5	5.3	6.1	6.9	3.5
Audio-visual technology	2.6	2.8	4.2	4.9	1.5	1.7	1.9	1.0	1.8	0.6
Telecommunications	1.6	2.2	2.0	2.4	0.9	1.4	1.4	0.6	1.2	1.3
Digital communication	5.0	7.8	3.0	5.7	2.1	3.1	2.7	1.5	2.5	0.9
Basic communication processes	0.4	0.8	0.7	0.5	0.6	0.6	0.7	0.4	0.8	0.8
Computer technology	12.1	12.9	6.1	8.9	4.0	5.0	8.6	2.9	6.0	3.2
IT methods for management	2.7	2.8	2.1	3.7	0.7	0.8	1.3	0.8	0.5	0.8
Semiconductors	1.8	2.6	5.2	6.7	1.8	2.4	1.4	0.9	3.0	0.8
Optics	1.5	2.0	5.4	2.7	1.8	2.1	1.9	1.0	5.5	0.8
Measurement	7.1	3.9	4.9	3.6	6.5	5.0	4.5	8.4	5.4	7.5
Analysis of biological materials	0.5	0.9	0.4	0.5	0.6	0.8	1.1	1.1	0.7	2.0
Control	2.6	2.2	2.7	2.0	2.5	1.5	1.6	1.6	1.2	1.9
Medical technology	3.4	9.4	3.7	4.3	4.5	5.4	7.6	9.8	13.2	8.8
Organic fine chemistry	1.6	2.6	1.4	2.0	2.7	4.5	3.7	5.2	4.1	1.6
Biotechnology	1.6	4.5	1.2	1.7	2.0	3.1	5.3	5.5	3.7	2.2
Pharmaceuticals	1.8	6.4	1.3	2.1	2.4	4.4	7.6	9.7	4.0	4.1
Macromolecular chemistry, polymers	1.5	1.2	2.5	1.5	1.9	2.0	0.7	1.7	2.5	0.8
Food chemistry	1.8	1.0	0.9	2.0	0.5	1.1	0.7	3.2	3.5	4.6
Basic materials chemistry	2.4	2.1	2.2	1.7	2.7	2.4	2.3	3.2	3.6	2.6
Materials, metallurgy	2.8	1.1	2.4	1.8	1.9	2.5	1.4	1.3	0.9	3.9
Surface technology, coating	1.4	1.2	2.5	1.4	1.6	1.8	1.0	1.4	1.9	1.4
Micro-structural and nano-technology	0.2	0.1	0.1	0.1	0.2	0.2	0.2	0.1	0.1	0.7
Chemical engineering	4.2	2.2	1.5	2.3	2.6	2.9	3.0	2.5	2.4	3.8
Environmental technology	2.8	1.1	1.1	1.6	1.4	1.4	1.6	0.8	1.3	2.7
Handling	3.6	2.1	3.3	2.2	3.4	2.5	2.5	5.4	2.9	1.3
Machine tools	4.8	1.5	2.5	1.8	3.6	1.3	1.2	1.8	1.3	2.4
Engines, pumps, turbines	1.3	1.7	2.4	1.5	4.5	4.5	3.6	1.4	0.9	7.4
Textile and paper machines	1.4	0.9	2.4	0.8	1.4	0.7	0.9	1.9	1.2	0.5
Other special machines	4.3	3.2	3.0	3.0	4.1	4.5	2.9	2.7	5.1	5.5
Thermal processes and apparatus	2.0	0.9	1.8	1.9	1.5	1.6	1.0	0.8	0.9	1.7
Mechanical elements	2.0	1.7	2.8	2.2	6.4	4.2	3.0	1.8	1.3	4.2
Transport	3.2	3.6	6.0	4.6	11.7	11.3	4.9	2.3	2.4	5.2
Furniture, games	1.8	2.1	4.6	2.6	1.8	1.4	2.5	2.2	2.1	1.2
Other consumer goods	1.6	1.8	1.6	3.1	1.7	2.6	6.0	6.9	2.2	1.1
Civil engineering	4.6	2.8	2.3	3.7	3.2	3.0	4.4	2.1	2.8	8.4

Note: Data refer to published patent applications. There is a minimum delay of 18 months between the application date and the publication date. WIPO's International Patent Classification (IPC) technology concordance table was used to convert IPC symbols into 35 corresponding fields of technology. For an electronic version of the IPC technology concordance table, visit www.wipo.int/ipstats. The top 10 origins were selected based on their 2019–2021 total published applications.
Sources: WIPO Statistics Database and EPO PATSTAT database, August 2023.

A31. Trend in patent applications in energy-related technologies, 2006–2021

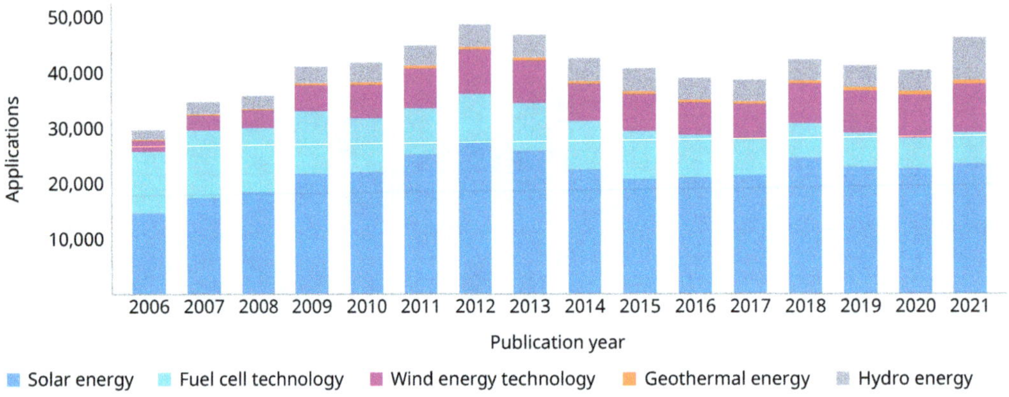

Note: For definitions of the technologies – fuel cell, geothermal, solar, wind and hydro energy – see annex A. The correspondence between International Patent Classification (IPC) symbols and technology fields is not always apparent (there is no one-to-one correspondence). It is therefore difficult to capture all patents in a specific technology field. Even so, the IPC-based definitions are likely to capture the vast majority of patent applications in these areas. Data refer to published patent applications.
Sources: WIPO Statistics Database and EPO PATSTAT database, August 2023.

A32. Share of patent applications in energy-related technologies for the top five origins, 2019–2021

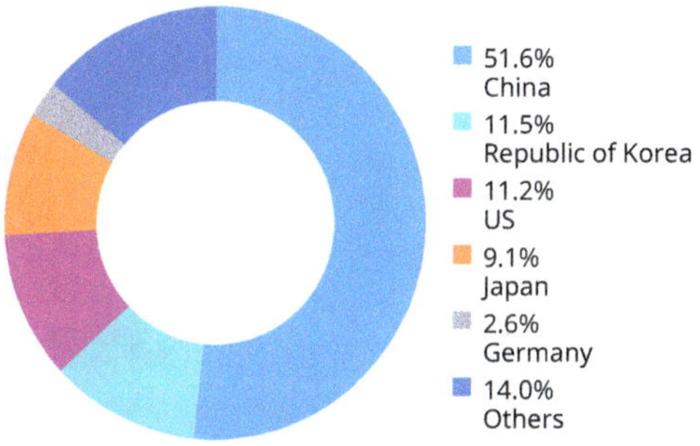

Solar energy

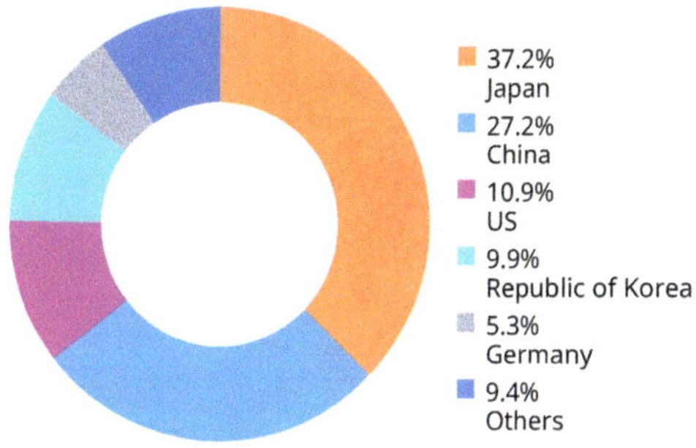

Fuel cell technology

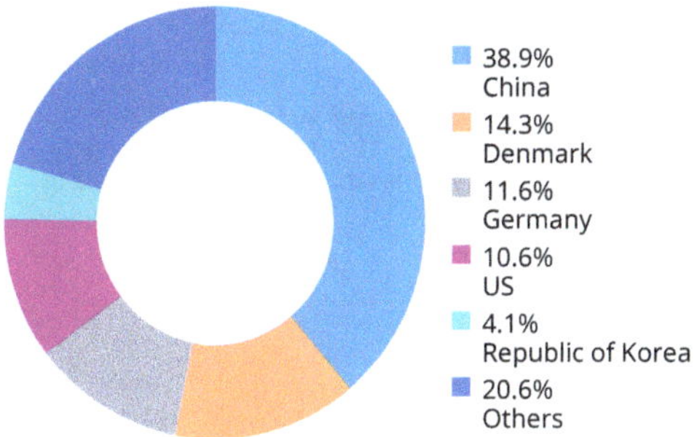

Wind energy technology

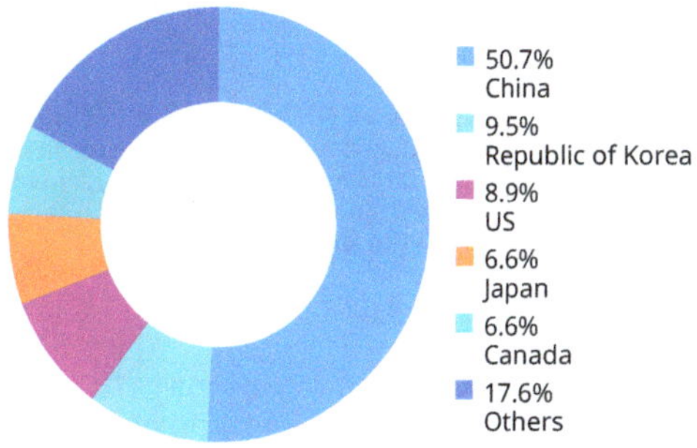

Geothermal energy

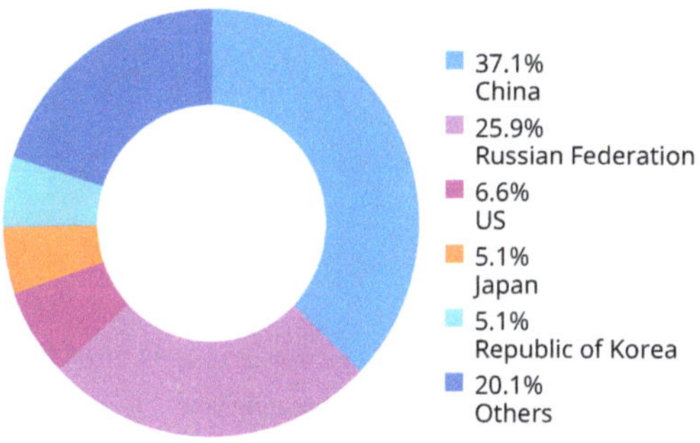

Hydro energy

Note: For definitions of the technologies – fuel cells, geothermal, solar, wind and hydro energy – see annex A. The correspondence between International Patent Classification (IPC) symbols and technology fields is not always apparent (there is no one-to-one correspondence). It is therefore difficult to capture all patents in a specific technology field. Even so, the IPC-based definitions are likely to capture the vast majority of patent applications in these areas. Data refer to published patent applications.
Sources: WIPO Statistics Database and EPO PATSTAT database, August 2023.

Participation of women inventors in published PCT applications

A33. Share of women among listed inventors in PCT applications, 2008–2022

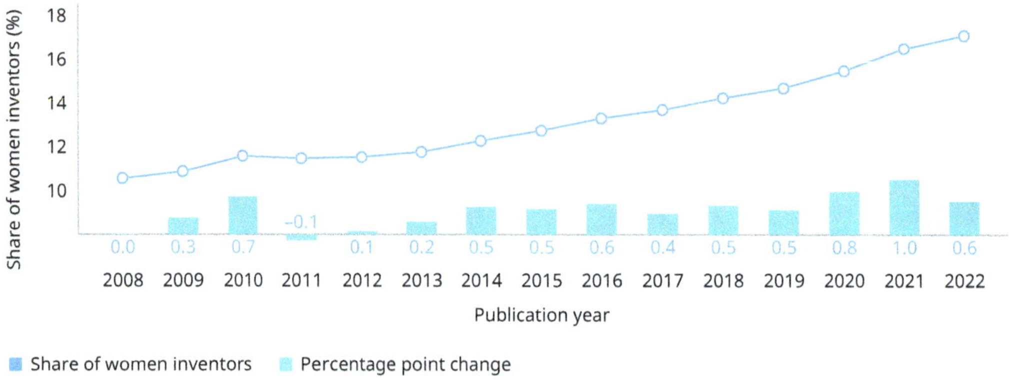

Note: Data refer to published PCT applications. In order to attribute gender to inventors' names recorded in PCT applications, WIPO produced a world gender-name dictionary based on information from 13 different public sources. Gender is attributed to a given name on a country-by-country basis, because certain names may be considered male in one country but female in another.
Source: WIPO Statistics Database, August 2023.

A34. Share of PCT applications with at least one woman as inventor and with at least one man as inventor, 2008–2022

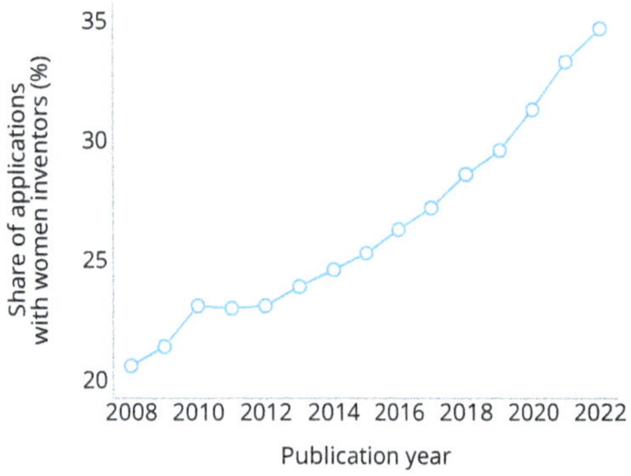

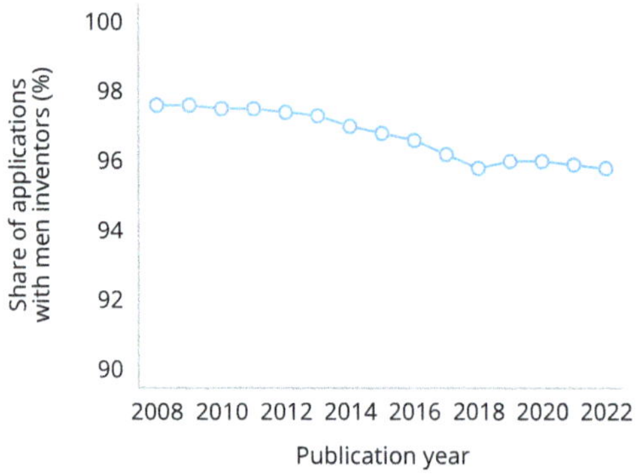

Note: Data refer to published PCT applications. In order to attribute gender to inventors' names recorded in PCT applications, WIPO produced a gender-name dictionary based on information from 13 different public sources. Gender is attributed to a given name on a country-by-country basis, because certain names may be considered male in one country but female in another.
Source: WIPO Statistics Database, August 2023.

A35. Share of women among listed inventors and share of PCT applications with at least one woman as inventor for the top 20 origins, 2022

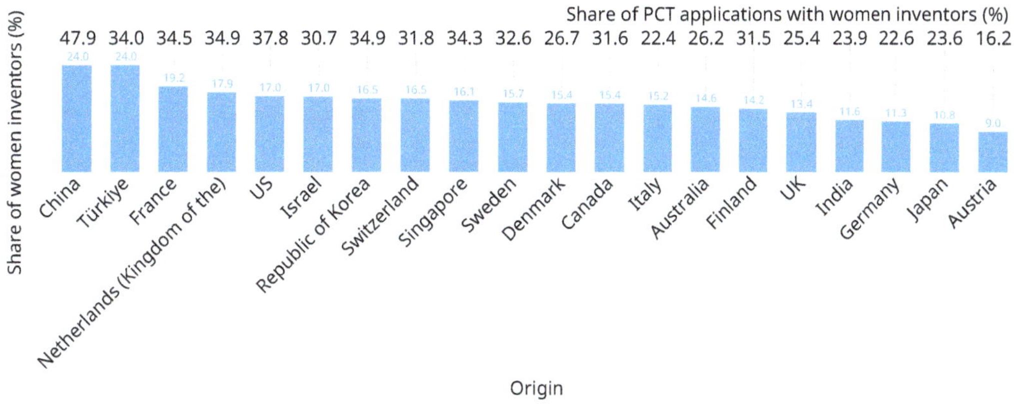

Note: Data refer to published PCT applications. In order to attribute gender to inventors' names recorded in PCT applications, WIPO produced a gender-name dictionary based on information from 13 different public sources. Gender is attributed to a given name on a country-by-country basis, because certain names may be considered male in one country but female in another.
Source: WIPO Statistics Database, August 2023.

A36. Share of PCT patent applications with women inventors by field of technology, 2022

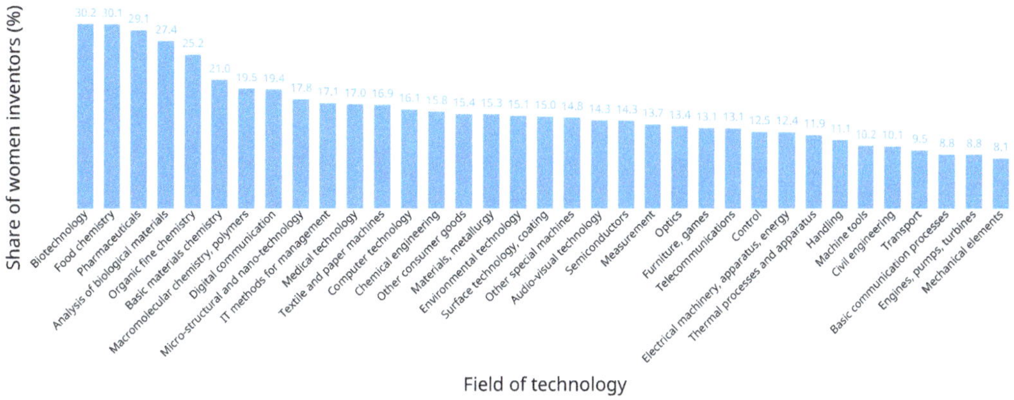

Note: Data refer to published PCT applications. WIPO's International Patent Classification (IPC) technology concordance table was used to convert IPC symbols into 35 corresponding fields of technology. For an electronic version of the IPC technology concordance table, visit www.wipo.int/ipstats.
Source: WIPO Statistics Database, August 2023.

Patent applications in relation to GDP and population

A37. Resident patent applications per USD 100 billion GDP for the top 20 origins, 2012 and 2022

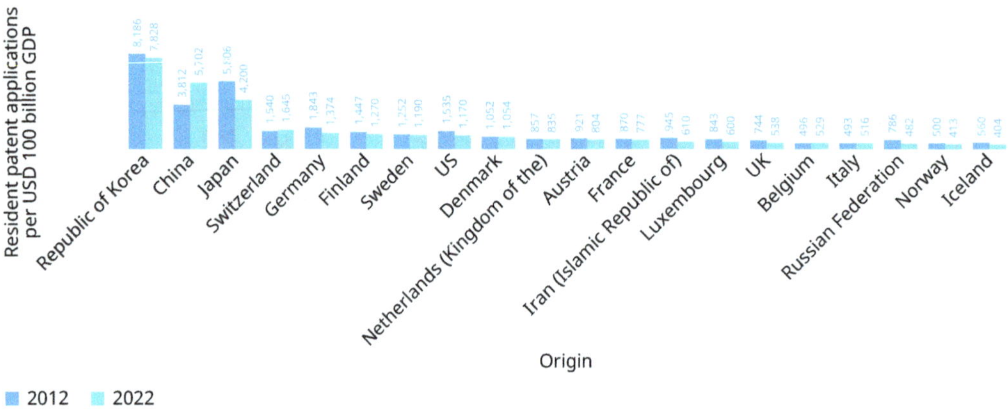

Note: GDP data are in 2017 US purchasing power parity (PPP) dollars. The top 20 origins were included if they had a GDP greater than USD 25 billion PPP and more than 100 resident patent applications. Because of space constraints, only the top 20 origins to fulfil these criteria are presented.
Sources: WIPO Statistics Database and World Bank, August 2023.

A38. Resident patent applications per million population for the top 20 origins, 2012 and 2022

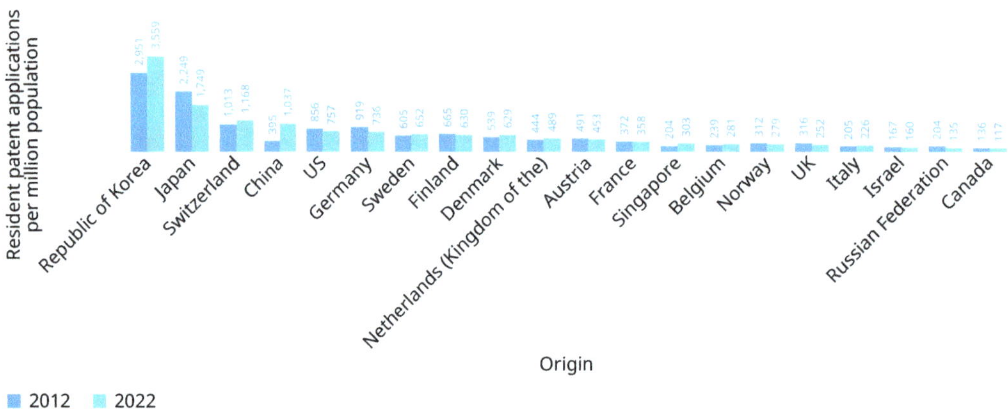

Note: The top 20 origins were included if they had a population greater than 5 million and if they had more than 100 resident patent applications. Because of space constraints, only the top 20 origins to fulfil these criteria are presented.
Sources: WIPO Statistics Database and World Bank, August 2023.

A39. Resident patent applications per capita and GDP per capita, 2018–2022

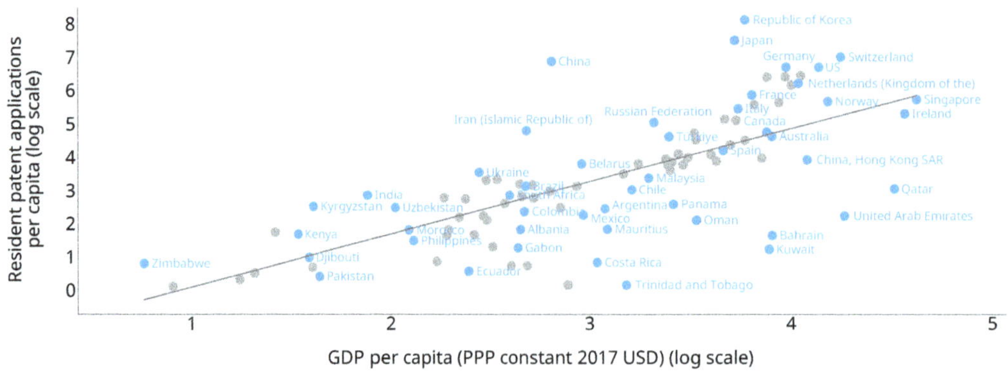

Sources: WIPO Statistics Database and World Bank, August 2023.

A40. Resident patent applications per capita and R&D expenditure per capita, 2018–2022

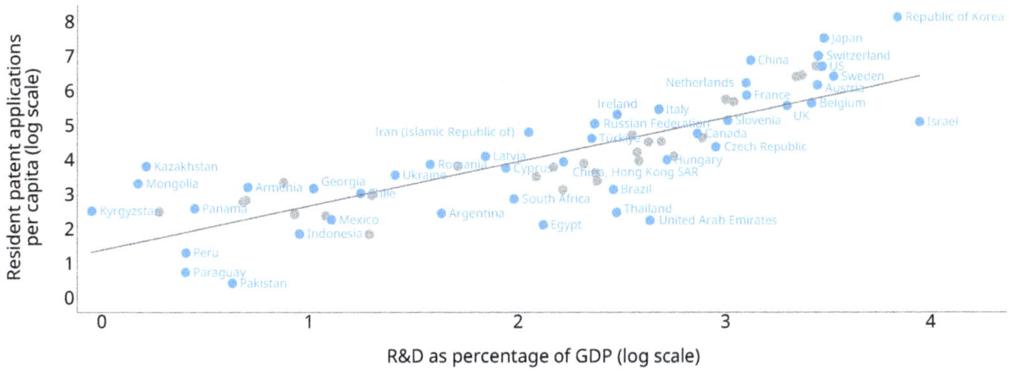

Note: R&D data refer to gross domestic expenditure on research and experimental development (GERD). R&D data lag by one year.
Sources: WIPO Statistics Database, OECD, UNESCO and World Bank, August 2023.

Patents in force

A41. Trend in patents in force worldwide, 2008–2022

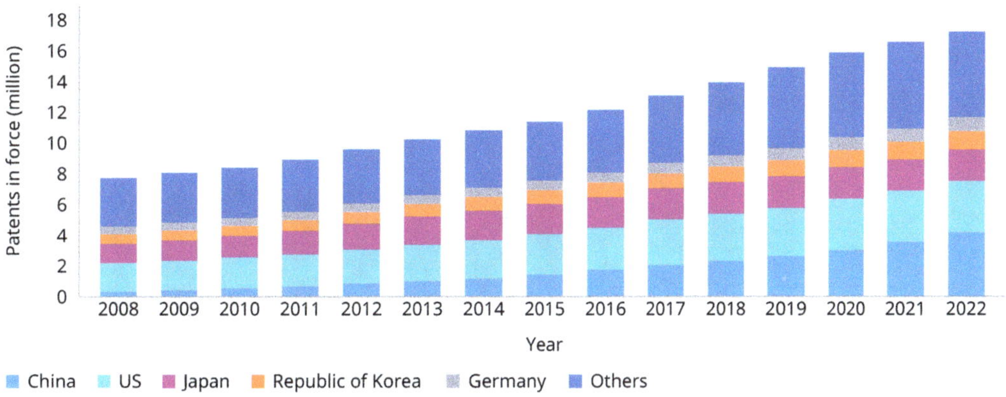

Note: World totals are WIPO estimates using data covering 137 offices.
Source: WIPO Statistics Database, August 2023.

A42. Patents in force at the top 20 offices, 2022

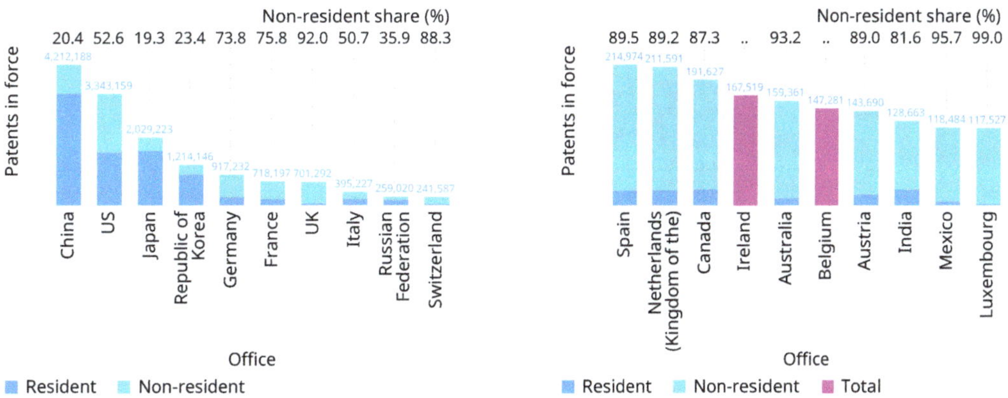

.. indicates not available.
Source: WIPO Statistics Database, August 2023.

A43. Flow of patents in force between selected origins and offices, 2022

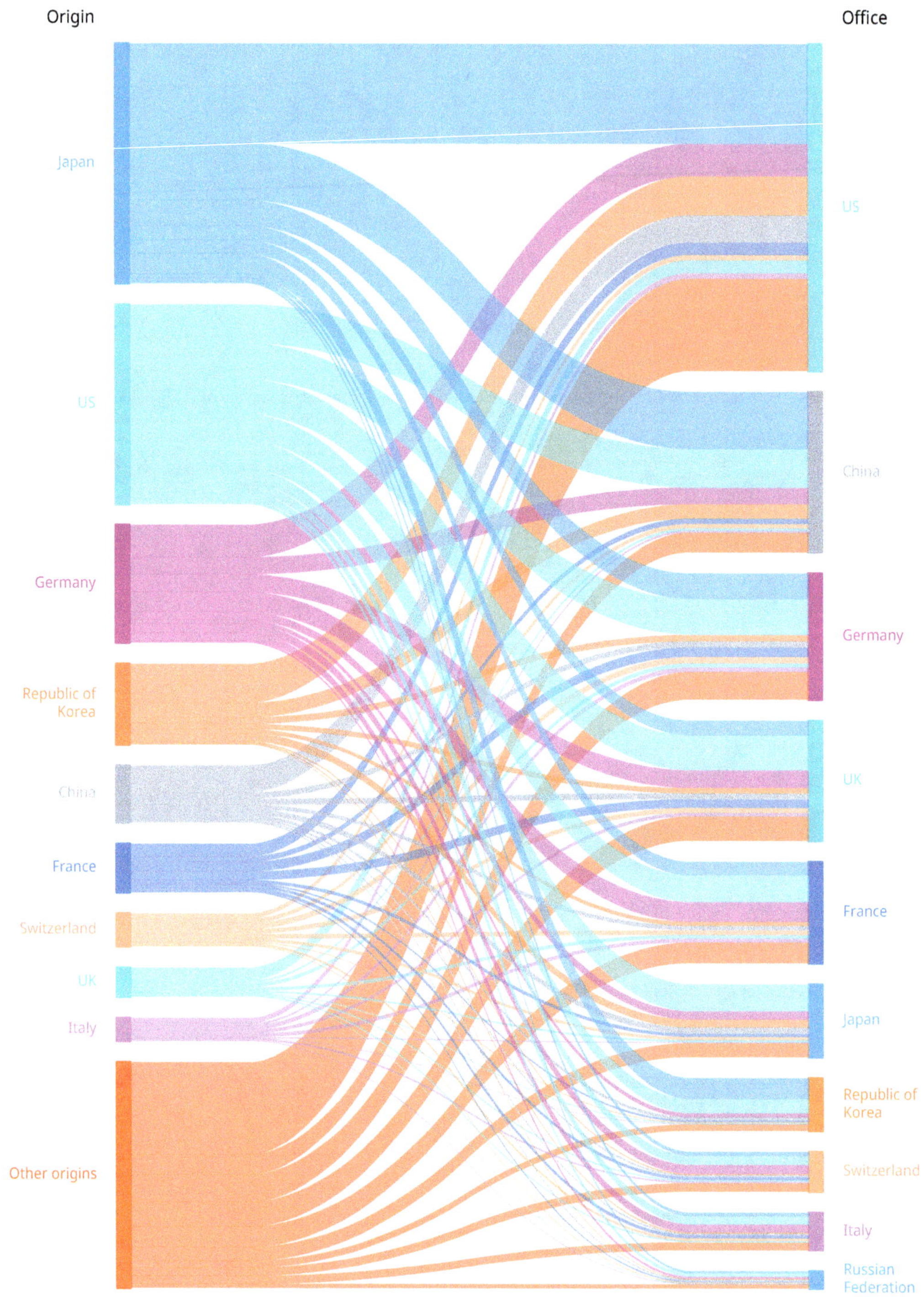

Source: WIPO Statistics Database, August 2023.

A44. Patents in force in 2022 as a percentage of total applications

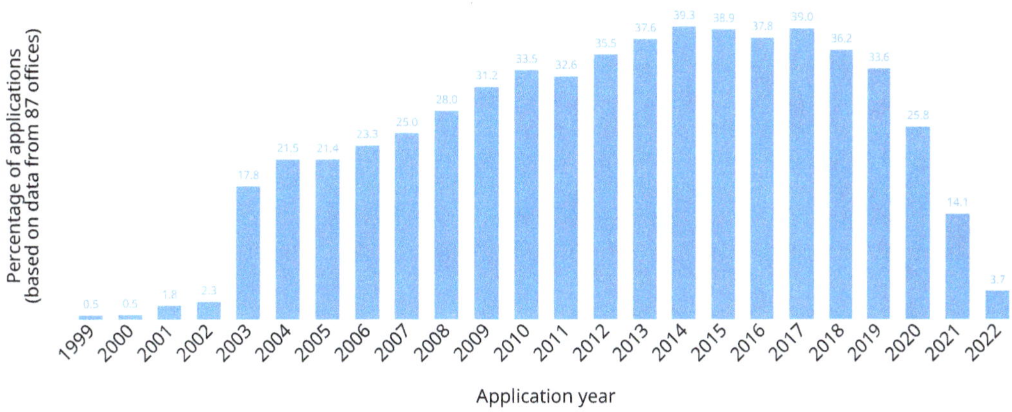

Note: Percentages are calculated as the number of patent applications filed in year *t* and in force in 2022, divided by the total number of patent applications filed in year *t*. Patent holders must pay maintenance fees to maintain the validity of their patents. Depending on technological and commercial considerations, patent holders may opt to let a patent lapse before the end of the full protection term. This figure shows the distribution of patents in force in 2022 as a percentage of total applications in the year of filing. However, not all offices provide these data. Data for 87 offices show that 39.3% of the applications for which patents were eventually granted remained in force for at least 9 years after the application date, and about 17.8% lasted the full 20-year term.
Source: WIPO Statistics Database, August 2023.

A45. Average age of patents in force at selected offices, 2017 and 2022

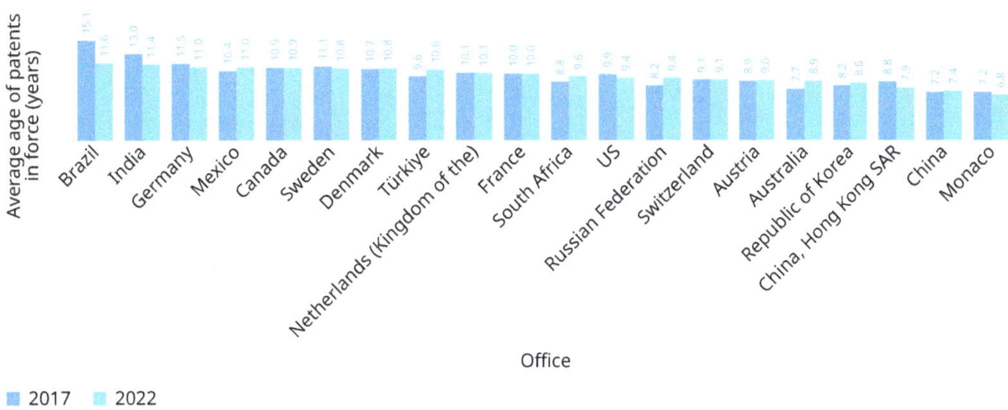

Note: The average age of patents in force is calculated using the following formula: $\Sigma(p*y)/\Sigma p$, where p is the number of patents in force and y the number of years between filing and reporting year.
Source: WIPO Statistics Database, August 2023.

Patent office procedural data

A46. Distribution of patent examination outcomes for selected offices, 2022

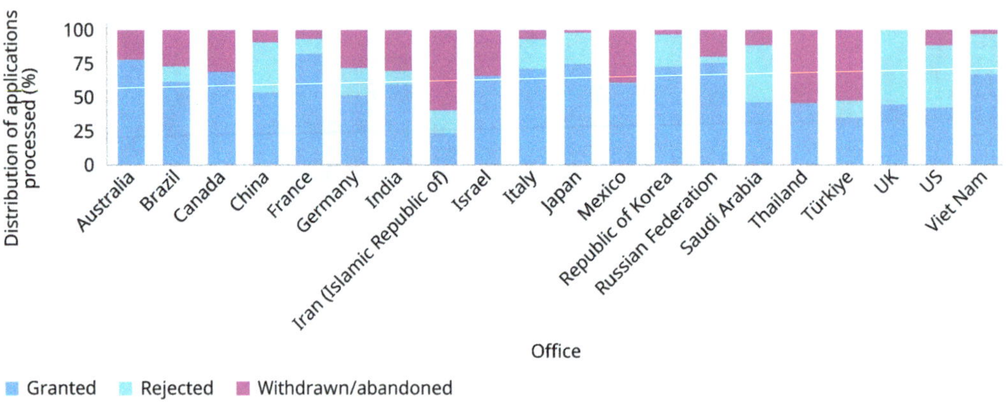

Note: The share of applications granted should not be interpreted as grant rates, as they are based on the examination date rather than the date when the application was filed. The number of grants in a given year relates to applications filed in previous years. WIPO collects data from IP offices using a common questionnaire and methodology. However, because of differences in patent procedures between offices, data cannot be fully harmonized. Therefore, caution should be exercised when making comparisons across offices.
Source: WIPO Statistics Database, August 2023.

A47. Potentially pending applications at the top 20 offices, 2022

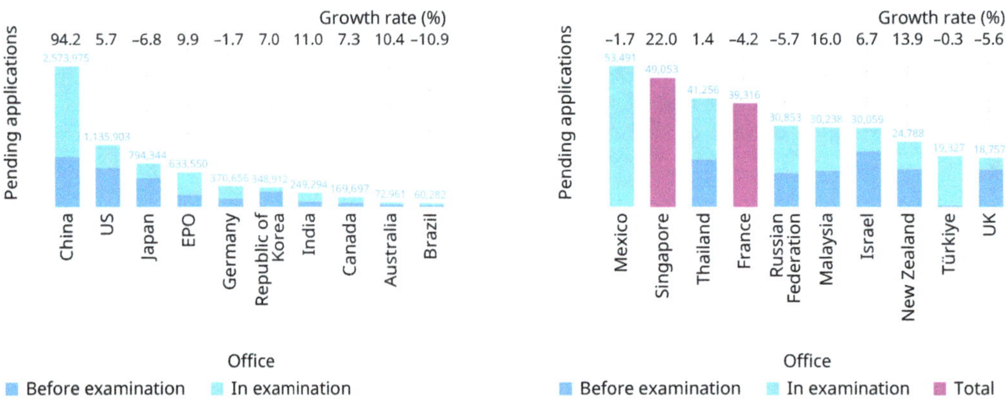

Note: EPO is the European Patent Office. Application processing varies between offices, making it difficult to measure pending applications. In some offices, patent applications automatically proceed to the examination stage, unless applicants withdraw them; in others, applications do not proceed to examination, unless applicants file a separate request for examination. To take account of procedural differences, pending application data are separated between (a) all patent applications, at any stage in the process, that are awaiting a final decision by a patent office, including those for which applicants have not filed a request for examination (where applicable), and (b) patent applications undergoing examination for which the applicant has requested examination (where such separate requests are necessary).
Source: WIPO Statistics Database, August 2023.

A48. Average pendency times for first office action and final decision at selected offices, 2022

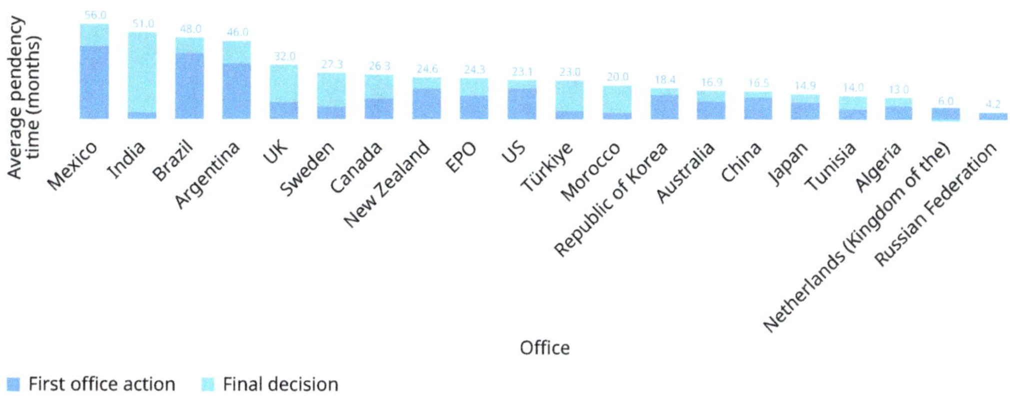

Note: EPO is the European Patent Office. WIPO collects data from IP offices using a common questionnaire and methodology. However, because of differences in patent procedures between offices, data cannot be fully harmonized. Therefore, caution should be exercised when making comparisons across offices.
Source: WIPO Statistics Database, August 2023.

A49. Number of patent examiners for selected offices, 2022

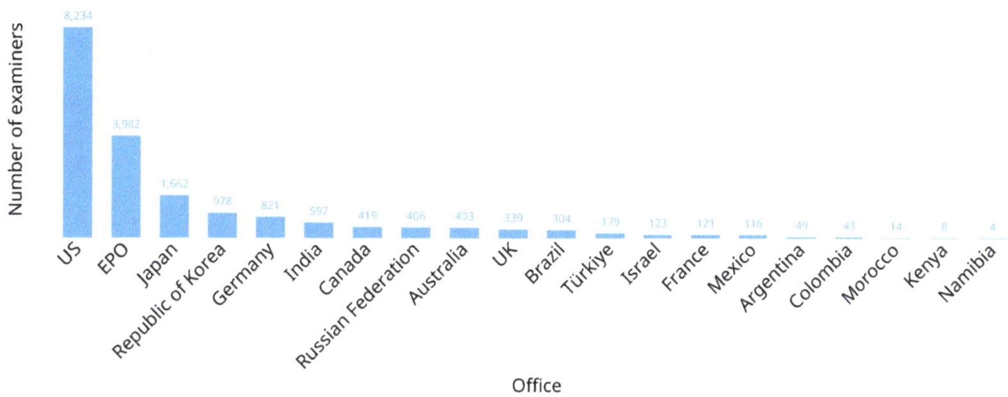

Note: EPO is the European Patent Office.
Source: WIPO Statistics Database, August 2023.

A50. Average years of experience of patent examiners for selected offices, 2022

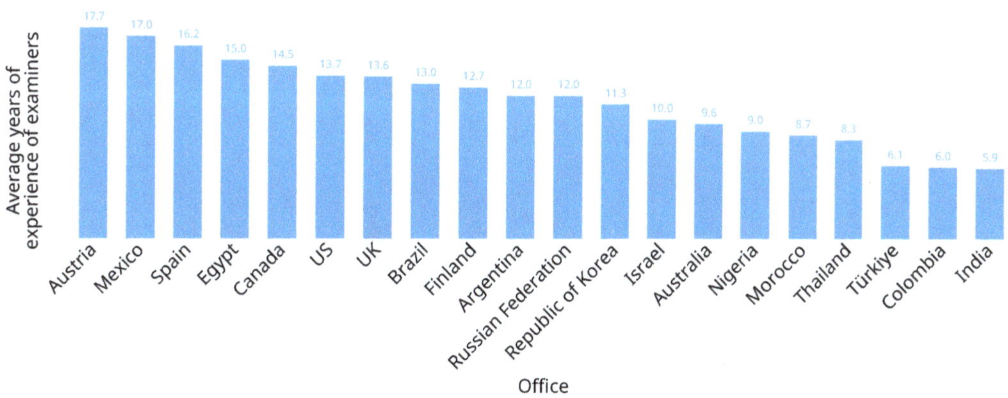

Source: WIPO Statistics Database, August 2023.

Patent prosecution highway (PPH)

A51. PPH requests by office of first filing and offices of later examination, 2022

	Office of first filing															
Office of later examination	**Australia**	**Canada**	**China**	**Denmark**	**EAPO**	**EPO**	**Germany**	**Israel**	**Japan**	**Republic of Korea**	**Singapore**	**UK**	**Unknown**	**US**	**Others**	**Total**
Australia	38	12	21	8		83	24	4	58	6	1	52	3	864	109	**1,283**
Brazil	1		63	4	118		5		64	40		21	2	422	51	**791**
Canada	74	123	82	1		489	6	20	92	43	8	29		2,327	50	**3,344**
China		20		24		857	68	10	1,323	275	24	44		2,451	71	**5,167**
EPO		40	230					16	293	134	2			690	25	**1,430**
Germany	1	4	31	1					177	20	1	61		609	14	**919**
Israel	14	3	13	1		140	1	32	22	9	5	3		296	5	**544**
Japan *	17	20	303	12	2	684	19	6	1,177	156	20	14	28	1,449	45	**3,952**
Mexico	2	1	26	3		63	27	1	48	3		12	3	390	91	**670**
New Zealand	19	2		1			2	2	10	3		5		109	6	**159**
Philippines									86	8				71		**165**
Republic of Korea	31	24	219	17	6	409	18	22	757	96	27	44	54	2,233	30	**3,987**
Russian Federation	5		55			97	3	1	40	58	1			85	3	**348**
Singapore	14	4	36			63		7	109	23	24	6		191	6	**483**
Thailand									381							**381**
Viet Nam									111	24						**135**
Others	16	5	37	3		47	4	3	195	3		12		203	783	**1,311**
Total	**232**	**258**	**1,116**	**75**	**126**	**2,932**	**177**	**124**	**4,943**	**901**	**113**	**303**	**90**	**12,390**	**1,289**	**25,069**

Note: EAPO is the Eurasian Patent Organization and EPO is the European Patent Office. A patent prosecution highway is a bilateral agreement between two offices that enables applicants to request a fast-track examination whereby patent examiners can use the work already undertaken by the other office.
* indicates data based on office of earlier examination rather than office of first filing.
Source: WIPO Statistics Database, August 2023.

A52. Flows of PPH requests between offices of first filing and offices of later examination, 2022

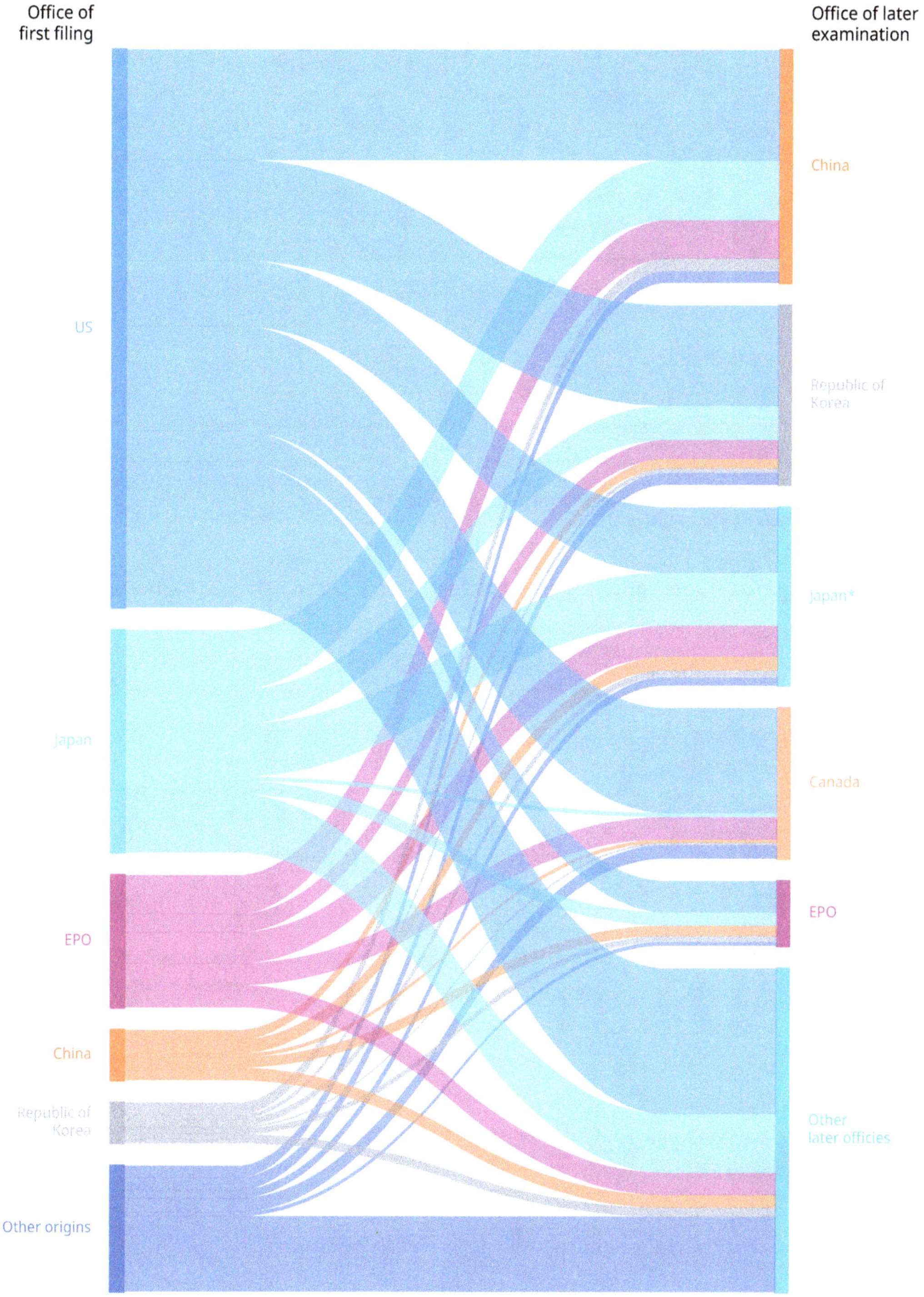

Note: EPO is the European Patent Office. Japan data refers to the office of earlier examination rather than the office of first filing. A patent prosecution highway (PPH) is a bilateral agreement between two offices that enables applicants to request a fast-track examination whereby patent examiners can use the work already undertaken by the other office. This graph shows the flows of PPH requests between offices of first filing and offices of later examination.
* indicates data based on office of earlier examination rather than office of first filing.
Source: WIPO Statistics Database, August 2023.

Utility model applications

A53. Trend in utility model applications worldwide, 2008–2022

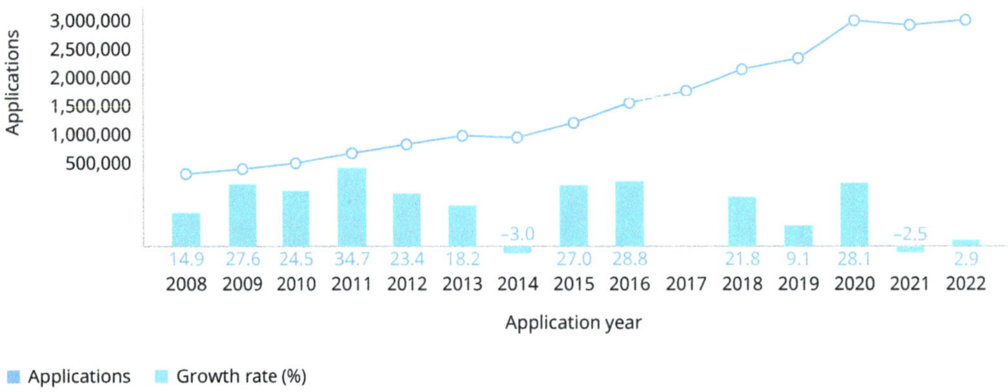

Note: World totals are WIPO estimates using data covering 83 patent offices. Totals include applications filed directly with national and regional offices and applications entering offices through the Patent Cooperation Treaty national phase (where applicable). China's pre-2017 data are not comparable owing to a change in methodology. Because of this break in the data series and to the large number of filings in China, it is not possible to report accurately the 2017 growth rate at world level (see data description section in Additional information for details).
Source: WIPO Statistics Database, August 2023.

A54. Utility model applications for the top 20 offices, 2022

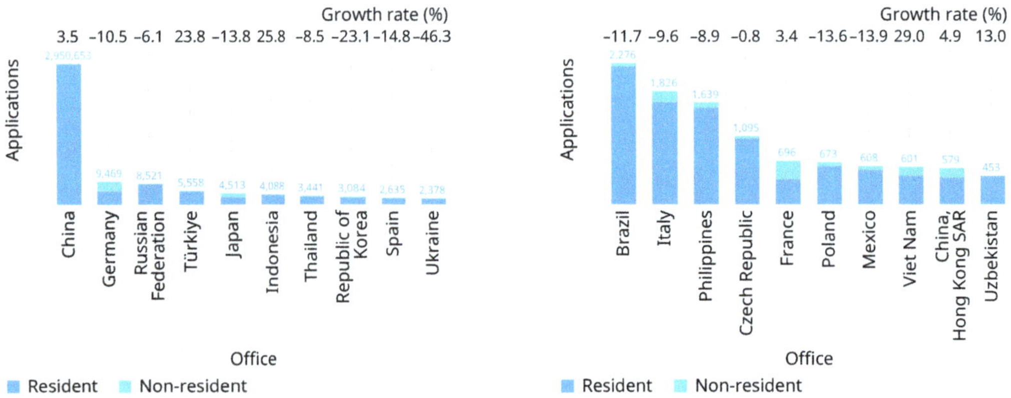

Source: WIPO Statistics Database, August 2023.

A55. Utility model applications for offices of selected low- and middle-income countries, 2022

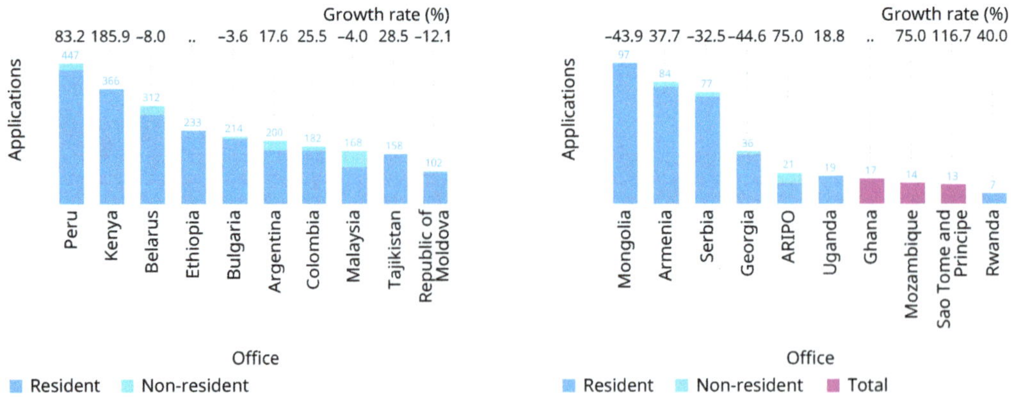

Note: ARIPO is the African Regional Intellectual Property Organization.
.. indicates not available.
Source: WIPO Statistics Database, August 2023.

Microorganisms

A56. Trend in microorganism deposits worldwide, 2008–2022

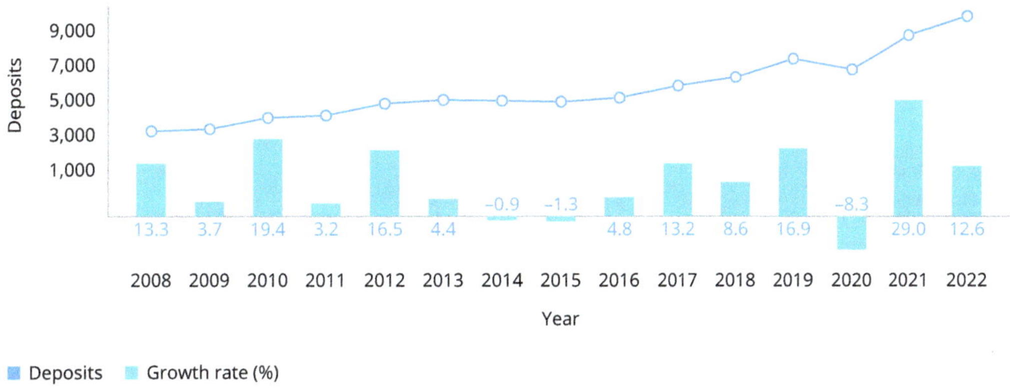

Note: Deposits of microorganisms for patent procedures are important for biotechnological inventions. Disclosing an invention is a requirement for receiving a patent.
Source: WIPO Statistics Database, August 2023.

A57. Deposits at the top international depositary authorities, 2022

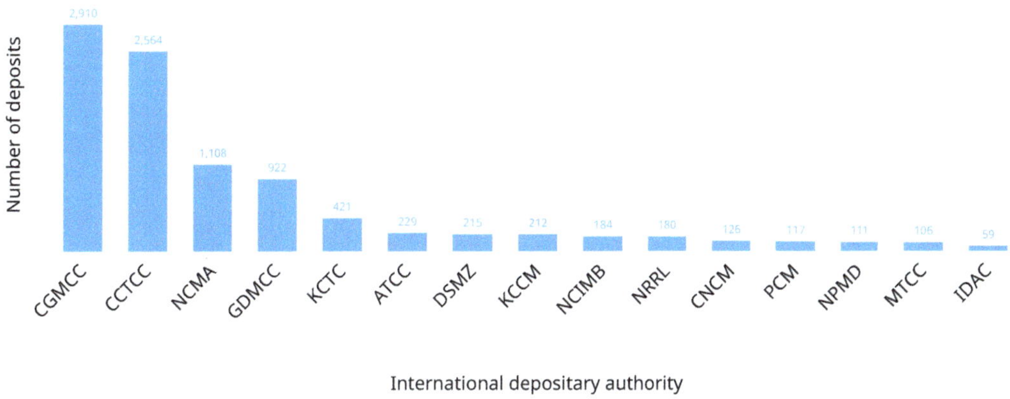

Note: ATCC is the American Type Culture Collection (US), CCTCC is the China Center for Type Culture Collection (China), CGMCC is the China General Microbiological Culture Collection Center (China), CNCM is the Collection Nationale de Cultures de Microorganisms (France), DSMZ is the Leibniz-Institut DSMZ (Deutsche Sammlung von Mikroorganismen und Zellkulturen GmbH; Germany), GDMCC is the Guangdong Microbial Culture Collection Center (China), IDAC is the International Depositary Authority of Canada (Canada), KCCM is the Korean Culture Center of Microorganisms (Republic of Korea), KCTC is the Korean Collection for Type Cultures (Republic of Korea), MTCC is the Microbial Type Culture Collection and Gene Bank (India), NCIMB is the National Collection of Industrial, Food and Marine Bacteria (UK), NCMA is the Provasoli-Guillard National Center for Marine Algae and Microbiota (US), NPMD is the National Institute of Technology and Evaluation, Patent Microorganisms Depositary (Japan), NRRL is the Agriculture Research Service Culture Collection (US) and PCM is the Polish Collection of Microorganisms (Poland).
Source: WIPO Statistics Database, August 2023.

Statistical tables

A58. Patent applications by office and origin, 2022

	Applications by office				Equivalent applications by origin		PCT national phase entry	
Name	Total	Resident	Non-resident	Change over previous year	Total (a)	Change over previous year	Office	Origin
Afghanistan (b)	..	..	..	..	17	..	..	..
African Intellectual Property Organization	549	161	388	-63	n.a.	n.a.	380	n.a.
African Regional Intellectual Property Organization	873	11	862	+40	n.a.	n.a.	833	n.a.
Albania	21	17	4	-3	35	-4	..	6
Algeria	1,118	471	647	+269	483	+202	627	5
Andorra	8	0	8	-3	19	-8	..	12
Angola	80	80	0	-6	82	+81	70	70
Antigua and Barbuda	6	0	6	-2	153	-255	5	66
Argentina	3,576	444	3,132	-93	763	+46	..	153
Armenia	34	20	14	-14	71	-35	7	9
Australia	32,284	2,465	29,819	-125	11,707	-1,118	23,707	7,928
Austria	1,887	1,710	177	-160	13,655	+183	420	7,175
Azerbaijan	213	165	48	+78	531	+193	40	2
Bahamas (b)	..	..	..	..	50	..	..	24
Bahrain	489	3	486	+160	30	+13	469	11
Bangladesh	418	76	342	-29	90	-1	..	3
Barbados	60	..	..	-13	795	+28	60	78
Belarus	342	279	63	-44	980	-138	44	36
Belgium	1,207	676	531	-7	14,290	+324	..	8,455
Belize	32	0	32	+5	17	-4	..	9
Benin (b,c)	n.a.	n.a.	n.a.	n.a.	71	-100	n.a.	20
Bhutan	5	0	5	-2	1	+1	..	..
Bolivia (Plurinational State of)	226	10	216	-6	14	+8	..	1
Bosnia and Herzegovina	51	36	15	-10	73	+9	10	14
Botswana	13	13	0	+10	17	+13	..	3
Brazil	24,759	4,398	20,361	+527	6,984	+75	19,191	1,692
Brunei Darussalam	155	0	155	+16	1	-4	149	..
Bulgaria	171	166	5	0	548	+82	..	207
Burkina Faso (b,c)	n.a.	n.a.	n.a.	n.a.	104	+19	n.a.	19
Cabo Verde	3	2	1	+1	2	+1	..	..
Cambodia	162	0	162	..	41	..	71	33
Cameroon (b,c)	n.a.	n.a.	n.a.	n.a.	803	-271	n.a.	3
Canada	38,052	4,564	33,488	+897	25,562	-963	31,604	11,676
Chad (b,c)	n.a.	n.a.	n.a.	n.a.	119	+68	n.a.	..
Chile	3,136	372	2,764	+54	823	-107	2,759	438
China	1,619,268	1,464,605	154,663	+33,605	1,586,339	+47,735	87,416	70,345
China, Hong Kong SAR	20,164	426	19,738	-1,779	2,459	-802	..	696
China, Macao SAR	31	7	24	-6	27	-136	..	3
Colombia	3,032	1,104	1,928	+745	1,317	+625	1,885	172
Congo (b,c)	n.a.	n.a.	n.a.	n.a.	52	-19	n.a.	..
Costa Rica	586	9	577	+5	135	+5	577	75
Côte d'Ivoire (b,c)	n.a.	n.a.	n.a.	n.a.	562	-135	n.a.	..
Croatia	130	122	8	+42	290	-14	3	72
Cuba (b)	..	..	..	..	196	..	..	171
Curaçao (b)	..	..	..	..	19	..	..	10
Cyprus	7	5	2	+4	295	-122	..	181
Czech Republic	551	505	46	-49	1,887	-35	27	809
Democratic People's Republic of Korea (b)	..	..	..	..	21	..	..	14
Democratic Republic of the Congo (b)	..	..	..	..	2	..	..	..
Denmark	1,227	1,052	175	-49	14,525	+425	74	8,847
Djibouti	7	0	7	-6	1	-2	7	1
Dominica	2	0	2	-9	1	-4	..	..
Dominican Republic	241	8	233	+14	51	+5	226	33
Ecuador	509	27	482	+101	45	-6	476	8

Name	Applications by office				Equivalent applications by origin		PCT national phase entry	
	Total	Resident	Non-resident	Change over previous year	Total (a)	Change over previous year	Office	Origin
Egypt	1,914	589	1,325	–310	866	–131	1,298	44
El Salvador	149	4	145	+3	4	+2	146	2
Estonia	15	10	5	–11	273	–77	4	156
Eswatini (b)	..	..	..	..	2	..	..	..
Ethiopia	64	16	48	..	39	..	..	..
Eurasian Patent Organization	3,731	645	3,086	+88	n.a.	n.a.	2,867	n.a.
European Patent Office	193,610	84,074	109,536	+4,832	n.a.	n.a.	120,634	n.a.
European Union (b)	..	..	..	..	26	..	..	25
Fiji (b)	..	..	..	..	4	..	..	3
Finland	1,447	1,361	86	–215	12,972	+146	34	7,468
France	14,746	13,322	1,424	–13	66,446	+309	..	34,366
Gabon (b,c)	n.a.	n.a.	n.a.	n.a.	103	–256	n.a.	..
Gambia	88	0	88	–3	..	..	88	..
Georgia	241	86	155	–13	97	–35	151	8
Germany	57,213	37,199	20,014	–1,356	157,652	–8,174	7,005	66,674
Ghana	21	7	14	..	11	..	14	1
Greece	1,085	437	648	+159	1,238	–149	..	292
Grenada	17	0	17	+1	..	..	6	..
Guatemala	289	7	282	+31	12	–3	282	1
Guinea (b,c)	n.a.	n.a.	n.a.	n.a.	51	–1	n.a.	..
Guyana (b)	..	..	..	..	1	..	..	..
Honduras	194	0	194	+6	2	0	189	..
Hungary	501	407	94	+55	1,145	–321	69	531
Iceland	39	37	2	+3	313	–58	2	167
India	77,068	38,551	38,517	+15,495	56,396	+13,233	31,577	5,668
Indonesia	9,967	1,549	8,418	+1,167	1,607	+162	7,533	59
Iran (Islamic Republic of)	8,681	8,267	414	–2,110	8,391	–1,959	412	74
Iraq (b)	..	..	..	..	23	..	..	..
Ireland	89	69	20	–28	7,464	+403	..	3,965
Israel	10,073	1,527	8,546	+464	17,327	–14	9,011	8,486
Italy	9,221	8,440	781	–1,857	32,021	–2,185	144	14,665
Jamaica	19	8	11	–57	13	–10	..	5
Japan	289,530	218,813	70,717	+330	406,374	–6,511	75,892	133,930
Jordan	350	25	325	+3	64	+11	299	9
Kazakhstan	838	713	125	..	1,297	..	107	16
Kenya	417	363	54	+220	396	+197	47	5
Kuwait	734	..	..	..	53	..	707	15
Kyrgyzstan	71	68	3	–16	132	+12	..	..
Lao People's Democratic Republic	61	0	61	..	..	..	45	..
Latvia	112	103	9	+4	246	–35	..	104
Lebanon (b)	..	..	..	..	30	..	..	14
Libya (b)	..	..	..	..	5	..	..	3
Liechtenstein (b)	..	..	..	..	1,480	..	..	816
Lithuania	77	69	8	–13	642	+165	..	145
Luxembourg	2,093	106	1,987	+540	2,580	–145	302	1,846
Madagascar	32	8	24	+4	9	+3	24	..
Malawi (b)	..	..	..	..	37	..	..	24
Malaysia	7,374	820	6,554	–160	1,760	–103	5,445	434
Mali (b,c)	n.a.	n.a.	n.a.	n.a.	55	–139	n.a.	..
Malta	16	8	8	+6	441	+34	..	207
Marshall Islands (b)	..	..	..	..	1	..	..	..
Mauritania (b,c)	n.a.	n.a.	n.a.	n.a.	85	+49	n.a.	..
Mauritius	8	0	8	–12	401	+236	..	321
Mexico	16,605	983	15,622	+444	1,815	–179	13,731	465
Monaco	4	4	0	–4	154	+17	..	94
Mongolia	192	112	80	+6	138	+25	76	24
Montenegro	7	7	0	..	11	..	..	3
Morocco	2,913	246	2,667	+110	363	–36	2,285	75
Mozambique	41	25	16	–5	25	–5	16	..
Myanmar (b)	..	..	..	..	1	..	..	..

Name	Applications by office				Equivalent applications by origin		PCT national phase entry	
	Total	Resident	Non-resident	Change over previous year	Total (a)	Change over previous year	Office	Origin
Namibia	32	16	16	..	39	..	3	12
Nepal (b)	..	..	..	..	5	..	..	..
Netherlands (Kingdom of the)	3,772	1,861	1,911	+302	32,738	-41	..	18,807
New Zealand	7,043	267	6,776	+191	2,588	-94	5,479	1,574
Niger (b,c)	n.a.	n.a.	n.a.	n.a.	87	+19	n.a.	1
Nigeria	1,104	..	..	..	16	..	828	1
North Macedonia	24	24	0	-18	53	-20	..	19
Norway	1,410	862	548	-170	5,974	+133	516	3,810
Oman	530	39	491	-19	88	-12	438	5
Pakistan	908	371	537	-85	416	-75	..	1
Palau (b)	..	..	..	..	2	..	..	..
Panama (b)	..	..	..	..	53	..	..	31
Papua New Guinea	32	1	31	+3	4	0	30	..
Paraguay	371	7	364	+7	11	-3	..	..
Peru	1,449	176	1,273	+214	234	+74	1,234	54
Philippines	4,765	533	4,232	+372	674	-21	3,982	16
Poland	3,323	3,240	83	-165	6,073	+157	39	1,293
Portugal	745	697	48	-8	2,035	+49	23	882
Qatar (b)	..	..	..	..	105	..	..	38
Republic of Korea	237,633	183,748	53,885	-365	272,675	+5,148	46,478	39,855
Republic of Moldova	59	49	10	-17	54	-21	6	2
Romania	843	806	37	+26	1,140	+26	9	98
Russian Federation	26,924	18,970	7,954	-4,053	25,188	-716	6,581	3,088
Rwanda	12	7	5	-4	9	-7	1	..
Saint Kitts and Nevis (b)	..	..	..	..	13	..	..	10
Saint Lucia (b)	..	..	..	..	1	..	..	..
Saint Vincent and the Grenadines	1	0	1	-10	2	+2	1	..
Samoa (b)	..	..	..	..	28	..	..	19
San Marino	502	9	493	-227	48	-10	..	17
Sao Tome and Principe	12	0	12	-2	..	..	..	..
Saudi Arabia	5,837	2,606	3,231	+1,858	5,019	+151	3,902	1,446
Senegal (b,c)	n.a.	n.a.	n.a.	n.a.	583	-23	n.a.	4
Serbia	148	127	21	-8	230	-41	14	49
Seychelles	25	1	24	-3	46	-5	13	12
Singapore	14,653	1,708	12,945	+63	8,599	-1,167	10,788	4,030
Slovakia	203	184	19	+44	557	+143	6	228
Slovenia	246	224	22	+7	811	+67	..	321
South Africa	13,990	1,651	12,339	+3,030	2,619	-132	6,432	930
Spain	1,318	1,150	168	-116	10,518	-362	87	5,370
Sri Lanka	431	171	260	-108	260	-69	249	69
Sudan (b)	..	..	..	..	1	..	..	1
Sweden	2,180	1,798	382	-16	28,184	+382	68	18,371
Switzerland	1,546	1,231	315	-9	51,445	+3,109	83	31,273
Syrian Arab Republic	139	126	13	+17	131	+25	13	2
Tajikistan	3	0	3	-6	33	-64	..	..
Thailand	8,607	772	7,835	+365	1,416	-132	7,090	465
Togo (b,c)	n.a.	n.a.	n.a.	n.a.	85	+4	n.a.	..
Trinidad and Tobago	149	1	148	-2	7	-8	148	..
Tunisia	366	200	166	..	225	..	166	15
Türkiye	9,119	8,837	282	+643	11,114	+245	334	1,931
Turkmenistan	62	..	..	+2	4	+1	..	3
Tuvalu	9	0	9	-2	..	..	..	..
Uganda	11	10	1	-7	16	-4	..	2
Ukraine	2,760	794	1,966	-633	1,080	-626	1,743	157
United Arab Emirates	2,848	112	2,736	+425	843	+188	2,620	448
United Kingdom	19,485	11,183	8,302	+630	54,620	+970	2,894	30,635
United Republic of Tanzania	62	..	..	+14	3	-15	..	3
United States of America	594,340	252,316	342,024	+2,867	515,281	+5,319	175,641	223,951
Uruguay (b)	..	..	..	..	95	..	..	45
Uzbekistan	674	458	216	+9	475	+47	196	4

Name	Applications by office: Total	Resident	Non-resident	Change over previous year	Equivalent applications by origin: Total (a)	Change over previous year	PCT national phase entry: Office	Origin
Vanuatu (b)	..	..	..	..	2	..	..	..
Venezuela (Bolivarian Republic of)	230	22	208	-61	29	+21	..	2
Viet Nam	8,707	895	7,812	+173	1,057	-148	6,966	48
Yemen	15	12	3	-27	13	-9	..	..
Zambia	19	10	9	-7	14	-1	9	1
Zimbabwe	41	33	8	-10	41	+31	3	2
Others/Unknown	..	..	..	..	48,265	+1,838	..	12,522
Total (2022 estimates)	**3,457,400**	**2,409,300**	**1,048,100**				**736,100**	

(a) Equivalent applications by origin data are incomplete, because some offices do not report by origin.
(b) The office did not report resident applications therefore the equivalent applications by origin data may be incomplete.
(c) The African Intellectual Property Organization (OAPI) acts as the national office for patent applications.
.. indicates not available.
n.a. indicates not applicable.
Source: WIPO Statistics Database, August 2023.

A59. Patent grants by office and origin, and patents in force, 2022

Name	Grants by office: Total	Resident	Non-resident	Change over previous year	Equivalent grants by origin: Total (a)	Change over previous year	In force by office: Total	Change over previous year
Afghanistan	..	..	..	..	4	..	..	..
African Intellectual Property Organization	530	120	410	+25	n.a.	n.a.	..	..
African Regional Intellectual Property Organization	640	1	639	+72	n.a.	n.a.	2,767	+409
Albania	4	4	0	+2	5	-2	8,497	+1,978
Algeria	610	118	492	-160	125	+21	..	..
Andorra	5	0	5	-7	18	0	40	+1
Angola	43	43	0	-6	43	+43	80	-6
Antigua and Barbuda	..	..	..	..	112	..	..	..
Argentina	1,949	166	1,783	-349	360	-142	12,976	-435
Armenia	3	2	1	-24	34	-33	12	0
Australia	16,407	1,046	15,361	-748	6,166	-188	159,361	+2,048
Austria	1,151	1,012	139	+113	8,176	-574	143,690	-8,415
Azerbaijan	108	83	25	-11	311	-11	250	-22
Bahamas	..	..	..	..	29	..	..	..
Bahrain	197	1	196	+130	15	+4	307	+193
Bangladesh	..	..	..	..	4	..	1,967	-147
Barbados	..	..	..	..	363	..	..	..
Belarus	302	238	64	-14	1,073	+122	1,490	-65
Belgium	1,081	753	328	+76	7,568	-614	..	..
Belize	4	0	4	-8	12	-1	61	+4
Benin (b)	n.a.	n.a.	n.a.	n.a.	119	+51	..	..
Bhutan	2	0	2	..	..	..	3	+2
Bolivia (Plurinational State of)	3	3	0	+2	3	0	224	+7
Bosnia and Herzegovina	7	0	7	+3	1	-4	119	-33
Botswana	..	..	..	..	4	..	..	..
Brazil	23,546	2,497	21,049	-3,326	3,559	-48	94,435	+18,906
Brunei Darussalam	60	1	59	+29	3	-5	962	-559
Bulgaria	78	75	3	-104	259	-176	14,922	-369
Burkina Faso (b)	n.a.	n.a.	n.a.	n.a.	68	-17	..	..
Cabo Verde	..	..	..	..	..	..	2	0
Cambodia	150	0	150	..	5	..	..	..
Cameroon (b)	n.a.	n.a.	n.a.	n.a.	714	+200	..	..
Canada	18,125	1,978	16,147	-4,562	14,556	+944	191,627	-11,976
Central African Republic (b)	n.a.	n.a.	n.a.	n.a.	17	0	..	..
Chad (b)	n.a.	n.a.	n.a.	n.a.	51	+51	..	..
Chile	2,668	331	2,337	+289	615	+55	20,328	+5,969
China	798,347	695,591	102,756	+102,401	760,953	+121,624	4,212,188	+615,287

Name	Grants by office Total	Resident	Non-resident	Change over previous year	Equivalent grants by origin Total (a)	Change over previous year	In force by office Total	Change over previous year
China, Hong Kong SAR	11,602	197	11,405	-3,060	962	-1,068	67,468	+6,022
China, Macao SAR	2	0	2	-13	36	-101	335	-13
Colombia	1,136	180	956	-127	284	-76	8,845	+388
Congo (b)	n.a.	n.a.	n.a.	n.a.	35	-135	..	..
Costa Rica	156	1	155	+26	37	-23	1,282	+94
Côte d'Ivoire (b)	n.a.	n.a.	n.a.	n.a.	374	-51	..	..
Croatia	11	6	5	+4	103	+36	12,597	+721
Cuba	..	..	..	..	77	..	..	..
Curaçao	..	..	..	..	22	..	..	..
Cyprus	1	0	1	..	203	..	11	-3
Czech Republic	352	307	45	-92	1,099	-149	50,974	-179
Democratic People's Republic of Korea	..	..	..	..	18	..	..	..
Democratic Republic of the Congo	..	..	..	..	1	..	..	..
Denmark	398	287	111	+30	6,202	-742	70,398	+614
Djibouti	2	0	2	-1	1	+1	7	-6
Dominican Republic	184	8	176	-43	15	+2	1,067	+129
Ecuador	41	9	32	+24	15	+8	66	-14
Egypt	495	88	407	-13	148	+19	5,267	-119
El Salvador	54	1	53	-4	6	+4	..	..
Estonia	9	9	0	+1	133	+11	11,752	-16
Eswatini	..	..	..	..	5	..	..	..
Ethiopia	23	6	17	..	6	..	264	..
Eurasian Patent Organization	2,766	654	2,112	+350	n.a.	n.a.	n.a.	n.a.
European Patent Office	81,086	36,626	44,460	-27,713	n.a.	n.a.	n.a.	n.a.
Finland	677	626	51	+132	6,878	-699	56,468	-379
France	12,421	10,762	1,659	-3,072	41,962	-7,186	718,197	+14,855
Gabon (b)	n.a.	n.a.	n.a.	n.a.	35	-84	..	..
Gambia	45	0	45	-9	..	..	639	+76
Georgia	122	37	85	-6	41	-20	892	-6
Germany	23,592	13,925	9,667	+2,479	87,659	-9,687	917,232	+39,469
Ghana	..	..	..	..	2	..	429	..
Greece	224	216	8	-28	624	-28	28,866	-362
Guatemala	47	2	45	+9	4	-2	205	-19
Guinea (b)	n.a.	n.a.	n.a.	n.a.	34	-17	..	..
Honduras	107	0	107	+15	..	..	379	+30
Hungary	132	114	18	+25	621	-5	35,746	+949
Iceland	10	5	5	+3	137	-26	9,457	+127
India	30,490	7,787	22,703	-231	17,038	+2,416	128,663	+17,784
Indonesia	9,970	1,547	8,423	+3,120	1,570	+814	84,540	..
Iran (Islamic Republic of)	2,250	2,051	199	-763	2,144	-644	38,762	+2,807
Iraq	..	..	..	..	2	..	..	..
Ireland	37	20	17	-6	3,576	-394	167,519	-29,735
Israel	5,358	1,003	4,355	-130	8,666	-366	38,145	+2,606
Italy	7,348	6,603	745	+94	21,645	-1,523	395,227	-14,469
Jamaica	11	1	10	+6	4	-2	245	-74
Japan	201,420	155,117	46,303	+17,048	281,597	+3,454	2,029,223	+8,799
Jordan	61	9	52	-105	31	-3	..	..
Kazakhstan	585	473	112	-66	988	+90	2,855	-282
Kenya	38	20	18	+3	42	-18	689	..
Kuwait	19	..	..	..	28	..	1,808	..
Kyrgyzstan	47	47	0	+8	82	+32	175	+2
Lao People's Democratic Republic	36	0	36	..	4	..	..	..
Latvia	71	66	5	-5	122	-22	11,282	+556
Lebanon	..	..	..	..	17	..	..	..
Liechtenstein	..	..	..	..	689	..	..	..
Lithuania	93	79	14	+10	254	+51	12,990	+272
Luxembourg	1,884	128	1,756	+848	1,852	-403	117,527	-26,461
Madagascar	55	1	54	+7	1	+1	217	-6

Name	Grants by office: Total	Resident	Non-resident	Change over previous year	Equivalent grants by origin: Total (a)	Change over previous year	In force by office: Total	Change over previous year
Malaysia	5,957	776	5,181	-919	1,351	-232	35,175	+1,034
Mali (b)	n.a.	n.a.	n.a.	n.a.	88	-69	..	..
Malta	13	7	6	+2	281	+16	1,131	+898
Marshall Islands	..	..	..	..	4	..	..	..
Mauritania (b)	n.a.	n.a.	n.a.	n.a.	34	+17	..	..
Mauritius	1	0	1	-3	41	-12	..	..
Mexico	9,698	507	9,191	-671	1,032	-275	118,484	+1,314
Monaco	2	2	0	-7	66	-27	69,300	-39,088
Mongolia	118	42	76	-68	46	-26	1,533	+88
Montenegro	7	7	0	..	11	..	..	..
Morocco	579	141	438	-166	230	+27	10,128	-87
Mozambique	..	..	..	..	1	..	4,753	+494
Namibia	29	16	13	..	25	..	2,195	..
Nepal	..	..	..	..	7	..	..	..
Netherlands (Kingdom of the)	2,815	1,742	1,073	+551	18,912	-2,032	211,591	-1,275
New Zealand	2,176	107	2,069	+27	1,322	-11	25,151	-598
Niger (b)	n.a.	n.a.	n.a.	n.a.	88	-33	..	..
Nigeria	1,081	..	..	-5	4	+2	..	..
North Macedonia	29	25	4	-22	41	-4	5,659	+756
Norway	761	460	301	+111	3,779	-250	51,035	+2,628
Oman	23	0	23	-13	6	-2	4,912	+483
Pakistan	189	24	165	-45	43	-20	2,062	+8
Panama	..	..	..	..	11	..	..	..
Papua New Guinea	14	0	14	+9	1	0	105	+14
Paraguay	34	0	34	+3	2	+1	..	..
Peru	588	32	556	+17	55	+7	3,998	+258
Philippines	2,004	72	1,932	+555	172	+5	28,755	+1,782
Poland	2,290	2,224	66	-1,029	3,407	-1,131	94,156	+792
Portugal	104	89	15	-87	552	-285	40,496	-1,431
Qatar	..	..	..	..	48	..	..	..
Republic of Korea	135,180	99,202	35,978	-10,702	147,790	-10,713	1,214,146	+60,826
Republic of Moldova	43	32	11	-26	38	-44	291	-2
Romania	364	353	11	-12	515	-22	27,931	+667
Russian Federation	23,315	15,307	8,008	-347	20,455	+1,263	259,020	-5,567
Rwanda	6	3	3	-2	3	-5	..	..
Saint Kitts and Nevis	..	..	..	..	12	..	..	..
Saint Vincent and the Grenadines	18	0	18	..	..	..	18	-2
Samoa	..	..	..	..	25	..	38	-13
San Marino	467	9	458	-262	36	+4	..	..
Sao Tome and Principe	12	0	12	-2	..	..	396	+9
Saudi Arabia	2,684	550	2,134	+938	2,438	+121	8,946	+2,929
Senegal (b)	n.a.	n.a.	n.a.	n.a.	359	+240	..	..
Serbia	30	28	2	-15	76	-33	8,613	+415
Seychelles	62	1	61	+36	17	-8	256	-8
Singapore	3,886	266	3,620	-2,602	3,602	-432	47,223	-578
Sint Maarten (Dutch Part)	..	..	..	..	1	..	..	..
Slovakia	95	75	20	-11	255	-51	21,829	-111
Slovenia	195	173	22	+37	398	-119	18,333	+29
South Africa	11,267	513	10,754	+5,160	1,175	-138	92,226	+6,795
Spain	714	651	63	-2	4,880	-503	214,974	-10,767
Sri Lanka	186	77	109	-8	107	+9	982	-13
Sweden	799	642	157	+82	16,449	-1,952	112,414	+379
Switzerland	782	528	254	+58	24,833	-1,949	241,587	-23,322
Syrian Arab Republic	65	59	6	+9	61	+9	451	-40
Tajikistan	8	0	8	+2	80	+24	..	..
Thailand	2,213	220	1,993	-781	579	-47	18,856	+39
Togo (b)	n.a.	n.a.	n.a.	n.a.	51	-34	..	..
Trinidad and Tobago	49	0	49	+9	1	-2	1,040	-35
Tunisia	..	..	..	..	13	..	..	..
Türkiye	3,449	3,231	218	+62	4,290	+138	80,347	-2,078

Name	Grants by office				Equivalent grants by origin		In force by office	
	Total	Resident	Non-resident	Change over previous year	Total (a)	Change over previous year	Total	Change over previous year
Tuvalu	9	0	9	-2	..	..	..	..
Uganda	..	..	..	..	2	..	22	0
Ukraine	1,566	630	936	-732	823	-417	18,806	+328
United Arab Emirates	1,048	11	1,037	+393	318	-58	3,265	+560
United Kingdom	10,578	4,894	5,684	-317	26,694	-2,368	701,292	+11,161
United Republic of Tanzania	34	..	..	+6	1	-5	..	..
United States of America	323,410	141,938	181,472	-3,897	277,988	-20,642	3,343,159	+15,619
Uruguay	..	..	..	..	79	..	..	..
Uzbekistan	559	354	205	+261	374	+141	1,413	+196
Vanuatu	..	..	..	..	3	..	..	..
Venezuela (Bolivarian Republic of)	317	5	312	..	15	..	450	+238
Viet Nam	3,868	153	3,715	+177	314	+87	19,028	+4,584
Yemen	3	0	3	-1	5	+4	102	+3
Zambia	12	4	8	+2	13	+12	8,537	+12
Zimbabwe	36	33	3	+32	42	+40	513	+36
Others/Unknown	..	..	..	..	20,318	-2,684	..	..
Total (2022 estimates)	**1,823,200**	**1,223,700**	**598,500**				**17,260,000**	

(a) Equivalent grants by origin data are incomplete, because some offices do not report by origin.
(b) The African Intellectual Property Organization (OAPI) acts as the national office for patent grants.
.. indicates not available.
n.a. indicates not applicable.
Source: WIPO Statistics Database, August 2023.

A60. Patent office procedural data, 2022

Office	Total applications processed	Granted	Rejected	Withdrawn or abandoned	Number of examiners (FTE)	First office action (months)	Final office decision (months)
Albania	..	4	7	..	2.0	45.0	180.0
Algeria	..	420	744	..	5.0	8.0	13.0
Antigua and Barbuda	..	..	..	..	2.0	..	..
Argentina	4,295	1,987	362	1,946	49.0	33.0	46.0
Armenia	19	5	2	12	4.0	3.5	7.7
Australia	20,938	16,407	39	4,492	403.3	10.5	16.9
Austria	2,279	1,151	1,013	115	110.0	8.7	23.6
Azerbaijan	137	83	2	52	11.0	4.0	7.0
Bahrain	..	197	..	22	5.0	4.0	12.0
Bangladesh	..	7	..	..	6.0	4.0	6.0
Belarus	366	306	56	4	11.0	10.5	..
Belize	..	..	..	..	1.0	..	..
Bhutan	..	2	..	..	1.0	24.0	48.0
Bolivia (Plurinational State of)	..	..	..	..	5.0	..	..
Bosnia and Herzegovina	..	7	..	..	4.0	2.0	30.0
Botswana	..	..	7	..	..	12.0	24.0
Brazil	38,118	23,546	4,468	10,104	304.0	39.0	48.0
Brunei Darussalam	..	60	..	..	..	3.0	39.0
Bulgaria	241	147	26	68	10.0	2.0	27.0
Cabo Verde	..	..	..	..	1.0	..	..
Cambodia	..	..	..	..	3.0	..	..
Canada	..	18,125	..	7,974	419.5	12.1	26.3
China	1,481,055	798,347	553,395	129,313	..	13.0	16.5
China, Hong Kong SAR	..	29	..	72	9.1	8.8	15.4
China, Macao SAR	..	2	41	..	..	5.4	12.3
Colombia	2,008	1,136	620	252	43.0	13.9	25.2
Costa Rica	..	156	393	..	..	..	..
Croatia	57	11	13	33	6.0	8.0	24.0
Czech Republic	759	352	164	243	32.0	..	..
Denmark	1,078	398	2	678	50.8	5.6	17.3
Djibouti	..	..	..	..	1.0	..	..

Office	Total applications processed	Granted	Rejected	Withdrawn or abandoned	Number of examiners (FTE)	First office action (months)	Final office decision (months)
Dominica	..	..	..	..	1.0	..	..
Dominican Republic	..	..	124	..	..	..	..
Ecuador	539	41	75	423	5.0	24.0	60.0
Egypt	1,328	461	319	548	100.0	18.0	..
El Salvador	..	..	..	..	2.0	6.0	7.0
Estonia	23	9	4	10	8.0	0.3	37.1
Ethiopia	..	23	3	..	7.0	24.0	36.0
European Patent Office	..	81,754	..	..	3,982.0	13.8	24.3
Finland	1,731	677	9	1,045	112.0	6.8	27.4
France	14,412	11,918	1,604	890	121.0	..	..
Georgia	255	122	11	122	18.0	15.0	21.0
Germany	45,506	23,592	9,300	12,614	821.8	..	..
Ghana	..	..	..	..	5.0	..	..
Guatemala	214	47	55	112	4.0	1.0	36.0
Honduras	..	..	46	..	..	..	..
Hungary	297	132	19	146	35.0	6.7	26.6
Iceland	..	..	..	..	..	0.3	4.0
India	51,025	30,490	5,198	15,337	597.0	4.0	51.0
Indonesia	30,028	29,619	85	324	..	..	..
Iran (Islamic Republic of)	6,334	1,515	1,080	3,739	18.0	3.0	6.0
Israel	8,091	5,358	10	2,723	123.0	26.4	39.5
Italy	10,234	7,321	2,267	646	18.0	24.0	..
Japan	249,732	187,794	57,927	4,011	1,662.0	10.1	14.9
Kazakhstan	751	585	14	152	31.0	..	13.0
Kenya	..	..	..	..	8.0	..	..
Kuwait	..	488	..	..	11.0	3.0	3.0
Kyrgyzstan	..	..	..	..	7.0	4.0	18.0
Lao People's Democratic Republic	..	93	..	32	4.0	6.0	8.0
Latvia	85	71	6	8	5.0	..	..
Lebanon	..	..	..	..	1.0	..	..
Lithuania	86	72	10	4	4.0	0.4	4.0
Madagascar	86	55	21	10	3.0	8.0	8.0
Mexico	17,569	10,639	123	6,807	116.0	43.0	56.0
Monaco	..	2	3	..	1.5	6.0	10.0
Mongolia	..	118	30	..	6.0	7.0	6.0
Montenegro	..	7	..	..	3.0	30.0	18.0
Morocco	768	580	146	42	14.0	4.0	20.0
Mozambique	..	..	..	..	2.0	..	..
Namibia	..	..	..	..	4.0	..	..
Netherlands (Kingdom of the)	3,372	2,815	239	318	20.0	7.0	6.0
New Zealand	..	2,145	..	1,888	79.0	18.2	24.6
Nigeria	..	1,104	23	..	9.0	2.0	3.0
North Macedonia	..	339	11	..	4.0	12.0	..
Norway	3,978	754	9	3,215	76.0	6.4	20.8
Oman	..	..	..	..	8.0	..	..
Pakistan	..	189	..	105	9.0	18.0	36.0
Papua New Guinea	..	..	..	..	2.0	..	..
Paraguay	..	..	..	..	2.0	..	..
Peru	..	584	130	..	29.0	36.2	39.2
Philippines	2,775	1,335	12	1,428	102.0	..	48.9
Poland	3,539	2,333	726	480	67.0	..	32.2
Portugal	260	93	161	6	15.0	..	37.4
Qatar	492	197	266	29	10.0	12.0	24.0
Republic of Korea	172,492	125,619	41,538	5,335	978.0	14.3	18.4
Republic of Moldova	94	52	23	19	10.0	3.0	14.0
Romania	1,080	351	395	334	42.0	12.0	45.0
Russian Federation	30,722	23,345	1,413	5,964	406.0	4.0	4.2
Rwanda	..	..	..	..	2.0	..	..
Saint Vincent and the Grenadines	..	1	..	2	2.0	0.2	6.0
Sao Tome and Principe	..	..	..	..	2.0	..	..
Saudi Arabia	5,769	2,684	2,462	623	96.0	5.9	14.8

Office	Total applications processed	Granted	Rejected	Withdrawn or abandoned	Number of examiners (FTE)	First office action (months)	Final office decision (months)
Serbia	161	30	57	74	12.0	12.0	18.0
Seychelles	26	24	1	1	2.0	1.0	1.0
Singapore	..	..	..	..	100.0	..	..
Slovakia	198	95	40	63	25.0	30.9	30.4
Slovenia	..	..	..	..	3.5	..	..
Spain	3,121	2,713	90	318	127.0	0.6	5.5
Sri Lanka	1,037	186	835	16	11.0	45.0	51.4
Sweden	2,085	799	22	1,264	104.6	7.4	27.3
Switzerland	1,545	782	650	113	15.0	2.5	12.0
Syrian Arab Republic	..	..	..	..	5.0	..	..
Tajikistan	..	..	..	..	9.0	..	..
Thailand	4,815	2,213	8	2,594	104.0	32.2	47.4
Trinidad and Tobago	..	..	..	..	7.0	..	..
Tunisia	..	..	..	..	4.0	6.0	14.0
Türkiye	9,108	3,225	1,148	4,735	179.0	5.0	23.0
Tuvalu	..	..	..	..	1.0	..	..
Uganda	..	..	..	..	2.0	..	..
Ukraine	2,093	1,742	23	328	109.0	15.4	18.4
United Arab Emirates	..	1,048	..	17	24.0	44.2	..
United Kingdom	..	10,578	12,925	..	339.0	10.0	32.0
United Republic of Tanzania	..	..	..	..	4.0	..	..
United States of America	758,520	322,963	350,300	85,257	8,234.0	18.3	23.1
Uzbekistan	837	578	109	150	10.0	2.0	31.9
Viet Nam	5,755	3,868	1,728	159	71.0	34.2	43.6
Zambia	..	..	..	..	2.0	..	..
Zimbabwe	..	..	..	..	1.0	..	..

Note: FTE is full time equivalent. Grant data differ slightly from grant data reported elsewhere in this report owing to different dates of extraction. Every effort has been made to compile procedural data based on common definitions and concepts, but procedural differences make it extremely difficult to fully harmonize such data. For instance, "rejection" is not recorded as a final decision in Canada, where applicants are informed of the action they must take or questions that they must answer in order for their application to be considered; and if an applicant cannot provide the required information, they are regarded as having abandoned the application. A similar situation exists in Australia.
.. indicates not available.
Source: WIPO Statistics Database, August 2023.

A61. Utility model applications and grants by office and origin, 2022

	Applications by office			Equivalent applications by origin	Grants by office		
Name	Total	Resident	Non-resident	Total (a)	Total	Resident	Non-resident
African Regional Intellectual Property Organization	21	14	7	n.a.	2	0	2
Albania	1	1	0	2	1	1	0
Algeria	..	..	..	3	..	..	..
Andorra	..	..	..	3	..	..	..
Argentina	200	171	29	186	86	66	20
Armenia	84	81	3	84	94	93	1
Australia	262	161	101	235	862	167	695
Austria	344	202	142	446	388	259	129
Azerbaijan	27	24	3	24	31	20	11
Barbados	..	..	..	13	..	..	..
Belarus	312	284	28	340	288	259	29
Belgium	..	..	..	77	..	..	..
Bolivia (Plurinational State of)	10	7	3	7	..	..	..
Bosnia and Herzegovina	..	..	..	1	..	..	..
Botswana	4	4	0	4	..	..	..
Brazil	2,276	2,230	46	2,259	758	689	69
Bulgaria	214	208	6	226	204	191	13
Cabo Verde	..	..	..	1	..	..	..
Cambodia	6	0	6	13	..	..	..

Name	Applications by office Total	Resident	Non-resident	Equivalent applications by origin Total (a)	Grants by office Total	Resident	Non-resident
Cameroon	..	..	..	6	..	..	..
Canada	..	..	..	54	..	..	..
Chile	115	95	20	116	46	32	14
China	2,950,653	2,944,139	6,514	2,946,816	2,804,155	2,796,049	8,106
China, Hong Kong SAR	579	424	155	472	535	371	164
China, Macao SAR	20	9	11	10	10	1	9
Colombia	182	170	12	176	122	114	8
Costa Rica	5	4	1	5	3	1	2
Côte d'Ivoire	..	..	..	1	..	..	..
Croatia	27	24	3	31	56	49	7
Cuba	..	..	..	2	..	..	..
Cyprus	..	..	..	22	..	..	..
Czech Republic	1,095	1,057	38	1,222	1,040	990	50
Democratic People's Republic of Korea	..	..	..	6	..	..	..
Democratic Republic of the Congo	..	..	..	6	..	..	..
Denmark	85	53	32	106	90	59	31
Dominican Republic	11	10	1	11	14	9	5
Ecuador	23	20	3	30	7	3	4
Egypt	..	..	..	3	..	..	..
El Salvador	2	1	1	1	1	1	0
Equatorial Guinea	..	..	..	1	..	..	..
Estonia	43	37	6	43	36	23	13
Ethiopia	233	233	0	233	62	62	0
Finland	235	214	21	324	235	215	20
France	696	396	300	848	503	247	256
Gambia	1	0	1	..	2	0	2
Georgia	36	34	2	35	37	33	4
Germany	9,469	5,523	3,946	6,349	8,765	4,913	3,852
Ghana	17	0	17	2	2	0	2
Greece	18	13	5	15	22	15	7
Guatemala	5	4	1	5	2	1	1
Honduras	2	0	2	..	2	0	2
Hungary	208	189	19	213	169	135	34
India	..	..	..	675	..	..	..
Indonesia	4,088	4,027	61	4,033	2,031	1,800	231
Iran (Islamic Republic of)	..	..	..	2	..	..	..
Iraq	..	..	..	3	..	..	..
Ireland	117	99	18	111	34	16	18
Israel	..	..	..	64	..	..	..
Italy	1,826	1,645	181	2,098	1,684	1,499	185
Japan	4,513	2,964	1,549	4,614	4,615	3,026	1,589
Jordan	..	..	..	3	..	..	..
Kazakhstan	..	..	..	14	864	840	24
Kenya	366	366	0	370	27	26	1
Kyrgyzstan	7	7	0	8	21	18	3
Lao People's Democratic Republic	9	6	3	7	25	0	25
Latvia	..	..	..	4	..	..	..
Lebanon	..	..	..	1	..	..	..
Liechtenstein	..	..	..	3	..	..	..
Luxembourg	..	..	..	29	..	..	..
Malaysia	168	116	52	164	248	180	68
Mali	..	..	..	1	..	..	..
Malta	..	..	..	7	..	..	..
Mauritius	..	..	..	1	..	..	..
Mexico	608	547	61	558	318	255	63
Mongolia	97	97	0	100	59	59	0
Mozambique	14	0	14	..	14	0	14
Namibia	4	4	0	4	4	4	0
Nepal	..	..	..	1	..	..	..

	Applications by office			Equivalent applications by origin	Grants by office		
Name	Total	Resident	Non-resident	Total (a)	Total	Resident	Non-resident
Netherlands (Kingdom of the)	..	..	..	310	..	..	..
New Zealand	..	..	..	42	..	..	..
Nigeria	..	..	..	1	..	..	..
North Macedonia	..	..	..	1	..	..	..
Norway	..	..	..	10	..	..	..
Oman	..	..	..	1	..	..	..
Pakistan	..	..	..	4	..	..	..
Panama	..	..	..	7	..	..	..
Paraguay	14	7	7	7	1	0	1
Peru	447	427	20	438	214	204	10
Philippines	1,639	1,555	84	1,558	914	852	62
Poland	673	610	63	687	556	511	45
Portugal	96	39	57	51	48	23	25
Qatar	..	..	..	1	..	..	..
Republic of Korea	3,084	2,784	300	4,019	1,452	1,288	164
Republic of Moldova	102	101	1	104	87	86	1
Romania	49	36	13	48	26	15	11
Russian Federation	8,521	8,368	153	8,457	7,178	7,025	153
Rwanda	7	7	0	11	1	1	0
Samoa	..	..	..	4	..	..	..
San Marino	..	..	..	5	..	..	..
Sao Tome and Principe	13	0	13	..	..	..	..
Saudi Arabia	..	..	..	56	..	..	..
Serbia	77	74	3	75	38	36	2
Seychelles	..	..	..	5	..	..	..
Singapore	..	..	..	223	..	..	..
Slovakia	288	236	52	255	262	218	44
Slovenia	..	..	..	13	..	..	..
Solomon Islands	..	..	..	1	..	..	..
South Africa	..	..	..	8	..	..	..
Spain	2,635	2,442	193	2,653	2,297	2,138	159
Sri Lanka	..	..	..	1	..	..	..
Sweden	..	..	..	127	..	..	..
Switzerland	..	..	..	415	..	..	..
Syrian Arab Republic	10	10	0	10	9	9	0
Tajikistan	158	158	0	159	92	92	0
Thailand	3,441	3,310	131	3,374	1,657	1,557	100
Trinidad and Tobago	..	..	..	..	1	1	0
Tunisia	..	..	..	2	..	..	..
Türkiye	5,558	5,502	56	5,546	2,369	2,302	67
Uganda	19	19	0	19	4	4	0
Ukraine	2,378	2,320	58	2,350	2,074	2,031	43
United Arab Emirates	9	2	7	33	5	0	5
United Kingdom	..	..	..	217	..	..	..
United States of America	..	..	..	2,102	..	..	..
Uruguay	..	..	..	13	..	..	..
Uzbekistan	453	447	6	450	419	410	9
Venezuela (Bolivarian Republic of)	84	46	38	46	46	8	38
Viet Nam	601	455	146	460	243	176	67
Zambia	..	..	..	3	..	..	..
Zimbabwe	..	..	..	20	..	..	..
Others/Unknown	..	..	..	1,343	..	..	..
Total (2022 estimates)	**3,010,510**	**2,995,570**	**14,950**				

(a) Equivalent applications by origin data are incomplete, because some offices do not report by origin.
.. indicates not available.
n.a. indicates not applicable.
Source: WIPO Statistics Database, August 2023.

Trademarks

Highlights

Applications declined sharply by 15.7% in 2022

An estimated 11.8 million trademark applications were filed worldwide in 2022. This is a decrease of 2.2 million on the previous year, marking a substantial decline of 15.7% (figure 2.1). In fact, this decline is so big that it mostly reverses the growth of the previous two years, the total trademark applications in 2022 being only around 315,000 or 2.7% higher than in 2019. This stands in stark contrast to a 16.6% surge in the number of trademark applications filed in 2020, amid the emergence of the COVID-19 pandemic and subsequent global economic slowdown, and to a lesser extent, the more modest growth of 4.6% observed in 2021. 2022's considerable decline is not readily attributable to any one factor, as various influences could be at play across different intellectual property (IP) offices. For instance, a drop in an office's numbers might stem from slowing economic expansion within its jurisdiction or changes to filing regulations, or both. However, this decrease could also reflect a return to normal filing levels after the surge in applications in 2020. The decline in 2022 brought to an end a 12-year growth streak that began after the global financial crisis ended in 2009, when annual growth fell by just 1.4%, and is the sharpest fall to have been recorded within the last four decades. However, it is important to note that trademark applications in 2022 were still roughly three and a half times greater than filed in 2008, mainly owing to the significant increases seen in seven of the last 15 years. And the long-term trend in trademark filing is nevertheless still positive, despite having been distorted by the pandemic.

During 2022, an estimated 11.8 million trademark applications were filed globally, down 2.2 million on the previous year

2.1. Trademark applications worldwide, 2008–2022

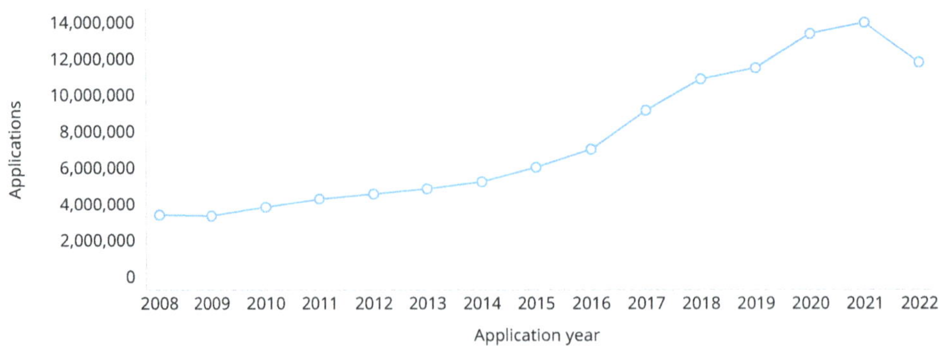

Source: Figure B1.

When differences between filing systems across national and regional offices are harmonized based on the application class count, the 2022 decrease in trademark filing becomes less pronounced, yet still a considerable 14.5% below the previous year's total. The total number of classes specified in applications – known as the application class count – declined from almost 18.2 million in 2021 to an estimated 15.5 million in 2022 (figure 2.2). As with trademark applications, this marks the first annual reduction in application class count since 2009.

From 2021 to 2022, there was a large decrease of 14.5% in the total number of classes specified in trademark applications

2.2. Trademark application class counts worldwide, 2008–2022

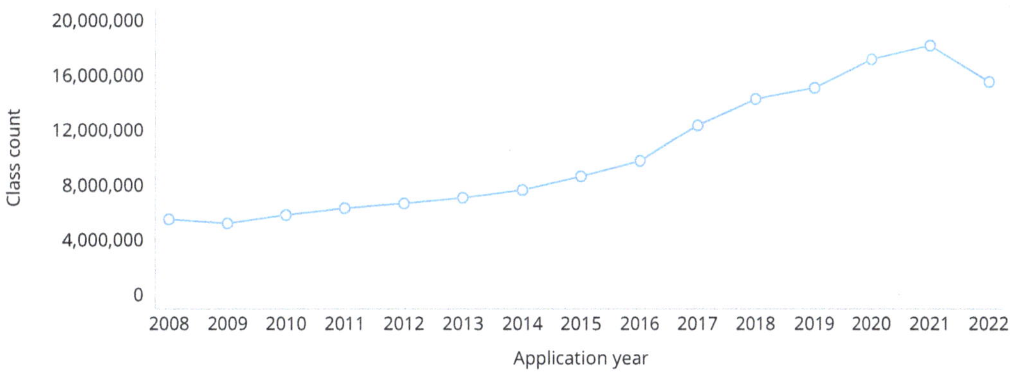

Source: Figure B2.

Class count

A trademark application can refer to different classes of goods or services. Many offices use the Nice Classification, an international classification of goods and services for registering trademarks and service marks. Applications received at these offices are classified according to one or more of the 45 Nice classes (see www.wipo.int/classifications/nice). Some offices allow only single-class filing, meaning applicants have to file a separate application for each class. Others permit multi-class filing, enabling applicants to file a single application in which a number of classes are specified. To improve international comparison of the number of applications received, it helps to compare class counts across offices. Class counts are also used to make trademark registration internationally comparable. This method of comparing offices began in 2004, the first year for which complete class count data are available.

Offices with the most trademark filing

Despite having filed one-fifth less than in 2021, Chinese applicants maintained their position as the world's most active filers in 2022. China's class count of just over 7.5 million was followed at a distance by that of the United States of America (US) at 767,375 (figure 2.3). These offices have between them consistently held the top two positions since the early 2000s. Notably, China's class count has seen remarkable growth over this period, increasing from under twice that of the US in 2008 to almost 10 times as many by 2022. This increase can be mostly attributed to the substantial number of trademark applications filed domestically by residents in China. Following behind these two top-ranked offices were those of India (500,305), Türkiye (485,779) and the European Union Intellectual Office (EUIPO) (448,807). Together, these five offices accounted for almost 63% of global trademark filing based on application class counts; a significant increase of 20 percentage points from the about 43% held by the top five offices a decade earlier in 2012, which then comprised the EUIPO, together with the offices of China, France, Türkiye and the US.

Among the top 20 offices, 14 experienced a decline in trademark filing in 2022 compared to the previous year (figure B10). Among these, 11 saw a notable decrease ranging from about 10% to 31%. The most sizeable reductions were at the offices of the Islamic Republic of Iran (–30.6%), the United Kingdom (UK) (–21.5%), China (–20.5%), Italy (–18.1%) and the US (–14.7%). They were followed by the offices of Germany (–14.2%), Australia (–13.4%) and Canada (–12.7%). The considerable decline in trademark filing at the office of the Islamic Republic of Iran was primarily because of a reduced demand from its residents in seeking protection for their marks domestically. This same was the case in China, where a considerable on-year decline was largely attributable to a decrease in filing by Chinese residents at their home office. In contrast, the declines seen at the offices of the US and the UK, which likewise saw a reduction in filing by residents, were driven more by a reduced demand from foreign applicants seeking trademark protection in these two countries. Contrary to the 14 that saw lower volumes of trademark filing in 2022 than the previous year, six top offices recorded an on-year increase. Among these, the highest growth rates were at the offices of Türkiye (+11.8%) and Indonesia (+10.4%), followed by the Russian Federation (+6.4%), Brazil (+2.6%), Viet Nam (+2.5%) and India (+2.4%). In all six offices bar Brazil, an increase in resident filing effectively offset a drop in non-resident filing, resulting in an overall net annual increase for each. Interestingly, Brazil stood out among the top 20 as the one office to see an increase in both resident and non-resident filing.

In 2022, 11 of the top 20 offices were in high-income economies, six in upper middle-income countries (Brazil, China, Indonesia, Mexico, the Russian Federation and Türkiye) and three in lower middle-income countries (India, the Islamic Republic of Iran and Viet Nam). Additionally, certain offices located within selected low- and middle-income countries not to appear in the top 20 list – specifically, Argentina (88,838), Colombia (72,641), the Philippines (67,078), Thailand (64,182) and Egypt (54,610) – experienced comparatively high levels of trademark filing (figure B11). Among the 20 selected offices within both income groups, notable double-digit annual growth rates were observed at the African Regional Intellectual Property Organization (ARIPO) (+12.9%) and at the offices of Cuba (+15.5%), Ethiopia (+19.3%) and Colombia (+30.7%). Conversely, there were declines of about 10% or more at the African Intellectual Property Organization (OAPI) (–18.1%) and at the offices of Egypt (–9.8%), Papua New Guinea (–40.5%) and Ukraine (–39.4%) (figure B12).

At most offices, the majority of applications stemmed from residents aiming to secure trademark protection within their domestic jurisdiction. In 2022, filing by residents at their home or regional office constituted 83.5% of the global total, with the remaining 16.5% attributable to non-resident filing (figure B3). Historically, up until 2020, year-on-year growth in domestic filing generally outpaced non-resident filing. Breaking with this trend, the growth in filing by non-residents surpassed that of residents in 2021, resulting in a remarkable 21.5% increase in the global non-resident application class count that year. But a decrease in demand from both residents and non-residents alike contributed to the overall decline in trademark filing in 2022, although the reduction in resident filing was the more significant in driving down the overall decrease. Among the 14 top offices to experience a net decrease in filing in 2022, 10 experienced a more substantial decline in resident as opposed to non-resident filing. In top offices China, France, Germany, Italy and the Islamic Republic of Iran, over 90% of the reduction in total filing for 2022 resulted from a decline in resident filing.

Due primarily to the large volume of resident trademark applications filed in China, the proportion of non-resident filing within the global total contracted in 2022 by nearly 16 percentage points, dropping from 32.2% in 2008 to the previously mentioned 16.5%. However, if China is excluded from the overall count, the decline in the non-resident share is no more than about five percentage points over this period.

Six of the top 20 offices attracted 35% or more of total filing from non-residents, largely in excess of the global non-resident share. The EUIPO (35.4%) and the offices of Australia (45.8%), Canada (64.9%), Switzerland (62.9%), the UK (47.5%) and the US (35.6%) stand out with the largest shares in this regard (figure B9). Conversely, those offices with the lowest non-resident shares were China (2.8%), France (5.2%), the Islamic Republic of Iran (3%) and Türkiye (8.1%). The relatively low non-resident shares for France and several other EU member state offices, including Germany (10%) and Italy (10.2%) are due to the fact that many non-resident applicants seek trademark protection within EU countries through the EUIPO. Those BRICS countries to feature among the top 20 offices for trademark filing – namely, Brazil (12%), India (10.3%) and the Russian Federation (10.8%) – also had relatively lower non-resident shares.

For China, the Islamic Republic of Iran and Türkiye, non-resident applicants constituted no more than around 3% to 8% of overall trademark filing

2.3. Trademark application class counts for the top 10 offices, 2022

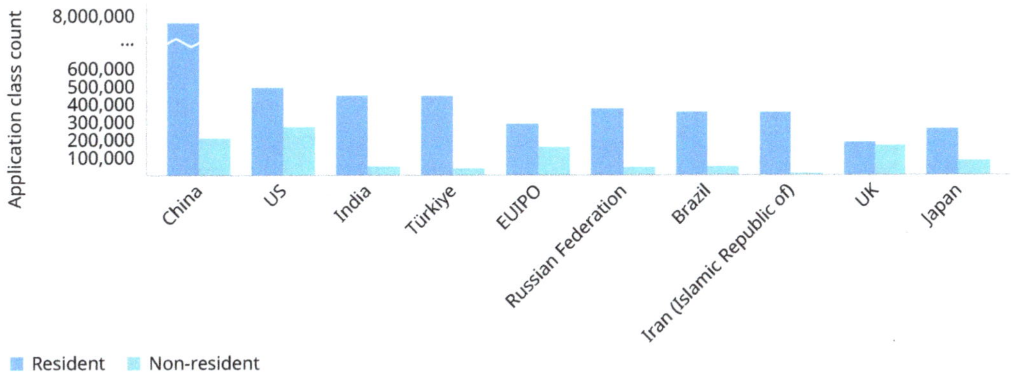

Note: EUIPO is the European Union Intellectual Property Office.
Source: Figure B9.

In 2022, the composition of the top 20 offices remained consistent with the year before, albeit with some noteworthy shifts within the ranking. The most significant move in ranking resulted from a big decline in resident trademark filing at the office of the Islamic Republic of Iran, causing it to drop from third position in 2021 to eighth spot in 2022. The UK dropped three places from sixth to ninth in the ranking. The EUIPO slipped one spot from fourth to fifth, while the office of Italy fell two places from 18th to 20th. Conversely, Türkiye climbed three places from seventh to fourth, through a combination of a decrease in the rankings among several top offices and a growth in resident filing. This same pattern applies to the office of India, advancing two positions from fifth to third, and to that of the Russian Federation, which climbed from eighth in 2021 to the sixth position in 2022. Similarly, Viet Nam's ranking improved from 20th to 18th place.

Trademark filing in Asia constituted 67.8% of the global total in 2022

2.4. Trademark application class counts by region, 2012 and 2022

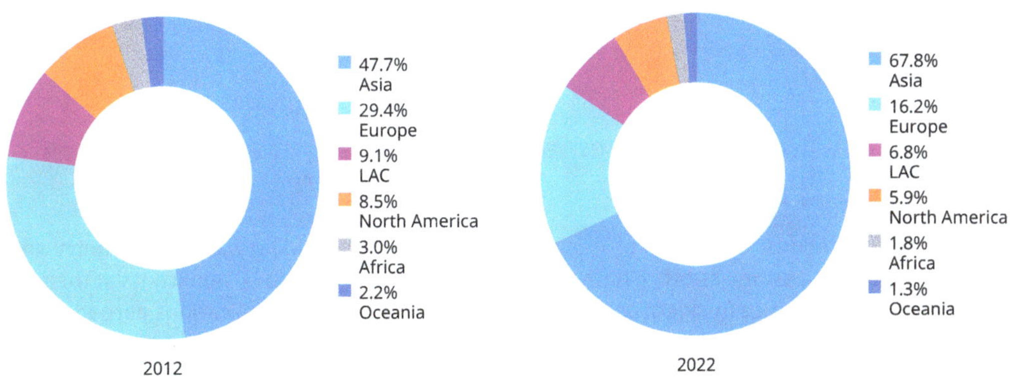

Note: LAC is Latin America and the Caribbean.
Source: Table B7.

Among top 20 offices in 2022, Asia was home to eight, Europe seven. Latin America and the Caribbean (LAC) and North America each accounted for two, and Oceania had one. Offices located in Asia dominated the global trademark filing landscape, constituting 67.8% of the total; a sizeable increase from its 47.7% share a decade earlier in 2012. This trend contributed to a decline in the overall shares of the other five geographical regions over the same period (figure 2.4). Offices located in Europe accounted for 16.2% of the world total in 2022, followed by LAC offices at 6.8% and the North American offices at 5.9%. The remaining shares were distributed between Africa (1.8%) and Oceania (1.3%).

Trademark applications filed since 1883

Trademark applications maintained a relatively steady but modest trajectory until the mid-1980s. A surge in applications at the China office began in the 1990s, surpassing those received by the US office in 2001 and establishing China as the largest office in terms of applications received. Even so, applications at the US office are two and a half times the number filed in 2001, despite a decrease in 2022 and earlier declines during the global financial crisis in 2008 and 2009 and at end of the dot-com era in 2001 and 2002. India's annual trademark applications, which had remained below 100,000 up until 2006, rose to nearly 480,000 in 2022. Brazil, with about 387,000 applications, and India stand out as the only two offices among the top five to have received more applications in 2022 than in 2021. Following behind Brazil, the Republic of Korea recorded approximately 256,000 applications.

Trend in trademark applications for the top five offices, 1883–2022

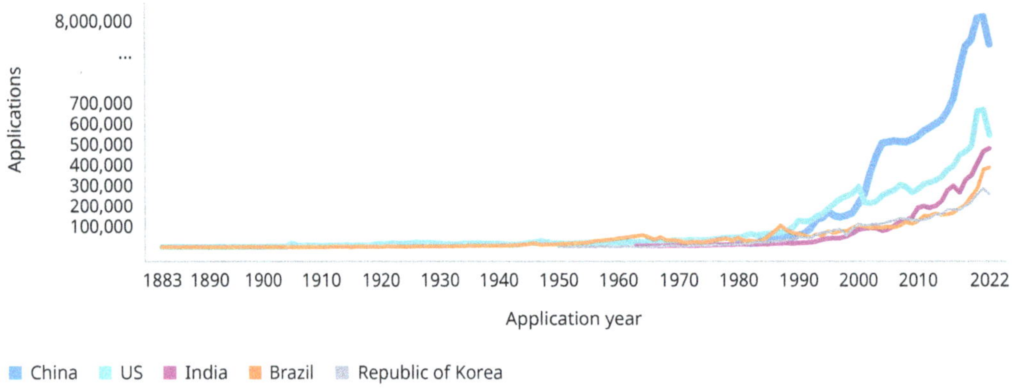

Source: Figure B8.

Equivalent application class count

Filing an application at a regional IP office is equivalent to filing an application in every member country of the organization that established that particular regional office. In the case of the EUIPO, for example, each application is multiplied by the corresponding number of EU member states. Thus, an application filed at the EUIPO in 2022 by an applicant residing outside the EU is counted as 27 applications abroad – equal to the number of EU member countries, whereas an application filed by an EU resident results in a count of 1 resident application and 26 applications abroad. This same multiplier is applied to the classes specified in such an application. The concept of equivalent application class count is employed for reporting data based on an applicant's origin.

Applicants from Germany remain the top filers of applications in foreign jurisdictions

Trademark applications received by offices both from applicants residing within the country and those outside are classified as office data. In contrast, applications filed by applicants at their national or regional office (resident applications) or at foreign offices (applications abroad) fall into the category of origin data. In this context, trademark statistics are presented based on an applicant's place of residence, so as to complement the picture of trademark filing worldwide.

When considering filing abroad based on equivalent class count, more applicants from Germany sought protection for their trademarks abroad than did applicants from any other origin. Germany has maintained its leading position since 2006. In 2022, filing abroad by German applicants reached an equivalent application class count of nearly 2.3 million. They were followed by applicants from the US, with an abroad equivalent application class count of just over 1.5 million, who moved ahead of applicants from China, whose almost 1.3 million secured China the third most active origin status for filing abroad. These top three countries of origin, Germany, the US and China, were followed by Italy (about 1.1 million), the UK (907,817) and

France (901,381) (figure B19).[1] The high equivalent class counts for applications filed abroad from these six origins can be attributed not only to high application class counts at numerous foreign offices, but also to the frequent use of the EUIPO – and its multiplier effect – for seeking protection within the European Union (EU) as a whole.

When looking at absolute counts – and in so doing removing the EUIPO's multiplier effect – a significant majority (95.1%) of filing (based on application class counts) undertaken by applicants based in China was destined solely for protection within China in 2022 (figure B17). Only 4.9% of these applicants' trademark filing was directed toward seeking protection abroad. In fact, this highly domestically-oriented trend has persisted for the past two and a half decades, with no less than 93% of China-based applicants filing within their own country each year during this period. Likewise, residents of many of the other middle-income countries with substantial trademark filing volumes, including Brazil, India, Indonesia, the Islamic Republic of Iran, Mexico, the Russian Federation, Türkiye and Viet Nam, directed only about 10% or less of their trademark filing toward seeking protection abroad. Notably, the lowest share was attributed to applicants based in the Islamic Republic of Iran, with a mere 0.5% of total filing directed abroad. Brazil (2.3%), India (4.1%) and Indonesia (2.1%) also registered relatively modest shares of filing abroad.

Among top 20 origins, 75.8% of filing by Switzerland-based applicants occurred outside the country, the largest share of absolute application class counts abroad as a proportion of total filing. Switzerland was followed by top origins the UK (50.7%), the US (47.7%), Canada (45.6%) and Germany (39.6%).

Trademark filing abroad behavior among applicants of selected middle-income countries displayed a range of patterns (figure B18). For instance, filing abroad accounted for no more than about 10% to 13% of total filing by applicants residing in middle-income countries Colombia (10.4%), Costa Rica (13.3%), Kazakhstan (13.2%), South Africa (10.3%) and Thailand (12.3%). Conversely, filing abroad as a proportion of total filing was particularly high for applicants based in Bulgaria (58.3%), Morocco (44.8%) and Serbia (57.6%). For a selection of low- and lower middle-income countries consisting of Algeria, Pakistan, the Philippines and Uganda, the share was about 3% or less.

When deciding where to pursue trademark protection, applicants weigh several factors, including the attractiveness of foreign markets for selling their goods and services, geographical proximity to those markets, and historical ties between the trademark holder's country of residence and the destination country. In 2022, almost a quarter (24.4%) of all non-resident trademark filing in China came from US applicants, followed by 11.7% from Japan and 8.5% from the UK. Collectively, applicants from these three countries accounted for 44.6% of all non-resident trademark filing in China for the year (figure 2.5). Conversely, non-resident filing in the US came primarily from China-based applicants, accounting for 43% of foreign filing. This was trailed by comparatively smaller volumes from applicants based in the UK (8.1%) and Canada (6.7%), for a combined share of over half (57.8%) of all filing received by the US office from abroad. In India, the three origins with the largest shares of total non-resident filing were the US (22.3%), followed by China and Germany, each constituting 8.6% of the total. Applicants from these three origins collectively accounted for 39.5% of all non-resident filing in India. In the case of the EUIPO, a remarkable 63.1% of its non-resident filing emanated from applicants based in just three countries: the US (25.2%), China (20.9%) and the UK (17%).

In 2022, US-based applicants were the primary source of non-resident filing at 10 of the other 19 top offices. They accounted for between around 18% of the total at the office of Türkiye to almost 39% at the offices of neighboring Canada and Mexico. Applicants from China were the most active non-residents filing at eight of the other 19 top offices. They accounted for between about 12% and 30% of application class counts in filings received from abroad by the offices of Germany, Indonesia, the Islamic Republic of Iran, Italy, Japan, the Russian Federation, the US and Viet Nam. Applicants residing in Germany played a significant role in non-resident filing at the Switzerland office, accounting for the largest volume at 32.8%. Beyond their sizeable

1 Equivalent application class counts differ from the absolute class counts presented in figure B17, which do not take into account the multiplying effect of regional offices.

presence in foreign filing in China, applicants located in Japan were the third largest origin of foreign filing at the offices of regional neighbors Indonesia, the Republic of Korea and Viet Nam.

US applicants were the most active non-resident filers at the offices of Brazil, China and India, as well as at the EUIPO

2.5. Share of total non-resident filing by origin at selected offices, 2022

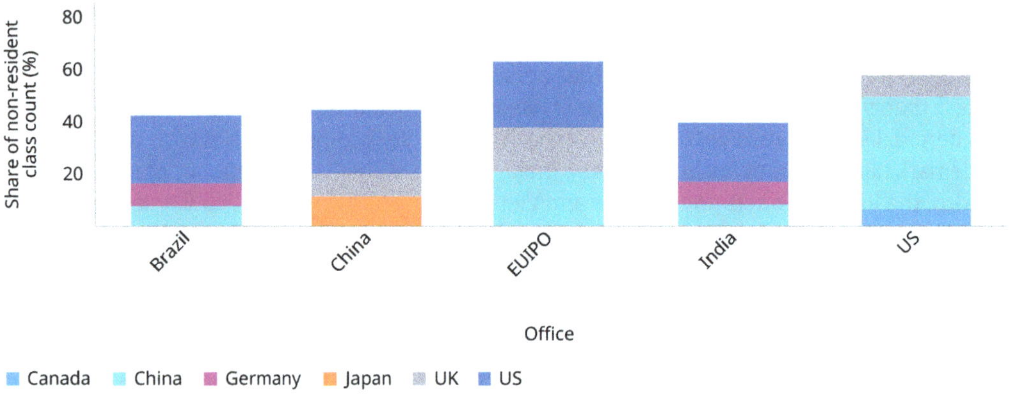

Note: EUIPO is the European Union Intellectual Property Office.
Source: Figure B22.

Adjusting for GDP and population

Variations in trademark filing across countries reflect differences in the size and structure of economies. It is therefore informative to examine resident application class counts with regard to gross domestic product (GDP) and population size.

When resident trademark applications are viewed as class counts and adjusted according to GDP, countries with a relatively lower number of classes specified in resident applications, like Australia and Chile, may rank above countries such as India and the US, which record higher class counts. Among selected origins, China (28,438), the Republic of Korea (11,431), Brazil (10,951), France (9,366) and the Russian Federation (9,331) exhibited some of the highest ratios of resident application class counts to GDP in 2022 (figure 2.6). Between 2012 and 2022, China (+17,738), Brazil (+7,043), the Russian Federation (+5,034) and the Republic of Korea (+3,645) all experienced considerable increases in resident application class counts per unit of GDP.

Between 2012 and 2022, Brazil, China, the Republic of Korea and the Russian Federation experienced a considerable increase in resident application class count per unit of GDP

2.6. Resident trademark application class count per USD 100 billion GDP for selected origins, 2012 and 2022

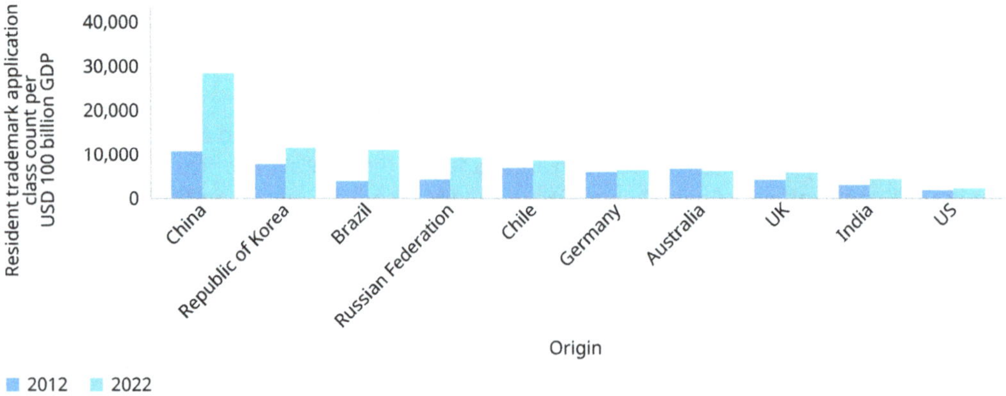

Source: Figure B30.

Analyzing application class count per million population data reveals that in 2022, Türkiye, with a population of about 85.3 million, recorded a particularly intensive resident application class count of 5,234 per million population – the highest ratio across all selected countries of origin (figure B31). The Republic of Korea, home to 51.6 million people, shared a similar class count per million population ratio of 5,197. It is worth noting that these ratios are closely aligned with China (5,172) and its much larger population of around 1.4 billion. Despite having a significantly smaller population of around 8.8 million in 2022, Switzerland displayed a relatively high ratio of resident application class count per million population at 4,508. Within other selected countries of origin, this ratio spanned from 2,226 to 3,934 for Australia (3,146), Chile (2,226), Germany (3,445), New Zealand (3,934), the Russian Federation (2,618), Singapore (2,429) and Sweden (2,252). Meanwhile, the range was between 1,081 and 1,632 for Canada (1,385), Costa Rica (1,632), Mexico (1,081) and the US (1,483). India, Israel, Malaysia, Morocco and South Africa had ratios of between about 315 and 550.

Which specific classes and industries saw the most intensive filing activity from applicants pursuing protection abroad?

Trademarks are registered in relation to particular classes of goods or services. The Nice Classification of goods and services is used in the international trademark system and at certain national and regional offices. Nice classification statistics provide insights into the relative importance of different goods and services. In 2022, goods class 9 – including scientific, photographic, measuring instruments, recording equipment, computers, and software – featured in 12% of all reported non-resident trademark filing by class (figure B23). Nice class 9 was followed by services class 35 (7.9%), which covers advertising, business management, business administration and office functions, and by services classes 42 (6.9%) and 41 (5.1%) and goods class 5 (5%). Services class 42 includes scientific and technological services, as well as the design and development of computer hardware and software, while services class 41 pertains to education, entertainment and sporting activities. Goods class 5 relates to pharmaceutical preparations, baby food, dietary supplements for humans and animals, disinfectants, fungicides and herbicides. Of 45 Nice classes, the top five (9, 35, 42, 41 and 5) were specified in over one-third (36.9%) of non-resident trademark filing worldwide.

In 2022, the 11 classes associated with services accounted for 32.8% of all Nice classes specified in applications filed abroad, up from the 29.5% reported in 2021 (figure B24). Across a selection of offices, services classes accounted for between about 31% and 34% of all filing in China, India and Indonesia, percentages that resemble the global services class share. This share increases to between about 36% and 41% for the EUIPO and the offices of Canada, the Russian Federation, the UK, the US and Viet Nam. However, at offices in countries that include Brazil, France, the Islamic Republic of Iran, Italy, Mexico, the Republic of Korea and Türkiye, services classes represented around 45% or more of the total. Among these top offices, Brazil held the largest share at 64.3% (figure B27).

Grouping the 45 Nice classes into 10 distinct industry sectors offers valuable insights. In 2022, the research and technology sector attracted the largest filing volumes by applicants seeking trademark protection abroad, constituting 22% of global reported non-resident trademark filing (figure B25). It was followed by the health (13%), clothing and accessories (11.9%) and leisure and education (10.9%) sectors. Trademarks relating to business services (10.5%), agriculture (9%) and household equipment (8%) accounted for the next largest shares of the total. In contrast, industries linked to chemicals (3.1%), construction (5.5%) and transportation (6.2%) received the smallest proportions of filing abroad.

Research and technology was the sector that attracted the biggest proportion of total filing at the EUIPO (23%), as well as at the offices of Japan (19.6%), the UK (22.1%) and the US (19.3%) (figure B26). In China (26.1%) and the Russian Federation (14.1%), the agricultural sector was the predominant choice, while also accounting for the second largest proportion in India (14.9%) and Türkiye (13.8%), and ranking third in the Islamic Republic of Iran (17.3%). Filing for trademarks associated with the health sector constituted the largest proportion of filing in India (23%) and the third largest in China (11.2%). Business services topped the list of industry sectors in Brazil (26.3%), the Islamic Republic of Iran (22.5%) and Türkiye (23.1%), accounting for the largest share of total trademark filing. Filing related to clothing and accessories featured as either the second or third top sector in India, the Russian Federation and the US.

In 2022, an estimated 9.3 million trademark registrations were recorded globally

After concluding the examination process, an office may decide to register a trademark. The number of registrations issued can fluctuate greatly from year to year, due in part not only to a rise or fall in the volume of applications received in any given year, but also to the amount of resources an office is able to dedicate to examining trademark applications. For this reason, it is not possible to accurately compare the number of applications filed at a particular office in any given year with the number of registrations issued by that office in the same year.

The estimated 9.3 million trademark registrations recorded worldwide in 2022 marks a significant decline of 15.5%, equivalent to 1.7 million fewer registrations compared to the previous year (figure B4). This shift is in stark contrast to the substantial 29% growth seen in 2021.

Just as class counts make application filing activity internationally comparable, they also enable a more meaningful comparison of registrations. In 2022, an estimated 12.4 million classes were specified in the above-mentioned 9.3 million trademark registrations, reflecting an 11.8% reduction compared to the previous year's total (figure B5). Notably, registrations measured in class counts at the office of China underwent a steep decline of 20.1%, equating to nearly 1.6 million fewer registrations from 2021 to 2022. This decrease contributed most to the overall reduction in global registration activity. Moreover, large drops in registration class counts, ranging from about 28,000 to 75,400, occurred at many top offices. The EUIPO recorded a decline of 28,716, while the offices of France (-48,773), Germany (-42,883), India (-75,422), Indonesia (-49,703), the Islamic Republic of Iran (-44,340) and the US (-28,020) also contributed to a worldwide decline in trademark registrations.

China's office registered trademarks in which about 6.2 million classes were specified, with that office accounting for about half (50.1%) of trademark registrations recorded worldwide in 2022. Following China were the office of the US (462,977), the EUIPO (426,961) and the offices of the UK (370,600) and Türkiye (366,875) (figure B15). Combined, these four offices accounted for 13.1% of all registration activity.

Apart from China, six additional offices among the top 20 in terms of registration activity experienced declines of about 10% or more in 2022. The most significant decrease was observed at the office of the Islamic Republic of Iran (-31.2%), followed by the offices of Indonesia (-28.4%), India (-21.2%) and Germany (-20.2%). In contrast, four top offices achieved double-digit growth compared to the previous year. This group comprised Canada (+12.2%), the Russian Federation (+16.8%), Spain (+20.8%) and Türkiye (+24.8%).

Active trademark registrations increased by 9.4% in 2022

Unlike most forms of IP, trademarks can be maintained indefinitely through the payment of renewal fees at defined time intervals. In 2022, there were an estimated 82.5 million active trademark registrations across 152 intellectual property offices globally, representing an increase of 9.4% compared to 2021 (figure B34). This growth occurred despite an annual decline in trademark registrations at a number of offices, suggesting that the increase in active registrations in 2022 resulted, in part, from examination decisions on trademark applications filed prior to that year.

Once again, the office of China had by far the highest number of trademark registrations in force in 2022, with a total of almost 42.7 million (figure B35). It was followed by the offices of the US, with 3.1 million registrations in force, India (nearly 2.9 million), the UK (2.5 million) and Japan (approximately 2.2 million). The EUIPO and the offices of Brazil, France, Mexico, the Republic of Korea and Türkiye reported figures ranging from between 1.2 to 1.7 million active trademark registrations. The offices of Argentina (936,624) and Germany (994,274) reported comparable stocks of trademark registrations in force, while Australia (820,805), Spain (832,268) and the Russian Federation (805,075) recorded similar counts.

The around 19.8 million trademark registrations in force at 82 offices lend themselves to be distributed according to the year of their initial registration. This represents about 61% of a total of approximately 32.7 million trademark registrations recorded at these offices between 1998 and 2022. Over one-fifth (22.1%) of the trademarks registered in 1998 remained in force in 2022, showcasing the enduring value of marks (figure B36). For trademarks registered in 2014 or later, the percentage surpasses 75%. More than half (54.1%) of the 19.8 million registrations in force were registered relatively recently, dating back to 2016.

Trademark statistics

Trademark applications and registrations worldwide **78**

B1. Trend in trademark applications worldwide, 2008–2022 78
B2. Trend in trademark application class counts worldwide, 2008–2022 78
B3. Resident and non-resident trademark application class counts worldwide, 2008–2022 78
B4. Trend in trademark registrations worldwide, 2008–2022 79
B5. Trend in trademark registration class counts worldwide, 2008–2022 79
B6. Resident and non-resident trademark registration class counts worldwide, 2008–2022 80

Trademark applications and registrations by office **80**

B7. Trademark application class counts by region, 2012 and 2022 80
B8. Trend in trademark applications for the top five offices, 1883–2022 80
B9. Trademark application class counts for the top 20 offices, 2022 81
B10. Contribution of resident and non-resident application class counts to total growth for the top 20 offices, 2021–2022 81
B11. Trademark application class counts for offices of selected low- and middle-income countries, 2022 81
B12. Contribution of resident and non-resident application class counts to total growth for offices of selected low- and middle-income countries, 2021–2022 82
B13. Trademark registration class counts by region, 2012 and 2022 82
B14. Trend in trademark registrations for the top five offices, 1883–2022 82
B15. Trademark registration class counts for the top 20 offices, 2022 83
B16. Trademark registration class counts for offices of selected low- and middle-income countries, 2022 83

Trademark applications by origin **84**

B17. Trademark application class counts for the top 20 origins, 2022 84
B18. Trademark application class counts for selected low- and middle-income origins, 2022 84
B19. Trademark application class counts abroad for the top 20 origins, 2022 85
B20. Trademark application class counts for the top 20 offices and origins, 2022 85
B21. Flows of non-resident trademark application class counts between selected top origins and offices, 2022 87
B22. Distribution of trademark application class counts for the top 15 offices and selected non-resident origins, 2022 88

Trademark applications by Nice class and industry sector **88**

B23. Distribution of non-resident trademark applications by top Nice classes, 2022 88
B24. Non-resident trademark applications by goods and services classes, 2022 89
B25. Non-resident trademark applications by industry sector, 2022 90
B26. Trademark applications by top three sectors at the top offices, 2022 91
B27. Distribution of trademark applications by goods and services at the top offices, 2022 91
B28. Trademark applications by top three sectors for the top origins, 2022 91
B29. Distribution of trademark applications by goods and services for the top origins, 2022 92

Trademark application class count in relation to GDP and population **92**

B30. Resident trademark application class count per USD 100 billion GDP for selected origins, 2012 and 2022 92
B31. Resident trademark application class count per million population for selected origins, 2012 and 2022 93

Collective and certification trademark applications by office **93**
B32. Collective trademark applications for the top 20 offices, 2022 93
B33. Certification trademark applications for the top 20 offices, 2022 94

Trademark registrations in force **94**
B34. Trend in trademark registrations in force worldwide, 2010–2022 94
B35. Trademark registrations in force for the top 20 offices, 2022 94
B36. Trademark registrations in force in 2022 as a percentage of total registrations recorded between 1998 and 2022 95
B37. Average age of trademarks in force at selected offices, 2017 and 2022 95

Trademark office procedural data **96**
B38. Distribution of trademark examination outcomes for selected offices, 2022 96
B39. Potentially pending trademark applications for selected offices, 2022 96
B40. Number of trademark examiners for selected offices, 2022 96
B41. Duration of trademark examination for selected offices, 2022 97
B42. Third-party oppositions for selected offices, 2022 97
B43. Appeals against decisions for selected offices, 2022 97

Statistical tables **98**
B44. Trademark applications by office and origin, 2022 98
B45. Trademark registrations by office and origin, and trademarks in force, 2022 101
B46. Trademark office procedural data, 2022 105

Trademark applications and registrations worldwide

B1. Trend in trademark applications worldwide, 2008–2022

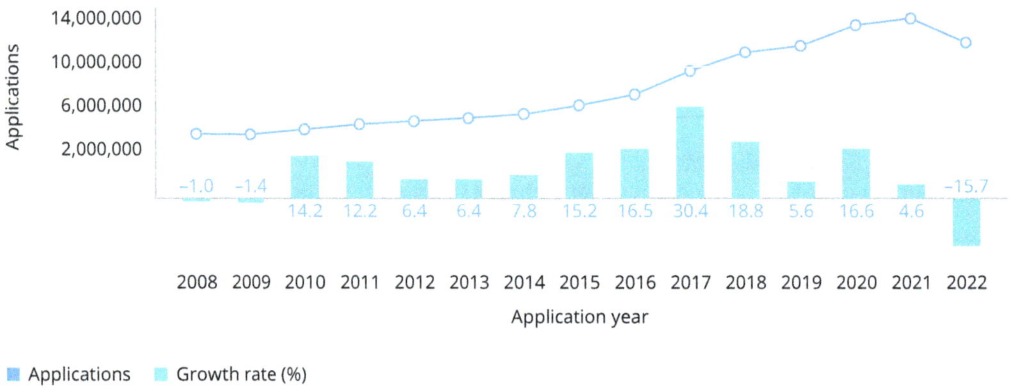

Note: World totals are WIPO estimates using data covering 168 IP offices. Each total includes the number of applications filed directly with national or regional offices (the Paris route), as well as the number of designations received by offices via the Madrid System (where applicable).
Source: WIPO Statistics Database, August 2023.

B2. Trend in trademark application class counts worldwide, 2008–2022

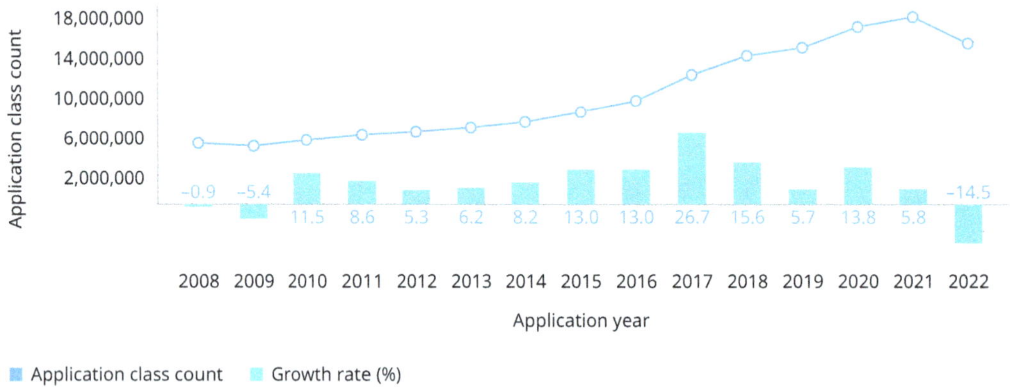

Note: World totals are WIPO estimates using data covering 168 IP offices. These totals include class counts in applications filed directly with national and regional offices (the Paris route), as well as class counts in designations received by offices via the Madrid System (where applicable). See glossary for the definition of class count.
Source: WIPO Statistics Database, August 2023.

B3. Resident and non-resident trademark application class counts worldwide, 2008–2022

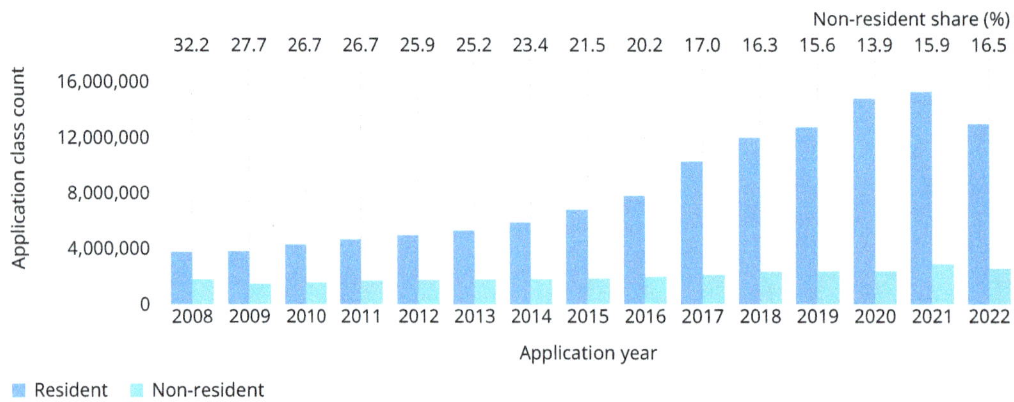

Note: World totals are WIPO estimates using data covering 168 IP offices. These totals include class counts in applications filed directly with national and regional offices (the Paris route), as well as class counts in designations received by offices via the Madrid System (where applicable). See glossary for definitions of class count, resident and non-resident.
Source: WIPO Statistics Database, August 2023.

B4. Trend in trademark registrations worldwide, 2008–2022

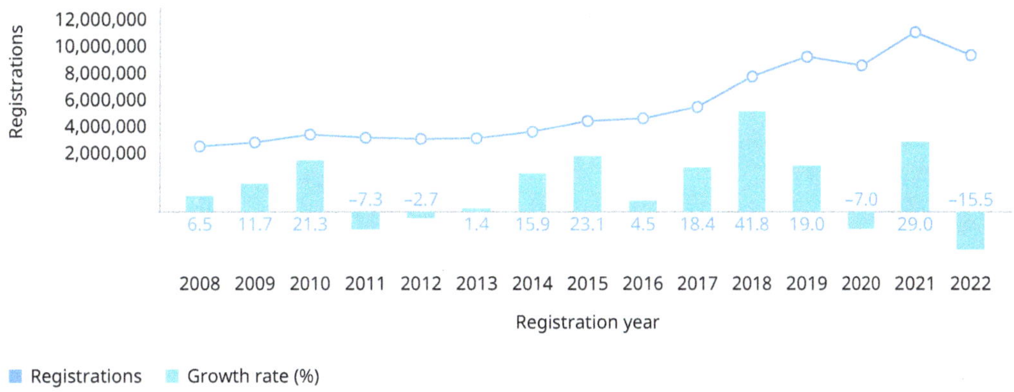

Note: World totals are WIPO estimates using data covering 168 IP offices. Each total includes the number of registrations issued by national and regional offices for applications filed directly with offices (the Paris route), as well as the number of designations received by offices via the Madrid System (where applicable).
Source: WIPO Statistics Database, August 2023.

B5. Trend in trademark registration class counts worldwide, 2008–2022

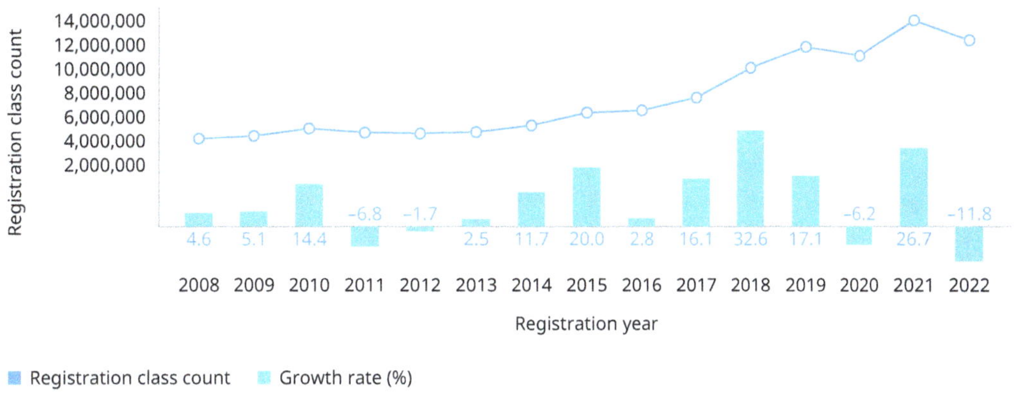

Note: World totals are WIPO estimates using data covering 168 IP offices. These totals include class counts in registrations issued by national and regional offices for applications filed directly with offices (the Paris route), as well as designations received by offices via the Madrid System (where applicable). See glossary for the definition of class count.
Source: WIPO Statistics Database, August 2023.

B6. Resident and non-resident trademark registration class counts worldwide, 2008–2022

Note: World totals are WIPO estimates using data covering 168 IP offices. These totals include class counts in registrations issued by national and regional offices for applications filed directly with offices (the Paris route), as well as for designations received by offices via the Madrid System (where applicable). See glossary for definitions of class count, resident and non-resident.
Source: WIPO Statistics Database, August 2023.

Trademark applications and registrations by office

B7. Trademark application class counts by region, 2012 and 2022

	Application class count		Resident share (%)		Share of world total (%)		Average growth (%)
Region	**2012**	**2022**	**2012**	**2022**	**2012**	**2022**	**2012–2022**
Africa	198,300	285,500	45.2	46.1	3.0	1.8	3.7
Asia	3,176,100	10,540,100	79.8	91.0	47.7	67.8	12.7
Europe	1,959,900	2,522,700	72.7	72.0	29.4	16.2	2.6
Latin America and the Caribbean	604,900	1,064,500	64.6	73.5	9.1	6.8	5.8
North America	568,300	920,900	71.6	59.5	8.5	5.9	4.9
Oceania	149,500	209,600	57.9	48.7	2.2	1.3	3.4
World	**6,657,000**	**15,543,300**	**74.1**	**83.5**	**100.0**	**100.0**	**8.8**

Note: Totals by geographical region are WIPO estimates using data covering 168 IP offices. Each region includes the following number of offices: Africa (36), Asia (45), Europe (42), Latin America and the Caribbean (36), North America (2) and Oceania (7).
Source: WIPO Statistics Database, August 2023.

B8. Trend in trademark applications for the top five offices, 1883–2022

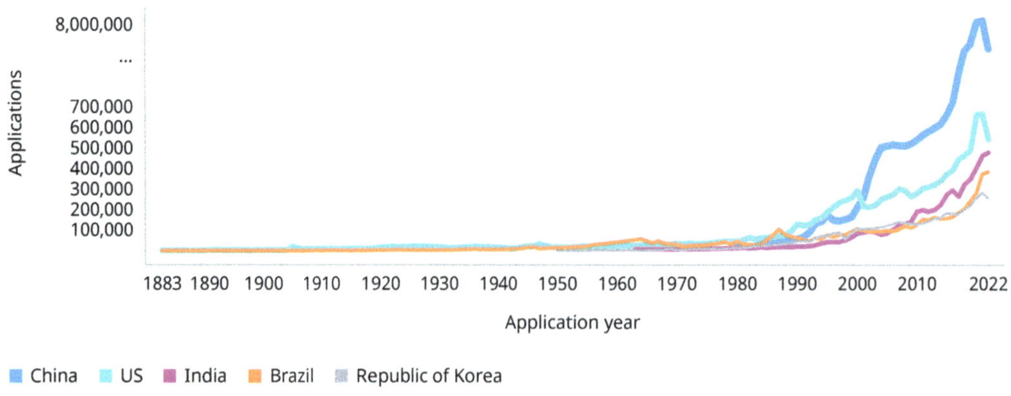

Note: Data are based on the numbers of applications filed; that is, differences between single-class and multi-class filing systems across IP offices are not taken into account. The top five offices were selected based on 2022 application totals.
Source: WIPO Statistics Database, August 2023.

B9. Trademark application class counts for the top 20 offices, 2022

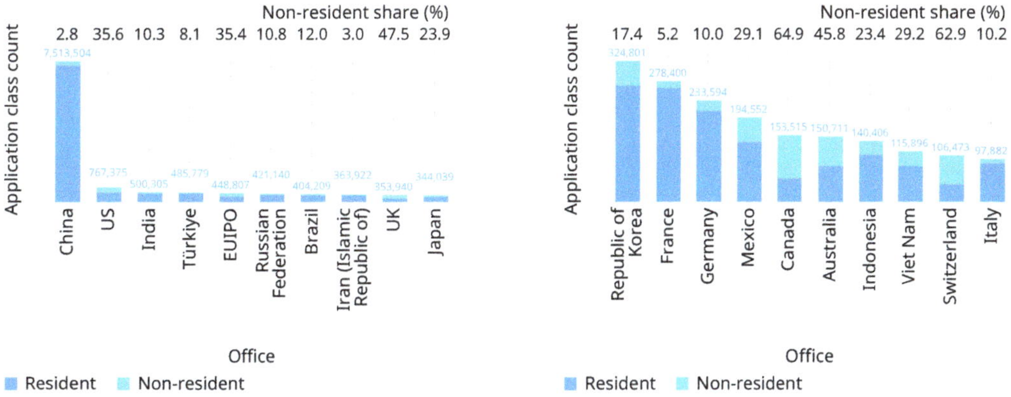

Note: EUIPO is the European Union Intellectual Property Office.
Source: WIPO Statistics Database, August 2023.

B10. Contribution of resident and non-resident application class counts to total growth for the top 20 offices, 2021–2022

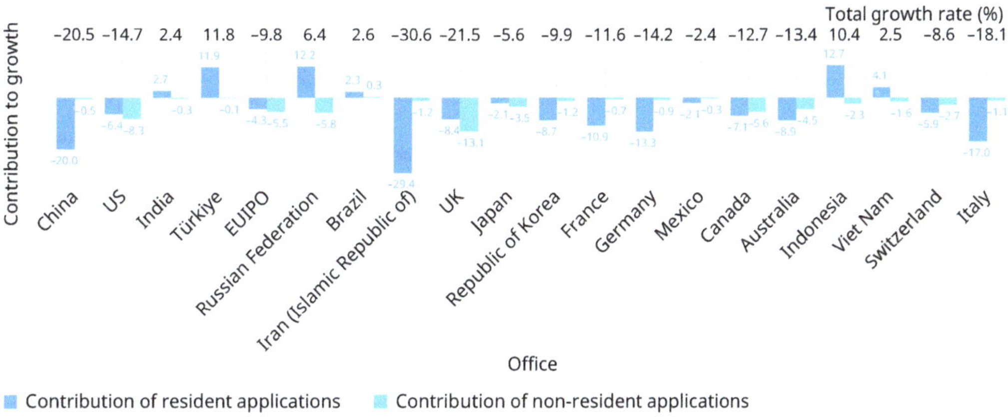

Note: EUIPO is the European Union Intellectual Property Office. This figure shows the total growth or decrease in application class counts for each office, broken down by the respective contributions made by resident and non-resident filing activity.
Source: WIPO Statistics Database, August 2023.

B11. Trademark application class counts for offices of selected low- and middle-income countries, 2022

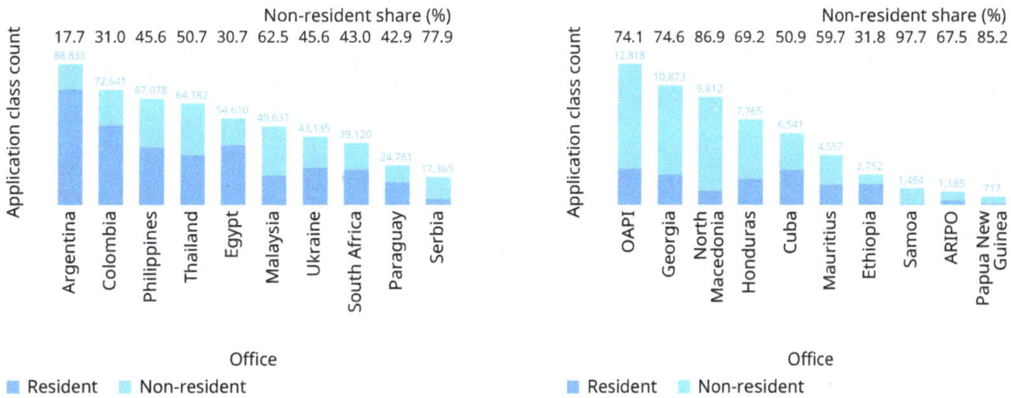

Note: The selected offices are from different world regions and income groups (low-income, lower middle-income and upper middle-income). ARIPO is the African Regional Intellectual Property Organization. OAPI is the African Intellectual Property Organization, which receives applications on behalf of its 17 member states. Where available, data for all offices are presented in statistical table B44 toward the end of this section.
Source: WIPO Statistics Database, August 2023.

B12. Contribution of resident and non-resident application class counts to total growth for offices of selected low- and middle-income countries, 2021–2022

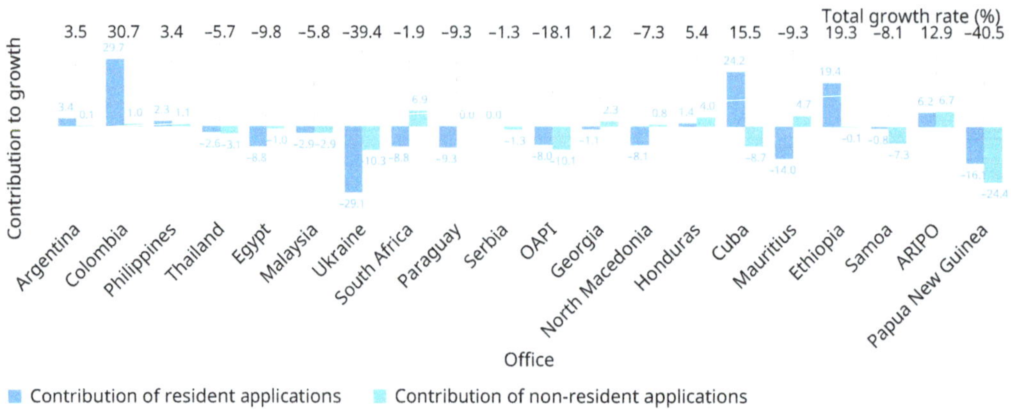

Note: The selected offices are from different world regions and income groups (low-income, lower middle-income and upper middle-income). ARIPO is the African Regional Intellectual Property Organization. OAPI is the African Intellectual Property Organization, which receives applications on behalf of its 17 member states. Where available, data for all offices are presented in statistical table B44 toward the end of this section. This figure shows the total growth or decrease in application class counts for each office, broken down by the respective contributions of resident and non-resident applications.
Source: WIPO Statistics Database, August 2023.

B13. Trademark registration class counts by region, 2012 and 2022

	Registration class count		Resident share (%)		Share of world total (%)		Average growth (%)
Region	**2012**	**2022**	**2012**	**2022**	**2012**	**2022**	**2012–2022**
Africa	160,000	245,500	32.7	33.8	3.4	2.0	4.4
Asia	2,000,400	8,351,400	72.3	88.1	43.1	67.4	15.4
Europe	1,608,300	2,297,800	66.0	66.4	34.6	18.6	3.6
Latin America and the Caribbean	434,600	677,300	58.2	61.4	9.4	5.5	4.5
North America	327,400	600,100	67.3	43.3	7.0	4.8	6.2
Oceania	113,400	211,700	48.9	43.8	2.4	1.7	6.4
World	**4,644,100**	**12,383,800**	**66.5**	**78.6**	**100.0**	**100.0**	**10.3**

Note: Totals by geographical region are WIPO estimates based on data covering 168 offices. Each region includes the following number of offices: Africa (36), Asia (45), Europe (42), Latin America and the Caribbean (36), North America (2) and Oceania (7).
Source: WIPO Statistics Database, August 2023.

B14. Trend in trademark registrations for the top five offices, 1883–2022

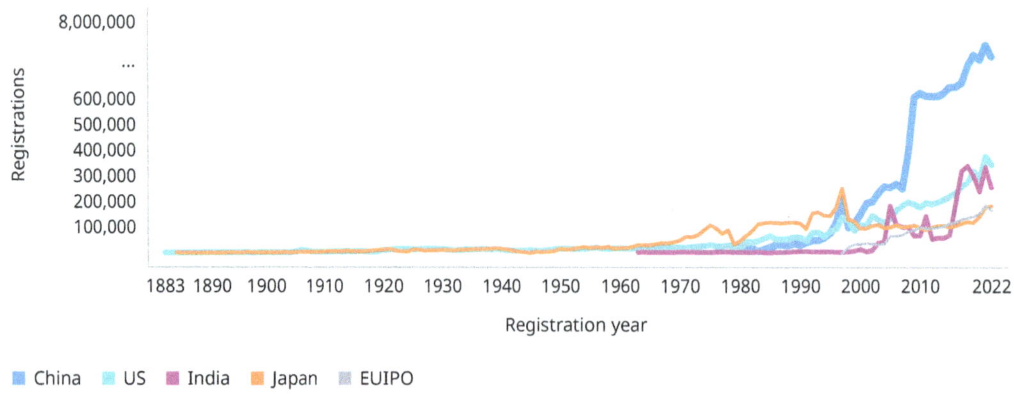

Note: EUIPO is the European Union Intellectual Property Office. Data are based on the numbers of registrations recorded; that is, differences between single-class and multi-class registration systems across IP offices are not taken into account. The top five offices were selected based on 2022 registration totals.
Source: WIPO Statistics Database, August 2023.

B15. Trademark registration class counts for the top 20 offices, 2022

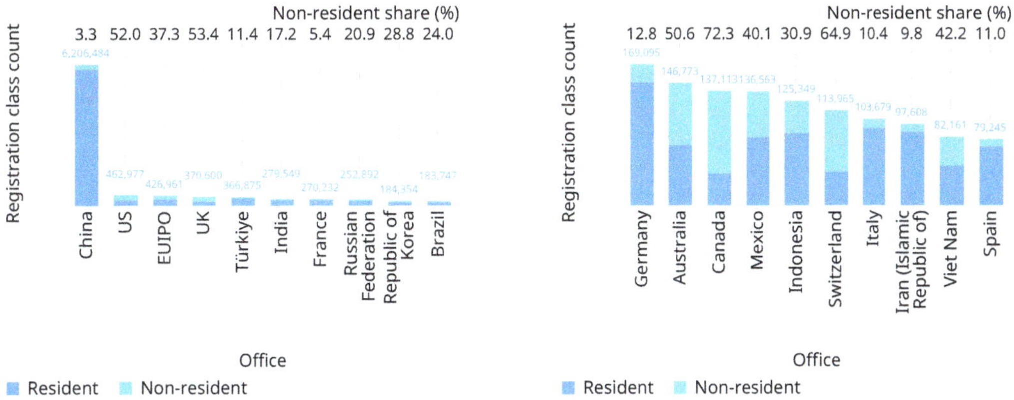

Note: EUIPO is the European Union Intellectual Property Office. On the basis of an examination, a registration may be issued for a trademark application. The number of registrations issued may fluctuate greatly from one year to the next, in part reflecting the amount of resources that IP offices dedicate to examining trademark applications.
Source: WIPO Statistics Database, August 2023.

B16. Trademark registration class counts for offices of selected low- and middle-income countries, 2022

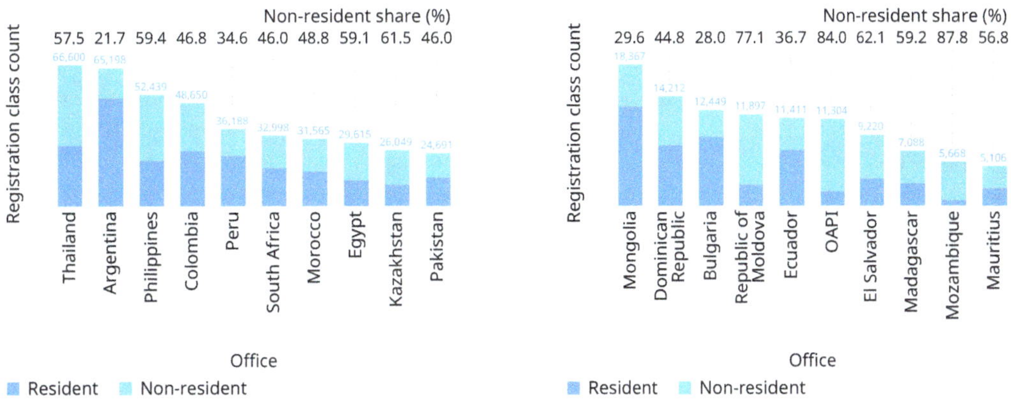

Note: The offices selected are from different world regions and income groups (low-income, lower middle-income and upper middle-income). OAPI is the African Intellectual Property Organization, which receives applications on behalf of its 17 member states. Where available, data for every office is presented in statistical table B45 toward the end of this section.
Source: WIPO Statistics Database, August 2023.

Trademark applications by origin

B17. Trademark application class counts for the top 20 origins, 2022

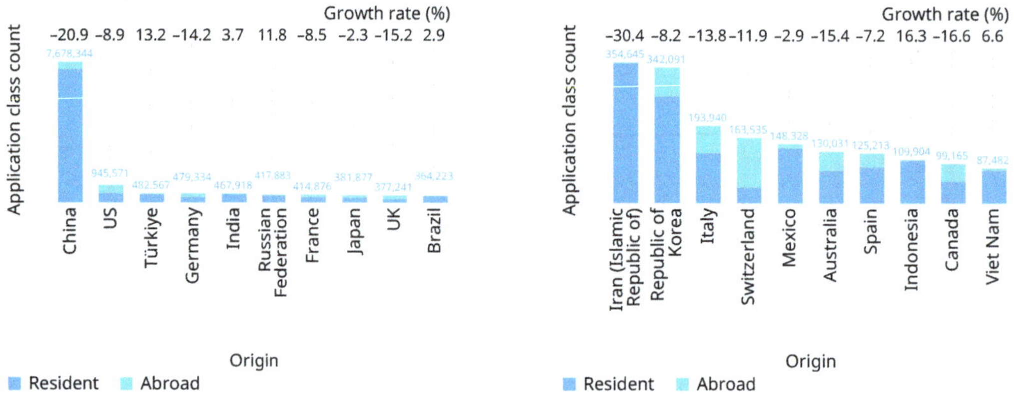

Note: In this figure, trademark application filing activity by origin includes the number of classes specified in resident applications and in applications filed abroad and is based on an absolute not equivalent count. The origin of a trademark application is determined by the residence of the applicant. An application filed at a regional office is considered a resident filing if the applicant is a resident of one of the relevant member states.
Source: WIPO Statistics Database, August 2023.

B18. Trademark application class counts for selected low- and middle-income origins, 2022

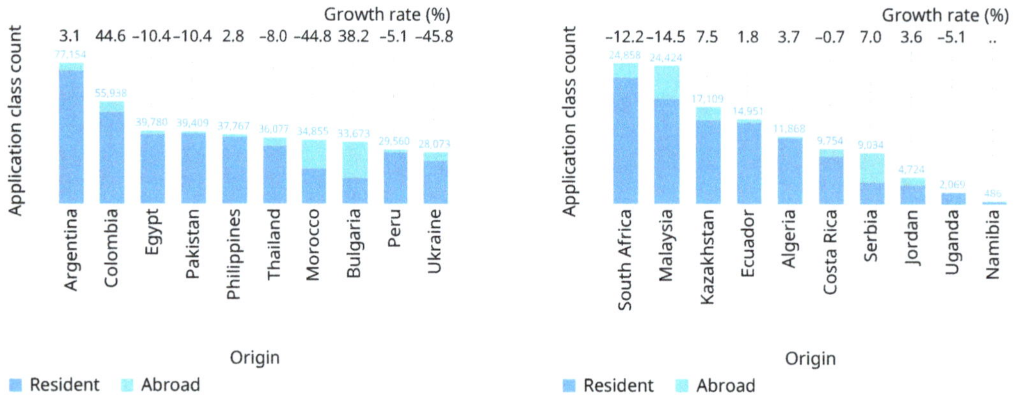

Note: In this figure, trademark application filing activity by origin includes the number of classes specified in resident applications and in applications filed abroad and is based on an absolute not equivalent count. The origin of a trademark application is determined by the residence of the applicant. The origins selected are from different world regions and income groups (low-income, lower middle-income and upper middle-income). Where available, data for all origins are presented in statistical table B44 toward the end of this section.
.. indicates not available.
Source: WIPO Statistics Database, August 2023.

B19. Trademark application class counts abroad for the top 20 origins, 2022

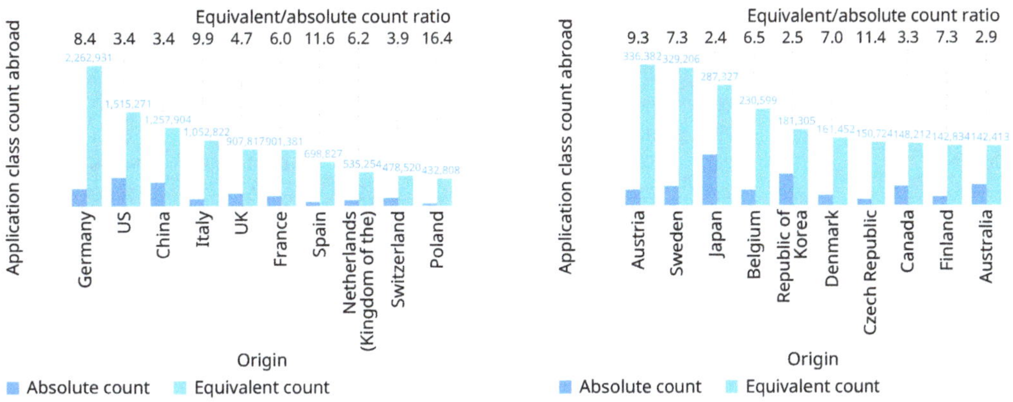

Note: This figure distinguishes between absolute and equivalent counts for filing activity abroad; that is, resident applications are excluded.
Source: WIPO Statistics Database, August 2023.

B20. Trademark application class counts for the top 20 offices and origins, 2022

	Office									
Origin	**Australia**	**Brazil**	**Canada**	**China**	**EUIPO**	**France**	**Germany**	**India**	**Indonesia**	**Iran (Islamic Republic of)**
Australia	81,740	538	2,628	6,348	3,572	113	156	1,041	831	50
Brazil	130	355,877	161	558	617	79	86	89	41	25
Canada	1,792	600	53,907	3,661	3,912	199	180	777	306	238
China	7,158	3,888	11,786	7,304,080	33,173	1,727	6,983	4,418	5,718	1,282
France	2,269	2,705	4,539	9,583	28,956	263,845	1,190	2,119	1,054	325
Germany	5,082	4,114	6,470	15,159	79,420	940	210,191	4,403	1,586	573
India	434	461	524	749	1,038	51	57	448,911	404	105
Indonesia	63	12	11	452	115	17	15	35	107,543	5
Iran (Islamic Republic of)	27		55	339	112	2	12	30		352,891
Italy	1,733	2,238	2,243	6,953	37,779	302	250	1,669	707	388
Japan	2,909	2,201	3,294	24,607	6,339	416	383	2,544	3,938	387
Mexico	69	415	260	453	552	42	23	106	29	1
Republic of Korea	1,463	760	1,583	15,149	4,049	206	306	1,190	2,113	250
Russian Federation	128	301	233	3,049	1,074	293	465	403	185	146
Spain	678	750	991	2,385	25,427	385	207	472	266	169
Switzerland	2,646	2,440	3,290	7,717	13,328	2,097	2,935	2,335	1,079	377
Türkiye	328	366	568	890	3,478	444	898	368	235	747
UK	7,432	3,526	7,176	17,706	27,045	916	1,163	3,906	1,863	570
US	19,873	12,570	38,510	51,142	40,119	1,642	1,624	11,450	4,896	702
Viet Nam	162	27	91	361	167	33	94	74	140	28
Others	14,595	10,420	15,195	42,163	138,535	4,651	6,376	13,965	7,472	4,663
Total	**150,711**	**404,209**	**153,515**	**7,513,504**	**448,807**	**278,400**	**233,594**	**500,305**	**140,406**	**363,922**

	Office									
Origin	**Italy**	**Japan**	**Mexico**	**Republic of Korea**	**Russian Federation**	**Switzerland**	**Türkiye**	**UK**	**US**	**Viet Nam**
Australia	43	1,402	483	1,038	262	296	256	4,642	7,138	776
Brazil	9	126	477	36	65	62	37	251	1,037	52
Canada	54	970	1,012	886	244	523	383	3,279	18,287	385
China	1,504	18,891	5,162	9,394	6,169	2,188	2,989	28,631	117,491	5,996
France	1,080	3,896	2,129	2,943	2,492	7,337	1,928	10,478	8,164	1,203
Germany	924	5,957	3,504	4,048	5,232	21,948	6,081	17,940	14,966	1,758
India	22	254	255	174	111	260	225	940	2,039	410
Indonesia	6	78	9	54	12	10	11	61	138	116
Iran (Islamic Republic of)	9	22		20	101	29	118	61	25	17
Italy	87,941	2,412	1,348	1,742	2,586	3,186	1,748	6,361	5,858	701
Japan	234	261,688	2,026	6,204	1,526	1,480	1,278	5,174	9,167	3,747
Mexico	42	32	137,882	34	38	45	205	160	2,769	47
Republic of Korea	174	5,879	836	268,334	1,288	404	651	2,451	8,798	3,123
Russian Federation	270	251	196	279	375,771	274	918	675	695	310
Spain	201	665	2,247	545	655	744	569	3,175	3,252	218
Switzerland	1,108	3,470	2,598	2,383	2,672	39,535	2,434	7,787	7,203	1,086
Türkiye	343	364	278	248	1,519	515	446,651	1,972	2,192	154
UK	692	5,071	2,608	3,669	2,236	3,657	2,732	185,858	22,097	1,670
US	865	18,538	21,813	13,629	5,187	8,071	6,922	35,892	494,216	4,896
Viet Nam	26	224	38	201	94	34	34	88	1,236	82,035
Others	2,335	13,849	9,651	8,940	12,880	15,875	9,609	38,064	40,607	7,196
Total	**97,882**	**344,039**	**194,552**	**324,801**	**421,140**	**106,473**	**485,779**	**353,940**	**767,375**	**115,896**

Note: EUIPO is the European Union Intellectual Property Office. The office and origin data shown consist of absolute rather than equivalent application class counts.
Source: WIPO Statistics Database, August 2023.

B21. **Flows of non-resident trademark application class counts between selected top origins and offices, 2022**

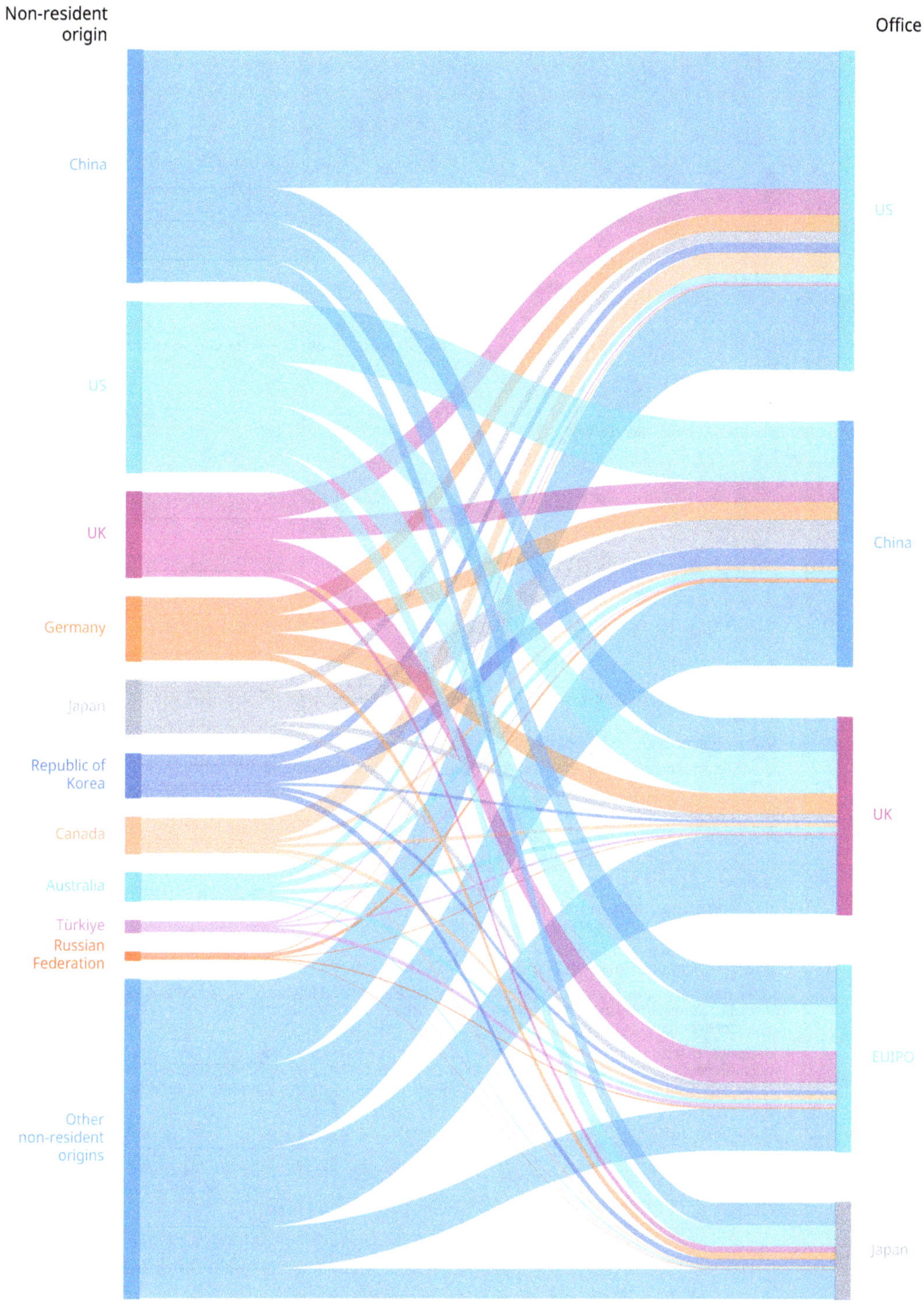

Note: EUIPO is the European Union Intellectual Property Office. The office and non-resident origin data shown consist of absolute rather than equivalent application class counts.
Source: WIPO Statistics Database, August 2023.

B22. Distribution of trademark application class counts for the top 15 offices and selected non-resident origins, 2022

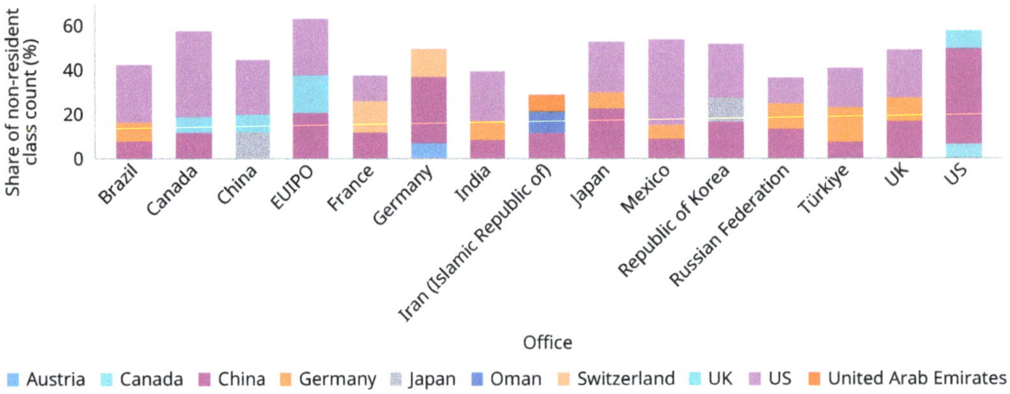

Note: EUIPO is the European Union Intellectual Property Office. The office and origin data shown consist of absolute rather than equivalent application class counts.
Source: WIPO Statistics Database, August 2023.

Trademark applications by Nice class and industry sector

B23. Distribution of non-resident trademark applications by top Nice classes, 2022

Rank	Class	Description	Share (%)
1	9	Scientific, photographic, measuring instruments; recording equipment; computers and software	12.0
2	35	Advertising, business management, business administration and office functions	7.9
3	42	Scientific and technological services, design and development of computer hardware and software	6.9
4	41	Education, entertainment and sporting activities	5.1
5	5	Pharmaceutical preparations, baby food, dietary supplements for humans and animals, disinfectants, fungicides and herbicides	5.0
6	25	Clothing, footwear, headwear	4.6
7	3	Bleaching preparations and other substances for laundry use; cleaning and abrasive preparations; soaps, perfumery and cosmetics	4.0
8	28	Games, toys and playthings; video game apparatus; gymnastic and sporting articles; decorations for Christmas trees	3.0
9	21	Small, hand-operated utensils and apparatus for household and kitchen use, as well as cosmetic and toilet utensils, glassware and certain goods made of porcelain, ceramic, earthenware, terra-cotta or glass	2.6
10	7	Machines, machine tools, power-operated tools; motors and engines, except for land vehicles; machine coupling and transmission components, except for land vehicles; agricultural implements, other than hand-operated hand tools; incubators for eggs; automatic vending machines	2.5
		Remaining classes	**46.3**

Note: Figures based on non-resident filing data from 137 IP offices. Some classes listed are abbreviated. See www.wipo.int/classifications/nice for a complete list of all classes.
Source: WIPO Statistics Database, August 2023.

B24. Non-resident trademark applications by goods and services classes, 2022

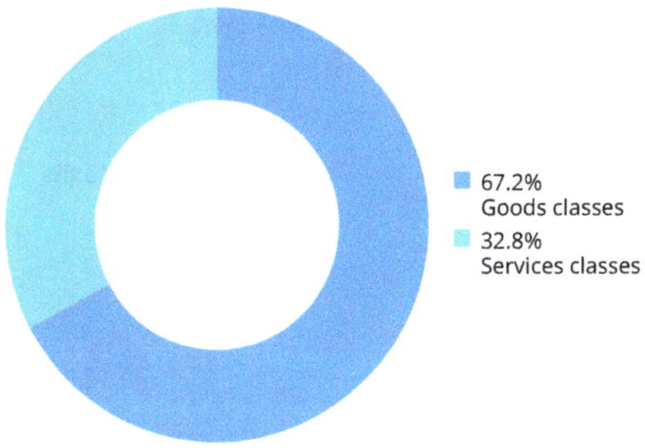

Note: In the 45-class Nice Classification, the first 34 classes indicate goods and the remaining 11 refer to services. See www.wipo.int/classifications/nice for a complete list of classes. These figures are based on non-resident filing data from 137 IP offices.
Source: WIPO Statistics Database, August 2023.

B25. Non-resident trademark applications by industry sector, 2022

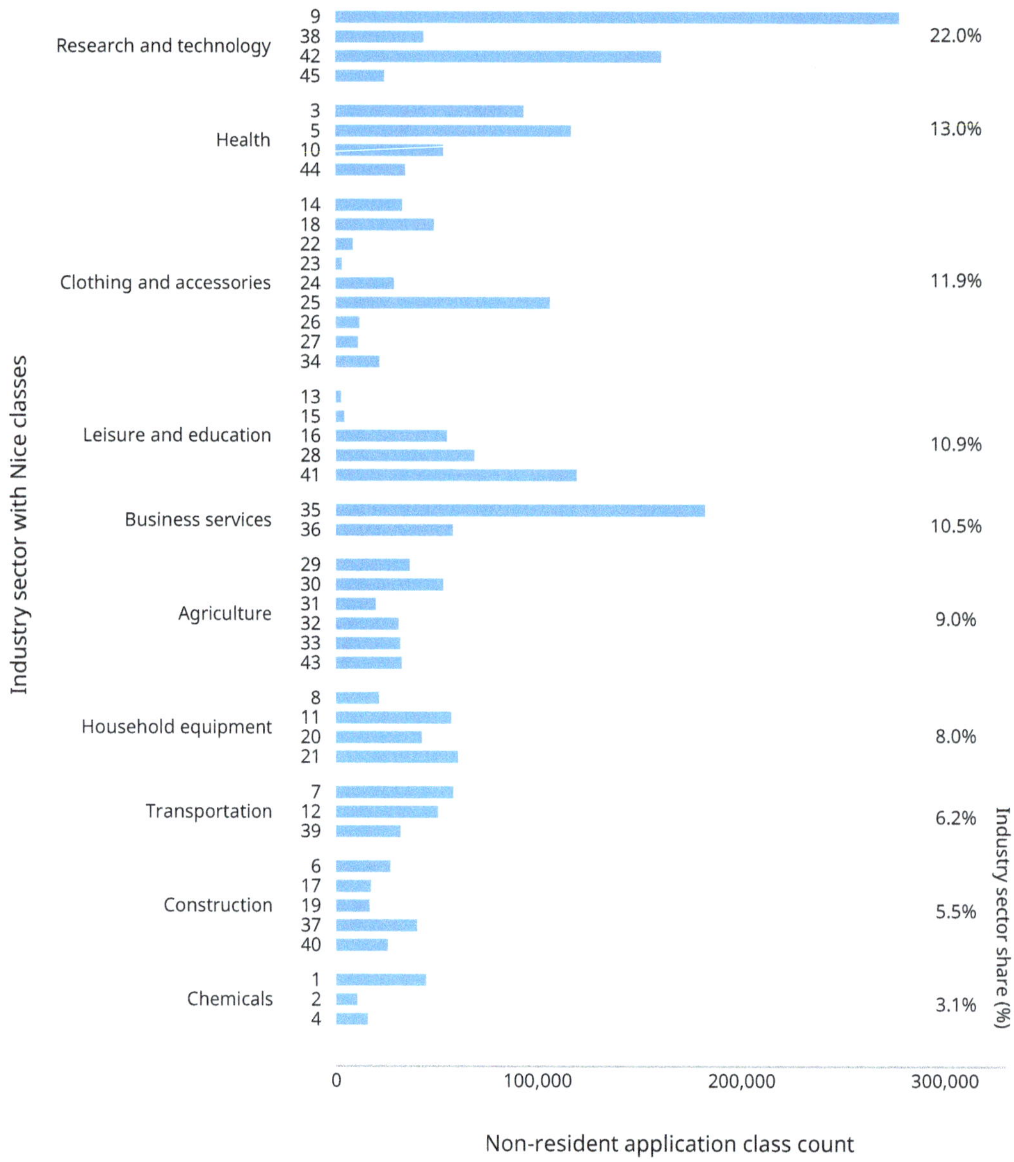

Note: Industry sectors based on class groups are those defined by Edital. Some industry sectors are abbreviated. See annex B for full definitions and the composition of Nice goods and services classes. Figures based on non-resident filing data from 137 IP offices.
Source: WIPO Statistics Database, August 2023.

B26. Trademark applications by top three sectors at the top offices, 2022

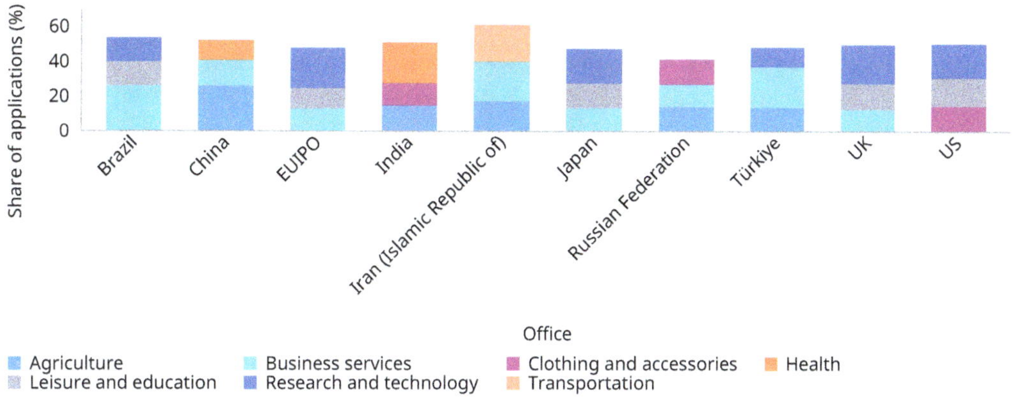

Note: EUIPO is the European Union Intellectual Property Office. Industry sectors based on class groups are those defined by Edital. Some industry sectors are abbreviated. See www.wipo.int/classifications/nice for a complete list of classes. The top three sectors and top offices were selected based on 2022 totals.
Source: WIPO Statistics Database, August 2023.

B27. Distribution of trademark applications by goods and services at the top offices, 2022

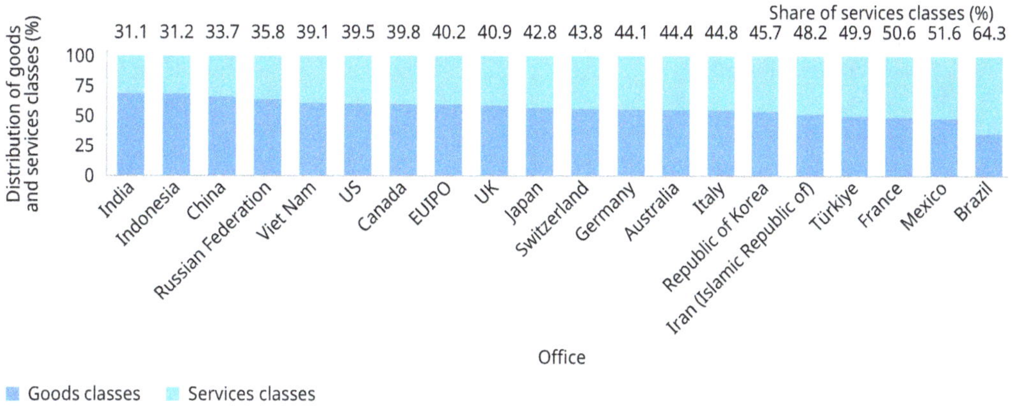

Note: EUIPO is the European Union Intellectual Property Office.
Source: WIPO Statistics Database, August 2023.

B28. Trademark applications by top three sectors for the top origins, 2022

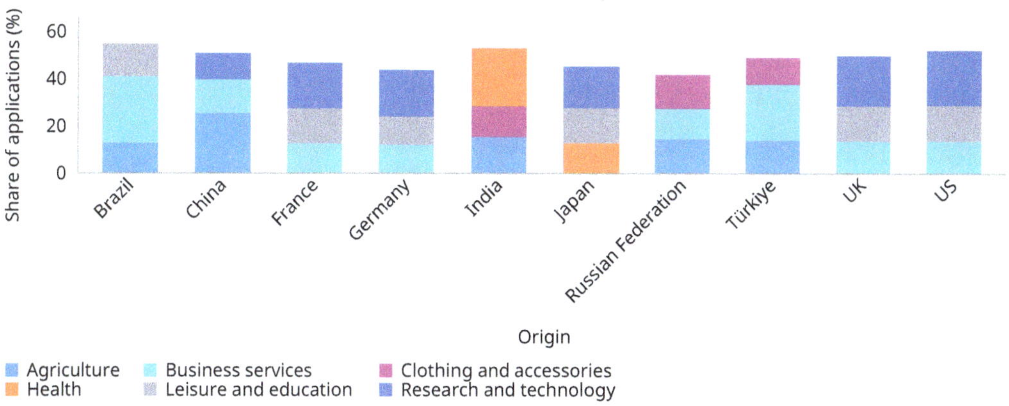

Note: Industry sectors based on class groups are those defined by Edital. Some industry sectors are abbreviated. See annex B for full definitions. The top three sectors and top origins were selected based on 2022 totals.
Source: WIPO Statistics Database, August 2023.

B29. Distribution of trademark applications by goods and services for the top origins, 2022

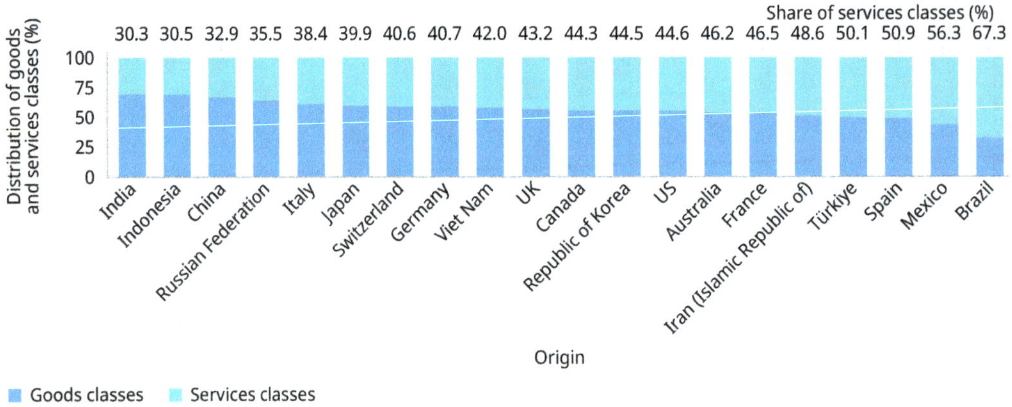

Source: WIPO Statistics Database, August 2023.

Trademark application class count in relation to GDP and population

B30. Resident trademark application class count per USD 100 billion GDP for selected origins, 2012 and 2022

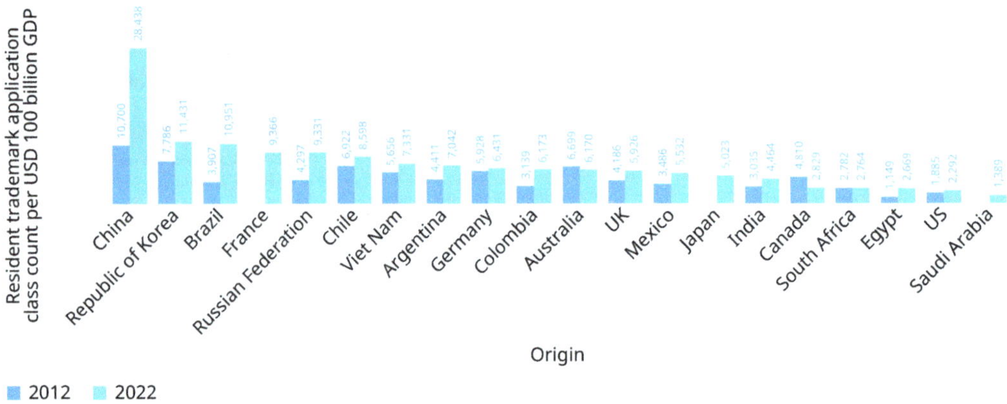

Note: GDP data are in 2017 US purchasing power parity (PPP) dollars. The selected 20 origins for 2022 were included if they had a GDP greater than USD 500 billion PPP and a resident trademark application class count of at least 20,000. This figure does not provide an overall ranking of all origins; rather, it shows a selection across geographical regions and income groups.
Sources: WIPO Statistics Database and World Bank, August 2023.

B31. Resident trademark application class count per million population for selected origins, 2012 and 2022

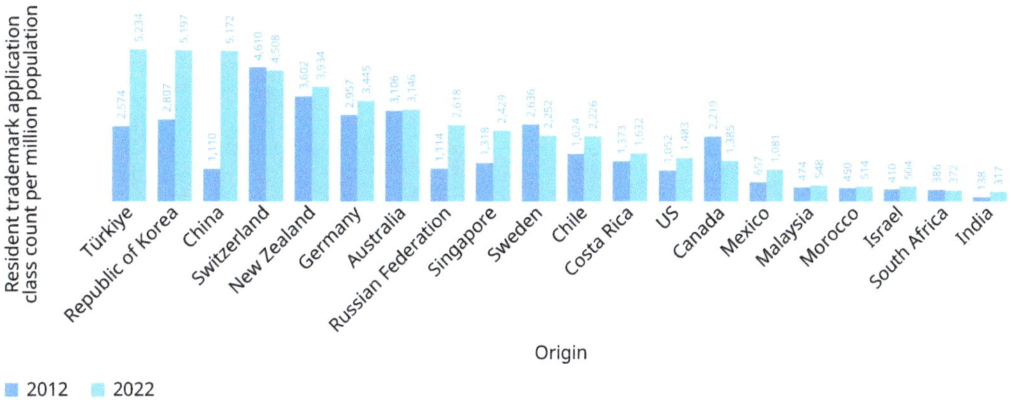

Note: The selected 20 origins for 2022 were included if they had a population greater than 5 million and a resident trademark application class count of at least 4,500. This figure does not provide an overall ranking of all origins; rather, it shows a selection across geographical regions and income groups.
Sources: WIPO Statistics Database and World Bank, August 2023.

Collective and certification trademark applications by office

B32. Collective trademark applications for the top 20 offices, 2022

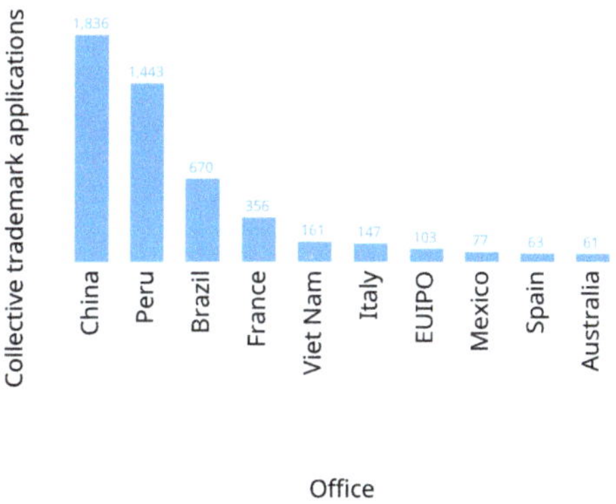

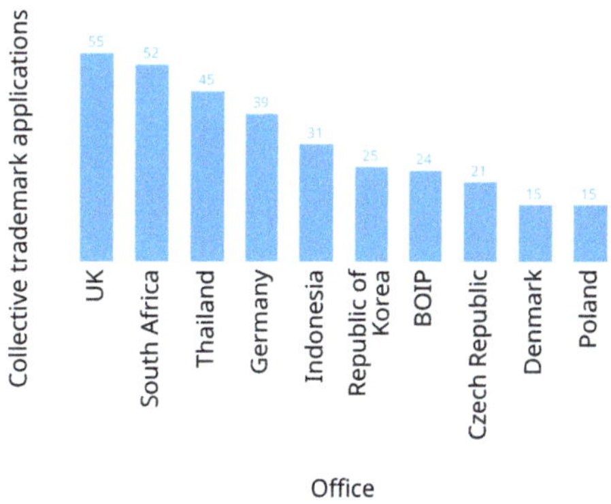

Note: EUIPO is the European Union Intellectual Property Office and BOIP is the Benelux Office for Intellectual Property.
Source: WIPO Statistics Database, August 2023.

B33. Certification trademark applications for the top 20 offices, 2022

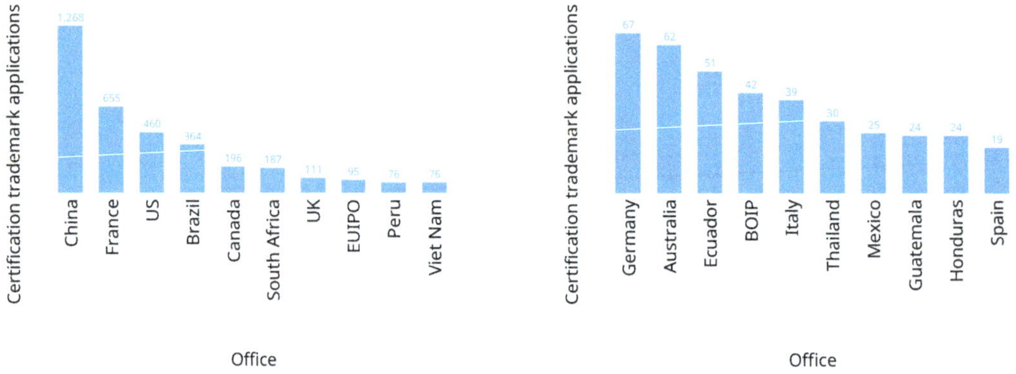

Note: EUIPO is the European Union Intellectual Property Office and BOIP is the Benelux Office for Intellectual Property.
Source: WIPO Statistics Database, August 2023.

Trademark registrations in force

B34. Trend in trademark registrations in force worldwide, 2010–2022

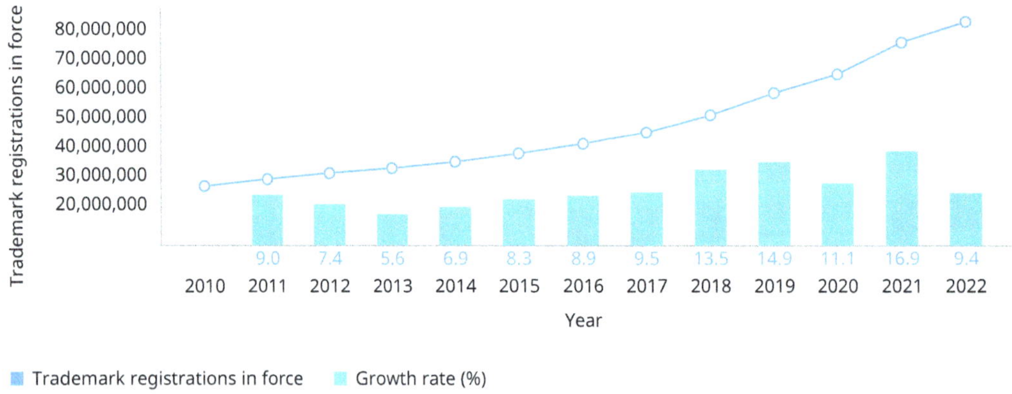

Note: World totals are WIPO estimates using data covering 152 IP offices. Data refer to the number of trademark registrations in force, not the number of classes specified in those registrations. Trademark rights can be maintained indefinitely by paying renewal fees at defined intervals. Trademarks in force provides information on the volume of trademark registrations currently active, as well as the historical trademark life cycle.
Source: WIPO Statistics Database, August 2023.

B35. Trademark registrations in force for the top 20 offices, 2022

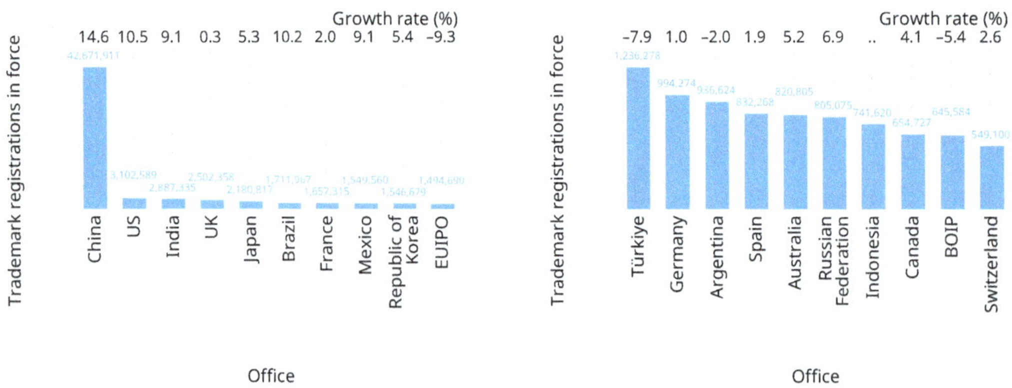

Note: EUIPO is the European Union Intellectual Property Office and BOIP is the Benelux Office for Intellectual Property. Data refer to the number of trademark registrations in force, not the number of classes specified in those registrations.
.. indicates not available.
Source: WIPO Statistics Database, August 2023.

B36. Trademark registrations in force in 2022 as a percentage of total registrations recorded between 1998 and 2022

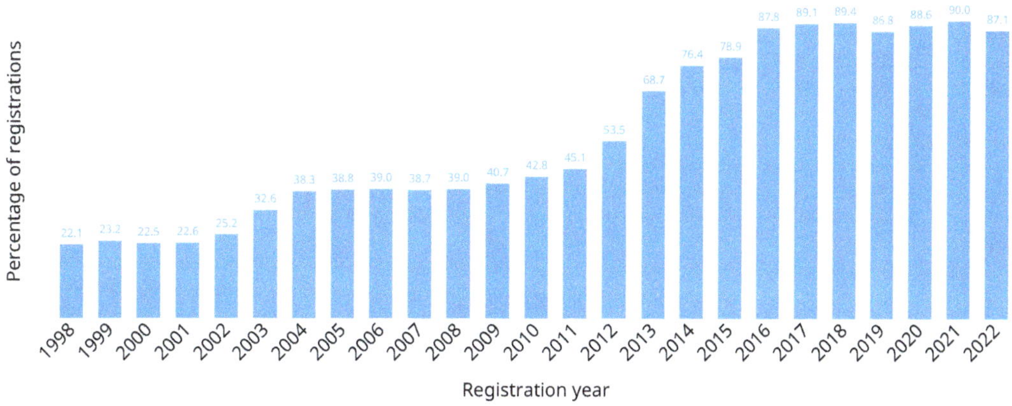

Note: Percentages are calculated as follows: the number of trademark registrations issued in year *t* and in force in 2022 divided by the total number of trademark registrations issued in year *t*. Trademark holders must pay renewal fees to maintain the validity of their marks, which in most cases can be maintained indefinitely. This figure is based on about 19.8 million active trademark registrations reported by the 82 offices that provided a breakdown by year of registration. Detailed data for several of the larger offices, such as those of China, Japan and Switzerland, are not available.
Source: WIPO Statistics Database, August 2023.

B37. Average age of trademarks in force at selected offices, 2017 and 2022

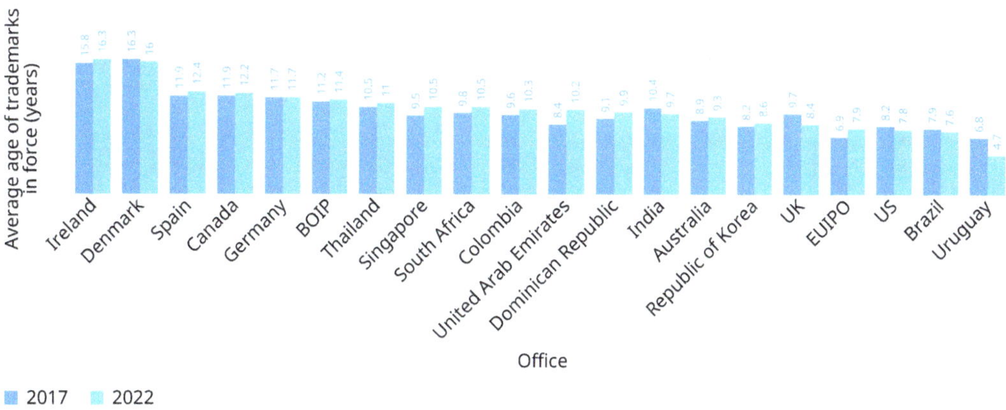

Note: BOIP is the Benelux Office for Intellectual Property and EUIPO is the European Union Intellectual Property Office.
Source: WIPO Statistics Database, August 2023.

Trademark office procedural data

B38. Distribution of trademark examination outcomes for selected offices, 2022

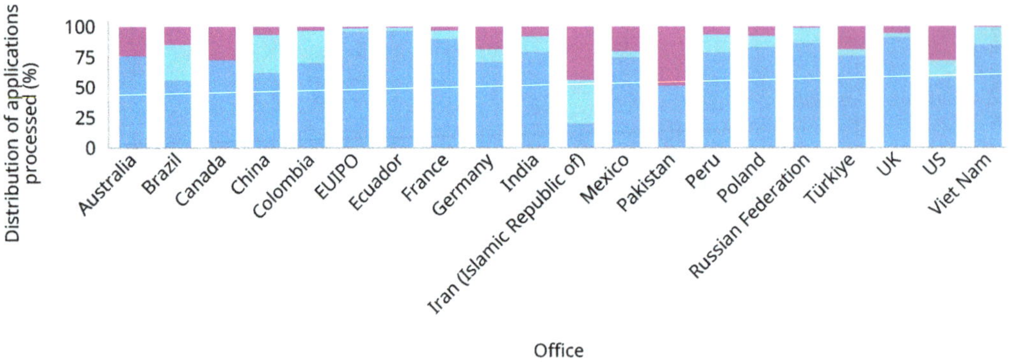

Note: EUIPO is the European Union Intellectual Property Office. WIPO collects data from IP offices using a common questionnaire and methodology. However, because of differences in the application processing procedures between offices, data cannot be fully harmonized. Therefore, caution should be exercised when making comparisons across offices.
Source: WIPO Statistics Database, August 2023.

B39. Potentially pending trademark applications for selected offices, 2022

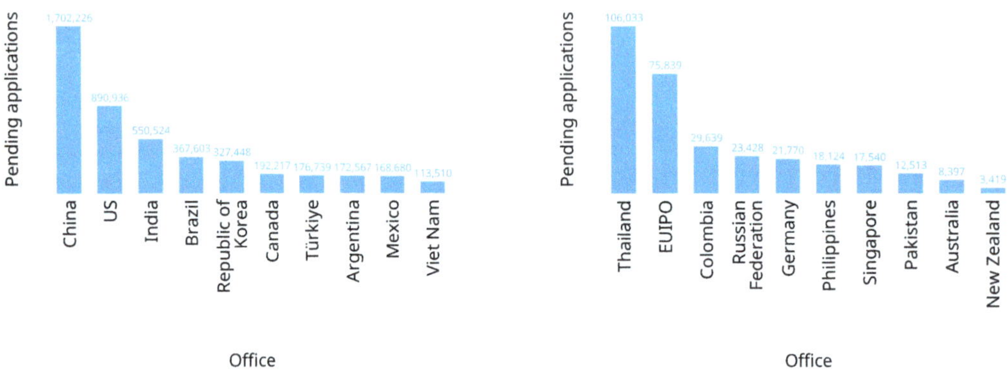

Note: EUIPO is the European Union Intellectual Property Office. WIPO collects data from IP offices using a common questionnaire and methodology. However, because of differences in the application processing procedures between offices, data cannot be fully harmonized. Therefore, caution should be exercised when making comparisons across offices. Detailed data for several larger offices, such as those of China and Japan, are not available.
Source: WIPO Statistics Database, August 2023.

B40. Number of trademark examiners for selected offices, 2022

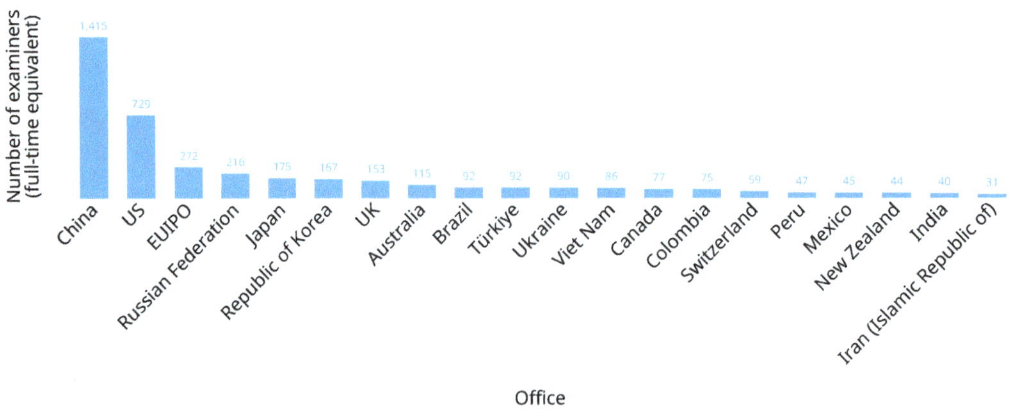

Note: EUIPO is the European Union Intellectual Property Office.
Source: WIPO Statistics Database, August 2023.

B41. Duration of trademark examination for selected offices, 2022

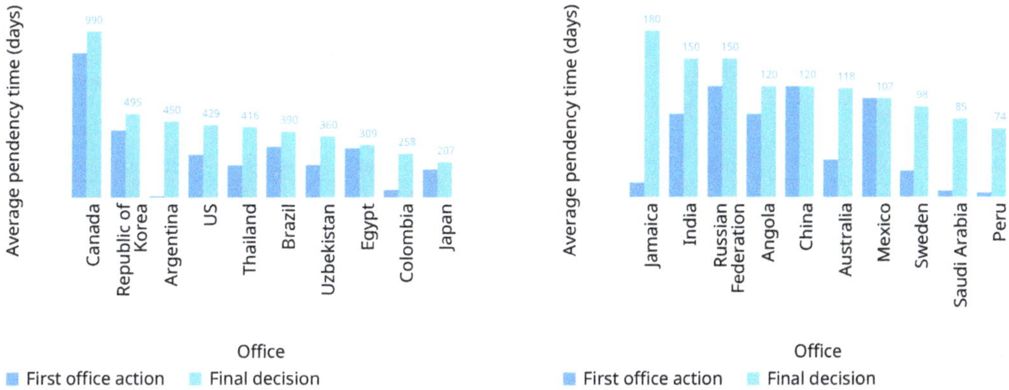

Note: WIPO collects data from IP offices using a common questionnaire and methodology. However, because of differences in application processing procedures between offices, data cannot be fully harmonized. Therefore, caution should be exercised when making comparisons across offices.
Source: WIPO Statistics Database, August 2023.

B42. Third-party oppositions for selected offices, 2022

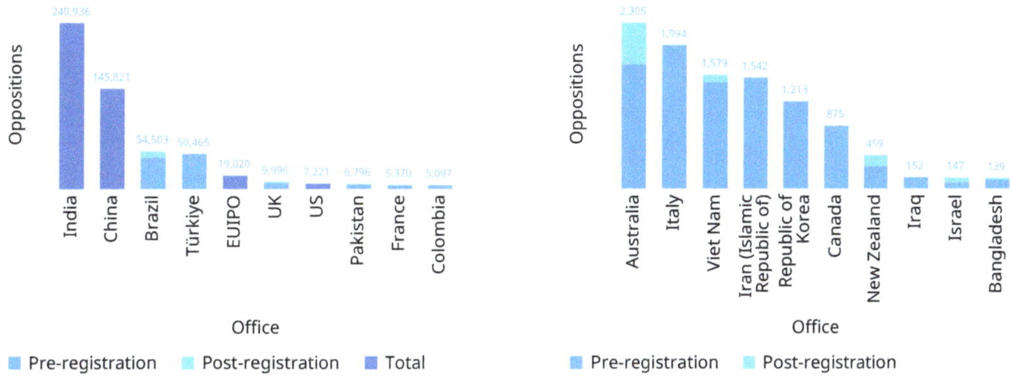

Note: EUIPO is the European Union Intellectual Property Office.
Source: WIPO Statistics Database, August 2023.

B43. Appeals against decisions for selected offices, 2022

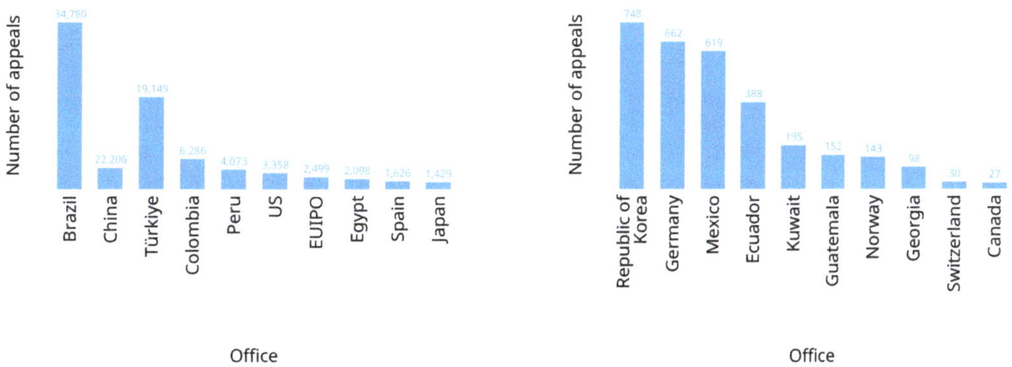

Note: EUIPO is the European Union Intellectual Property Office.
Source: WIPO Statistics Database, August 2023.

Statistical tables

B44. Trademark applications by office and origin, 2022

	Application class count by office				Application class count by origin	Equivalent application class count by origin	
Name	Total	Resident	Non-resident	Change over previous year	Total (a)	Total (a)	Change over previous year
Afghanistan (b)	..	..	..	..	760	790	..
African Intellectual Property Organization	12,818	3,326	9,492	-2,825	n.a.	n.a.	n.a.
African Regional Intellectual Property Organization	1,185	385	800	+135	n.a.	n.a.	n.a.
Albania	8,595	1,405	7,190	-824	1,523	1,655	-1,111
Algeria	25,905	11,678	14,227	+5,561	11,868	12,252	+395
Andorra	3,018	1,242	1,776	-195	2,177	8,885	+1,297
Angola (f)	5,180	..	..	+956	279	583	+380
Antigua and Barbuda	2,188	477	1,711	-9	1,199	1,555	-385
Argentina	88,838	73,082	15,756	+2,994	77,154	83,214	+746
Armenia	13,358	5,692	7,666	+1,477	7,312	8,278	+2,627
Australia	150,711	81,740	68,971	-23,301	130,031	224,153	-27,335
Austria	21,673	13,499	8,174	-4,614	49,765	361,857	-50,340
Azerbaijan	15,938	7,209	8,729	+1,258	8,410	8,602	+2,437
Bahamas (b)	..	..	..	..	1,015	4,213	..
Bahrain	14,272	416	13,856	+164	885	1,945	+619
Bangladesh	13,687	8,928	4,759	-1,840	9,105	9,439	-1,571
Barbados	1,282	110	1,172	+295	930	2,646	-14,414
Belarus	16,618	3,590	13,028	-2,926	6,333	7,985	-4,287
Belgium (c)	n.a.	n.a.	n.a.	n.a.	35,464	250,062	-31,921
Belize (b)	..	..	..	..	214	440	..
Benelux Office for Intellectual Property (d)	53,023	44,179	8,844	-10,706	n.a.	n.a.	n.a.
Benin (b,g)	n.a.	n.a.	n.a.	n.a.	165	2,677	-919
Bhutan	2,193	92	2,101	-7	93	93	-64
Bolivia (Plurinational State of)	8,558	4,761	3,797	+59	4,884	4,910	-25
Bonaire, Sint Eustatius and Saba (b,h)	..	..	..	..	1	27	..
Bosnia and Herzegovina	10,265	837	9,428	-683	1,413	2,035	+156
Botswana (f)	4,998	..	..	-995	39	96	+21
Brazil	404,209	355,877	48,332	+10,184	364,223	380,501	+10,343
Brunei Darussalam	4,015	178	3,837	-341	201	227	-510
Bulgaria	14,035	10,536	3,499	-947	33,673	131,517	+26,393
Burkina Faso (b,g)	n.a.	n.a.	n.a.	n.a.	198	3,270	-2,878
Cabo Verde	857	105	752	+586	110	110	-37
Cambodia (f)	11,528	..	..	-1,281	79	147	-10
Cameroon (b,g)	n.a.	n.a.	n.a.	n.a.	673	11,159	-2,086
Canada	153,515	53,907	99,608	-22,278	99,165	202,119	-33,780
Central African Republic (b,g)	n.a.	n.a.	n.a.	n.a.	17	97	+27
Chad (b,g)	n.a.	n.a.	n.a.	n.a.	7	129	-34
Chile	60,757	43,634	17,123	-8,358	48,342	53,486	-12,719
China	7,513,504	7,304,080	209,424	-1,941,231	7,678,344	8,561,984	-2,608,640
China, Hong Kong SAR	64,266	25,839	38,427	-12,434	46,115	112,271	-27,288
China, Macao SAR	12,432	2,122	10,310	-2,311	2,614	3,108	-552
Colombia	72,641	50,117	22,524	+17,060	55,938	61,046	+18,303
Comoros (b)	..	..	..	..	4	36	..
Congo (b,g)	n.a.	n.a.	n.a.	n.a.	29	421	-286
Cook Islands (b)	..	..	..	..	38	38	..
Costa Rica	15,872	8,454	7,418	-97	9,754	11,990	+1,076
Côte d'Ivoire (b,g)	n.a.	n.a.	n.a.	n.a.	904	14,692	-4,939
Croatia	7,550	3,942	3,608	+226	9,139	36,255	+5,476
Cuba	6,541	3,211	3,330	+879	3,435	4,161	+1,640
Curaçao (h)	2,713	258	2,455	-70	799	4,315	+1,912
Cyprus	3,797	1,493	2,304	-113	17,109	81,971	-9,812
Czech Republic	20,960	16,960	4,000	-6,905	30,162	173,176	-26,358

Name	Application class count by office				Application class count by origin	Equivalent application class count by origin	
	Total	Resident	Non-resident	Change over previous year	Total (a)	Total (a)	Change over previous year
Democratic People's Republic of Korea (b)	..	..	..	..	301	327	..
Democratic Republic of the Congo (b)	..	..	..	..	32	440	..
Denmark	7,965	4,346	3,619	-1,843	27,490	171,314	-24,607
Djibouti	408	43	365	+57	52	52	+11
Dominica	369	4	365	+179	19	19	-74
Dominican Republic	16,677	10,202	6,475	+901	10,731	12,135	+1,041
Ecuador	22,076	14,357	7,719	+424	14,951	15,367	-130
Egypt	54,610	37,867	16,743	-5,927	39,780	43,102	-3,582
El Salvador	12,293	5,028	7,265	-485	5,441	5,441	-170
Equatorial Guinea (b,g)	n.a.	n.a.	n.a.	n.a.	27	459	+272
Eritrea (b)	..	..	..	..	2	2	..
Estonia	4,151	1,836	2,315	-2,284	7,282	70,390	-4,206
Eswatini (b)	..	..	..	..	57	57	..
Ethiopia	2,752	1,876	876	+446	1,898	1,924	+481
European Union Intellectual Property Office (e)	448,807	289,725	159,082	-48,594	n.a.	n.a.	n.a.
Fiji (b)	..	..	..	..	24	24	..
Finland	7,867	4,756	3,111	-1,450	24,259	152,511	-22,325
France	278,400	263,845	14,555	-36,571	414,876	1,194,182	-56,865
Gabon (b,g)	n.a.	n.a.	n.a.	n.a.	83	1,299	+71
Gambia	2,201	199	2,002	-996	211	405	+284
Georgia	10,873	2,758	8,115	+127	3,304	3,750	-868
Germany	233,594	210,191	23,403	-38,800	479,334	2,552,542	-395,038
Ghana	6,169	670	5,499	..	749	1,097	..
Greece (b)	..	..	..	..	6,672	101,296	..
Grenada	331	6	325	+29	10	10	-16
Guatemala (f)	12,851	..	..	-799	2,147	2,329	-105
Guinea (b,g)	n.a.	n.a.	n.a.	n.a.	255	4,175	-870
Guinea-Bissau (b,g)	n.a.	n.a.	n.a.	n.a.	23	391	-35
Guyana	1,103	109	994	-112	117	117	+87
Haiti (b)	..	..	..	..	44	70	..
Honduras	7,765	2,395	5,370	+397	2,672	3,062	+112
Hungary	9,856	6,492	3,364	-2,212	12,644	63,856	-6,091
Iceland	10,614	1,377	9,237	-71	2,111	5,747	-386
India	500,305	448,911	51,394	+11,846	467,918	499,674	+22,553
Indonesia	140,406	107,543	32,863	+13,284	109,904	113,162	+15,992
Iran (Islamic Republic of)	363,922	352,891	11,031	-160,207	354,645	357,669	-154,199
Iraq	2,891	0	2,891	+759	907	1,193	-1,563
Ireland (f)	7,081	..	..	-1,288	15,503	101,653	-22,435
Israel	24,684	4,812	19,872	-1,372	15,766	48,990	+4,930
Italy	97,882	87,941	9,941	-21,692	193,940	1,178,542	-59,539
Jamaica (b)	..	..	..	..	177	281	..
Japan	344,039	261,688	82,351	-20,303	381,877	549,015	-6,258
Jordan	7,942	3,398	4,544	+178	4,724	6,366	+45
Kazakhstan	30,437	14,843	15,594	+1,375	17,109	18,309	+1,200
Kenya	13,020	5,172	7,848	..	5,233	5,475	..
Kuwait	12,673	4,842	7,831	..	6,173	7,801	..
Kyrgyzstan	8,203	730	7,473	+92	981	981	+136
Lao People's Democratic Republic (b)	..	..	..	..	111	111	..
Latvia	4,834	2,187	2,647	-790	4,528	26,106	-1,668
Lebanon (b)	..	..	..	..	974	3,100	..
Lesotho (b)	..	..	..	..	3	3	..
Liberia (b)	..	..	..	..	4	4	..
Libya (b)	..	..	..	..	196	222	..
Liechtenstein	10,011	621	9,390	+814	2,991	12,723	-2,605
Lithuania	5,503	2,992	2,511	-1,111	6,393	61,635	-1,300
Luxembourg (c)	n.a.	n.a.	n.a.	n.a.	14,384	88,768	-9,293
Madagascar	6,906	3,424	3,482	+254	3,441	3,441	+166
Malawi (b)	..	..	..	..	17	29	..

	Application class count by office				Application class count by origin	Equivalent application class count by origin	
Name	Total	Resident	Non-resident	Change over previous year	Total (a)	Total (a)	Change over previous year
Malaysia	49,637	18,597	31,040	-3,077	24,424	27,650	-6,046
Maldives (b)	..	..	..	..	32	32	..
Mali (b,g)	n.a.	n.a.	n.a.	n.a.	250	3,514	-2,246
Malta	1,763	1,397	366	+191	8,418	67,790	-11,143
Marshall Islands (b)	..	..	..	..	359	3,235	..
Mauritania (b,g)	n.a.	n.a.	n.a.	n.a.	102	982	-1,484
Mauritius	4,557	1,837	2,720	-466	3,342	5,798	-2,809
Mexico	194,552	137,882	56,670	-4,784	148,328	162,780	-2,767
Monaco	9,278	1,474	7,804	-764	3,437	15,953	+569
Mongolia	14,617	10,043	4,574	-9,472	10,221	10,415	-9,072
Montenegro (b)	..	..	..	..	123	487	..
Morocco	32,520	19,247	13,273	-2,491	34,855	52,405	-54,017
Mozambique	4,932	712	4,220	-1,604	788	788	-818
Myanmar (b)	..	..	..	..	209	251	..
Namibia	3,726	381	3,345	..	486	488	..
Nepal (b)	..	..	..	..	72	98	..
Netherlands (Kingdom of the) (c)	n.a.	n.a.	n.a.	n.a.	86,893	582,247	-26,875
New Zealand	56,091	20,160	35,931	-10,574	29,801	48,773	-6,841
Nicaragua (b)	..	..	..	..	90	142	..
Niger (b,g)	n.a.	n.a.	n.a.	n.a.	57	809	-6
Nigeria (b)	..	..	..	..	247	1,037	..
North Macedonia	9,812	1,285	8,527	-770	4,514	8,860	+4,275
Norway	48,003	9,088	38,915	-4,509	19,838	78,970	-15,181
Oman	15,007	6,254	8,753	-877	7,762	8,074	+1,255
Pakistan	49,923	38,445	11,478	-1,389	39,409	39,967	-4,628
Palau (b)	..	..	..	..	1	1	..
Panama (b)	..	..	..	..	3,494	7,952	..
Papua New Guinea	717	106	611	-489	112	112	-217
Paraguay	24,781	14,138	10,643	-2,526	14,609	14,791	-2,398
Peru	40,875	28,108	12,767	-1,730	29,560	31,278	-1,038
Philippines	67,078	36,497	30,581	+2,175	37,767	38,417	+807
Poland	34,613	28,683	5,930	-8,131	55,007	477,735	-22,746
Portugal	34,185	29,384	4,801	-3,565	37,953	146,295	-22,348
Qatar	10,568	1,666	8,902	+981	3,849	8,241	-2,481
Republic of Korea	324,801	268,334	56,467	-35,646	342,091	449,639	-22,086
Republic of Moldova	11,146	3,224	7,922	-1,265	4,367	5,257	-996
Romania	26,160	21,637	4,523	+591	29,217	162,185	+31,448
Russian Federation	421,140	375,771	45,369	+25,470	417,883	447,229	+29,347
Rwanda	3,277	771	2,506	-1,444	777	777	+56
Saint Kitts and Nevis (b)	..	..	..	..	373	1,621	..
Saint Lucia (b)	..	..	..	..	125	307	..
Saint Vincent and the Grenadines	567	11	556	+9	107	601	+215
Samoa	1,484	34	1,450	-130	386	880	+15
San Marino (b)	..	..	..	..	537	3,299	..
Sao Tome and Principe	1,997	41	1,956	-800	48	48	+44
Saudi Arabia	40,287	25,303	14,984	+2,157	31,151	39,991	+7,728
Senegal (b,g)	n.a.	n.a.	n.a.	n.a.	622	9,702	-2,858
Serbia	17,369	3,830	13,539	-223	9,034	14,102	-2,671
Seychelles	611	54	557	+167	1,451	4,641	-899
Sierra Leone	2,613	203	2,410	-874	211	237	+216
Singapore	58,631	13,690	44,941	-3,815	56,788	109,348	+4,050
Sint Maarten (Dutch Part) (b,h)	..	..	..	..	1	1	..
Slovakia	11,345	7,633	3,712	-3,536	10,882	53,820	-8,273
Slovenia	5,577	2,695	2,882	-1,202	10,003	53,579	+5,200
Solomon Islands (b)	..	..	..	..	2	2	..
Somalia	410	30	380	+258	30	30	+15
South Africa	39,120	22,297	16,823	-743	24,858	32,164	-4,687
South Sudan (b)	..	..	..	..	1	1	..
Spain	73,711	64,777	8,934	-8,429	125,213	789,031	-5,313
Sri Lanka	9,465	6,245	3,220	-482	6,532	6,980	-745

Name	Application class count by office: Total	Resident	Non-resident	Change over previous year	Application class count by origin: Total (a)	Equivalent application class count by origin: Total (a)	Change over previous year
Sudan (b)	..	..	..	..	27	43	..
Suriname	237	16	221	-885	50	116	-413
Sweden	16,361	12,285	4,076	-3,610	57,081	352,825	-47,908
Switzerland	106,473	39,535	66,938	-10,038	163,535	518,055	-49,054
Syrian Arab Republic (f)	12,214	..	..	-2,226	774	1,948	-486
Tajikistan (b)	..	..	..	..	405	1,367	..
Thailand	64,182	31,630	32,552	-3,907	36,077	39,009	-4,538
Timor-Leste (b)	..	..	..	..	9	9	..
Togo (b,g)	n.a.	n.a.	n.a.	n.a.	216	3,390	-3,592
Tonga	448	1	447	-37	5	5	-2
Trinidad and Tobago	6,604	659	5,945	+2,106	973	1,443	+487
Tunisia	11,093	2,988	8,105	..	3,464	5,760	..
Türkiye	485,779	446,651	39,128	+51,400	482,567	579,543	+75,802
Turkmenistan (f)	4,971	..	..	-143	67	67	0
Tuvalu	171	0	171	-15	..	..	..
Uganda	3,860	2,049	1,811	-63	2,069	2,186	-47
Ukraine	43,135	23,469	19,666	-28,054	28,073	46,691	-17,510
United Arab Emirates	40,344	8,159	32,185	+14,768	26,769	60,177	+14,286
United Kingdom	353,940	185,858	168,082	-96,738	377,241	1,093,675	-105,196
United Republic of Tanzania (f)	4,746	..	..	+369	122	482	+429
United States of America	767,375	494,216	273,159	-132,124	945,571	2,009,487	-159,978
Uruguay	10,905	4,856	6,049	-170	6,774	8,386	-671
Uzbekistan	20,816	12,292	8,524	+2,461	13,499	13,879	+2,924
Vanuatu	54	1	53	-103	24	362	+166
Venezuela (Bolivarian Republic of)	12,143	7,817	4,326	+2,621	8,147	8,329	+7,657
Viet Nam	115,896	82,035	33,861	+2,844	87,482	92,118	+6,009
Yemen	4,960	3,290	1,670	-1,608	3,650	3,702	-2,007
Zambia	5,151	1,038	4,113	-780	1,134	1,264	-20
Zimbabwe	3,913	667	3,246	-703	1,018	1,341	+682
Others/Unknown	..	..	..	..	83,016	189,766	+40,104
Total (2022 estimates)	**15,543,300**	**12,976,000**	**2,567,300**		**15,543,300**		

(a) Data on application class count by origin are incomplete, because some offices do not report detailed statistics containing the origin of application class counts.
(b) Only Madrid designation data are available therefore application class count by office and origin data are incomplete.
(c) This country does not have a national trademark office. All applications for trademark protection are filed at the Benelux Office for Intellectual Property or the European Union Intellectual Property Office.
(d) Resident applications include those filed by residents of Belgium, Luxembourg and the Kingdom of the Netherlands.
(e) Resident applications include those filed by residents of EU member states.
(f) Total includes an aggregate direct application class count that cannot be broken down into direct and non-resident components.
(g) The African Intellectual Property Office (OAPI) is the competent office for processing applications.
(h) This country or municipality is not a Madrid member. The Kingdom of the Netherlands has extended the application of the Madrid Protocol to the territories of Curaçao and Sint Maarten, Bonaire, Sint Eustatius and Saba.
n.a. indicates not applicable.
.. indicates not available.
Source: WIPO Statistics Database, August 2023.

B45. Trademark registrations by office and origin, and trademarks in force, 2022

Name	Registration class count by office: Total	Resident	Non-resident	Registration class count by origin: Total (a)	Equivalent registration class count by origin: Total (a)	In force by office: Total	Change over previous year
Afghanistan (b)	..	..	..	150	150	..	..
African Intellectual Property Organization	11,304	1,811	9,493	n.a.	n.a.	..	..
African Regional Intellectual Property Organization	1,004	276	728	n.a.	n.a.	2,983	+170
Albania	9,849	1,128	8,721	1,305	1,707	10,397	-124
Algeria	21,655	6,315	15,340	6,427	6,653	53,620	+9,081
Andorra	3,014	1,242	1,772	2,036	5,832	21,553	+554

Name	Registration class count by office: Total	Registration class count by office: Resident	Registration class count by office: Non-resident	Registration class count by origin: Total (a)	Equivalent registration class count by origin: Total (a)	In force by office: Total	In force by office: Change over previous year
Angola (f)	5,174	..	..	247	497	68,587	+4,164
Antigua and Barbuda (b)	..	..	..	438	794	..	..
Argentina	65,198	51,069	14,129	54,950	60,570	936,624	-19,457
Armenia	11,508	3,189	8,319	4,123	4,713	25,001	+1,898
Australia	146,773	72,469	74,304	125,428	229,886	820,805	+40,444
Austria	21,076	12,892	8,184	54,242	354,768	98,131	-553
Azerbaijan	14,838	4,686	10,152	5,675	5,831	80,496	+2,644
Bahamas (b)	..	..	..	635	2,585	..	..
Bahrain	16,449	321	16,128	633	1,517	81,716	+4,288
Bangladesh	3,454	878	2,576	976	1,284	70,956	+3,454
Barbados (b)	..	..	..	813	5,503	..	..
Belarus	17,985	3,845	14,140	6,864	9,754	129,031	-294
Belgium (c)	n.a.	n.a.	n.a.	37,849	242,705	n.a.	n.a.
Belize (b)	..	..	..	205	379	..	..
Benelux Office for Intellectual Property (d)	50,876	42,039	8,837	n.a.	n.a.	645,584	-36,681
Benin (b,g)	n.a.	n.a.	n.a.	85	1,237	..	..
Bhutan	1,985	41	1,944	42	42	..	..
Bolivia (Plurinational State of)	7,160	4,755	2,405	4,855	4,855	..	..
Bonaire, Sint Eustatius and Saba (b,h)	..	..	..	9	35	..	..
Bosnia and Herzegovina	12,422	1,138	11,284	1,594	2,014	83,059	+806
Botswana (f)	5,530	..	..	40	92	..	..
Brazil	183,747	139,682	44,065	145,348	158,154	1,711,967	+159,126
Brunei Darussalam	4,027	139	3,888	240	474	22,016	+2,437
Bulgaria	12,449	8,967	3,482	30,327	114,117	54,534	-2,105
Burkina Faso (b,g)	n.a.	n.a.	n.a.	197	3,269	..	..
Burundi (b)	..	..	..	3	3	..	..
Cabo Verde	694	41	653	46	124	2,981	+213
Cambodia (f)	11,591	..	..	31	83	..	..
Cameroon (b,g)	n.a.	n.a.	n.a.	371	5,819	..	..
Canada	137,113	37,997	99,116	74,133	184,607	654,727	+25,534
Chad (b,g)	n.a.	n.a.	n.a.	4	62	..	..
Chile	35,541	22,715	12,826	26,531	30,281	397,497	+6,876
China	6,206,484	6,001,772	204,712	6,382,160	7,362,312	42,671,911	+5,432,391
China, Hong Kong SAR	66,376	26,406	39,970	43,418	110,608	489,300	+12,857
China, Macao SAR	13,558	2,163	11,395	2,662	3,026	151,232	+6,337
Colombia	48,650	25,871	22,779	29,185	32,525	387,687	+23,366
Comoros (b)	..	..	..	2	18	..	..
Congo (b,g)	n.a.	n.a.	n.a.	35	523	..	..
Cook Islands (b)	..	..	..	76	76	..	..
Costa Rica	12,971	5,711	7,260	6,430	8,042	161,159	+35,770
Côte d'Ivoire (b,g)	n.a.	n.a.	n.a.	511	8,251	..	..
Croatia	6,785	3,022	3,763	7,848	31,090	95,369	-3,774
Cuba	4,817	1,355	3,462	1,479	1,843	16,891	-30,007
Curaçao (h)	2,780	230	2,550	639	2,543	33,058	+10,445
Cyprus	3,486	1,463	2,023	16,592	78,068	44,573	-7,765
Czech Republic	25,366	20,957	4,409	33,353	168,713	126,999	-273
Democratic People's Republic of Korea (b)	..	..	..	277	277	..	..
Democratic Republic of the Congo (b)	..	..	..	29	453	..	..
Denmark	7,858	4,174	3,684	29,813	171,533	108,863	-3,924
Djibouti	408	43	365	51	51	..	..
Dominica	214	0	214	6	6	..	..
Dominican Republic	14,212	7,848	6,364	8,120	9,004	138,925	+4,797
Ecuador	11,411	7,223	4,188	7,695	8,345	159,876	+11,409
Egypt	29,615	12,117	17,498	13,781	16,297	96,037	+7,436
El Salvador	9,220	3,490	5,730	3,846	3,950	97,685	+2,787
Equatorial Guinea (b,g)	n.a.	n.a.	n.a.	1	1	..	..
Eritrea (b)	..	..	..	1	1	..	..

Name	Registration class count by office Total	Resident	Non-resident	Registration class count by origin Total (a)	Equivalent registration class count by origin Total (a)	In force by office Total	Change over previous year
Estonia	4,726	2,353	2,373	8,021	65,699	52,262	-839
Eswatini (b)	..	..	..	16	16	..	..
Ethiopia	2,731	1,880	851	1,893	1,919	..	..
European Union Intellectual Property Office (e)	426,961	267,793	159,168	n.a.	n.a.	1,494,690	-152,953
Fiji (b)	..	..	..	15	15	..	..
Finland	6,453	3,599	2,854	23,329	149,013	90,354	-3,203
France	270,232	255,576	14,656	413,646	1,160,956	1,657,315	+32,950
Gabon (b,g)	n.a.	n.a.	n.a.	33	561	..	..
Gambia	2,505	86	2,419	89	89	..	..
Georgia	10,907	1,575	9,332	2,039	2,649	67,899	+1,836
Germany	169,095	147,434	21,661	450,785	2,443,971	994,274	+9,924
Ghana	6,280	298	5,982	357	723	55,617	..
Greece (b)	..	..	..	6,505	94,021	..	..
Grenada	198	6	192	11	11	..	..
Guatemala (f)	10,292	..	..	1,714	2,000	109,608	..
Guernsey (b)	..	..	..	n.a.	n.a.	..	..
Guinea (b,g)	n.a.	n.a.	n.a.	126	1,918	..	..
Guinea-Bissau (b,g)	n.a.	n.a.	n.a.	12	188	..	..
Guyana	1,764	108	1,656	165	165	..	..
Haiti (b)	..	..	..	51	77	..	..
Holy See (b)	..	..	..	5	5	..	..
Honduras	5,740	1,275	4,465	1,537	1,953	94,671	+2,977
Hungary	8,801	5,437	3,364	11,991	56,969	53,673	-451
Iceland	11,311	866	10,445	1,725	5,527	60,966	-153
India	279,549	231,365	48,184	245,376	267,164	2,887,335	+239,765
Indonesia	125,349	86,637	38,712	88,950	90,718	741,620	..
Iran (Islamic Republic of)	97,608	88,073	9,535	89,888	92,448	380,882	+47,112
Iraq (b)	..	..	..	546	812	58,364	..
Ireland (f)	6,580	..	..	15,240	95,950	71,036	-187
Israel	26,936	4,162	22,774	15,369	48,071	145,915	-348
Italy	103,679	92,906	10,773	211,037	1,118,661	523,923	+6,312
Jamaica (b)	..	..	..	144	170	..	..
Japan (b)	..	..	..	131,292	306,112	2,180,817	+109,940
Jordan (b)	..	..	..	671	2,503	..	..
Kazakhstan	26,049	10,034	16,015	12,668	14,446	109,821	+25,591
Kenya (b)	..	..	..	66	228	..	..
Kuwait (f)	9,962	..	..	891	3,309	..	..
Kyrgyzstan	8,546	522	8,024	793	793	11,995	+508
Lao People's Democratic Republic (b)	..	..	..	33	33	..	..
Latvia	4,639	2,154	2,485	4,491	22,517	25,009	-811
Lebanon	7,030	3,800	3,230	4,353	6,177	..	..
Lesotho (b)	..	..	..	6	6	..	..
Liberia (b)	..	..	..	674	938	..	..
Libya (b)	..	..	..	80	158	..	..
Liechtenstein (b)	..	..	..	2,325	11,407	..	..
Lithuania	5,748	3,110	2,638	6,634	54,524	37,062	+37
Luxembourg (c)	n.a.	n.a.	n.a.	16,133	83,037	n.a.	n.a.
Madagascar	7,088	2,890	4,198	2,925	2,925	25,804	+537
Malawi (b)	..	..	..	7	13	..	..
Malaysia	54,088	16,783	37,305	23,560	27,026	432,502	+18,239
Maldives (b)	..	..	..	12	12	..	..
Mali (b,g)	n.a.	n.a.	n.a.	166	2,070	..	..
Malta	1,104	841	263	8,170	65,778	24,328	+595
Marshall Islands (b)	..	..	..	286	1,586	..	..
Mauritania (b,g)	n.a.	n.a.	n.a.	113	1,169	..	..
Mauritius	5,106	2,206	2,900	3,838	5,750	..	..
Mexico	136,563	81,819	54,744	89,298	100,150	1,549,560	+129,894
Micronesia (Federated States of) (b)	..	..	..	1	1	..	..

Name	Registration class count by office			Registration class count by origin	Equivalent registration class count by origin	In force by office	
	Total	Resident	Non-resident	Total (a)	Total (a)	Total	Change over previous year
Monaco	10,060	1,298	8,762	3,498	13,446	10,554	+65
Mongolia	18,367	12,925	5,442	13,085	13,215	19,317	+1,510
Montenegro (b)	..	..	..	83	161	79,816	..
Morocco	31,565	16,148	15,417	39,380	64,172	..	..
Mozambique	5,668	690	4,978	724	724	34,991	+2,299
Myanmar (b)	..	..	..	95	95	..	..
Namibia	5,131	401	4,730	527	641	..	..
Nepal (b)	..	..	..	39	39	..	..
Netherlands (Kingdom of the) (c)	n.a.	n.a.	n.a.	88,840	533,280	n.a.	n.a.
New Zealand	61,955	20,036	41,919	30,537	49,953	320,065	+18,146
Nicaragua (b)	..	..	..	49	49	..	..
Niger (b,g)	n.a.	n.a.	n.a.	29	317	..	..
Nigeria (b)	..	..	..	136	948	..	..
North Macedonia	11,102	1,509	9,593	2,388	3,760	91,013	+72,649
Norway	50,541	8,224	42,317	20,732	76,860	240,828	+4,427
Oman	12,647	2,746	9,901	3,186	3,628	..	..
Pakistan	24,691	13,336	11,355	13,695	14,247	240,493	+19,973
Panama (b)	..	..	..	2,497	5,675	..	..
Papua New Guinea	1,087	188	899	201	201	..	..
Paraguay	19,938	10,495	9,443	10,840	11,022	..	..
Peru	36,188	23,677	12,511	25,179	26,683	419,662	+16,382
Philippines	52,439	21,302	31,137	22,953	23,891	184,640	+12,315
Poland	32,087	25,933	6,154	51,439	403,693	250,903	+2,600
Portugal	28,500	23,885	4,615	33,271	140,317	233,399	−268
Qatar	7,355	864	6,491	2,703	8,523	..	..
Republic of Korea	184,354	131,299	53,055	194,448	292,288	1,546,679	+78,951
Republic of Moldova	11,897	2,724	9,173	4,137	5,143	76,424	+1,164
Romania	27,291	22,626	4,665	28,640	119,516	93,208	+5,546
Russian Federation	252,892	199,926	52,966	238,237	266,599	805,075	+51,690
Rwanda	3,974	771	3,203	778	804	9,837	+998
Saint Kitts and Nevis (b)	..	..	..	271	381	..	..
Saint Lucia (b)	..	..	..	100	178	..	..
Saint Vincent and the Grenadines	43	0	43	68	708	..	..
Samoa	1,450	26	1,424	162	812	..	..
San Marino (b)	..	..	..	511	2,233	..	..
Sao Tome and Principe	2,141	41	2,100	44	44	8,048	+749
Saudi Arabia	26,398	13,101	13,297	15,363	20,949	172,779	..
Senegal (b,g)	n.a.	n.a.	n.a.	301	4,313	..	..
Serbia	19,063	3,075	15,988	7,440	11,892	32,987	+722
Seychelles	543	50	493	1,448	3,384	8,714	+2,400
Sierra Leone	2,861	203	2,658	206	206	..	..
Singapore	54,910	10,171	44,739	44,245	88,885	360,815	+3,413
Sint Maarten (Dutch Part) (b,h)	..	..	..	..	..	..	..
Slovakia	11,000	7,267	3,733	10,863	49,697	47,485	−57
Slovenia	6,108	3,164	2,944	11,671	48,899	25,506	−54
Somalia	374	20	354	21	21	515	+378
South Africa	32,998	17,809	15,189	19,882	27,168	398,390	+14,795
South Sudan (b)	..	..	..	1	1	..	..
Spain	79,245	70,521	8,724	131,684	709,920	832,268	+15,149
Sri Lanka	3,640	1,847	1,793	2,110	2,892	59,293	+4,639
Sudan (b)	..	..	..	12	12	..	..
Suriname	659	166	493	187	229	12,072	−328
Sweden	12,550	8,540	4,010	56,684	338,578	119,354	−6,076
Switzerland	113,965	40,004	73,961	170,545	509,471	549,100	+14,140
Syrian Arab Republic (f)	9,643	..	..	409	1,413	78,398	+5,155
Tajikistan (b)	..	..	..	6	6	..	..
Thailand	66,600	28,308	38,292	32,125	35,223	458,967	+24,789
Timor-Leste (b)	..	..	..	7	7	..	..
Togo (b,g)	n.a.	n.a.	n.a.	143	1,717	..	..

	Registration class count by office			Registration class count by origin	Equivalent registration class count by origin	In force by office	
Name	Total	Resident	Non-resident	Total (a)	Total (a)	Total	Change over previous year
Tonga	318	16	302	24	24	..	..
Trinidad and Tobago	4,786	413	4,373	544	598	25,925	+1,201
Tunisia (b)	..	..	..	394	1,972	..	..
Türkiye	366,875	325,018	41,857	365,644	460,142	1,236,278	-106,770
Turkmenistan (b)	..	..	..	31	31	..	..
Tuvalu	171	0	171	1	1	..	..
Uganda	3,511	1,289	2,222	1,303	1,359	..	..
Ukraine	46,885	22,370	24,515	28,117	41,783	224,188	+12,456
United Arab Emirates (b)	..	..	..	11,899	38,313	322,268	+16,250
United Kingdom	370,600	172,844	197,756	333,258	1,034,206	2,502,358	+7,332
United Republic of Tanzania (f)	3,222	..	..	43	52	..	..
United States of America	462,977	222,104	240,873	656,061	1,716,495	3,102,589	+294,258
Uruguay	20,532	8,522	12,010	9,998	11,922	91,650	+8,047
Uzbekistan	17,052	7,875	9,177	8,709	8,929	31,107	+2,966
Vanuatu	13	3	10	24	284	..	..
Venezuela (Bolivarian Republic of)	11,312	5,656	5,656	5,851	6,007	..	..
Viet Nam	82,161	47,453	34,708	52,139	56,873	329,472	+36,894
Yemen	3,486	2,347	1,139	2,538	2,832	..	..
Zambia	5,775	1,050	4,725	1,129	1,161	39,529	+986
Zimbabwe	5,790	1,567	4,223	1,831	2,080	..	..
Others/Unknown	..	..	..	62,946	142,928	..	..
Total (2022 estimates)	**12,383,800**	**9,730,500**	**2,653,300**	**12,383,800**		**82,495,504**	

(a) Data on registration class count by origin are incomplete, because some offices do not report detailed statistics containing the origin of registration class counts.
(b) Only Madrid designation data are available therefore registration class count by office and origin data are incomplete.
(c) This country does not have a national trademark office. All trademark registrations for this country are issued by the Benelux Office for Intellectual Property or the European Union Intellectual Property Office.
(d) Resident registrations include those issued to residents of Belgium, Luxembourg and the Kingdom of the Netherlands.
(e) Resident registrations include those issued to residents of EU member states.
(f) Total includes an aggregate direct registration class count that cannot be broken down into direct and non-resident components.
(g) The African Intellectual Property Office (OAPI) is the competent office for issuing registrations.
(h) This country or municipality is not a Madrid member. The Kingdom of the Netherlands has extended the application of the Madrid Protocol to the territories of Curaçao and Sint Maarten, Bonaire, Sint Eustatius and Saba.
n.a. indicates not applicable.
.. indicates not available.
Source: WIPO Statistics Database, August 2023.

B46. Trademark office procedural data, 2022

Office	Total applications processed	Registered	Total rejections	Withdrawn or abandoned	Applications pending	Number of examiners (FTE)	First office action (days)	Final office decision (days)
Albania	738	675	52	11	427	4	45	180
Algeria	5,025	4,400	625	..	..	6	90	..
Andorra	1,096	1,087	5	4	..	3	1	..
Angola	5,541	5,174	318	49	361	8	90	120
Antigua and Barbuda	..	..	..	..	150	4	..	..
Argentina	75,536	65,206	8,433	1,897	172,567	15	4	450
Armenia	2,256	1,898	324	34	806	11	10	100
Australia	67,339	51,366	84	15,889	8,397	114.6	39.9	118
Austria	5,445	4,564	628	253	965	10	3	63
Azerbaijan	4,593	3,133	620	840	274	8	20	90
Bangladesh	13,687	3,454	287	9,946	36,124	10	30	50
Belarus	7,457	7,266	..	191	..	23	60	250
Belize	..	..	..	..	218	2	..	..
Bhutan	889	831	58	..	5	2	30	90
Bolivia (Plurinational State of)	..	..	..	..	245	12	..	..
Bosnia and Herzegovina	1,227	1,060	29	138	911	5	210	400

Office	Total applications processed	Registered	Total rejections	Withdrawn or abandoned	Applications pending	Number of examiners (FTE)	First office action (days)	Final office decision (days)
Botswana	450	387	63	..	509	4	5	3
Brazil	270,222	152,154	78,924	39,144	367,603	92	300	390
Brunei Darussalam	389	321	..	68	257	4	7	105
Bulgaria	..	..	..	..	..	..	..	136
Cabo Verde	..	..	..	..	1,978	4	..	..
Cambodia	4,959	3,583	..	1,376	1,156	5	90	90
Canada	43,194	31,406	73	11,715	192,217	77	860	990
China	7,515,961	4,687,280	2,368,381	460,300	1,702,226	1,415.00	120	120
China, Hong Kong SAR	32,053	28,501	2,648	904	8,055	39	32	114
China, Macao SAR	14,298	13,558	682	58	3,249	7	179	179
Colombia	47,190	33,299	12,544	1,347	29,639	75	41	258
Croatia	803	707	69	27	399	3	20	36
Cuba	1,387	595	209	583	3,403	8	90	1,095.00
Curaçao	349	344	..	5	21	4	60	60
Cyprus	848	823	..	25	97	7	2	30
Czech Republic	6,705	6,049	581	75	3,451	20	..	273
Denmark	2,413	2,030	225	158	1,174	11	1	..
Djibouti	..	..	..	..	..	1	..	..
Dominica	..	..	..	..	49	1	..	..
Ecuador	11,784	11,411	335	38	10,665	4	20	150
Egypt	..	..	..	..	..	..	291	309
El Salvador	..	..	..	..	..	13	5	5
Estonia	1,278	1,117	8	153	514	9	3	73.5
European Union Intellectual Property Office	138,433	133,452	3,827	1,154	75,839	272	24	13
Finland	2,500	1,918	130	452	821	6	36	58
France	103,971	93,935	7,188	2,848	45,350	84	..	181
Gambia	..	..	..	..	225	2	..	..
Georgia	2,183	1,457	155	571	870	10	40	210
Germany	75,056	53,625	7,793	13,638	21,770	81	47.4	81.6
Guatemala	10,738	10,292	223	223	2,336	6	3	20
Hungary	3,800	2,862	112	826	1,695	14	15	178
Iceland	1,247	993	214	40	60	5	50	90
India	301,583	239,765	39,089	22,729	550,524	40	90	150
Iran (Islamic Republic of)	106,033	21,661	37,934	46,438	..	31	28	58
Iraq	10,598	9,035	1,563	..	15	8	..	..
Israel	5,437	4,606	..	831	4,528	17	106	186.8
Italy	47,024	41,371	4,287	1,366	..	10	..	180
Jamaica	2,247	2,247	..	..	..	3	15	180
Japan	192,228	169,054	23,174	..	..	175	164	207
Kazakhstan	5,697	5,165	489	43	4,878	39	30	210
Kenya	..	..	..	..	..	7	..	..
Kuwait	12,494	11,645	849	..	131	11	1	1
Kyrgyzstan	994	917	65	12	567	7	360	240
Latvia	1,118	969	83	66	136	5	1	82
Lebanon	..	..	..	..	..	11	..	..
Lithuania	2,172	2,035	109	28	238	4	3	24
Madagascar	1,158	1,093	51	14	288	3	240	220
Malta	1,322	1,104	76	142	..	4	1	60
Mexico	137,601	103,184	6,996	27,421	168,680	45	107	107
Monaco	571	512	49	10	..	2	5	36
Mongolia	2,571	2,248	307	16	1,877	3	144	168
Montenegro	148	138	..	10	702	3	30	270
Mozambique	..	..	..	..	140	10	..	..
Namibia	..	..	..	..	10	4	..	..
New Zealand	8,285	7,981	..	304	3,419	44	20	21
North Macedonia	1,081	1,035	26	20	492	3	30	180
Norway	6,505	5,317	103	1,085	2,618	20	63	..
Oman	..	..	..	..	3	21	..	..
Pakistan	35,278	18,058	144	17,076	12,513	3	50	240
Papua New Guinea	..	..	..	..	151	3	..	..
Paraguay	..	..	..	..	..	5	..	..

Office	Total applications processed	Registered	Total rejections	Withdrawn or abandoned	Applications pending	Number of examiners (FTE)	First office action (days)	Final office decision (days)
Peru	43,492	34,346	6,463	2,683	10,242	47	4	74
Philippines	37,332	26,760	625	9,947	18,124	29	33	130.2
Poland	14,430	12,042	1,339	1,049	9,975	42	..	249.9
Portugal	20,199	15,919	4,054	226	1,373	23	10	90
Qatar	10,568	9,855	666	47	192	9	30	180
Republic of Korea	243,844	204,848	38,996	..	327,448	167	398	495
Republic of Moldova	2,123	1,844	224	55	2,042	8	11	241
Romania	8,642	7,771	774	97	2,084	48	3	499
Russian Federation	81,072	70,261	10,302	509	23,428	216	120	150
Rwanda	..	..	..	..	17	2	..	..
Saint Vincent and the Grenadines	47	34	12	1	209	4	7	14
Samoa	..	..	..	..	..	4	..	..
Sao Tome and Principe	..	..	..	..	..	8	..	..
Saudi Arabia	30,082	26,398	3,645	39	..	17	6	84.9
Seychelles	513	507	1	5	5	2	2	5
Sierra Leone	..	..	..	..	..	3	..	..
Singapore	..	..	..	..	17,540	24.8	..	..
Slovakia	2,613	2,351	224	38	477	8	4	150
Slovenia	..	..	..	..	1,144	9.5	..	..
Somalia	..	..	..	..	31	5	..	..
Spain	15,255	14,036	630	589	29,972	49	30	193
Sri Lanka	4,030	3,640	30	360	11,352	18	180	270
Suriname	..	..	..	..	1,190	3	..	..
Sweden	6,409	4,569	286	1,554	1,707	21	28	98
Switzerland	16,890	16,890	..	..	6,539	58.6	112	112
Syrian Arab Republic	..	..	..	..	57	5	..	..
Thailand	65,318	..	41,494	23,824	106,033	36	189	416
Tonga	..	..	..	..	27	3	..	..
Trinidad and Tobago	..	..	..	..	1,750	7	..	..
Türkiye	189,815	144,916	9,813	35,086	176,739	92	6	34
Tuvalu	..	..	..	..	..	1	..	..
Uganda	..	..	..	..	16	4	..	..
Ukraine	25,984	19,415	558	6,011	45,379	90	583	584
United Kingdom	136,880	125,021	4,841	7,018	3,074	153	12	13
United Republic of Tanzania	..	..	..	..	93	14	..	..
United States of America	96,035	55,866	13,659	26,510	890,936	729	252	429
Uzbekistan	5,820	4,516	240	1,064	3,194	9	190	360
Vanuatu	..	..	..	..	143	1	..	..
Venezuela (Bolivarian Republic of)	10,366	8,185	2,044	137	10,456	6	30	180
Viet Nam	44,647	38,119	6,371	157	113,510	86	725.6	757.4
Zambia	..	..	..	..	..	5	..	..
Zimbabwe	..	..	..	..	362	6	..	..

Note: FTE is full time equivalent. WIPO collects data from IP offices using a common questionnaire and methodology. Every effort has been made to compile procedural data based on common definitions and concepts, but procedural differences make it extremely difficult to fully harmonize such data. Therefore, caution should be exercised when making comparisons across offices. The total number of applications processed for a given office may be incomplete owing to the omission of one or several elements by the office.
.. indicates not available.
Source: WIPO Statistics Database, August 2023.

Industrial designs

Highlights

Industrial design applications worldwide fell by 3% in 2022

In 2022, about 1.1 million industrial design applications were filed worldwide. This represents a decrease of 3% on 2021, marking a first drop in filings since 2014 (figure 3.1). About 61% of offices worldwide reported lower filing activity in 2022 than in the previous year. Notably, the office of China received almost 9,500 fewer applications than in 2021. The Republic of Korea (-8,019 applications) and the Islamic Republic of Iran (-5,804) also received substantially fewer applications in 2022.

Statistics based on the number of designs contained in industrial design applications - known as application design counts - improve comparability worldwide by harmonizing data between offices that allow several designs to be contained within a single application and those that allow only one. An estimated 1.5 million designs were contained in applications filed worldwide in 2022 (figure 3.2). This corresponds to a decrease of 2.1% on 2021, marking a first drop since 2014.

Overall, the number of designs contained within both resident and non-resident applications declined by 1% and 6.7%, respectively. The global reduction in resident activity was mainly driven by a decrease in activity in China, the Islamic Republic of Iran and the Republic of Korea. Following a remarkable growth of 29.5% in 2021, designs in non-resident applications underwent the most substantial decrease recorded since 2009. Two other drops in non-resident design count have been recorded over the past decade, once in 2018 (-1.9%) and again in 2020 (-5.5%). The primary contributors to the overall decline in non-resident filing activity in 2022 were the United Kingdom (UK) (-5,996 designs in non-resident applications), the European Union Intellectual Property Office (EUIPO) (-5,165) and the Russian Federation (-2,225).

In 2022, the Hague System filing route accounted for approximately one-third (33.8%) of global non-resident filing activity (figure C15). Designs in non-resident applications filed directly at offices accounted for the remaining two-thirds. The 2022 Hague share is the second highest recorded since 2008. This contrasts with the 2021 share of 29.5%, which was the lowest within this timeframe, and largely the result of a sharp increase in non-resident applications filed directly at the UK office following Brexit.

Filings at the office of Türkiye grew sharply in 2022

The office of China received 798,112 designs in applications in 2022, constituting over half (53.8%) of global activity. It was followed by the EUIPO (109,132), Türkiye (84,111), the UK (69,004) and the Republic of Korea (61,136) (figure 3.3). Notably, designs within applications filed at the office of Türkiye increased sharply in comparison to 2021, propelling it two positions higher in the global ranking within a year.

Combined, the top 20 offices accounted for 94.6% of global application design count activity. Of these, only six recorded a rise in application design count, half of which were double-digit increases (figure C10). The three offices at which growth was strongest were Türkiye (+27.6%), Morocco (+11.3%) and Italy (+10.9%). Conversely, 14 offices experienced a decline, the most substantial being at the offices of the Islamic Republic of Iran (-41.4%), the Russian Federation (-24.7%) and the Republic of Korea (-11.7%).

Among top 20 offices, only France and Italy reported an increase in the number of designs contained in both resident and non-resident applications in 2022. Conversely, six offices saw a decline in design count in resident as well as non-resident design activity, among which were the EUIPO, and the offices of Germany and the United States of America (US). Growth in resident designs was particularly strong at the offices of Türkiye (+28.8%), Morocco (+16.1%) and Brazil (+11.4%). The most notable increase in non-resident design count among top 20 offices was the modest 2.6% observed at the office of Australia.

Industrial design applications filed worldwide totaled 1.1 million in 2022

3.1. Industrial design applications worldwide, 2008–2022

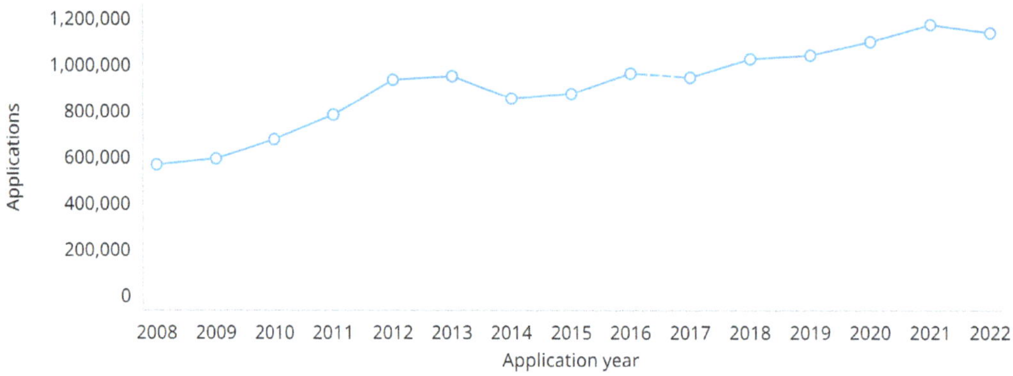

Source: Figure C1.

Designs contained in applications dropped by 2.1% in 2022

3.2. Number of designs in industrial design applications worldwide, 2008–2022

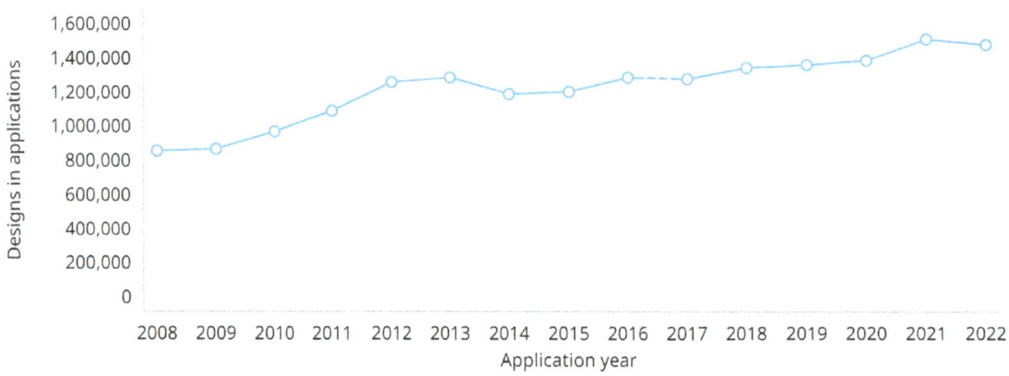

Source: Figure C2.

The office of Türkiye moved up two positions to rank third in 2022

3.3. Application design counts for the top 10 offices, 2022

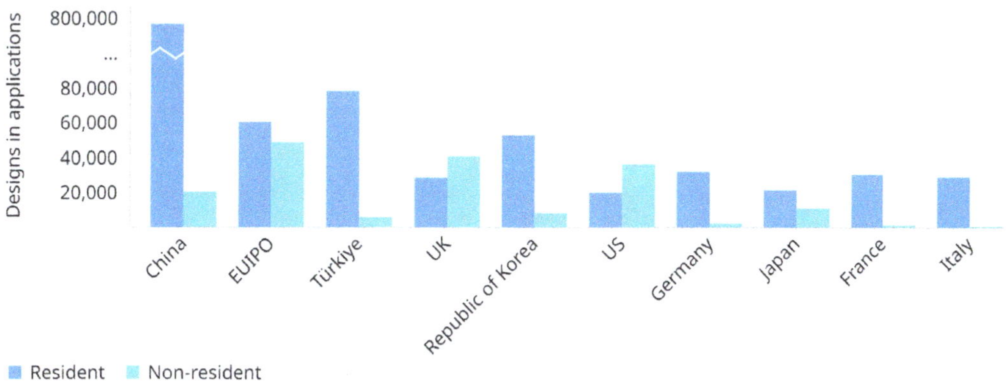

Note: EUIPO is the European Union Intellectual Property Office.
Source: Figure C9.

Among offices located in low- and middle-income economies beyond the top 20 offices, annual growth rates in 2022 were especially high at the African Regional Intellectual Property Organization (ARIPO) (+49.4%), the offices of Indonesia (+11.3%) and South Africa (+8.9%), and at the African Intellectual Property Organization (OAPI) (+8.8%). Conversely, Ukraine (-37.5%), Belarus (-28.7%), Mongolia (-17.5%) and Mexico (-13.4%) all experienced a steep decline in design count (figure C12).

Designs contained in resident applications accounted for 82.8% of the world design count in 2022. A notably substantial resident design share at the China office (97.5%) is primarily responsible for a proportionately high resident design share at the global level. Resident design counts accounted for a majority of filing activity at 15 of the top 20 offices (figure C9). However, resident activity constituted less than one-third of the total at the offices of Canada (8.2%), Switzerland (26%) and Australia (26.9%).

Asia accounted for 70.3% of all designs in applications filed worldwide in 2022 (figure 3.4). Asia was followed by Europe (22.4%) and North America (4.4%). The combined share for Africa, Latin America and the Caribbean (LAC) and Oceania was 2.9% in 2022, down from 3.4% a decade ago. Over that same period, from 2012 to 2022, North America (+5.5%) and Asia (+2.1%) were the two regions to observe the most substantial average increase in design count.

Design count

Some offices allow industrial design applications to contain more than one design for the same good or in the same class; others allow only one design per application. In order to capture differences in application filing systems across offices, the respective application and registration design counts needed to be compared.

Equivalent design count

Designs in applications filed at some regional offices are equivalent to multiple designs in applications filed in the respective member states of those offices. To calculate the number of equivalent designs for the OAPI (17 member states), the Benelux Office for Intellectual Property (BOIP) (3) and the EUIPO (27), each design is multiplied by the corresponding number of member states. However, the African Regional Intellectual Property Organization (ARIPO) and the Eurasian Patent Organization (EAPO) do not register industrial designs with an automatic region-wide applicability. Therefore, for these offices, each application is counted as one application abroad, if the applicant does not reside within a member state, or as one resident application and one application abroad, if the applicant resides within a member state.

Offices located in Asia and Europe accounted for 92.7% of total filing activity in 2022

3.4. Application design counts by region, 2012 and 2022

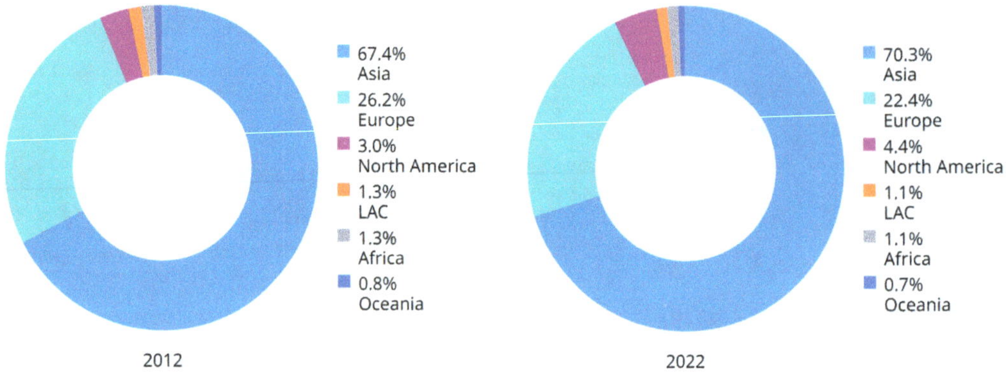

Note: LAC is Latin America and the Caribbean.
Source: Table C7.

Industrial design applications filed since 1883

Between 1883 and the early 1950s, the offices of Japan and the United States of America (US) averaged a similar number of applications, rarely exceeding 10,000. The office of Japan received the highest number of applications per year from the 1950s thru to the late 1990s, reaching approximately 50,000 annual filings at its peak. The office of China, which received 640 applications when it first began receiving applications in 1985, has seen an unprecedented rate of growth, peaking at 805,710 applications filed in 2021. The office of the Republic of Korea surpassed the office of Japan in 2004 and has remained in second position ever since. In 2012, the office of the US moved ahead of Japan to become the third largest globally. The EUIPO began receiving applications in 2003 and moved up to fourth position in 2019. Among these top five offices, the EUIPO is the only one to have a multiple design system. Applications filed at the EUIPO contained 109,132 designs in 2022.

Trend in industrial design applications for the top five offices, 1883–2022

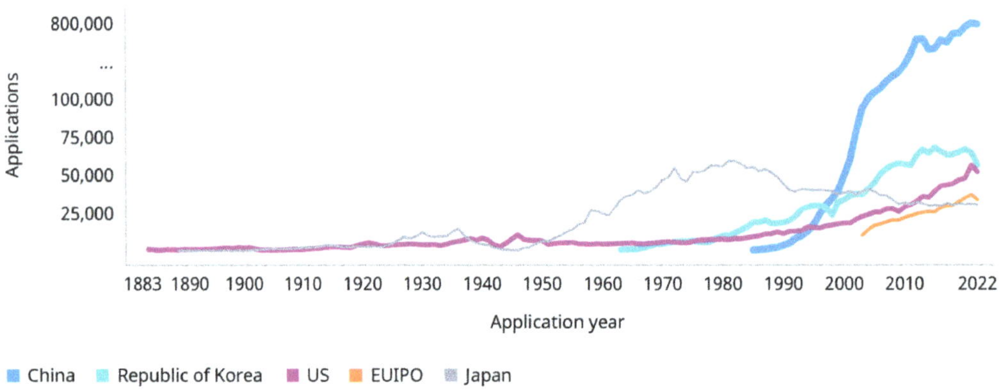

Note: EUIPO is the European Union Intellectual Property Office.
Source: Figure C8.

The top five countries of origin accounted for three-quarter of global industrial design activity in 2022

Applications received by offices from resident and non-resident applicants are referred to as office data, whereas applications filed by applicants at their home office(s) (resident applications) or at foreign offices (applications abroad) are referred to as origin data. Industrial design statistics based on office data provides information on the destination of industrial design activity, whereas statistics based on the origin of residence of the first named applicant complement the picture by providing information on the source of industrial design activity.

With 841,164 designs in applications filed, applicants residing in China were the most active in the world in terms of design count in 2022. They were followed by applicants from Türkiye (80,559), Germany (70,346), the US (67,349) and the Republic of Korea (62,014) (figure C16). Together, these top five countries accounted for 75.6% of the global design count in 2022. Driven mainly by a rapid increase in filings by applicants from China, the combined share of the top five origins has grown by 4.6 percentage points over the last decade.

When applying the equivalent count concept, applications filed by applicants at some regional offices are treated as being equivalent to multiple applications across the member states of those offices. Applicants from China had the highest equivalent application design count in 2022, with 1.4 million. They were followed by applicants residing in Germany (489,507), Italy (369,347), the US (366,686) and France (217,619) (figure C17).

Among the top 10 origins, only Spain (+16.5%) and Italy (+5.4%) recorded an increase in equivalent design count in 2022. In contrast, the steepest falls were observed at the offices of the Republic of Korea (–11.6%), Germany (–9.5%), China (–6.9%) and the US (–6.5%). Expanding the scope to all top 20 origins, just five origins recorded an increase in equivalent design count, among which the sharpest were at the offices of Bulgaria (+120.6%) and Türkiye (+20.3%).

Of the top 20 origins, 14 are European countries, five are from Asia and one from North America. In terms of income group, 17 of the top 20 origins are high-income countries, while Bulgaria, China and Türkiye are upper middle-income countries.

Equivalent designs in applications filed abroad accounted for over three-quarters of total filing activity at every top 20 origin, apart from Türkiye (17.4%), China (44.8%) and the Republic of Korea (48.8%). In 2022, applicants from China had 631,108 equivalent designs in applications filed abroad. China was followed by Germany (441,555), the US (346,758), Italy (328,321) and France (180,738). Of these top five origins, Italy (5.1%) was the only one to see its equivalent designs in applications filed abroad grow in 2022. In contrast, China (–13.2%), Germany (–9.8%), the US (–6.4%) and France (–5.3%) all experienced a steep drop compared to 2021.

Madagascar's industrial design activity is intense when compared to its level of development

Adjusting resident filing activity according to gross domestic product (GDP) and population helps when comparing the intensity of industrial design filing by residents across origins.

China (3,028) had the highest resident design count per USD 100 billion of GDP in 2022 (figure 3.5). China was followed by Türkiye (2,781) and the Republic of Korea (2,252). In contrast, the US (92), Indonesia (104) and the Russian Federation (140) exhibited notably lower ratios. Compared to 2012, ratios for 2022 increased sharply for the UK (+537) and Türkiye (+416). Conversely, during this same decade, China (–1,546), the Republic of Korea (–1,111) and Germany (–568) experienced a marked decrease in their respective ratios.

In 2022, the Republic of Korea stood out as having the most substantial resident design count per million population, with a ratio of 1,024 (figure C27). It was followed by Türkiye (918), Italy (697), Germany (570) and China (551). When comparing 2022 ratios to a decade ago, in 2012, those of Türkiye (+387) and the UK (+268) are shown to have increased substantially.

Plotting the resident application design count per capita and GDP per capita makes it possible to visualize an economy's industrial design output compared to its development level (figure C28). Countries whose points lie above the sloping fitted line, which reflects the positive correlation between the two variables, exhibit intense industrial design activity for their level of development. Over the 2018-2022 period, Brazil sat precisely on that line, indicating that the country's industrial design activity was consistent with its development level. Countries such as China, Madagascar, Mongolia, Morocco and the Republic of Korea are shown to have had a high degree of industrial design activity with respect to their GDP. Conversely, industrial design activity for economies like Chile, Costa Rica and the United Arab Emirates was low in comparison to their development level.

Most filing activity worldwide is concentrated within just four industry sectors

Grouping the 32 Locarno classes into 12 industry sectors serves to highlight the most important industry sectors for designs contained within industrial design applications filed.

In 2022, those sectors with the biggest shares of the world total were furniture and household goods (17.2%), textiles and accessories (15.6%), tools and machines (12.4%), and electricity and lighting (9.1%). Combined, these four sectors accounted for a majority (54.3%) of all classes recorded globally (figure C23).

All top 10 offices for which data were available had between 39% and 67% of total classes concentrated in just three sectors, although the specific top sectors varied between offices (figure 3.6). Furniture and household goods made up a substantial share of the total at the offices of the Islamic Republic of Iran (23.6%), Germany (22.5%) and Brazil (22.2%). The textiles and accessories sector dominated at the offices of Germany (25.9%), India (21.8%) and the Republic of Korea (20.4%). However, advertising and tools and machines were the main sectors for Türkiye (31.6%) and the EUIPO (21.7%), respectively (figure C24).

The respective top three sectors for each of the top 10 origins accounted for over 44% of the total application design count (figure C25). Notably, textiles and accessories was among the top three sectors for every top 10 origin, followed by furniture and household goods for seven of the origins and tools and machines for six.

Applications registered worldwide drop by 5.2% in 2022

Approximately 1 million industrial design applications were registered globally in 2022. This represents a decrease of 5.2% on 2021 (figure C4). Between 2010 and 2022, the number of applications registered worldwide almost doubled, mainly due to a considerable rise in registrations issued by the office of China. The decline seen in 2022 - the first since 2016 - brings the number of registrations back down to close to the 2020 level.

About 1.3 million designs were contained in applications registered in 2022, down 2.6% on the previous year (figure C5). The office of China accounted for 54.8% of all designs in applications registered worldwide, while the top 20 offices combined accounted for 95.3% of the total. Among top 20 offices, 13 recorded annual growth, including sharp increases at the offices of India (+53.2%), France (+50.8%), Canada (+39.3%) and Türkiye (+27.6%). In contrast, among top five offices, China (-7.9%), the EUIPO (-7.9%) and the Republic of Korea (-4.1%) all saw a decline in registration design count (figure C13).

About 5.8 million registrations were active worldwide in 2022

Industrial design rights generally last for up to 15 years from the date an application is filed, although they last up to 25 years in most European countries and up to 10 years in China.

In 2022, there were an estimated 5.8 million active industrial design registrations worldwide based on data provided by 136 offices (figure C29). This represents an increase of 8.8% on 2021.

Registrations in force in China grew by 9.7%, reaching 2.8 million and contributing to nearly half (49%) of the global total in 2022 (figure C30). China was followed by the Republic of Korea (406,009), the US (389,540), the EUIPO (296,912) and Japan (270,073). Combined, the top 20 offices accounted for 93.5% of active industrial design registrations globally.

China had the most designs per unit of GDP in 2022

3.5. Resident application design count per USD 100 billion GDP for selected origins, 2012 and 2022

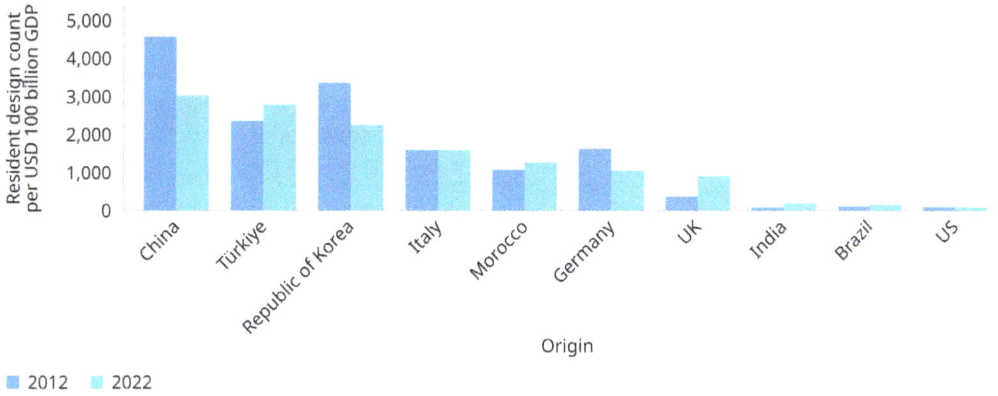

Source: Figure C26.

The top three sectors accounted for two-thirds of application designs in Türkiye

3.6. Distribution of application design counts by the top three sectors for selected offices, 2022

Note: EUIPO is the European Union Intellectual Property Office.
Source: Figure C24.

Figure C31 shows the distribution of about 2.4 million active industrial design registrations in 2022 recorded at 90 offices according to the year in which they were first registered. Nearly a quarter of the industrial design applications registered in 2005 remained valid in 2022. The majority of applications registered in 2013 remained active in 2022 and more than two-thirds of those registered in 2017 continued to be in force in 2022.

The average age of active industrial design registrations varied widely across offices. For instance, in 2022, the average age of all industrial design registrations in force in Spain stood at 10.3 years, while in the UK it was 2.9 years (figure C32).

The EUIPO registered almost 97% of applications in 2022

An industrial design office examines applications and decides whether to register them. Examination processes between offices vary, making cross-office comparison difficult. Every effort has been made to compile examination outcome data based on common definitions and concepts.

The distribution of examination outcomes differs widely across offices. Among the top five offices, the EUIPO (96.7%) registered the largest proportion of processed applications in 2022. It was followed by the offices of the UK (94.8%), China (90.6%), Türkiye (89%) and the Republic of Korea (85.7%) (figure C33). Beyond the top five offices, those of India (97.8%) and Switzerland (96.8%) also registered a large proportion of processed applications. In contrast, the share of applications rejected was particularly high at the offices of the US (23.7%), Jamaica (20.7%) and Indonesia (19.1%). Applications withdrawn or abandoned constituted a large share of total applications processed in Thailand (31.5%), Mexico (24.4%) and the US (18.1%).

Türkiye and the UK had relatively few potentially pending applications in 2022

In general, for an industrial design to be eligible for protection, it typically needs to meet criteria such as being new, original and of an individual character. However, examination procedures vary widely between offices. At some offices, no search is made and no examination as to substance is carried out prior to registration. At other offices, a substantive examination is conducted, whereby the design is checked against designs on the register for novelty and/or originality. Here, potentially pending applications are taken to be all industrial design applications, at any stage in the process, awaiting a final decision by an office.

In 2022, the US had 75,587 potentially pending applications (figure C34). The Republic of Korea followed with 20,538. Türkiye and the UK, which ranked as the third and fourth largest offices in terms of application design count for 2022, had much smaller volumes of pending applications, with 1,664 and 2,098, respectively. Among middle-income countries, India (14,992) and Thailand (6,560) had a notable number of potentially pending applications in 2022.

On average, an industrial design application was processed in under five days following its filing at the EUIPO in 2022. In contrast, at the office of Thailand, the processing time was 915 days (figure C35). The average time between a first office action and a final office decision was less than one day at both the EUIPO and the office of France. However, in Thailand, final office decisions were made 455 days after the first office action, on average.

Industrial design statistics

Industrial design applications and registrations worldwide 119

C1. Trend in industrial design applications worldwide, 2008–2022 119
C2. Trend in application design counts worldwide, 2008–2022 119
C3. Resident and non-resident application design counts worldwide, 2008–2022 120
C4. Trend in industrial design registrations worldwide, 2008–2022 120
C5. Trend in registration design counts worldwide, 2008–2022 120
C6. Resident and non-resident registration design counts worldwide, 2008–2022 121

Industrial design applications and registrations by office 121

C7. Application design counts by region, 2012 and 2022 121
C8. Trend in industrial design applications for the top five offices, 1883–2022 121
C9. Application design counts for the top 20 offices, 2022 122
C10. Contribution of resident and non-resident application design counts to total growth for the top 20 offices, 2021–2022 122
C11. Application design counts for offices of selected low- and middle-income countries, 2022 122
C12. Contribution of resident and non-resident application design counts to total growth for offices of selected low- and middle-income countries, 2021–2022 123
C13. Registration design counts for the top 20 offices, 2022 123
C14. Registration design counts for offices of selected low- and middle-income countries, 2022 124
C15. Non-resident application design counts by filing route, 2008–2022 124

Application design counts by origin 125

C16. Application design counts for the top 20 origins, 2022 125
C17. Equivalent application design counts for the top 20 origins, 2022 125
C18. Application design counts for selected low- and middle-income origins, 2022 126
C19. Equivalent application design counts for selected low- and middle-income origins, 2022 126
C20. Flows of non-resident application design counts for the top five origins and the top 10 offices of high-income economies, 2022 127
C21. Flows of non-resident application design counts for the top five origins and the top 10 offices of low- and middle-income economies, 2022 128

Application design counts by Locarno class and industry sector 129

C22. Application design counts for the top 10 Locarno classes, 2022 129
C23. Application design counts by industry sector, 2022 129
C24. Distribution of application design counts by the top three sectors for the top 10 offices, 2022 129
C25. Distribution of application design counts by the top three sectors for the top 10 origins, 2022 130

Application design count in relation to GDP and population 130

C26. Resident application design count per USD 100 billion of GDP for the top 20 origins, 2012 and 2022 130
C27. Resident application design count per million population for the top 20 origins, 2012 and 2022 131
C28. Resident application design count per capita and GDP per capita for selected origins, 2018–2022 131

Industrial design registrations in force 131

C29. Trend in industrial design registrations in force worldwide, 2012–2022 131
C30. Industrial design registrations in force for the top 20 offices, 2022 132
C31. Industrial design registrations in force in 2022 as a percentage of total registrations 132
C32. Average age of industrial design registrations in force at selected offices, 2017 and 2022 132

Industrial design office procedural data 133
C33. Distribution of industrial design examination outcomes for selected offices, 2022 133
C34. Potentially pending applications for selected offices, 2022 133
C35. Average pendency times from filing date to first office action and to final decision at selected offices, 2022 134
C36. Number of industrial design examiners for selected offices, 2022 134

Statistical tables 135
C37. Industrial design applications by office and origin, 2022 135
C38. Industrial design registrations by office and origin, and registrations in force, 2022 138
C39. Industrial design office procedural data, 2022 141

Industrial design applications and registrations worldwide

C1. Trend in industrial design applications worldwide, 2008–2022

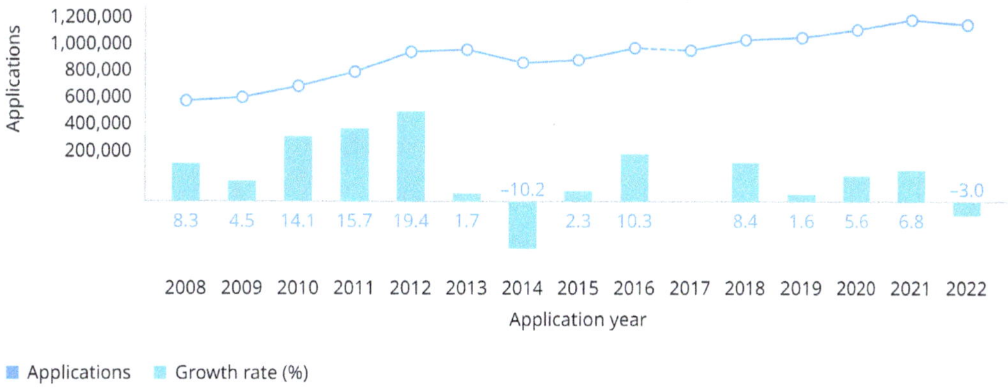

Note: From 2017 onwards, industrial design application data provided by the IP office of China include only those applications for which the necessary application fees has been paid. Because China accounts for most of the global total, this means it is not possible to report the 2017 worldwide application growth rate. World totals are WIPO estimates using data covering 157 IP offices. These totals include applications filed directly with national and regional offices (known as the Paris route), as well as the designations received via the Hague System (where applicable).
Source: WIPO Statistics Database, August 2023.

C2. Trend in application design counts worldwide, 2008–2022

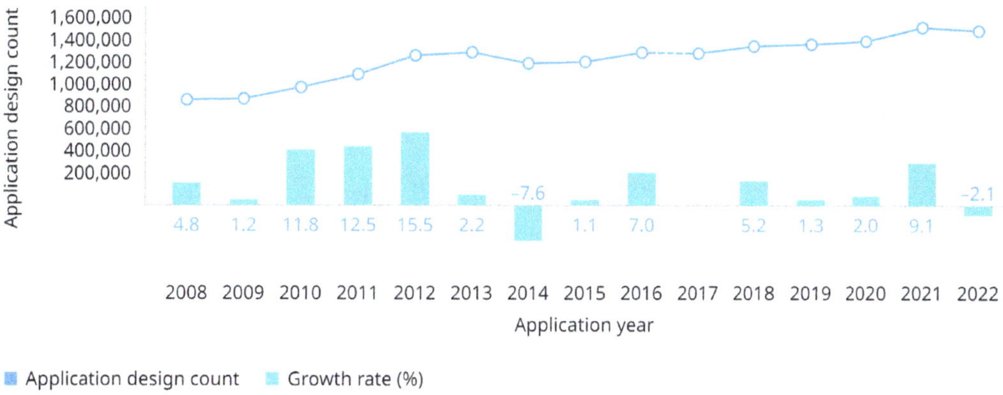

Note: From 2017 onwards, industrial design application data provided by the IP office of China include only those applications for which the necessary application fees have been paid. Because China accounts for most of the global total, this means it is not possible to report the 2017 worldwide application growth rate. World totals are WIPO estimates using data covering 157 IP offices. These totals include designs contained in applications filed directly with national and regional offices (known as the Paris route), as well as designs contained in designations received via the Hague System (where applicable). See glossary for the definition of design count.
Source: WIPO Statistics Database, August 2023.

C3. Resident and non-resident application design counts worldwide, 2008–2022

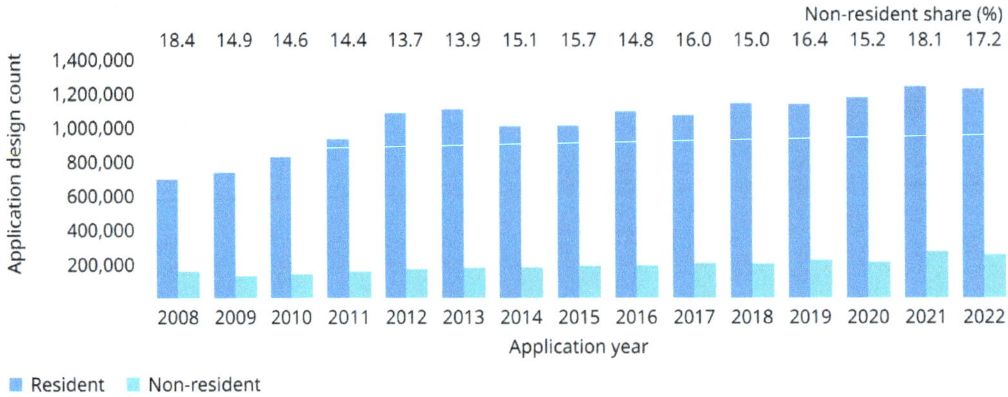

Note: World totals are WIPO estimates using data covering 157 IP offices. These totals include designs contained in applications filed directly with national and regional offices (known as the Paris route), as well as designs contained in designations received via the Hague System (where applicable). See glossary for the definition of design count.
Source: WIPO Statistics Database, August 2023.

C4. Trend in industrial design registrations worldwide, 2008–2022

Note: World totals are WIPO estimates using data covering 157 IP offices. These totals include the registrations issued by national and regional offices for applications filed directly with offices (known as the Paris route), as well as for designations received via the Hague System (where applicable).
Source: WIPO Statistics Database, August 2023.

C5. Trend in registration design counts worldwide, 2008–2022

Note: World totals are WIPO estimates using data covering 157 IP offices. These totals include designs contained in registrations issued by national and regional offices for applications filed directly with offices (known as the Paris route), as well as for designations received via the Hague System (where applicable). See glossary for the definition of design count.
Source: WIPO Statistics Database, August 2023.

C6. Resident and non-resident registration design counts worldwide, 2008–2022

Note: World totals are WIPO estimates using data covering 157 IP offices. These totals include designs contained in registrations issued by national and regional offices for applications filed directly with offices (known as the Paris route), as well as for designations received via the Hague System (where applicable). See glossary for the definition of design count.
Source: WIPO Statistics Database, August 2023.

Industrial design applications and registrations by office

C7. Application design counts by region, 2012 and 2022

	Application design count		Resident share (%)		Share of world total (%)		Average growth (%)
Region	**2012**	**2022**	**2012**	**2022**	**2012**	**2022**	**2012–2022**
Africa	16,200	16,400	51.3	64.7	1.3	1.1	0.1
Asia	848,200	1,042,800	93.6	93.5	67.4	70.3	2.1
Europe	329,900	331,600	56.7	63.4	26.2	22.4	0.1
Latin America and the Caribbean	15,800	17,000	48.1	52.1	1.3	1.1	0.7
North America	38,200	65,100	51.5	31.7	3.0	4.4	5.5
Oceania	10,300	9,700	38.2	26.2	0.8	0.7	-0.6
World	**1,258,600**	**1,482,600**	**77.7**	**85.0**	**100.0**	**100.0**	**1.7**

Note: Totals by geographical region are WIPO estimates using data covering 157 IP offices. Each region includes the following number of offices: Africa (37), Asia (43), Europe (42), Latin America and the Caribbean (27), North America (2) and Oceania (6). For information on geographical region classification, see data description section.
Source: WIPO Statistics Database, August 2023.

C8. Trend in industrial design applications for the top five offices, 1883–2022

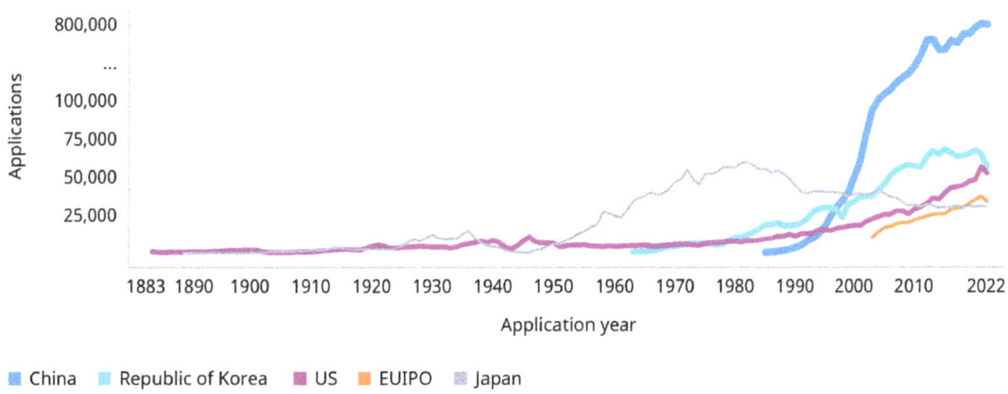

Note: The decrease in applications at the IP office of China in 2017 is most likely explained by the new way in which that office counts applications data. Starting from 2017, China's application count data include only those applications for which the necessary application fees have been paid. EUIPO is the European Union Intellectual Property Office. Data are based on the numbers of applications filed; this means that differences between single-design and multiple-design filing systems across IP offices are not taken into account. The top five offices are selected based on 2022 totals.
Source: WIPO Statistics Database, August 2023.

C9. Application design counts for the top 20 offices, 2022

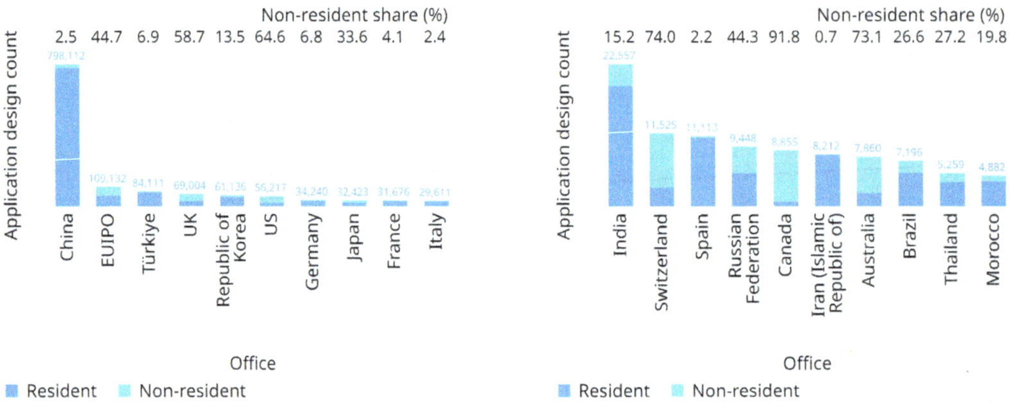

Note: EUIPO is the European Union Intellectual Property Office.
Source: WIPO Statistics Database, August 2023.

C10. Contribution of resident and non-resident application design counts to total growth for the top 20 offices, 2021–2022

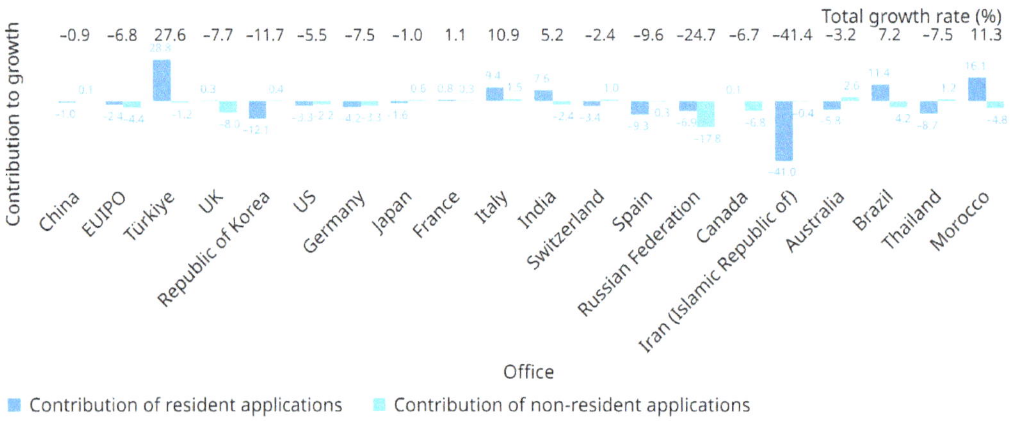

Note: EUIPO is the European Union Intellectual Property Office. This figure shows total growth in application design counts, broken down by the respective contributions of resident and non-resident applicants. For example, total design counts in the US decreased by 5.5%, with resident applicants contributing 3.3 percentage points to the overall decline and non-resident applicants 2.2 percentage points.
Source: WIPO Statistics Database, August 2023.

C11. Application design counts for offices of selected low- and middle-income countries, 2022

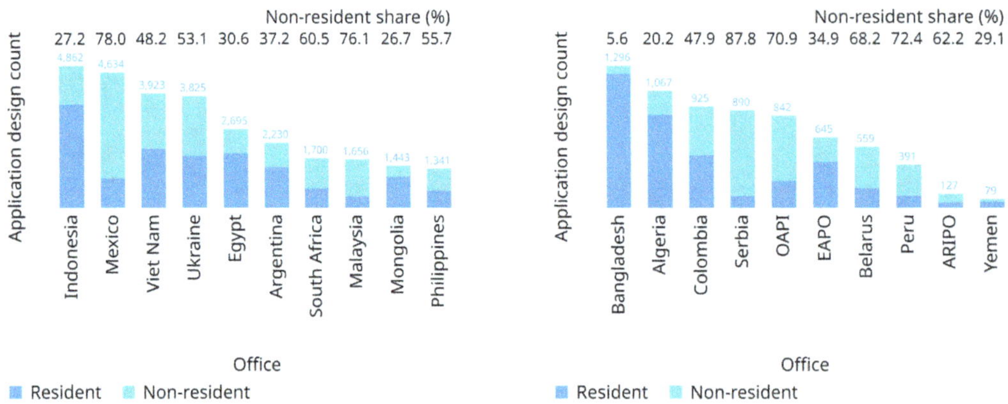

Note: ARIPO is the African Regional Intellectual Property Organization, EAPO is the Eurasian Patent Organization and OAPI is the African Intellectual Property Organization. The selected offices are from different world regions and income groups (low-income, lower middle-income and upper middle-income). Where available, data for all offices are presented in the statistical table C37 at the end of this section.
Source: WIPO Statistics Database, August 2023.

C12. Contribution of resident and non-resident application design counts to total growth for offices of selected low- and middle-income countries, 2021–2022

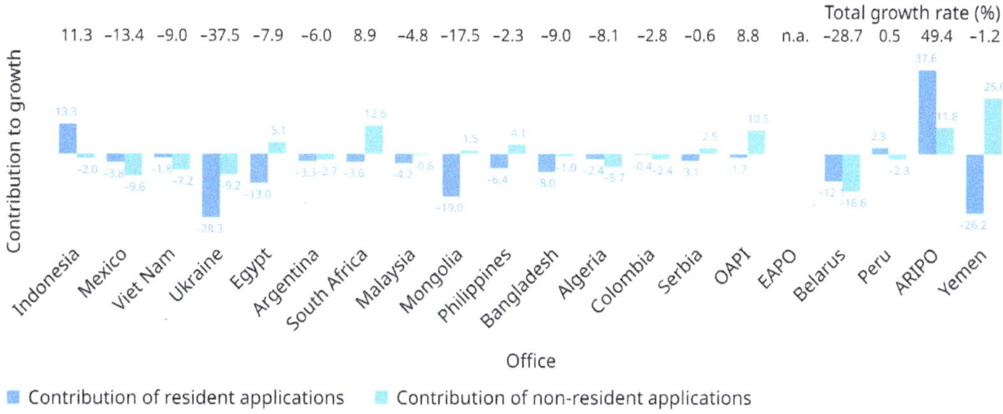

Note: ARIPO is the African Regional Intellectual Property Organization, EAPO is the Eurasian Patent Organization and OAPI is the African Intellectual Property Organization. The selected offices are from different world regions and income groups (low-income, lower middle-income and upper middle-income). Where available, data for all offices are in the statistical table C37 at the end of this section. This figure shows total growth in design counts, broken down by the respective contributions made by resident and non-resident applicants. For example, the total design count in Viet Nam dropped by 9%, with resident applicants contributing 1.8 percentage points to overall decrease and non-resident applicants 7.2 percentage points.
n.a. indicates not applicable.
Source: WIPO Statistics Database, August 2023.

C13. Registration design counts for the top 20 offices, 2022

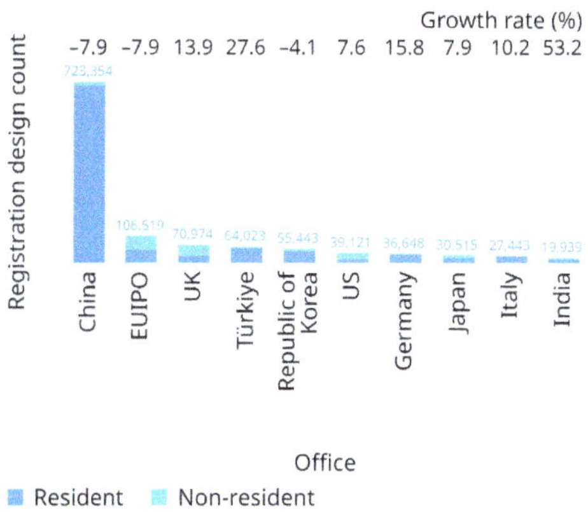

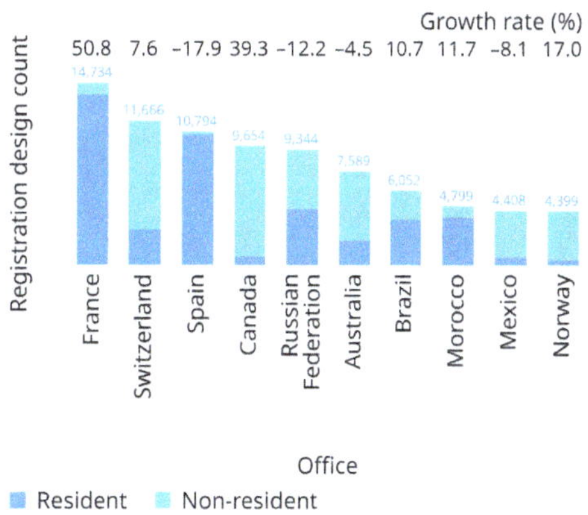

Note: EUIPO is the European Union Intellectual Property Office.
Source: WIPO Statistics Database, August 2023.

C14. Registration design counts for offices of selected low- and middle-income countries, 2022

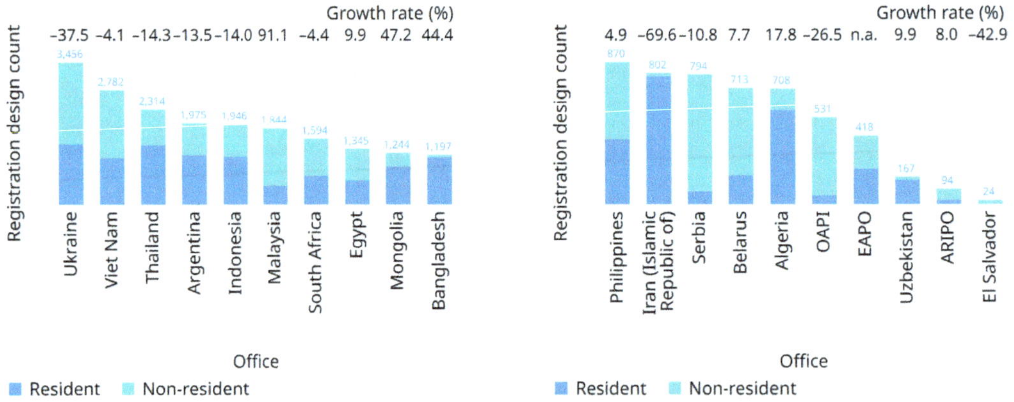

Note: ARIPO is the African Regional Intellectual Property Organization, EAPO is the Eurasian Patent Organization and OAPI is the African Intellectual Property Organization. The selected offices are from different world regions and income groups (low-income, lower middle-income and upper middle-income). Where available, data for all offices are presented in statistical table C38 at the end of this section.
n.a. indicates not applicable.
Source: WIPO Statistics Database, August 2023.

C15. Non-resident application design counts by filing route, 2008–2022

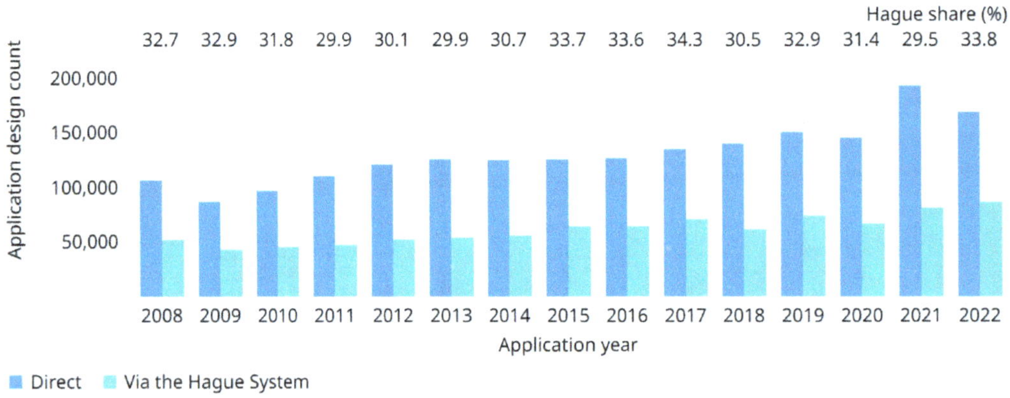

Source: WIPO Statistics Database, August 2023.

Application design counts by origin

C16. Application design counts for the top 20 origins, 2022

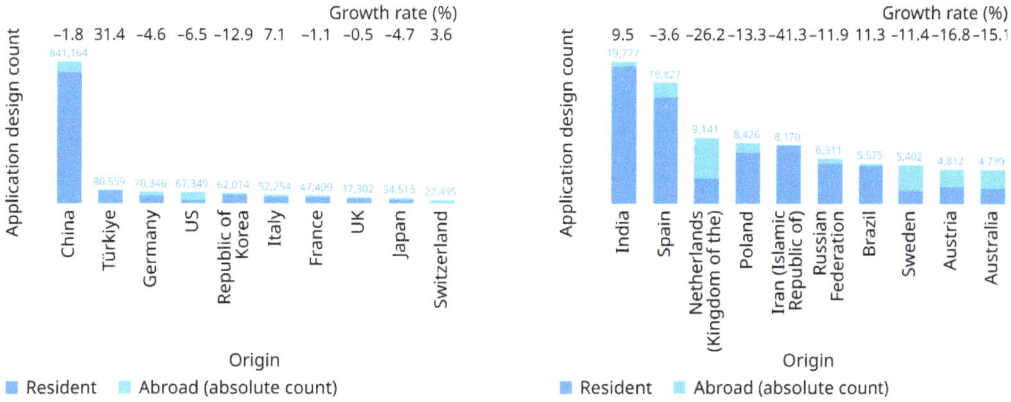

Note: Data are based on an absolute not an equivalent count. The origin of an industrial design application is determined by the residence of the first named applicant. An application filed at a regional office is considered to be a resident filing, if the applicant resides in one of that office's member states.
Source: WIPO Statistics Database, August 2023.

C17. Equivalent application design counts for the top 20 origins, 2022

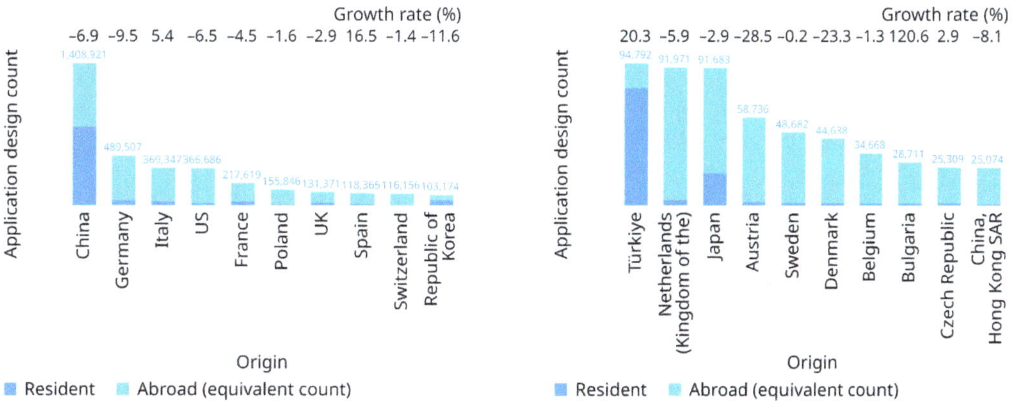

Note: The origin of an industrial design application is determined by the residence of the first named applicant. An application filed at a regional office is considered to be a resident filing, if the applicant resides in one of that office's member states. Applications filed at some regional offices are considered equivalent to multiple applications in the member states of those offices. See glossary for the definition of equivalent application and design count.
Source: WIPO Statistics Database, August 2023.

C18. Application design counts for selected low- and middle-income origins, 2022

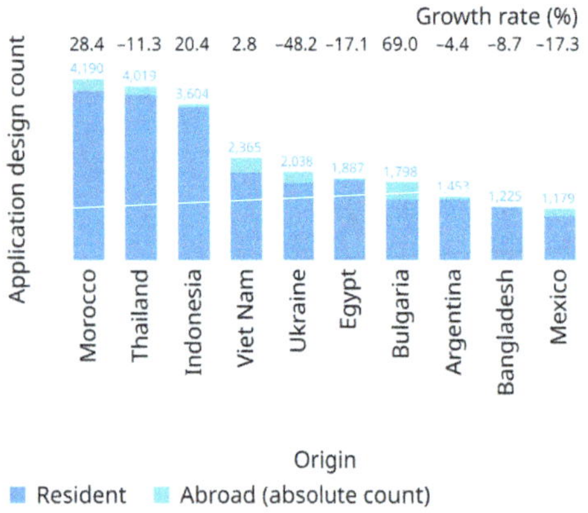

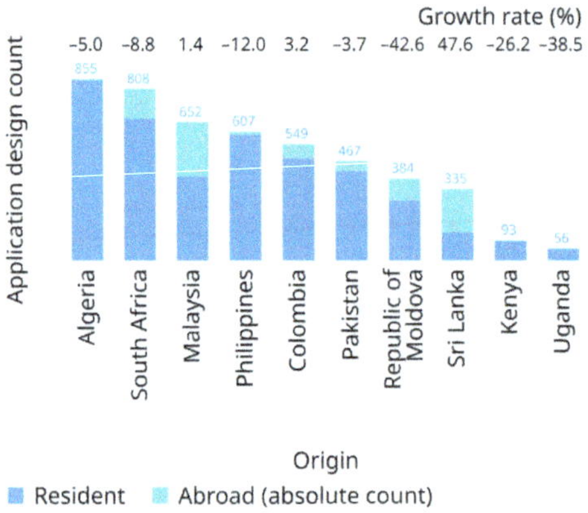

Note: Data are based on an absolute count not an equivalent count. The selected origins are from different world regions and income groups (low-income, lower middle-income and upper middle-income). Where available, data for all origins are presented in statistical table C37 at the end of this section. The origin of an industrial design application is determined by the residence of the first named applicant.
Source: WIPO Statistics Database, August 2023.

C19. Equivalent application design counts for selected low- and middle-income origins, 2022

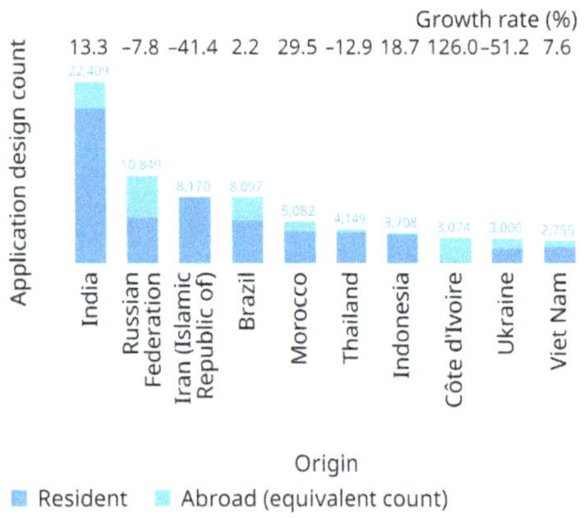

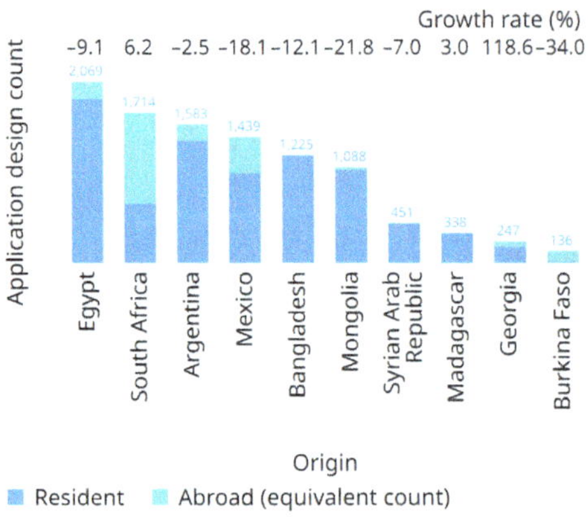

Note: The selected origins are from different world regions and income groups (low-income, lower middle-income and upper middle-income). Where available, data for all origins are presented in statistical table C37 at the end of this section. The origin of an industrial design application is determined by the residence of the first named applicant. Applications filed at some regional offices are considered equivalent to multiple applications in the member states of those offices. See glossary for the definition of equivalent application and design count.
Source: WIPO Statistics Database, August 2023.

C20. Flows of non-resident application design counts for the top five origins and the top 10 offices of high-income economies, 2022

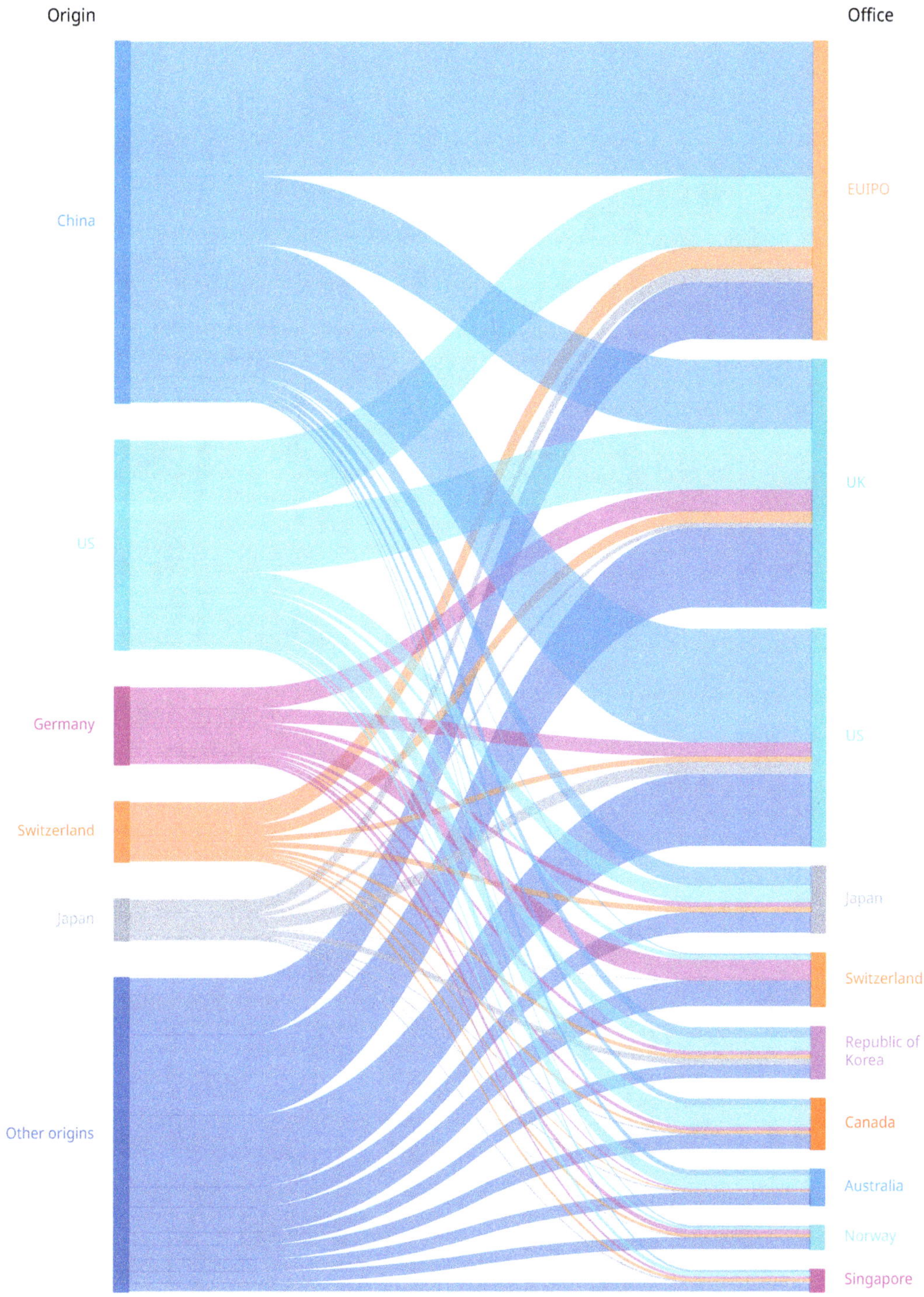

Note: EUIPO is the European Union Intellectual Property Office.
Source: WIPO Statistics Database, August 2023.

C21. Flows of non-resident application design counts for the top five origins and the top 10 offices of low- and middle-income economies, 2022

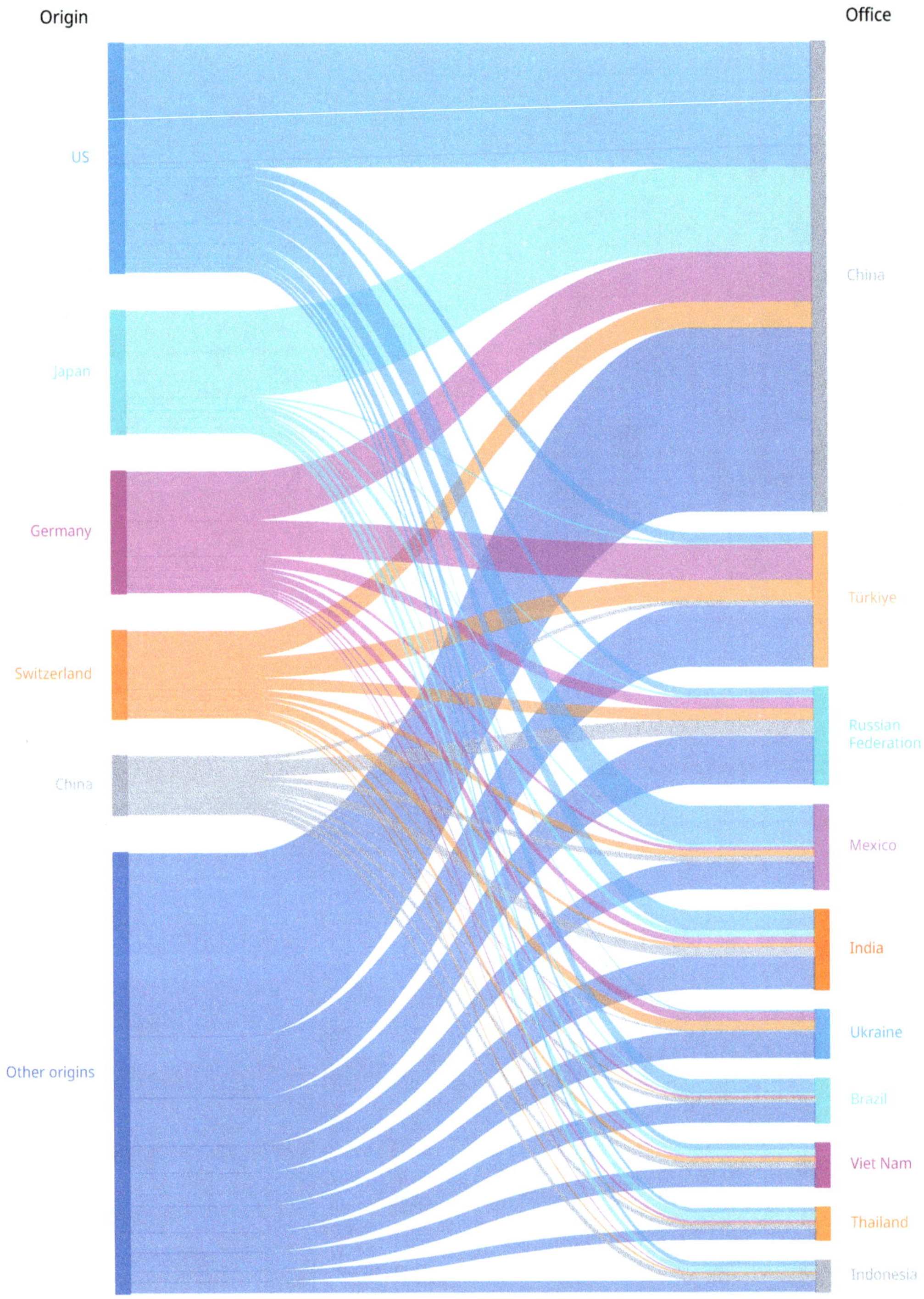

Source: WIPO Statistics Database, August 2023.

Application design counts by Locarno class and industry sector

C22. Application design counts for the top 10 Locarno classes, 2022

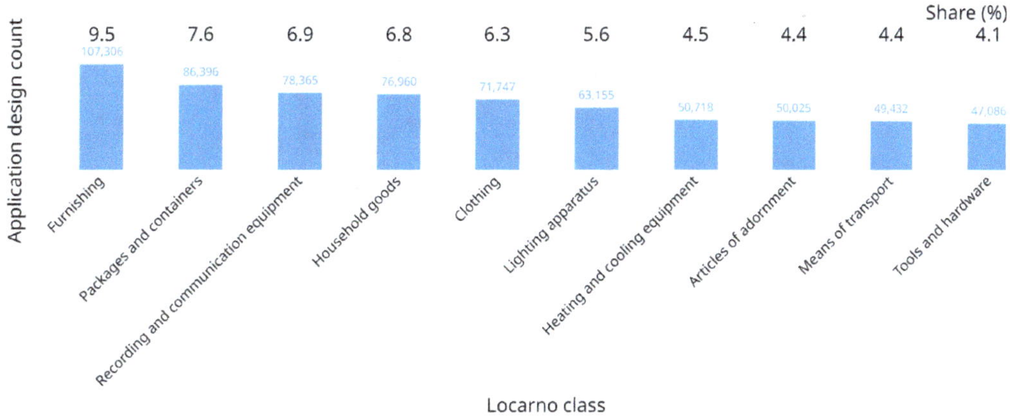

Note: See annex C for class numbers. These figures are based on data from 115 IP offices. Data for several of the larger offices are either not available or incomplete, including for the offices of Japan and the US.
Source: WIPO Statistics Database, August 2023.

C23. Application design counts by industry sector, 2022

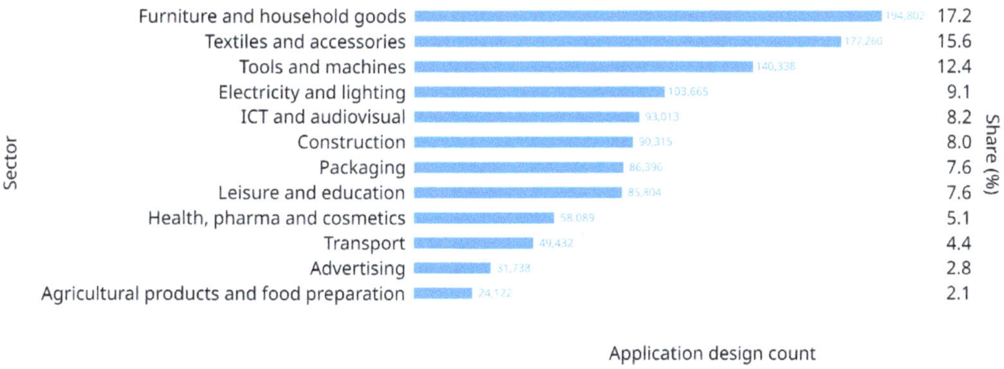

Note: A concordance table produced by the Organisation for Economic Co-operation and Development (OECD) was used to convert the 32 classes into 12 industry sectors (see annex C for definitions). These figures are based on data from 115 IP offices. Data for several of the larger offices are either not available or incomplete, including for the offices of Japan and the US.
Source: WIPO Statistics Database, August 2023.

C24. Distribution of application design counts by the top three sectors for the top 10 offices, 2022

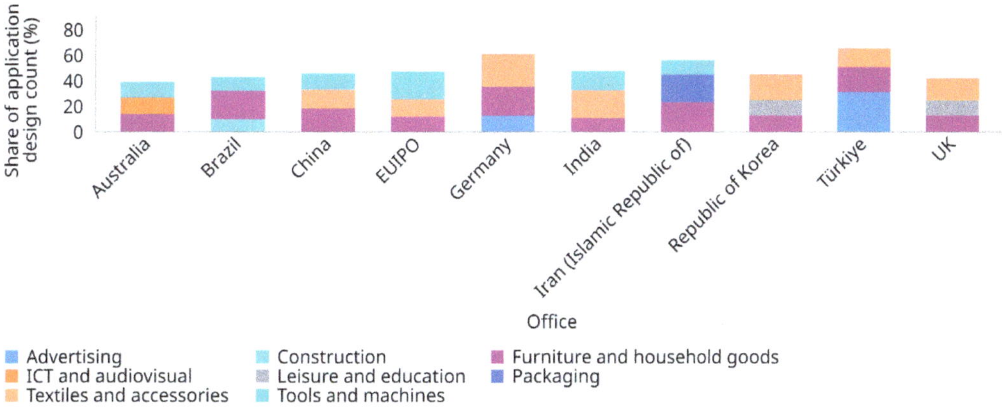

Note: EUIPO is the European Union Intellectual Property Office. A concordance table produced by the Organisation for Economic Co-operation and Development (OECD) was used to convert the 32 classes into 12 industry sectors (see annex C for definitions). The top three sectors and top 10 offices were selected based on 2022 totals. Data for several of the larger offices are either not available or incomplete, including for the offices of Japan and the US.
Source: WIPO Statistics Database, August 2023.

C25. Distribution of application design counts by the top three sectors for the top 10 origins, 2022

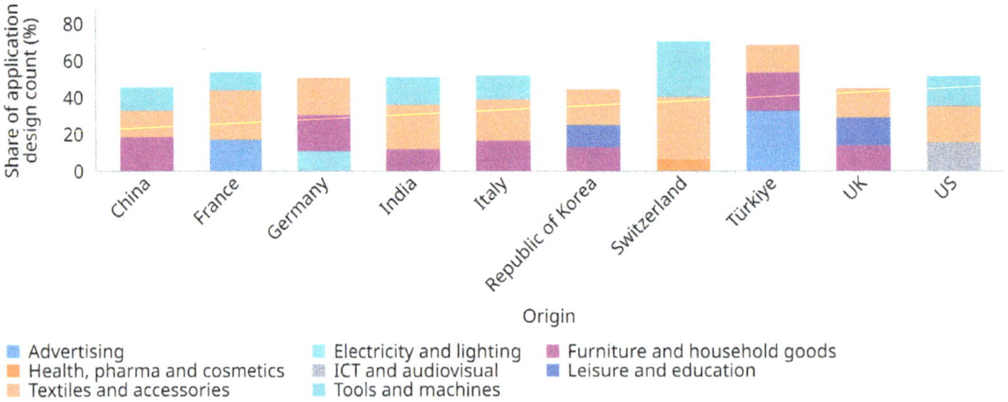

Note: A concordance table produced by the Organisation for Economic Co-operation and Development (OECD) was used to convert the 32 classes into 12 industry sectors (see annex C for definitions). These figures are based on data from 115 IP offices. Data for several of the larger offices are either not available or incomplete, including for the offices of Japan and the US.
Source: WIPO Statistics Database, August 2023.

Application design count in relation to GDP and population

C26. Resident application design count per USD 100 billion of GDP for the top 20 origins, 2012 and 2022

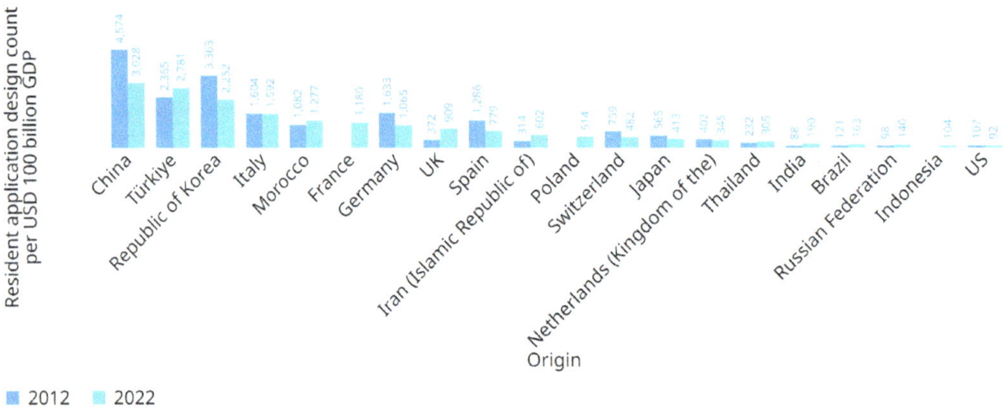

Note: GDP data are in constant 2017 US PPP dollars. Origins were selected based on the top origins list in terms of application design count and on GDP data availability.
Sources: WIPO Statistics Database and World Bank, August 2023.

C27. Resident application design count per million population for the top 20 origins, 2012 and 2022

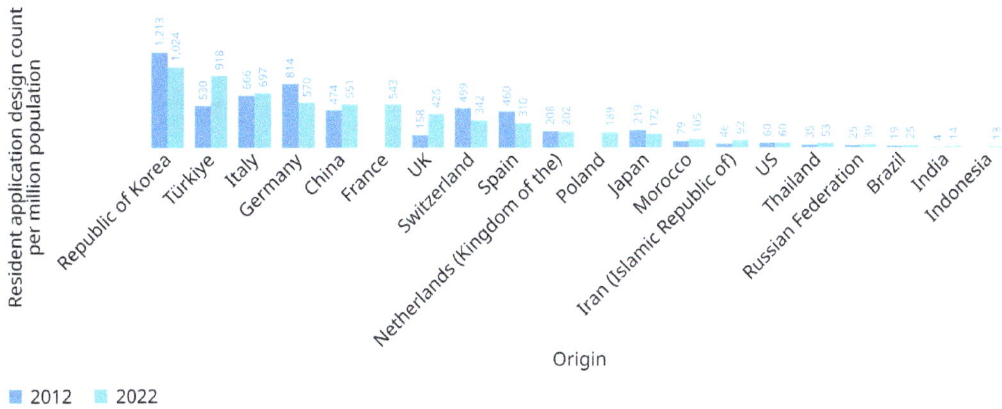

Note: Origins were selected based on the top origins list in terms of application design count and on population data availability.
Sources: WIPO Statistics Database and World Bank, August 2023.

C28. Resident application design count per capita and GDP per capita for selected origins, 2018–2022

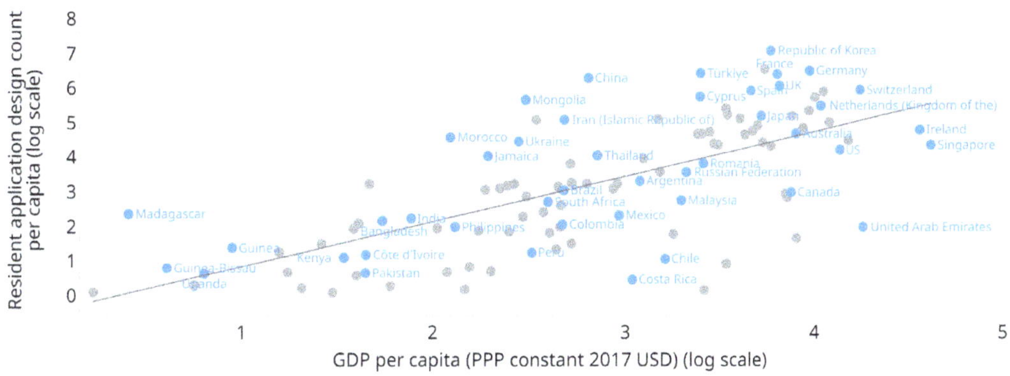

Note: The selected origins are from different world regions and income groups.
Sources: WIPO Statistics Database and World Bank, August 2023.

Industrial design registrations in force

C29. Trend in industrial design registrations in force worldwide, 2012–2022

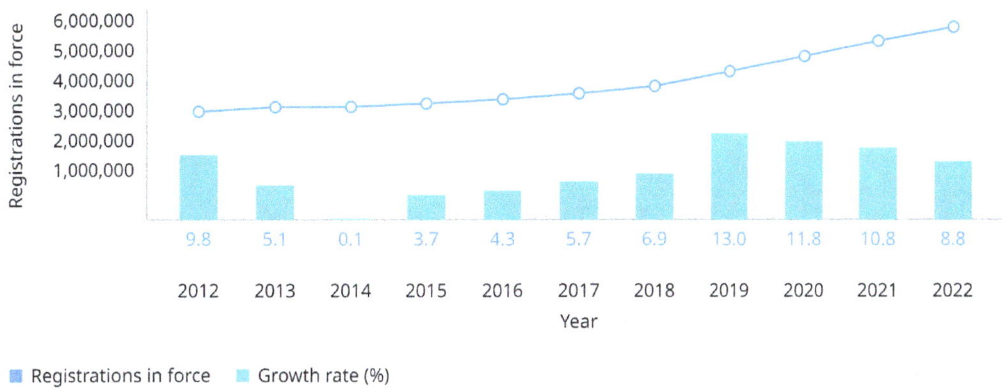

Note: WIPO estimates cover 136 IP offices and include direct national and regional applications, as well as designations received via the Hague System. Data refer to the number of industrial design registrations in force and not the number of designs contained in those registrations.
Source: WIPO Statistics Database, August 2023.

C30. Industrial design registrations in force for the top 20 offices, 2022

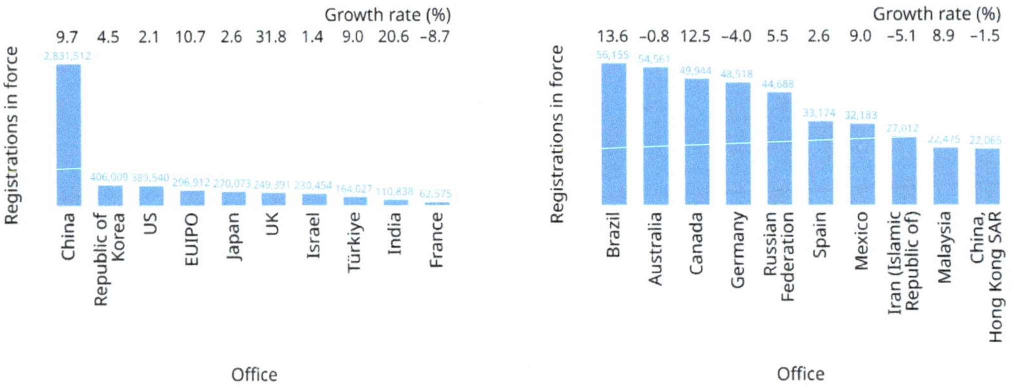

Note: EUIPO is the European Union Intellectual Property Office. Data refer to the number of industrial design registrations in force and not the number of designs contained in those registrations.
Source: WIPO Statistics Database, August 2023.

C31. Industrial design registrations in force in 2022 as a percentage of total registrations

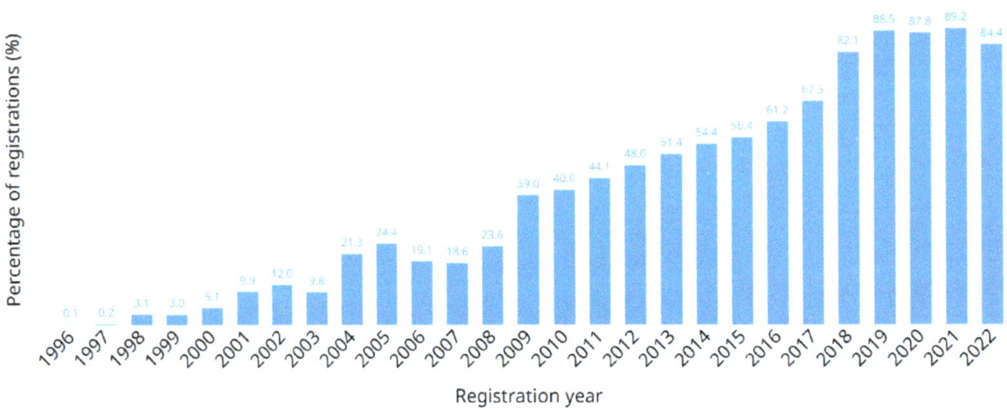

Note: Percentages are calculated using the number of industrial designs registered in year *t* and in force in 2022 divided by the total number of industrial designs registered in year *t*. The graph is based on data from 90 offices (including most of the larger offices) for which a breakdown of industrial design registrations in force by year of registration was available. Industrial design rights generally last for up to 15 years from the filing date. In China that protection period is limited to 10 years. Because China accounts for most of the global total, it was excluded from this figure.
Source: WIPO Statistics Database, August 2023.

C32. Average age of industrial design registrations in force at selected offices, 2017 and 2022

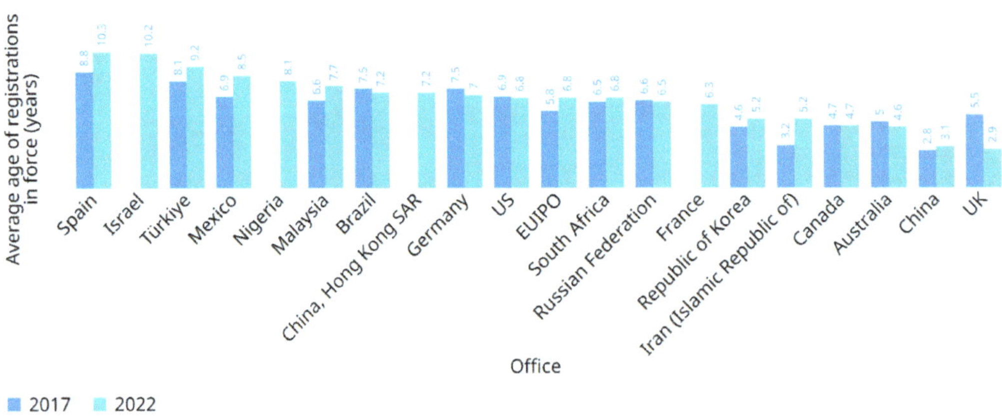

Note: EUIPO is the European Union Intellectual Property Office. Percentages are calculated using the number of industrial designs registered in year *t* and in force in 2022 divided by the total number of industrial designs registered in year *t*.
Source: WIPO Statistics Database, August 2023.

Industrial design office procedural data

C33. Distribution of industrial design examination outcomes for selected offices, 2022

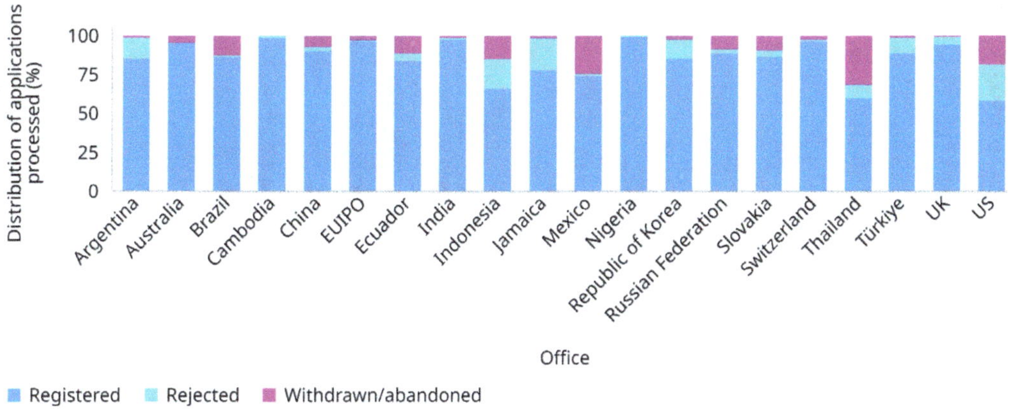

Note: EUIPO is the European Union Intellectual Property Office. WIPO collects data from offices using a common questionnaire and methodology. However, because of differences in industrial design procedures between offices, data cannot be fully harmonized. Therefore, caution should be exercised when making comparisons across offices.
Source: WIPO Statistics Database, August 2023.

C34. Potentially pending applications for selected offices, 2022

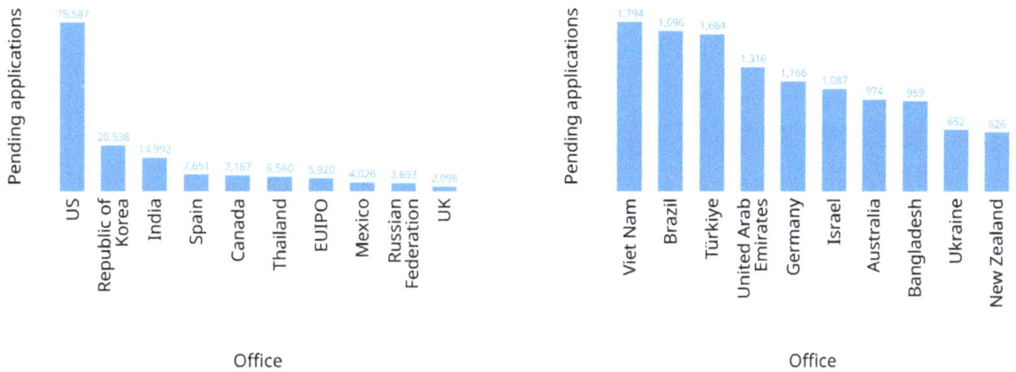

Note: EUIPO is the European Union Intellectual Property Office. WIPO collects data from offices using a common questionnaire and methodology. However, because of differences in industrial design procedures between offices, data cannot be fully harmonized. Therefore, caution should be exercised when making comparisons across offices. Data for some large offices are missing, such as for China, Italy and Japan.
Source: WIPO Statistics Database, August 2023.

C35. Average pendency times from filing date to first office action and to final decision at selected offices, 2022

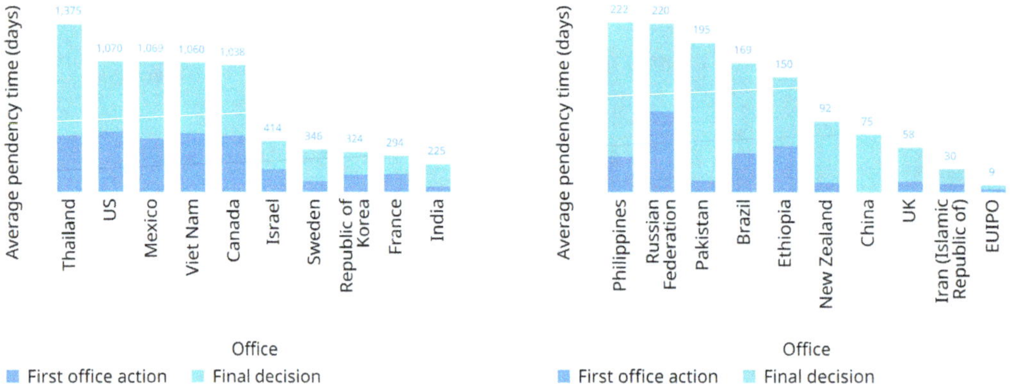

Note: EUIPO is the European Union Intellectual Property Office. WIPO collects data from IP offices using a common questionnaire and methodology. However, because of differences in industrial design procedures between offices, data cannot be fully harmonized. Therefore, caution should be exercised when making comparisons across offices.
Source: WIPO Statistics Database, August 2023.

C36. Number of industrial design examiners for selected offices, 2022

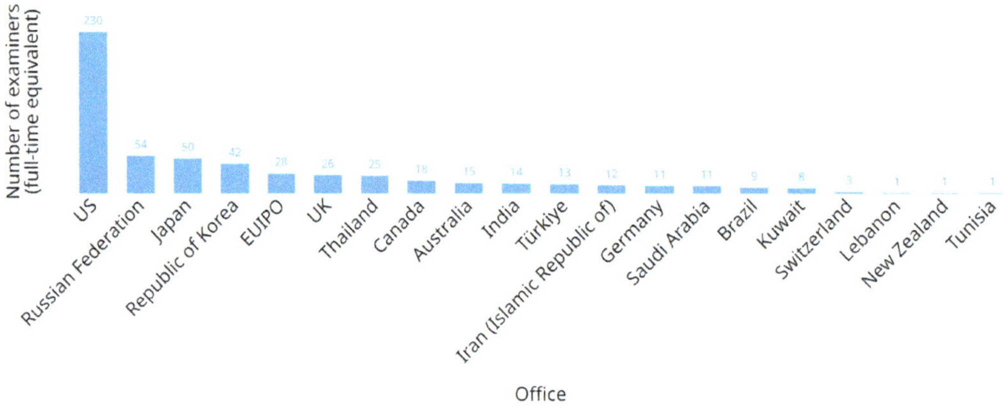

Note: EUIPO is the European Union Intellectual Property Office. WIPO collects data from IP offices using a common questionnaire and methodology. However, because of differences in industrial design procedures between offices, data cannot be fully harmonized. Therefore, caution should be exercised when making comparisons across offices.
Source: WIPO Statistics Database, August 2023.

C37. Industrial design applications by office and origin, 2022

Name	Application design count by office: Total	Resident	Non-resident	Change over previous year	Application design count by origin: Total (a)	Equivalent application design count by origin: Total (a)	Change over previous year
Afghanistan (b)	..	..	..	..	5	5	..
African Intellectual Property Organization	842	245	597	+68	n.a.	n.a.	n.a.
African Regional Intellectual Property Organization	127	48	79	+42	n.a.	n.a.	n.a.
Albania	407	18	389	-83	50	778	+720
Algeria	1,067	851	216	-94	855	855	-45
Andorra (b)	..	..	..	..	6	136	..
Angola	46	46	0	..	46	46	..
Argentina	2,230	1,400	830	-142	1,453	1,583	-41
Armenia	383	111	272	+23	129	129	+48
Australia	7,860	2,114	5,746	-260	4,739	15,867	-2,194
Austria	370	320	50	-30	4,812	58,736	-23,449
Azerbaijan	416	73	343	-244	89	96	+15
Bahamas (b)	..	..	..	..	21	21	..
Bahrain	88	3	85	-36	9	35	+20
Bangladesh	1,296	1,224	72	-128	1,225	1,225	-168
Barbados (b)	..	..	..	..	214	1,930	..
Belarus	559	178	381	-225	292	670	+208
Belgium (d)	n.a.	n.a.	n.a.	n.a.	2,966	34,668	-447
Belize (b)	..	..	..	..	..	..	..
Benelux Office for Intellectual Property	874	660	214	-321	n.a.	n.a.	n.a.
Benin (b,c)	n.a.	n.a.	n.a.	n.a.	3	51	-34
Bhutan (b)	..	..	..	..	1	1	..
Bolivia (Plurinational State of)	89	31	58	+28	31	31	+8
Bonaire, Sint Eustatius and Saba (b)	..	..	..	..	2	54	..
Bosnia and Herzegovina	632	63	569	-98	68	172	-499
Botswana	92	5	87	+22	5	5	-13
Brazil	7,196	5,282	1,914	+485	5,575	8,097	+177
Brunei Darussalam	231	0	231	+159	..	..	..
Bulgaria	463	364	99	-11	1,798	28,711	+15,697
Burkina Faso (b,c)	n.a.	n.a.	n.a.	n.a.	8	136	-70
Cambodia	200	0	200	..	1	1	..
Cameroon (b,c)	n.a.	n.a.	n.a.	n.a.	26	426	-205
Canada	8,855	723	8,132	-636	3,327	15,352	-2,633
Central African Republic (b,c)	n.a.	n.a.	n.a.	n.a.	1	17	+17
Chad (b,c)	n.a.	n.a.	n.a.	n.a.	3	51	-68
Chile	506	54	452	+118	66	92	-97
China	798,112	777,813	20,299	-7,598	841,164	1,408,921	-103,940
China, Hong Kong SAR	3,286	723	2,563	-572	2,473	25,074	-2,221
China, Macao SAR	268	13	255	+4	14	14	-231
Colombia	925	482	443	-27	549	783	+147
Cook Islands (b)	..	..	..	..	1	1	..
Costa Rica	64	3	61	-11	4	4	-9
Côte d'Ivoire (b,c)	n.a.	n.a.	n.a.	n.a.	150	3,074	+1,714
Croatia	604	253	351	-109	783	5,281	-586
Cuba (b)	..	..	..	..	5	5	..
Curaçao (b)	..	..	..	..	12	324	..
Cyprus	221	221	0	+201	808	4,604	-4,580
Czech Republic	490	377	113	-118	2,273	25,309	+704
Democratic People's Republic of Korea (b)	..	..	..	..	258	284	..
Denmark	328	81	247	+8	3,910	44,638	-13,591
Djibouti	9	9	0	+1	9	9	+9

Name	Application design count by office				Application design count by origin	Equivalent application design count by origin	
	Total	Resident	Non-resident	Change over previous year	Total (a)	Total (a)	Change over previous year
Dominica (b)	..	..	..	..	3	3	..
Dominican Republic	26	10	16	+5	12	64	+20
Ecuador	164	85	79	+3	89	89	–18
Egypt	2,695	1,871	824	–231	1,887	2,069	–207
El Salvador	52	20	32	+12	20	20	+4
Estonia	76	27	49	–50	321	4,845	–928
Eswatini (b)	..	..	..	..	3	3	..
Ethiopia	66	55	11	..	60	60	..
Eurasian Patent Organization	645	420	225	+455	n.a.	n.a.	n.a.
European Union Intellectual Property Office	109,132	60,301	48,831	–7,917	n.a.	n.a.	n.a.
Finland	178	97	81	–46	1,527	19,972	–5,483
France	31,676	30,376	1,300	+332	47,409	217,619	–10,271
Gabon (b,c)	n.a.	n.a.	n.a.	n.a.	5	85	–119
Gambia	6	0	6	–4	..	..	..
Georgia	518	183	335	+36	235	247	+134
Germany	34,240	31,907	2,333	–2,757	70,346	489,507	–51,193
Ghana	827	648	179	..	661	673	..
Greece	1,026	858	168	+143	1,715	11,803	+45
Guatemala	56	17	39	–36	19	19	–64
Guinea (b,c)	n.a.	n.a.	n.a.	n.a.	60	1,020	+17
Guinea-Bissau (b,c)	n.a.	n.a.	n.a.	n.a.	5	85	+34
Honduras	21	1	20	..	1	1	..
Hungary	235	194	41	–672	640	6,274	+1,142
Iceland (b)	..	..	..	..	82	680	..
India	22,557	19,130	3,427	+1,111	19,777	22,409	+2,635
Indonesia	4,862	3,538	1,324	+494	3,604	3,708	+585
Iran (Islamic Republic of)	8,212	8,154	58	–5,804	8,170	8,170	–5,767
Iraq (b)	..	..	..	..	10	10	..
Ireland	106	77	29	–8	985	9,799	–5,826
Israel	2,025	580	1,445	+70	1,917	10,107	–56
Italy	29,611	28,903	708	+2,917	52,254	369,347	+18,910
Jamaica	218	154	64	+118	154	154	+60
Japan	32,423	21,515	10,908	–324	34,515	91,683	–2,691
Jordan	123	68	55	–6	95	251	–71
Kazakhstan	192	93	99	–138	156	231	–52
Kenya	122	85	37	–31	93	99	–27
Kuwait	308	14	294	–84	17	17	–97
Kyrgyzstan	339	10	329	+18	20	20	–10
Lao People's Democratic Republic	1	1	0	..	1	1	..
Latvia	129	85	44	+2	245	2,481	–23
Lebanon (b)	..	..	..	..	14	92	..
Libya (b)	..	..	..	..	1	1	..
Liechtenstein	830	78	752	+138	563	2,853	–362
Lithuania	397	152	245	+53	437	5,055	–272
Luxembourg (d)	n.a.	n.a.	n.a.	n.a.	742	6,304	–2,688
Madagascar	360	338	22	+32	338	338	+10
Malaysia	1,656	395	1,261	–83	652	990	+269
Mali (b,c)	n.a.	n.a.	n.a.	n.a.	9	121	–85
Malta	12	11	1	–5	902	4,802	–9,020
Mauritania (b,c)	n.a.	n.a.	n.a.	n.a.	2	34	+34
Mauritius	27	25	2	0	73	115	+52
Mexico	4,634	1,020	3,614	–719	1,179	1,439	–317
Monaco	781	10	771	+138	73	229	–202
Mongolia	1,443	1,058	385	–306	1,062	1,088	–303
Montenegro	589	2	587	..	2	2	..
Morocco	4,882	3,914	968	+496	4,190	5,082	+1,158
Mozambique	110	51	59	+45	52	52	+17
Namibia	154	37	117	..	38	38	..

Name	Application design count by office: Total	Resident	Non-resident	Change over previous year	Application design count by origin: Total (a)	Equivalent application design count by origin: Total (a)	Change over previous year
Netherlands (Kingdom of the) (d)	n.a.	n.a.	n.a.	n.a.	9,141	91,971	-5,799
New Zealand	1,736	400	1,336	+305	1,424	6,666	+674
Nicaragua (b)	..	..	..	..	6	6	..
Niger (b,c)	n.a.	n.a.	n.a.	n.a.	..	..	..
Nigeria (b)	..	..	..	..	11	53	..
North Macedonia	513	14	499	-109	31	265	+93
Norway	4,116	392	3,724	-288	1,346	6,936	-1,568
Oman	535	9	526	-27	30	108	+91
Pakistan	478	421	57	-94	467	467	-18
Panama (b)	..	..	..	..	95	95	..
Paraguay	83	1	82	+5	1	1	-8
Peru	391	108	283	+2	117	117	+19
Philippines	1,341	594	747	-31	607	685	-35
Poland	1,630	1,442	188	-1,125	8,426	155,846	-2,495
Portugal	1,051	968	83	-78	2,151	23,863	-834
Qatar (b)	..	..	..	..	19	19	..
Republic of Korea	61,136	52,866	8,270	-8,112	62,014	103,174	-13,519
Republic of Moldova	740	281	459	-392	384	528	-221
Romania	617	335	282	-64	959	14,391	+4,705
Russian Federation	9,448	5,259	4,189	-3,094	6,311	10,849	-924
Rwanda	93	3	90	+37	4	5	-5
Samoa	59	5	54	..	9	9	..
San Marino	178	3	175	+92	553	605	+119
Sao Tome and Principe (b)	..	..	..	..	..	..	..
Saudi Arabia	1,508	906	602	+108	942	968	-128
Senegal (b,c)	n.a.	n.a.	n.a.	n.a.	29	493	+68
Serbia	890	109	781	-5	227	685	-248
Seychelles (b)	..	..	..	..	330	1,344	..
Sierra Leone (b)	..	..	..	..	1	1	..
Singapore	3,787	333	3,454	-807	1,631	6,519	-8,782
Slovakia	352	244	108	-56	454	3,808	-2,690
Slovenia	373	21	352	-3	556	7,638	+3,187
Somalia (b)	..	..	..	..	1	1	..
South Africa	1,700	672	1,028	+139	808	1,714	+100
Spain	11,113	10,866	247	-1,181	16,827	118,365	+16,777
Sri Lanka	159	132	27	+20	335	361	+134
Sudan (b)	..	..	..	..	2	2	..
Suriname (b)	..	..	..	..	..	..	..
Sweden	200	189	11	-219	5,402	48,682	-118
Switzerland	11,525	2,998	8,527	-283	22,495	116,156	-1,657
Syrian Arab Republic	517	446	71	+49	451	451	-34
Tajikistan	184	0	184	+36	..	..	..
Thailand	5,259	3,828	1,431	-428	4,019	4,149	-615
Togo (b,c)	n.a.	n.a.	n.a.	n.a.	2	34	-51
Tonga	4	4	0	..	4	4	..
Trinidad and Tobago	12	11	1	-47	12	12	-48
Tunisia	1,321	478	843	..	547	547	..
Türkiye	84,111	78,308	5,803	+18,187	80,559	94,792	+15,963
Turkmenistan (b)	..	..	..	..	..	..	..
Uganda	58	54	4	-32	56	56	-35
Ukraine	3,825	1,793	2,032	-2,297	2,038	3,000	-3,149
United Arab Emirates	902	56	846	-70	244	1,326	+61
United Kingdom	69,004	28,519	40,485	-5,776	37,302	131,371	-3,874
United Republic of Tanzania (b)	..	..	..	..	1	1	..
United States of America	56,217	19,928	36,289	-3,260	67,349	366,686	-25,572
Uruguay (b)	..	..	..	..	19	45	..
Uzbekistan	255	234	21	-18	236	236	-4
Vanuatu	6	6	0	+2	6	6	+2

Name	Application design count by office: Total	Resident	Non-resident	Change over previous year	Application design count by origin: Total (a)	Equivalent application design count by origin: Total (a)	Change over previous year
Venezuela (Bolivarian Republic of)	33	17	16	–258	19	19	+14
Viet Nam	3,923	2,031	1,892	–387	2,365	2,755	+194
Yemen	79	56	23	–1	56	56	–24
Zambia	42	42	0	–4	62	81	+35
Zimbabwe	17	17	0	+3	28	38	+19
Others/Unknown	..	..	..	..	3,655	18,449	+1,822
Total (2022 estimates)	**1,482,600**	**1,227,200**	**255,400**		**1,482,600**		

(a) Design count by origin data are incomplete, because some offices do not report the origin of applications.
(b) Only Hague designation data are available and/or this office has not reported the origin of applications therefore the design count by office and origin data may be incomplete.
(c) The African Intellectual Property Organization (OAPI) is the competent office for processing applications.
(d) The Benelux Office for Intellectual Property is the competent office for processing applications.
n.a. indicates not applicable.
.. indicates not available.
Source: WIPO Statistics Database, August 2023.

C38. Industrial design registrations by office and origin, and registrations in force, 2022

Name	Registration design count by office: Total	Resident	Non-resident	Registration design count by origin: Total (a)	Equivalent registration design count by origin: Total (a)	In force by office: Total	Change over previous year
Afghanistan (b)	..	..	..	1	1	..	..
African Intellectual Property Organization	531	55	476	n.a.	n.a.	..	..
African Regional Intellectual Property Organization	94	26	68	n.a.	n.a.	553	–27
Albania	384	44	340	70	694	89	+14
Algeria	708	576	132	595	595	2,188	+575
Andorra (b)	..	..	..	3	29	..	..
Angola (b)	..	..	..	..	..	742	..
Argentina	1,975	1,193	782	1,245	1,323	14,501	..
Armenia	266	37	229	39	39	263	+1
Australia	7,589	1,993	5,596	4,274	14,362	54,561	–434
Austria	315	249	66	4,363	55,803	6,855	–527
Azerbaijan	340	13	327	15	15	1,739	+63
Bahamas (b)	..	..	..	9	9	..	..
Bahrain	91	3	88	9	35	782	+24
Bangladesh	1,197	1,141	56	1,146	1,276	3,235	–2,086
Barbados (b)	..	..	..	189	2,113	12	0
Belarus	713	178	535	244	340	1,476	+37
Belgium (d)	n.a.	n.a.	n.a.	2,713	31,683	n.a.	n.a.
Belize (b)	..	..	..	..	..	..	..
Benelux Office for Intellectual Property	867	662	205	n.a.	n.a.	3,389	+98
Benin (b,c)	n.a.	n.a.	n.a.	..	..	..	..
Bhutan (b)	..	..	..	1	1	28	–5
Bolivia (Plurinational State of)	21	7	14	7	7	..	..
Bonaire, Sint Eustatius and Saba (b)	..	..	..	2	54	..	..
Bosnia and Herzegovina	522	12	510	15	41	524	+19
Botswana (b)	..	..	..	..	..	210	–12
Brazil	6,052	3,715	2,337	4,070	8,074	56,155	+6,703
Brunei Darussalam	172	0	172	..	..	447	+71
Bulgaria	442	366	76	1,362	23,588	1,741	–204
Burkina Faso (b,c)	n.a.	n.a.	n.a.	4	36	..	..
Cabo Verde (b)	..	..	..	..	..	4	0
Cambodia	180	3	177	3	3	1,101	+83
Cameroon (b,c)	n.a.	n.a.	n.a.	3	51	..	..

Name	Registration design count by office			Registration design count by origin	Equivalent registration design count by origin	In force by office	
	Total	Resident	Non-resident	Total (a)	Total (a)	Total	Change over previous year
Canada	9,654	704	8,950	2,768	15,384	49,944	+5,530
Chad (b,c)	n.a.	n.a.	n.a.	1	17	..	..
Chile	275	15	260	44	70	2,871	+197
China	723,354	709,659	13,695	760,234	1,175,896	2,831,512	+250,980
China, Hong Kong SAR	3,319	703	2,616	1,925	16,485	22,065	-342
China, Macao SAR	262	30	232	30	30	1,585	+160
Colombia	479	234	245	274	378	5,522	+318
Cook Islands (b)	..	..	..	1	1	..	..
Costa Rica	28	3	25	5	5	467	-98
Côte d'Ivoire (b,c)	n.a.	n.a.	n.a.	72	1,764	..	..
Croatia	628	279	349	888	6,140	3,033	-288
Cyprus	220	220	0	686	4,248	65	+15
Czech Republic	693	591	102	2,439	22,641	2,283	-96
Democratic People's Republic of Korea (b)	..	..	..	218	244	..	..
Denmark	277	65	212	3,924	40,024	1,127	-618
Djibouti	9	9	0	10	10	..	..
Dominican Republic	22	1	21	13	39	142	-46
Ecuador	144	77	67	81	107	1,311	+430
Egypt	1,345	592	753	607	789	5,852	+233
El Salvador	24	2	22	2	2	..	..
Estonia	70	31	39	276	3,396	806	-428
Ethiopia	29	25	4	30	30	396	..
Eurasian Patent Organization	418	218	200	n.a.	n.a.	..	..
European Union Intellectual Property Office	106,519	51,178	55,341	n.a.	n.a.	296,912	+28,762
Finland	140	72	68	1,350	16,098	1,443	-172
France	14,734	13,814	920	29,338	188,100	62,575	-5,952
Gabon (b,c)	n.a.	n.a.	n.a.	4	68	..	..
Gambia	6	0	6	..	..	..	..
Georgia	401	102	299	150	162	2,643	-106
Germany	36,648	34,274	2,374	68,602	426,542	48,518	-2,013
Ghana	149	0	149	14	25	..	..
Greece	1,075	909	166	1,733	10,911	1,192	-51
Grenada (b)	..	..	..	2	2	..	..
Guatemala	4	1	3	9	9	125	-87
Guinea (b,c)	n.a.	n.a.	n.a.	19	323	..	..
Guinea-Bissau (b,c)	n.a.	n.a.	n.a.	2	34	..	..
Honduras	18	1	17	1	1	135	..
Hungary	244	226	18	524	4,490	2,406	-99
Iceland (b)	..	..	..	45	539	1,461	+129
India	19,939	15,478	4,461	15,942	16,998	110,838	+18,951
Indonesia	1,946	1,159	787	1,213	1,317	..	..
Iran (Islamic Republic of)	802	785	17	789	789	27,012	-1,455
Iraq (b)	..	..	..	9	9	..	..
Ireland	102	77	25	887	8,817	1,587	+11
Israel	1,592	441	1,151	1,819	8,657	230,454	+3,193
Italy	27,443	27,343	100	49,168	342,240	8,811	-191
Jamaica	156	111	45	121	121	..	..
Japan	30,515	20,208	10,307	31,971	87,667	270,073	+6,799
Jordan	55	33	22	64	220	1,284	+226
Kazakhstan	176	65	111	102	212	2,354	-1,386
Kenya	97	71	26	76	81	..	..
Kuwait	308	14	294	19	19	308	..
Kyrgyzstan	271	7	264	11	11	54	-2
Lao People's Democratic Republic	76	1	75	1	1	73	..
Latvia	100	65	35	228	2,308	342	-29
Lebanon	64	30	34	37	115	..	..
Libya (b)	..	..	..	18	18	..	..

Name	Registration design count by office Total	Resident	Non-resident	Registration design count by origin Total (a)	Equivalent registration design count by origin Total (a)	In force by office Total	Change over previous year
Liechtenstein (b)	..	..	..	486	2,802	..	..
Lithuania	416	170	246	368	3,140	283	–7
Luxembourg (d)	n.a.	n.a.	n.a.	724	6,500	n.a.	n.a.
Madagascar	295	284	11	284	284	1,281	+3
Malaysia	1,844	455	1,389	566	748	22,475	+1,844
Mali (b,c)	n.a.	n.a.	n.a.	2	18	..	..
Malta	11	10	1	2,025	10,137	105	–33
Mauritius	13	9	4	33	59	141	–7
Mexico	4,408	637	3,771	766	1,000	32,183	+2,649
Monaco	686	10	676	62	166	202	–13
Mongolia	1,244	920	324	924	950	767	+121
Montenegro	527	3	524	3	3	..	..
Morocco	4,799	3,898	901	4,172	5,032	..	..
Mozambique	110	51	59	52	52	1,154	+110
Myanmar (b)	..	..	..	1	1	..	..
Namibia	141	34	107	37	37	144	..
Netherlands (Kingdom of the) (d)	n.a.	n.a.	n.a.	8,792	70,042	n.a.	n.a.
New Zealand	1,448	300	1,148	1,221	6,447	12,164	+208
Nicaragua (b)	..	..	..	6	6	..	..
Niger (b,c)	n.a.	n.a.	n.a.	..	..	..	..
Nigeria	1,213	..	..	4	4	15,276	..
North Macedonia	544	59	485	74	282	2,097	–217
Norway	4,399	378	4,021	1,281	6,559	12,123	+388
Oman	457	19	438	38	116	17	–13
Pakistan	247	192	55	232	232	8,167	..
Panama (b)	..	..	..	73	73	..	..
Papua New Guinea (b)	..	..	..	..	..	13	+5
Paraguay	122	0	122	3	3	..	..
Peru	366	91	275	94	94	3,042	+7
Philippines	870	398	472	412	490	..	..
Poland	1,688	1,475	213	6,399	101,999	8,357	–298
Portugal	958	912	46	1,769	15,505	3,220	–150
Qatar (b)	..	..	..	36	36	..	..
Republic of Korea	55,443	47,464	7,979	55,430	93,512	406,009	+17,509
Republic of Moldova	568	192	376	292	384	2,827	–96
Romania	354	177	177	535	7,571	3,078	+88
Russian Federation	9,344	4,581	4,763	5,332	8,450	44,688	+2,312
Rwanda	77	1	76	1	1	..	..
Saint Vincent and the Grenadines (b)	..	..	..	..	..	2	0
Samoa	48	5	43	12	12	..	..
San Marino	109	3	106	29	81	..	..
Sao Tome and Principe (b)	..	..	..	..	..	640	+58
Saudi Arabia	1,112	576	536	611	637	5,786	+948
Senegal (b,c)	n.a.	n.a.	n.a.	6	86	..	..
Serbia	794	81	713	199	563	5,381	–89
Seychelles (b)	..	..	..	161	1,175	21	0
Singapore	3,597	354	3,243	1,752	7,966	11,928	–1,310
Slovakia	297	198	99	381	3,163	1,008	+3
Slovenia	331	22	309	451	4,771	430	+13
South Africa	1,594	699	895	860	1,562	18,361	–2,878
Spain	10,794	10,597	197	15,577	97,219	33,174	+837
Sri Lanka	96	74	22	86	112	1,292	–175
Sudan (b)	..	..	..	1	1	..	..
Suriname (b)	..	..	..	..	..	..	..
Sweden	276	265	11	5,007	39,577	2,826	–276
Switzerland	11,666	2,863	8,803	21,824	122,630	9,429	–116
Syrian Arab Republic	225	171	54	175	175	904	+237
Tajikistan	119	0	119	..	..	..	..
Thailand	2,314	1,439	875	1,557	1,583	..	..

Name	Registration design count by office			Registration design count by origin	Equivalent registration design count by origin	In force by office	
	Total	Resident	Non-resident	Total (a)	Total (a)	Total	Change over previous year
Tonga	5	0	5	..	..	..	..
Trinidad and Tobago	50	42	8	42	42	110	+34
Tunisia (b)	..	..	..	23	23	..	..
Türkiye	64,023	58,409	5,614	60,565	76,089	164,027	+13,558
Turkmenistan (b)	..	..	..	2	2	..	..
Uganda	17	17	0	19	19	179	+17
Ukraine	3,456	1,463	1,993	1,654	2,488	13,730	+104
United Arab Emirates	942	45	897	179	387	4,907	+490
United Kingdom	70,974	27,118	43,856	35,013	123,565	249,391	+60,120
United Republic of Tanzania (b)	..	..	..	1	2	..	..
United States of America	39,121	14,601	24,520	60,582	350,200	389,540	+7,991
Uruguay (b)	..	..	..	22	48	..	..
Uzbekistan	167	150	17	152	152	379	–188
Vanuatu	6	6	0	6	6	..	..
Viet Nam	2,782	1,124	1,658	1,342	1,524	13,711	–356
Yemen	24	23	1	23	23	122	+1
Zambia	21	21	0	28	35	744	+7
Zimbabwe	3	3	0	5	7	125	..
Others/Unknown	..	..	..	16,368	375,662	..	..
Total (2022 estimates)	**1,320,100**	**1,076,500**	**243,600**	**1,320,100**		**5,774,900**	

(a) Design count by origin data are incomplete, because some offices do not report the origin of registrations.
(b) Only Hague designation data are available and/or the office has not reported the origin of registrations therefore design count by office and origin data may be incomplete.
(c) The African Intellectual Property Organization (OAPI) is the competent office for registering applications.
(d) The Benelux Office for Intellectual Property is the competent office for processing applications.
n.a. indicates not applicable.
.. indicates not available.
Source: WIPO Statistics Database, August 2023.

C39. Industrial design office procedural data, 2022

Office	Total applications processed	Registered	Rejected	Withdrawn or abandoned	Applications pending	Number of examiners (FTE)	First office action from filing date (days)	Final office decision from filing date (days)
Albania	..	5	..	..	14	1.0	30.0	180.0
Algeria	..	248	226	..	219	2.0	180.0	180.0
Angola	..	..	..	..	..	5.0	180.0	720.0
Antigua and Barbuda	..	..	..	..	1	2.0	..	..
Argentina	2,287	1,951	313	23	1	4.0	2.0	3.0
Armenia	..	43	..	5	14	1.0	10.0	171.3
Australia (a)	..	7,595	..	322	974	15.0	31.5	56.0
Austria	320	315	3	2	10	3.0	12.0	59.0
Azerbaijan	15	5	1	9	16	2.0	90.0	180.0
Bangladesh	1,267	1,197	10	60	959	2.0	90.0	270.0
Belarus	..	171	15	..	38	1.0	35.0	55.0
Belize	..	..	..	..	..	1.0	..	..
Bhutan	..	3	..	..	7	1.0	1.0	360.0
Bolivia (Plurinational State of)	..	..	..	..	64	2.0	..	..
Bosnia and Herzegovina	..	19	2	..	5	1.0	1.0	120.0
Botswana	..	..	1	..	4	4.0	3.0	30.0
Brazil	6,991	6,052	53	886	1,696	8.5	51.3	117.4
Brunei Darussalam	..	2	..	..	5	..	14.0	91.0
Cabo Verde	..	..	..	..	15	4.0	..	..
Cambodia	..	83	1	..	11	2.0	60.0	180.0
Canada	6,323	6,008	7	308	7,167	18.0	460.0	578.0
China	795,457	720,907	19,967	54,583	..	..	..	75.0
China, Hong Kong SAR	3,394	3,319	2	73	276	2.0	36.3	60.7

Office	Total applications processed	Registered	Rejected	Withdrawn or abandoned	Applications pending	Number of examiners (FTE)	First office action from filing date (days)	Final office decision from filing date (days)
China, Macao SAR	..	262	9	..	287	1.0	22.8	22.8
Colombia	637	479	107	51	478	1.0	..	169.0
Croatia	123	100	19	4	20	2.0	14.0	82.0
Cyprus	..	16	..	..	..	1.0	25.0	40.0
Czech Republic	295	209	48	38	71	3.0	..	321.0
Denmark	67	59	2	6	16	3.0	1.0	61.0
Djibouti	..	..	..	..	..	2.0	..	..
Dominica	..	..	..	..	..	1.0	..	..
Ecuador	171	144	8	19	43	1.0	30.0	180.0
El Salvador	..	..	..	..	..	1.0	5.0	180.0
Estonia	..	45	..	5	3	1.0	7.5	47.5
Ethiopia	..	29	4	..	37	1.0	60.0	90.0
Finland	..	58	..	9	16	0.1	41.0	63.0
France	5,817	5,580	177	60	442	6.5	147.0	147.0
Gambia	..	..	..	..	6	2.0	..	..
Georgia	38	29	1	8	4	2.0	100.0	195.0
Germany	4,837	4,213	162	462	1,166	11.2	..	126.0
Ghana	..	..	..	..	10	3.0	..	..
Guatemala	..	4	..	..	367	1.0	30.0	1,825.0
Honduras	..	18	1	..	..	1.0	5.0	15.0
Hungary	103	52	3	48	44	2.0	5.0	254.0
Iceland	..	63	..	..	..	0.2	4.0	25.0
India	20,379	19,939	199	241	14,992	14.0	45.0	180.0
Indonesia	2,867	1,897	548	422	..	..	..	..
Iran (Islamic Republic of)	8,212	785	6,161	1,266	..	12.0	11.0	19.0
Israel	..	1,380	338	..	1,087	4.0	188.0	226.0
Italy	1,018	1,011	1	6	..	3.0	30.0	60.0
Jamaica	145	113	30	2	..	2.0	15.0	60.0
Japan	..	29,540	..	..	..	50.0	..	..
Jordan	..	55	36	..	36	1.0	15.0	275.0
Kazakhstan	165	150	6	9	86	3.0	210.0	210.0
Kenya	..	..	..	..	..	4.0	..	..
Kuwait	..	635	45	..	..	8.0	1.0	3.0
Kyrgyzstan	..	..	..	..	..	7.0	60.0	180.0
Lao People's Democratic Republic	..	73	1	..	4	3.0	60.0	180.0
Latvia	..	23	..	5	28	1.0	3.0	10.0
Lebanon	..	..	..	..	..	1.0	..	..
Lithuania	..	21	..	3	4	2.0	7.0	63.0
Madagascar	..	295	57	..	4	3.0	210.0	210.0
Mexico	3,930	2,921	50	959	4,026	8.0	437.0	632.0
Monaco	..	8	..	1	..	2.0	17.0	40.0
Mongolia	..	177	37	..	154	2.0	144.0	216.0
Montenegro	..	7	..	..	3	1.0	30.0	240.0
Mozambique	..	..	..	..	..	3.0	..	..
Namibia	..	..	..	..	..	1.0	..	..
New Zealand	..	1,448	..	146	626	1.0	12.9	79.2
Nigeria	..	1,181	5	..	27	2.0	7.0	3.0
North Macedonia	..	24	..	..	..	1.0	4.0	180.0
Norway	..	325	..	35	74	1.5	75.0	..
Pakistan	..	243	..	..	..	1.0	15.0	180.0
Papua New Guinea	..	..	..	..	25	2.0	..	..
Paraguay	..	..	..	..	10	1.0	..	..
Peru	..	366	17	..	246	7.0	275.0	275.0
Philippines	..	934	..	245	375	5.0	46.5	175.2
Poland	807	663	31	113	222	3.0	..	41.4
Portugal	205	190	8	7	8	4.0	10.0	100.0
Republic of Korea	63,940	54,775	7,743	1,422	20,538	42.0	144.0	180.0
Republic of Moldova	52	39	11	2	58	3.0	4.0	240.0
Romania	172	138	22	12	85	3.0	2.9	173.0
Russian Federation	6,583	5,854	180	549	3,693	54.0	106.0	114.0
Rwanda	..	..	..	..	..	2.0	..	..

Office	Total applications processed	Registered	Rejected	Withdrawn or abandoned	Applications pending	Number of examiners (FTE)	First office action from filing date (days)	Final office decision from filing date (days)
Saint Vincent and the Grenadines	..	..	..	..	..	2.0	..	..
Samoa	..	..	..	..	..	4.0	..	..
Sao Tome and Principe	..	..	..	..	..	1.0	..	..
Saudi Arabia	..	1,112	314	..	..	11.0	1.0	56.0
Serbia	111	74	4	33	30	1.0	30.0	150.0
Seychelles	..	..	..	..	..	2.0	2.0	5.0
Singapore	1,333	1,302	4	27	104	..	..	..
Slovakia	98	85	4	9	13	2.0	1.0	180.0
Slovenia	..	..	..	..	6	0.5	..	..
Spain	1,865	1,723	57	85	7,651	8.0	16.0	17.0
Sri Lanka	754	96	56	602	76	2.0	7.0	60.0
Sweden	221	171	45	5	43	2.0	91.0	255.0
Switzerland	634	614	6	14	16	2.5	1.0	14.0
Syrian Arab Republic	..	..	..	..	18	2.0	..	..
Thailand	3,857	2,314	329	1,214	6,560	25.0	460.0	915.0
Tonga	..	..	..	..	1	1.0	..	..
Trinidad and Tobago	..	..	..	..	43	7.0	..	..
Tunisia	..	145	..	2	..	1.0	..	90.0
Türkiye	15,475	13,775	1,557	143	1,664	13.0	45.0	45.0
Uganda	..	..	..	..	25	2.0	..	..
Ukraine	..	739	..	126	652	4.0	..	148.0
United Arab Emirates	717	713	3	1	1,316	8.0	242.0	242.0
United Kingdom	59,556	56,434	2,889	233	2,098	26.0	14.0	44.0
United States of America	55,441	32,227	13,154	10,060	75,587	230.0	492.9	577.5
Uzbekistan	236	159	28	49	79	2.0	65.0	190.0
Vanuatu	..	..	..	..	2	1.0	..	..
Viet Nam	2,752	1,819	866	67	1,794	12.0	480.0	580.0
Zimbabwe	..	..	..	..	14	1.0	..	..

Note: FTE is full time equivalent. WIPO collects data from offices using a common questionnaire and methodology. Every effort has been made to compile procedural data based on common definitions and concepts, but procedural differences make it extremely difficult to fully harmonize such data. Therefore, caution should be exercised when making comparisons across offices. The total number of applications processed for any given office may be incomplete due to the omission of one or several elements by the office.
(a) data are for formalities examinations only.
.. indicates not available.
Source: WIPO Statistics Database, August 2023.

Plant varieties

Highlights

Plant variety applications sustain their strong growth

Around 27,260 plant variety applications were filed worldwide in 2022, up 8.2% on 2021 – a seventh consecutive year of growth (figure 4.1). China contributed the majority of global growth, followed by the United Kingdom (UK).

Applications grew by 8.2% in 2022

4.1. Plant variety applications worldwide, 2008–2022

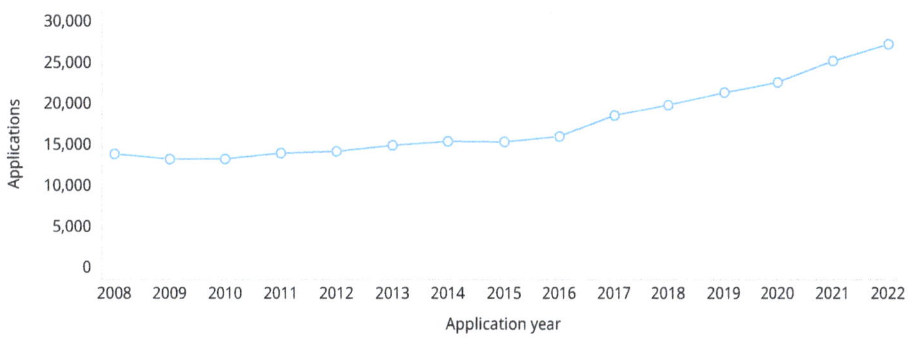

Source: Figure D1.

China received 47.8% of all plant variety applications filed worldwide

China remained the top destination in 2022, receiving 13,027 plant variety applications. China accounts for over two-fifths of the plant varieties filed worldwide. The Community Plant Variety Office of the European Union (CPVO) received 3,193 applications, accounting for 11.7% of global filings. Following the CPVO were the UK (1,702), the United States of America (US) (1,375) and the Russian Federation (865) (figure 4.2). Filings in China grew sizably for a ninth straight year, increasing by 16.4% on 2021, driven almost entirely by resident filings (figure D6). Among top 10 offices, the UK experienced significant growth (+316.1%), as did the Russian Federation (+28.7%). The UK's sizeable increase in filings was partially due to pending CPVO applications prior to December 2020 opting to extend their application request to the UK, which were processed in 2022. Russia's increase in filings marked a return to trend after a steep decline in 2021.

Seven of the top 10 offices underwent a decline in applications in 2022. The CPVO declined by 8.2%, with applicants from the US, Netherlands and Italy being the primary reason for this drop. Similarly, the US recorded a 27.7% decline, driven by a decrease in applications from residents. Ukraine saw a decline of 16.2%, primarily from non-resident filers. The Kingdom of the Netherlands (–18.2%), Japan (–12%), the

Republic of Korea (–10.9%) and Argentina (–9.6%) were the other top 10 offices to see a decrease in applications in 2022.

In 2022, the combined share of applications received at the top five jurisdictions worldwide grew by 1.6 percentage points to 74.0%, owing to a big increase in filings at China and UK offices.

Nine of the top 10 jurisdictions received more applications from residents than from non-residents. China's resident share (94.7%) was the highest among top 10 offices. Ukraine was the only office in the top 10 to receive more applications from non-residents than from residents, with 62.4% of applications originating from abroad.

China continues to be the top destination for plant variety applications

4.2. Plant variety applications for the top 10 offices, 2022

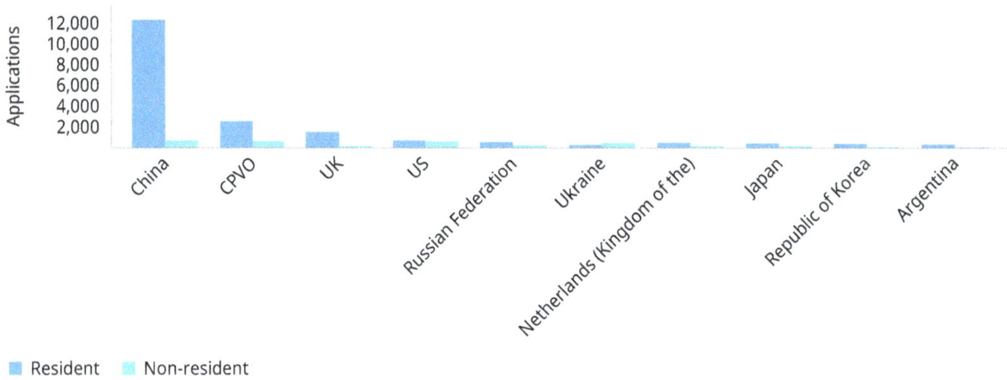

Note: CPVO is the Community Plant Variety Office of the European Union.
Source: Figure D5.

Asia is the top region, with 54.6% of all applications

4.3. Plant variety applications by region, 2012 and 2022

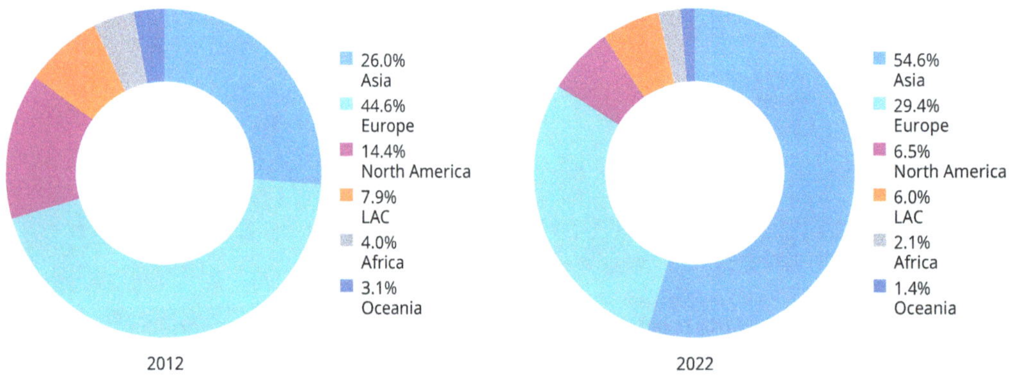

Note: LAC is Latin America and the Caribbean.
Source: Figure D3.

Asia was the region that received the most filings, representing 54.6% of all plant variety applications in 2022. Filings in Asia have more than quadrupled since 2012, equating to a more than doubling of the region's global share from 26.0% in 2012 (figure 4.3). Europe was the second largest region in terms of total plant filings, accounting for roughly 29% of the world total in 2022. That said, the surge in filings within Asia witnessed during this period has caused Europe's collective share to decline from the 44.6% of total filings it accounted for back in 2012. In addition to Asia (+15.0%), Latin America and the Caribbean (+3.9%) and Europe (+2.4%) have both experienced positive average annual growth over the 10 years from 2012 to 2022. In contrast, three regions have undergone a modest decline over the same period, namely, Africa (–0.1%), Oceania (–1.1%), and North America (–1.4%) all displaying a negative average annual growth rate.

China-based applicants were the most active filers worldwide

Applications received by offices from resident and non-resident applicants are referred to as office data, whereas applications filed by applicants at a national or regional office (resident applications) or at a foreign office (applications abroad) are referred to as origin data. Here, plant variety statistics based on the origin of residence are reported in order to complement the global picture. Note that for applicants domiciled within European Union (EU) member states, filing at the CPVO regional office is regarded as a resident filing.

Applicants based in China were the most active in the world in 2022, filing 12,357 plant variety applications (figure 4.4). This represents growth of 16.9% on the previous year, driven by resident filings. China-based applicants were followed by applicants from the Kingdom of the Netherlands, who submitted 2,874 applications, 10.6% fewer than the year before. Applicants from the US (2,120), the UK (1,657) and France (1,167) were the next three largest origins, respectively.

Half of the top 10 origins experienced strong positive growth compared to the previous year. In addition to China, the UK (+377.5%), France (+9.9%), Switzerland (+21.9%), and the Russian Federation (+23.1%) registered a significant increase in their application filings. In the case of the UK, this surge was predominantly fueled by applications within its jurisdiction, whereas Switzerland-based applicants achieved strong growth through an expansion in filings abroad. Conversely, applicants based in the Russian Federation grew their filings exclusively through domestic applications. Collectively, the top five origin countries represented 74% of total plant variety filings worldwide in 2022, with China (45.3% of the total) and the Kingdom of the Netherlands (10.5%) contributing the majority.

Whereas applicants from four of the top five origins filed most applications either abroad or at a regional office, applicants from China filed almost exclusively at home. Like China, applicants from Japan, the Republic of Korea, the Russian Federation and Argentina also filed predominantly at home.

Applicants from China filed primarily at their home office

4.4. Plant variety applications for the top 10 origins, 2022

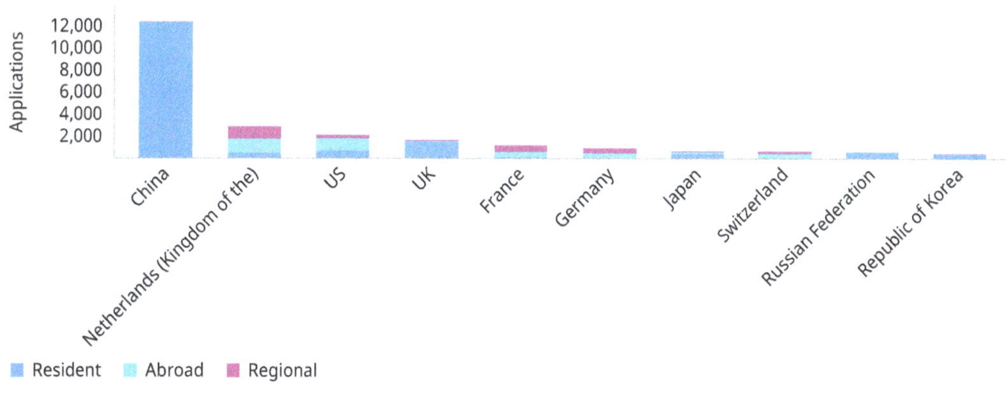

Source: Figure D11.

Equivalent count

Origin data are compiled using two different counting methods – absolute counts and equivalent counts. The difference between the two lies in the treatment of regional office data (the CPVO and the African Intellectual Property Organization (OAPI)). For absolute counts, an application received by a regional office is counted only once. For the equivalent count, a single application filed at a regional office is equivalent to multiple applications. To calculate the number of equivalent applications at a regional office in 2022, each application has been multiplied by the corresponding number of member states of the regional office. For CPVO applications, if the applicant resided in one of the 27 EU member states, the application was counted as one resident filing and 26 filings abroad. If the applicant did not reside in an EU member state, the application was counted as 27 filings abroad. The same methodology was applied to OAPI member states.

Equivalent counts take multiple members of the regional office into account. One would expect to see those country origins whose applicants filed intensively at the CPVO move up the ranking when this counting method is applied (figure D12). It is not therefore surprising that European countries topped the list of origins based on an equivalent count. Applicants from the Kingdom of the Netherlands once again ranked first, with 31,240 equivalent applications filed worldwide. They were followed by applicants from France (15,125). China-based applicants emerged as the number three origin when using an equivalent count, with 12,546. China-based applicants moved ahead of those in Germany (11,684) and the US (9,750), both of whom experiencing a year-over-year decline. China was placed among the top five origins by equivalent count, despite only 1.7% of its applicants' filings being equivalent filings abroad. This is in marked contrast to the Kingdom of the Netherlands, for which the abroad share was 94.9%.

Plant variety titles issued decreased by 1.4% in 2022

4.5. Plant variety titles issued worldwide, 2008–2022

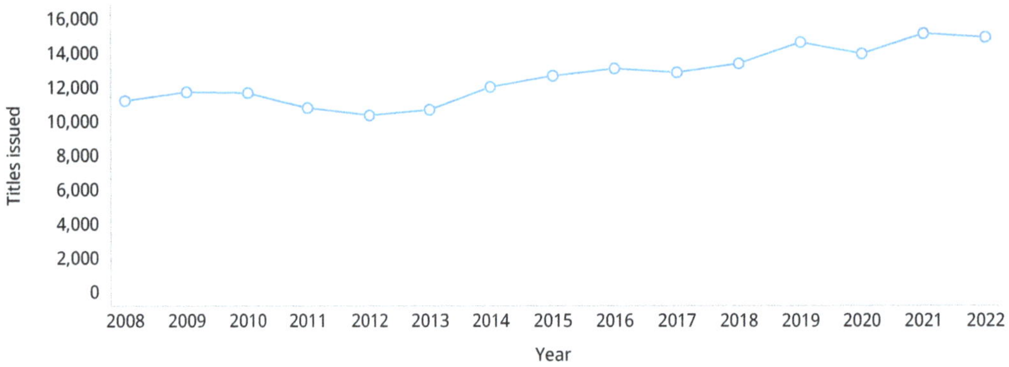

Source: Figure D2.

The number of titles issued declined slightly in 2022

The total number of plant variety titles issued decreased by 1.4% in 2022. The 14,920 plant variety titles issued in 2022 is lower than last year's total, but still represents the second highest number of titles issued in a single year (figure 4.5). China issued the most titles, with 4,026, up 1.2% on the previous year. China was followed by the CPVO (2,964), the US (1,544), Ukraine (956) and Japan (672) (figure D9). Similarly to China, the CPVO also experienced a moderate increase in titles issued, growing 3.9%. Japan experienced some of the strongest year-on-year growth, with +13.9%. In contrast, the US (-4%) and the Ukraine (-17.7%) experienced a decline in titles issued compared to 2021.

Note that the grant or registration process takes time, so fluctuations in the volume of plant variety titles granted may be a consequence of changes in processing capacity or procedural delay.

Steady growth in plant varieties in force continues

Around 161,210 plant variety titles were in force at the end of 2022, up 4.5% on 2021 (figure D16). The CPVO (30,562), the US (28,442) and China (23,585) had the highest number of active titles (figure D17). Other offices maintaining at least 5,000 active titles included Ukraine (11,880), the Kingdom of the Netherlands (9,742), Japan (7,599) the Russian Federation (6,592) and the Republic of Korea (6,238).

Plant variety statistics

Plant variety applications and titles issued worldwide **150**
D1. Trend in plant variety applications worldwide, 2008–2022 150
D2. Trend in plant variety titles issued worldwide, 2008–2022 150

Plant variety applications and titles issued by office **150**
D3. Plant variety applications by region, 2012 and 2022 150
D4. Trend in plant variety applications for the top five offices, 2000–2022 151
D5. Plant variety applications for the top 20 offices, 2022 151
D6. Contribution of resident and non-resident applications to total growth for the top 20 offices, 2021–2022 151
D7. Plant variety applications for offices of selected low- and middle-income countries, 2022 152
D8. Flow of non-resident applications for the top offices, 2022 153
D9. Plant variety titles issued by the top 20 offices, 2022 154
D10. Trend in plant variety titles issued for the top five offices, 2000–2022 154

Plant variety applications and titles issued by origin **154**
D11. Plant variety applications for the top 20 origins, 2022 154
D12. Plant variety equivalent applications for the top 20 origins, 2022 155
D13. Plant variety applications abroad for the top 20 origins, 2022 155
D14. Plant variety titles issued for the top 20 origins, 2022 155
D15. Plant variety titles issued abroad for the top 20 origins, 2022 156

Plant varieties in force **156**
D16. Trend in plant varieties in force worldwide, 2008–2022 156
D17. Plant varieties in force at selected offices, 2022 156

Statistical table **157**
D18. Plant variety applications and titles issued by office and origin, and plant variety titles in force by office, 2022 157

Plant variety applications and titles issued worldwide

D1. Trend in plant variety applications worldwide, 2008–2022

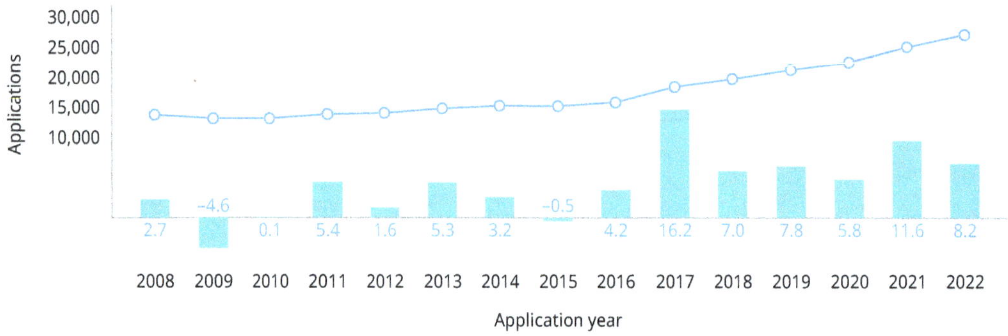

Note: World totals are WIPO estimates using data covering 72 offices.
Source: WIPO Statistics Database, September 2023.

D2. Trend in plant variety titles issued worldwide, 2008–2022

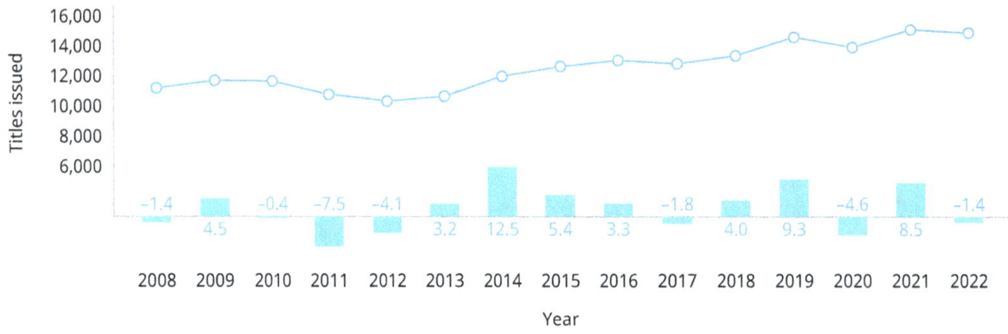

Note: World totals are WIPO estimates using data covering 72 offices.
Source: WIPO Statistics Database, September 2023.

Plant variety applications and titles issued by office

D3. Plant variety applications by region, 2012 and 2022

Region	Number of applications		Resident share (%)		Share of world total (%)		Average growth (%)
	2012	2022	2012	2022	2012	2022	2012-2022
Africa	571	564	42.0	17.9	4.0	2.1	-0.1
Asia	3,672	14,883	80.1	91.4	26.0	54.6	15.0
Europe	6,310	8,026	67.8	75.1	44.6	29.4	2.4
Latin America and the Caribbean	1,117	1,633	46.5	47.2	7.9	6.0	3.9
North America	2,034	1,765	43.2	45.8	14.4	6.5	-1.4
Oceania	436	389	42.4	38.0	3.1	1.4	-1.1
World	**14,140**	**27,260**	**63.9**	**78.7**	**100.0**	**100.0**	**6.8**

Note: Totals by geographic region are WIPO estimates using data covering 72 offices. Each region includes the following number of offices: Africa (7), Asia (12), Europe (34), Latin America and the Caribbean (14), North America (3) and Oceania (2).
Source: WIPO Statistics Database, September 2023.

D4. Trend in plant variety applications for the top five offices, 2000–2022

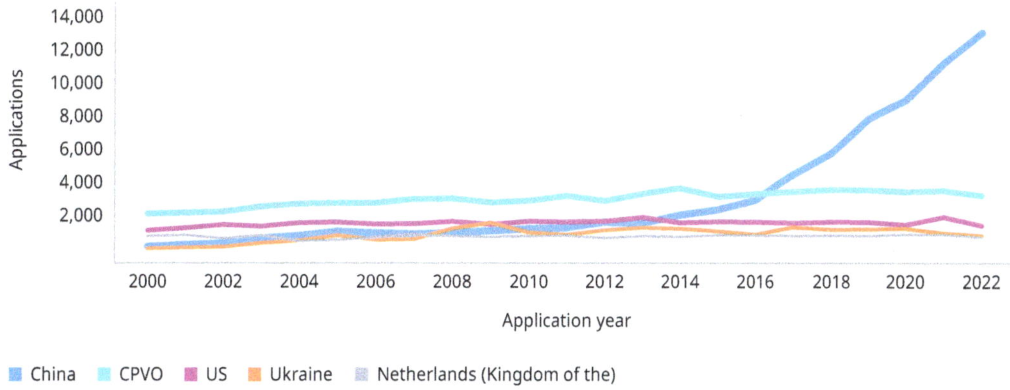

Note: CPVO is the Community Plant Variety Office of the European Union. The top five offices were selected based on their 2022 totals.
Source: WIPO Statistics Database, September 2023.

D5. Plant variety applications for the top 20 offices, 2022

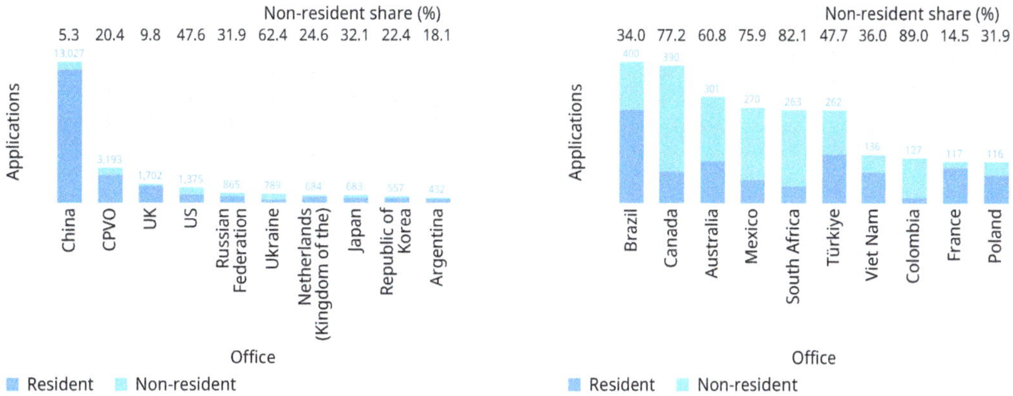

Note: CPVO is the Community Plant Variety Office of the European Union. In general, the national offices of CPVO member states receive lower volumes of applications, because applicants may choose to apply via the CPVO when seeking protection within any CPVO member state.
Source: WIPO Statistics Database, September 2023.

D6. Contribution of resident and non-resident applications to total growth for the top 20 offices, 2021–2022

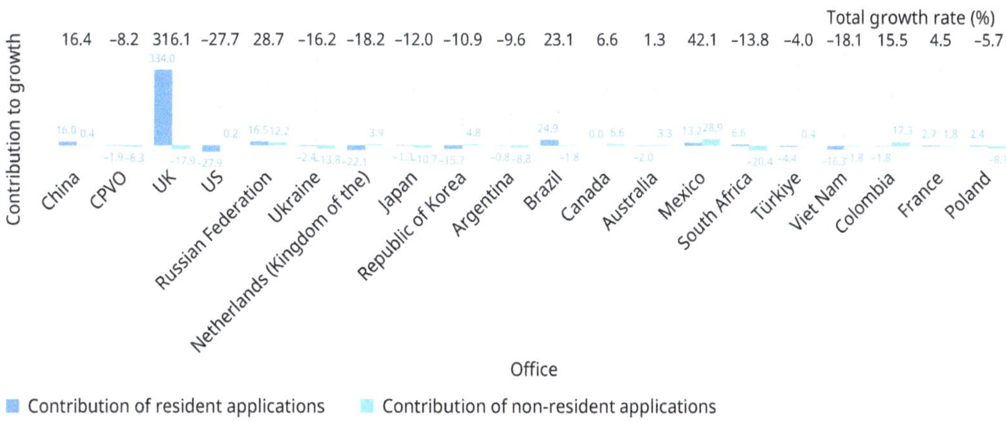

Note: CPVO is the Community Plant Variety Office of the European Union. This figure shows total growth in plant variety applications broken down by the respective contributions of resident and non-resident filings. For example, applications in Brazil grew by +23.1%, with resident applications contributing 24.9 percentage points to total growth and non-resident applications accounting for the other –1.8 percentage points.
Source: WIPO Statistics Database, September 2023.

D7. Plant variety applications for offices of selected low- and middle-income countries, 2022

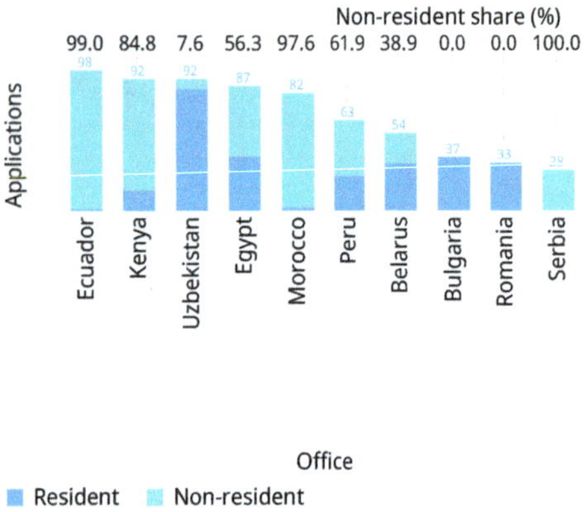

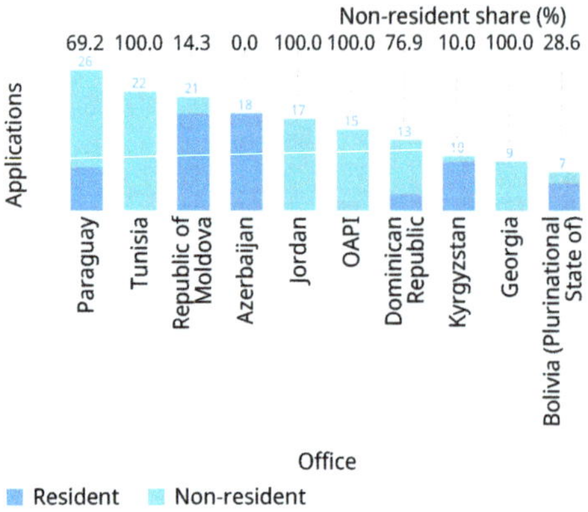

Note: OAPI is the African Intellectual Property Organization. The selected offices are from different world regions and income groups. Where available, data for all offices can be found in the statistical table at the end of this section.
Source: WIPO Statistics Database, September 2023.

D8. Flow of non-resident applications for the top offices, 2022

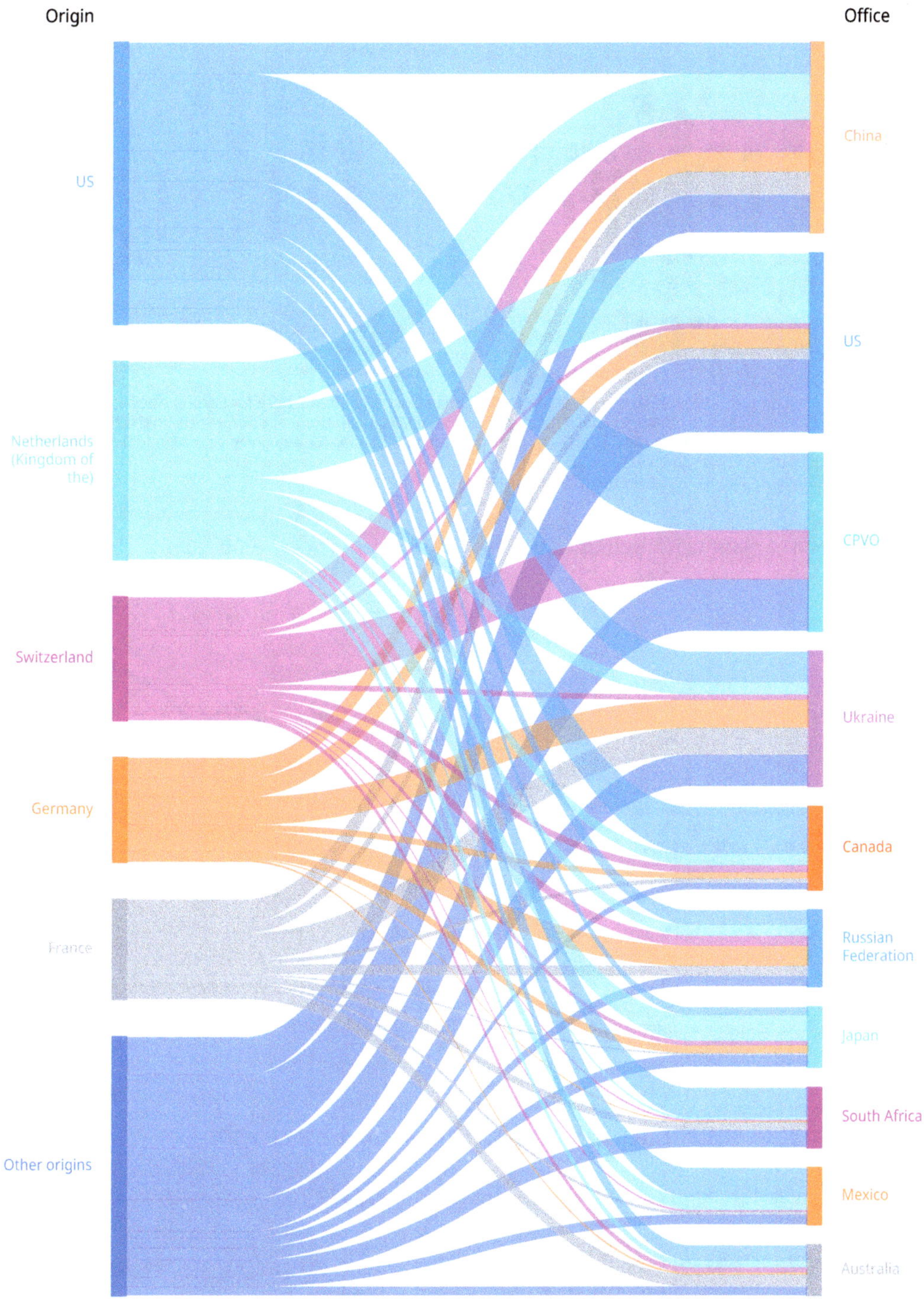

Note: CPVO is the Community Plant Variety Office of the European Union.
Source: WIPO Statistics Database, September 2023.

D9. Plant variety titles issued by the top 20 offices, 2022

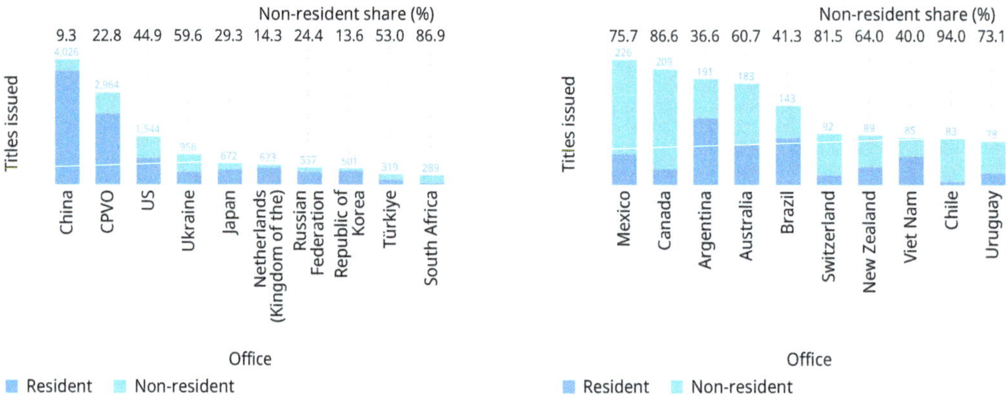

Note: CPVO is the Community Plant Variety Office of the European Union. The procedure for issuing titles varies across offices, and factors such as examination capacity and procedural delays mean there are differences in the time lag between application and title issue dates. For this reason, data on applications for any given year should not be compared with data on titles issued that same year.
Source: WIPO Statistics Database, September 2023.

D10. Trend in plant variety titles issued for the top five offices, 2000–2022

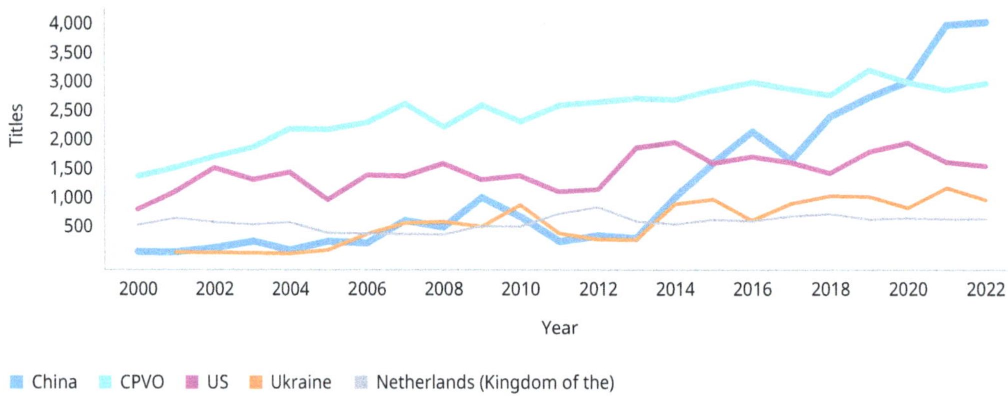

Note: CPVO is the Community Plant Variety Office of the European Union. The top five offices were selected based on their 2022 totals.
Source: WIPO Statistics Database, September 2023.

Plant variety applications and titles issued by origin

D11. Plant variety applications for the top 20 origins, 2022

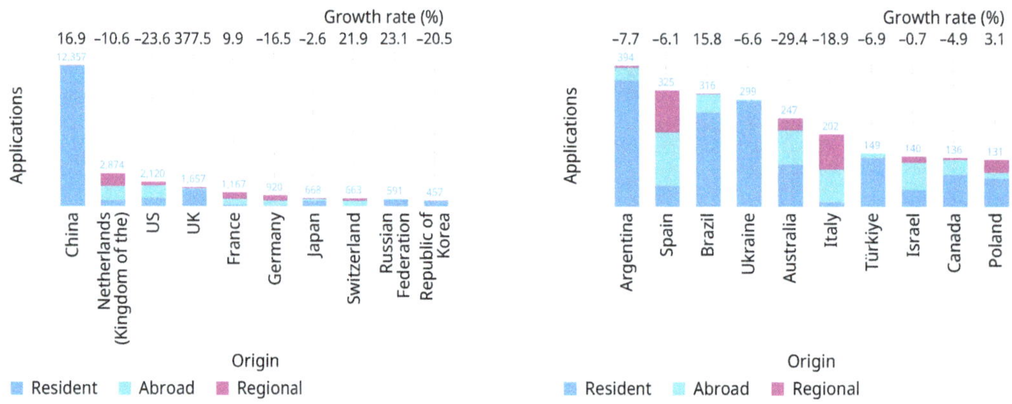

Note: Data are based on absolute count, not equivalent count. Applications by origin include resident applications and applications filed abroad. The origin of an application is determined by the residence of the applicant. Regional refers to applications filed at the Community Plant Variety Office of the European Union.
Source: WIPO Statistics Database, September 2023.

D12. Plant variety equivalent applications for the top 20 origins, 2022

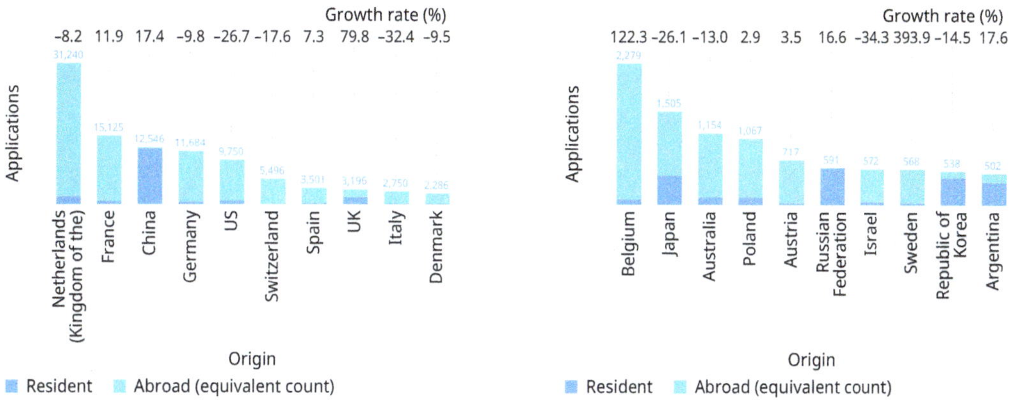

Note: Data are based on equivalent count (see glossary for the definition of equivalent applications). Applications by origin include resident applications and applications filed abroad. The origin of an application is determined by the residence of the applicant.
Source: WIPO Statistics Database, September 2023.

D13. Plant variety applications abroad for the top 20 origins, 2022

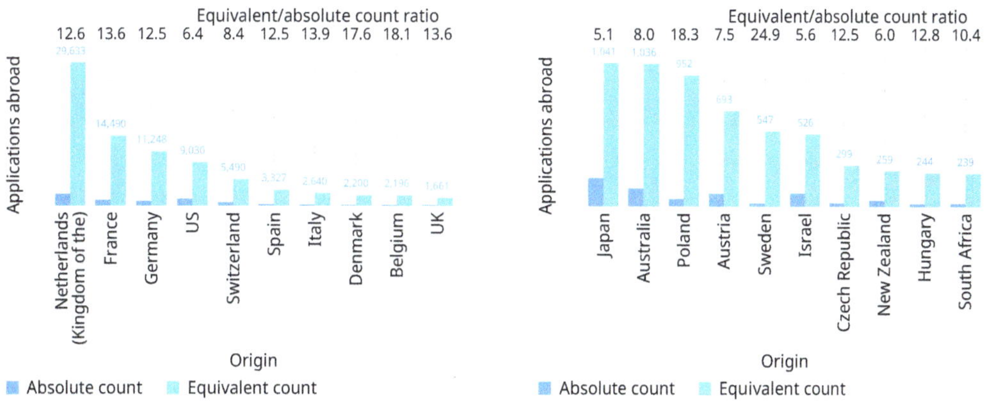

Note: The origin of an application is determined by the residence of the applicant. Applications filed at regional offices are considered equivalent to multiple applications in the relevant member states. See glossary for the definition of equivalent applications.
Source: WIPO Statistics Database, September 2023.

D14. Plant variety titles issued for the top 20 origins, 2022

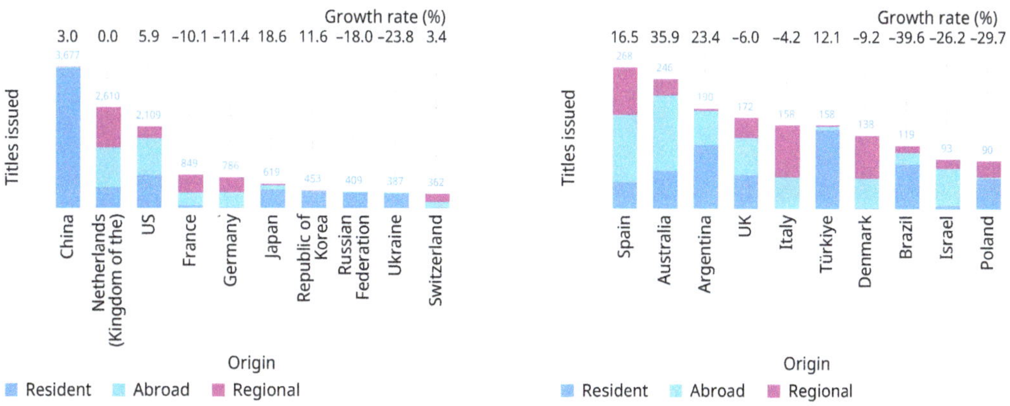

Note: Data are based on an absolute count not an equivalent count. The origin of titles issued is determined by the residence of the applicant. Regional refers to titles issued by the Community Plant Variety Office of the European Union.
Source: WIPO Statistics Database, September 2023.

D15. Plant variety titles issued abroad for the top 20 origins, 2022

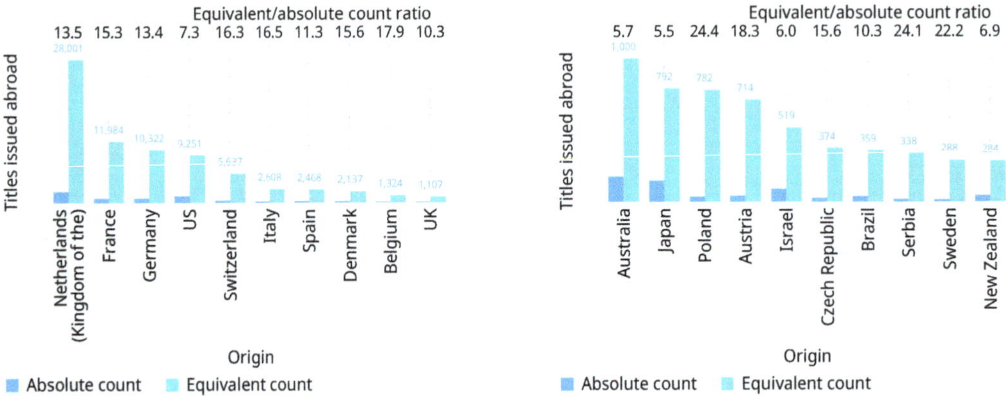

Note: The origin of titles issued is determined by the residence of the applicant. Titles issued by regional offices are considered equivalent to multiple titles in the relevant member states. See glossary for the definition of equivalent count.
Source: WIPO Statistics Database, September 2023.

Plant varieties in force

D16. Trend in plant varieties in force worldwide, 2008–2022

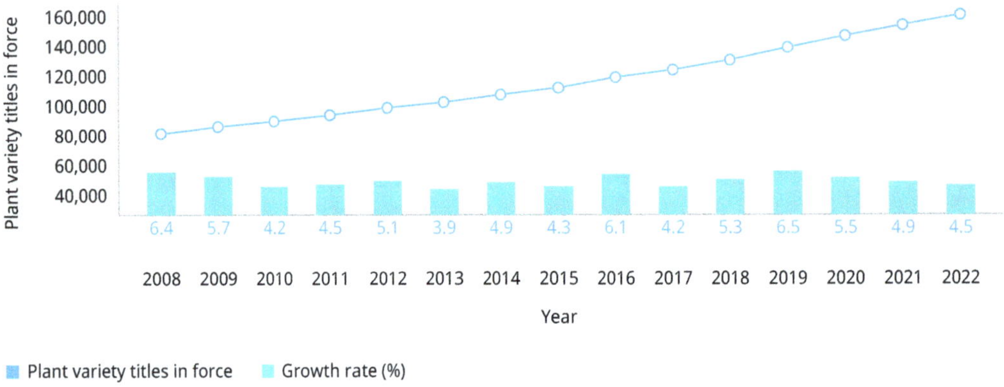

Note: World totals are WIPO estimates using data covering 70 offices.
Source: WIPO Statistics Database, September 2023.

D17. Plant varieties in force at selected offices, 2022

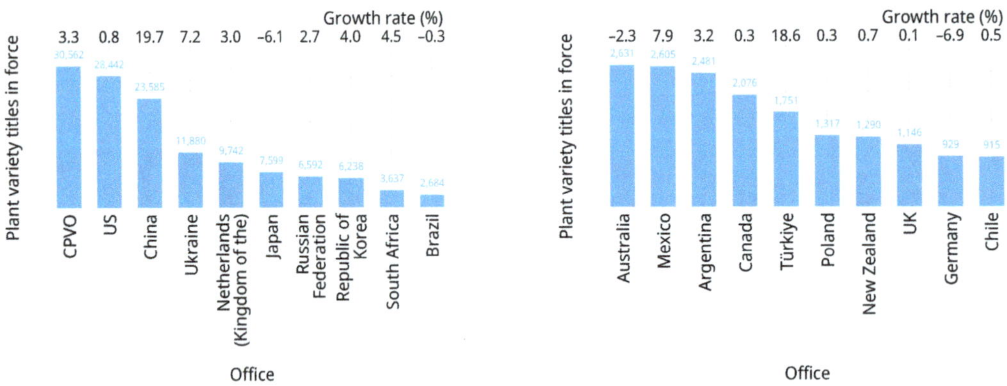

Note: CPVO is the Community Plant Variety Office of the European Union.
Source: WIPO Statistics Database, September 2023.

Statistical table

D18. Plant variety applications and titles issued by office and origin, and plant variety titles in force by office, 2022

	Applications by office			Applications by origin	Equivalent applications by origin	Titles issued by office			Plant varieties in force
Name	Total	Resident	Non-resident	Total	Total	Total	Resident	Non-resident	Office
African Intellectual Property Organization	15	0	15	..	..	2	1	1	7
Argentina	432	354	78	394	502	191	121	70	2,481
Australia	301	118	183	247	1,154	183	72	111	2,631
Austria (a)	..	..	..	93	717	..	..	..	15
Azerbaijan	18	18	0	18	18	18	18	0	247
Belarus	54	33	21	45	45	42	28	14	270
Belgium (a)	..	..	..	121	2,279	3	3	0	36
Bolivia (Plurinational State of)	7	5	2	5	5	7	5	2	67
Bosnia and Herzegovina	3	3	0	3	3	..	..	..	..
Brazil	400	264	136	316	343	143	84	59	2,684
Bulgaria	37	37	0	39	91	18	18	0	288
Canada	390	89	301	136	244	209	28	181	2,076
Chile	111	15	96	19	19	83	5	78	915
China	13,027	12,333	694	12,357	12,546	4,026	3,651	375	23,585
Colombia	127	14	113	21	21	74	16	58	770
Community Plant Variety Office	3,193	2,543	650	n.a.	..	2,964	2,288	676	30,562
Costa Rica	7	0	7	1	1	6	0	6	26
Croatia (a)	..	..	..	1	1	..	..	..	67
Czech Republic	59	56	3	80	366	43	37	6	804
Denmark	6	3	3	128	2,286	7	1	6	44
Dominican Republic	13	3	10	3	3	17	5	12	35
Ecuador	98	1	97	6	6	19	1	18	403
Egypt	87	38	49	38	38	46	8	38	496
Estonia	5	2	3	3	29	6	1	5	94
Finland	5	5	0	5	5	8	5	3	211
France	117	100	17	1,167	15,125	70	65	5	905
Georgia	9	0	9	..	..	10	0	10	217
Germany	27	22	5	920	11,684	22	14	8	929
Greece (b)	..	..	..	3	81	..	..	..	..
Honduras (b)	..	..	..	1	1	..	..	..	..
Hungary	30	30	0	49	283	14	13	1	200
India (b)	..	..	..	3	57	..	..	..	..
Ireland	10	10	0	25	207	5	5	0	54
Israel	74	46	28	140	572	15	6	9	774
Italy	16	12	4	202	2,750	..	..	..	41
Jamaica (b)	..	..	..	1	1	..	..	..	..
Japan	683	464	219	668	1,505	672	475	197	7,599
Jordan	17	0	17	..	..	17	0	17	76
Kazakhstan (b)	..	..	..	2	2	..	..	..	..
Kenya	92	14	78	14	14	32	0	32	518
Kyrgyzstan	10	9	1	9	9	..	..	..	9
Lao People's Democratic Republic (b)	..	..	..	3	3	..	..	..	..
Latvia	7	7	0	8	34	1	1	0	187
Lithuania	4	4	0	4	4	4	4	0	130
Mauritius (b)	..	..	..	6	6	..	..	..	..
Mexico	270	65	205	74	155	226	55	171	2,605
Morocco	82	2	80	4	4	56	0	56	669
Netherlands (Kingdom of the)	684	516	168	2,874	31,240	623	534	89	9,742
New Zealand	88	30	58	73	289	89	32	57	1,290
Nicaragua	4	4	0	4	4	3	3	0	20
Norway	15	0	15	..	..	19	0	19	227
Panama (a)	..	..	..	..	..	6	1	5	25
Paraguay	26	8	18	10	10	23	7	16	223
Peru	63	24	39	25	25	62	18	44	369

Name	Applications by office Total	Resident	Non-resident	Applications by origin Total	Equivalent applications by origin Total	Titles issued by office Total	Resident	Non-resident	Plant varieties in force Office
Poland	116	79	37	131	1,067	65	58	7	1,317
Portugal	1	0	1	2	54	..	..	..	9
Republic of Korea	557	432	125	457	538	501	433	68	6,238
Republic of Moldova	21	18	3	18	18	14	7	7	293
Romania	33	33	0	45	45	41	41	0	510
Russian Federation	865	589	276	591	591	537	406	131	6,592
Saudi Arabia (b)	..	..	..	2	2	..	..	..	..
Serbia	28	0	28	14	14	44	0	44	516
Singapore	3	0	3	1	1	1	0	1	14
Slovakia	2	2	0	17	17	7	7	0	283
Slovenia (a)	..	..	..	6	162	..	..	..	9
South Africa	263	47	216	70	286	289	38	251	3,637
Spain	72	58	14	325	3,501	70	50	20	442
Sweden (a)	..	..	..	22	568	3	1	2	79
Switzerland	53	6	47	663	5,496	92	17	75	647
Thailand (b)	..	..	..	22	211	..	..	..	..
Tunisia	22	0	22	..	..	6	1	5	231
Türkiye	262	137	125	149	149	319	150	169	1,751
Ukraine	789	297	492	299	299	956	386	570	11,880
United Kingdom	1,702	1,535	167	1,657	3,196	67	64	3	1,146
United Republic of Tanzania	3	0	3	..	..	7	0	7	133
United States of America (PPA) (c)	945	403	542	n.a.	..	1,109	491	618	20,025
United States of America (PVPA)	430	317	113	2,120	9,750	435	359	76	8,417
Uruguay	69	14	55	23	77	78	21	57	627
Uzbekistan	92	85	7	85	85	50	47	3	201
Viet Nam	136	87	49	87	87	85	51	34	612
Others/Unknown	..	..	..	13	94	..	..	..	..
Total (2022 estimates)	**27,260**	**21,500**	**5,760**	**27,260**	**n.a.**	**14,920**	**9,500**	**2,510**	**161,210**

(a) This office did not report data; therefore, applications by origin data may be incomplete.
(b) This office is not a member of the International Union for the Protection of New Varieties of Plants (UPOV).
(c) Applications by origin are reported under United States of America Plant Varieties Protection Act (PVPA).
n.a. indicates not applicable.
.. indicates not available.
Source: WIPO Statistics Database, September 2023.

Geographical indications

Highlights

Introduction[1]

A geographical indication (GI) is a sign identifying a good as having originated from a specific geographical area and possessing a given quality, reputation or other characteristic essentially attributable to that geographical origin. Thus, the main function of a GI is to identify goods whose quality, reputation or other characteristics are strongly connected to their territory of origin.

GIs can be protected through a variety of legal means (e.g., *sui generis* systems, trademark law, regional systems, international agreements, other national legal means, etc.). In addition, the protection of GIs at a national level is often shared among several agencies. WIPO has made a major effort to gather data from all relevant sources, but in many instances it has not been possible to obtain the necessary data from every source. For instance, many countries are unable to identify GIs protected through the trademark system. Nonetheless, the statistics gathered afford a valuable insight into how this form of intellectual property (IP) is being used in different parts of the world.

How many GIs are in force worldwide?

Data received by WIPO from a total of 91 national and regional authorities show there were an estimated 58,400 protected GIs in existence in 2022. To minimize double counting, GIs in force through the European Union (EU) (5,176 GIs in force) regional system and the Lisbon System (1,039) are counted once only, rather than multiplied by the number of member states party to each system. That notwithstanding, the overall total of around 58,400 will inevitably include a degree of double counting, as GIs in force through bilateral, plurilateral or multilateral agreements could potentially be included multiple times. If GIs in force through various international agreements are excluded, then around 22,000 GIs were in force in 2022.

Of the 58,400 GIs in force in 2022, upper middle-income economies accounted for 46.3% of the world total, followed by high-income (43.1%) and lower middle-income economies (10.6%).[2] In terms of regional distribution, Europe had the most GIs in force, amounting to 53.1%, followed by Asia (36.3%), Latin America and the Caribbean (4.3%), Oceania (3.6%), North America (2.6%) and Africa 0.1%.[3]

1 Of the 91 responses received from authorities worldwide, six – Bahrain, Barbados, Kyrgyzstan, Lebanon, South Africa and Zambia – replied saying there were no GIs in force within their respective jurisdictions in 2022.

2 Each category includes the following number of economies: high-income economies (43), upper middle-income (31), lower middle-income (16) and low-income (5). European Union data are allocated to the high-income group, because most of its member states are high-income countries. Venezuela is unclassified pending release of revised national accounts statistics.

3 Regions include the following number of offices: Africa (10), Asia (25), Europe (41), Latin America and the Caribbean (16), North America (2) and Oceania (2).

Figure 5.1 shows the total number of GIs in force within selected national and regional authorities, while figure 5.2 reports data on GIs in force within EU member states. In 2022, China (9,571) had the most GIs in force within its territory, followed by Hungary (7,843), Germany (7,386) and the Czech Republic (6,383). The high rankings achieved by EU countries is explained by the fact that the 5,176 GIs in force throughout the EU regional system are in force in every member state. In addition, some EU member states, such as the Czech Republic and Hungary, are party to the Lisbon System; therefore GIs in force via the Lisbon System (1,039 appellations of origin and geographical indications, excluding domestic and refusals) are also included in the total. Several middle-income economies had a high number of GIs in force within their jurisdiction in 2022; for example, there were 5,991 GIs in force in Bulgaria, 4,602 in the Republic of Moldova and 4,534 in Bosnia and Herzegovina. Again, these countries' high ranking in terms of GIs in force is because of their being party to the Lisbon System. In contrast, Brazil (109) and India (429) had considerably fewer GIs in force, which could be explained by them having no GIs protected through international agreements in 2022 (see table 5.7).

China had over 9,500 GIs in force in 2022, three-quarters of which were protected through the trademark system

5.1. Geographical indications in force for selected national and regional authorities, 2022

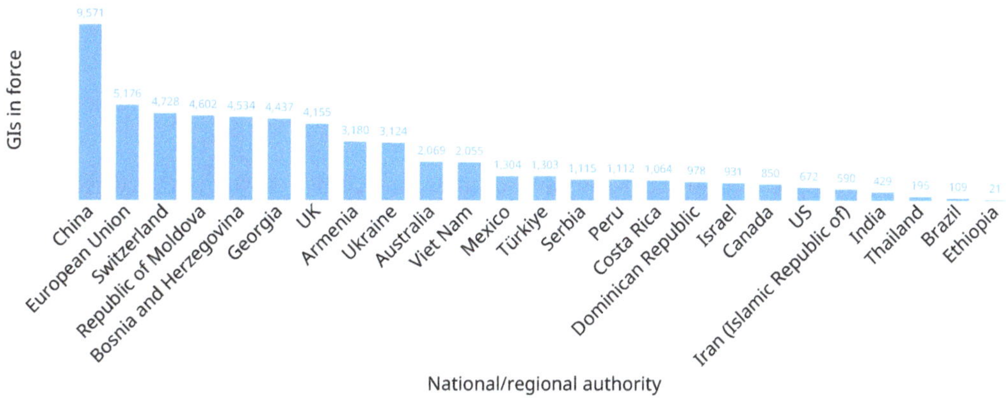

Source: Table 5.7.

Among EU member states, Germany and Hungary had the highest number of GIs in force in 2022

5.2. Geographical indications in force for EU member states, 2022

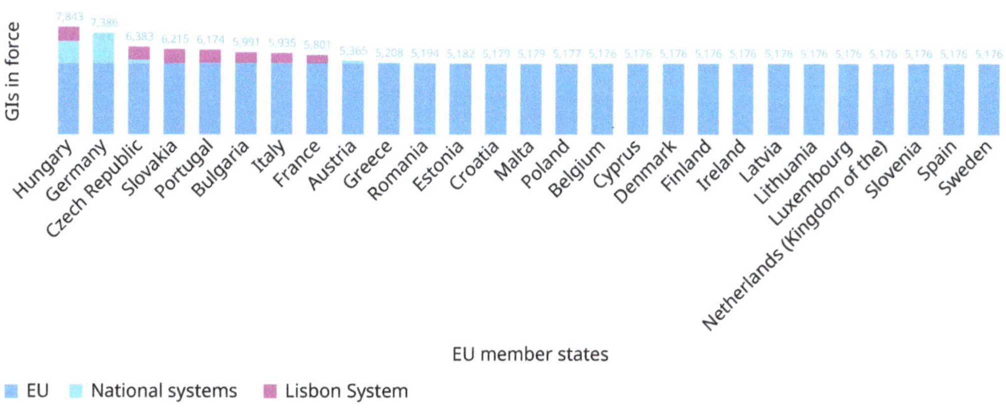

Note: The EU's regional system for the protection of GIs cover agricultural products and foodstuffs, wines and spirits.
Source: Table 5.7.

Figure 5.3 shows the total number of GIs in force broken down by the legal means of protection for selected national and regional authorities. All GIs in force in Brazil, Colombia, India, Malaysia and the United States of America (US) were protected through national systems, whereas the bulk of GIs in force in Costa Rica (96.9%), the Dominican Republic (97.5%) and Israel (99.2%) were protected through the Lisbon System. In contrast, almost every GI in force in Armenia (99.7%) and the United Kingdom (UK) (99.9%) was protected via international agreements.

Most of the GIs in force in Costa Rica, the Dominican Republic and Israel were protected by the Lisbon System

5.3. Distribution of geographical indications in force by legal means of protection for selected national and regional authorities, 2022

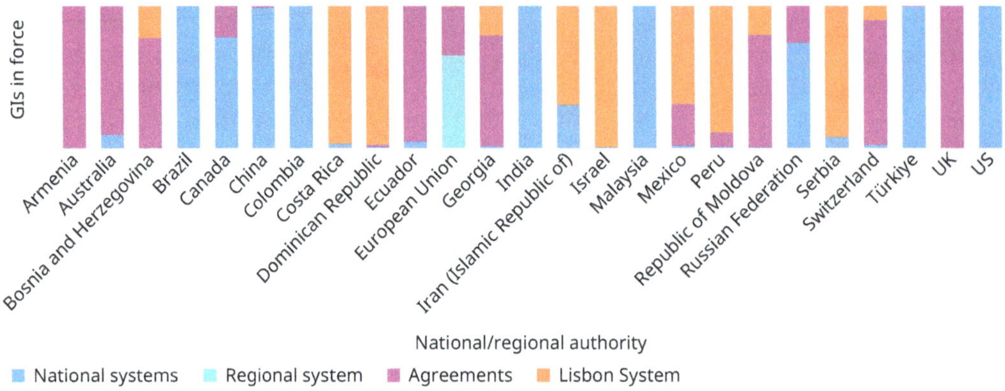

Source: Table 5.7.

A number of authorities provided data on GIs broken down according to source (i.e., whether they are a national or foreign GI). Figure 5.4 shows data for selected national and regional authorities. The share of national GIs ranged from as low as 0.3% in Bosnia and Herzegovina to as high as 99.8% in Türkiye. More than 90% of the GIs in force in Brazil (91.7%), China (94.4%), India (92.8%), Malaysia (94.5%), Thailand (90.8%) and Türkiye (99.8%) were national GIs, whereas almost all those in force in Bosnia and Herzegovina (99.7%) and Costa Rica (99.6%) were foreign GIs.

GIs in force relating to wines and spirits (50.7%) accounted for half of the 2022 global total, while agricultural products and foodstuffs accounted for 43.1% and handicrafts 4.2% of the total (figure 5.5). In terms of absolute numbers, Bosnia and Herzegovina (5,416) reported the highest number of GIs in force for agricultural products and foodstuffs, followed by the EU (1,909), China (1,839), the UK (1,722) and Switzerland (1,657). When it comes to the category of wines and spirits, the EU (3,267) had the most GIs in force, followed by the Republic of Moldova (2,882), Switzerland (2,646), the UK (2,433) and Ukraine (2,289). Switzerland (425), India (232), Austria (189) and Türkiye (145) each had a considerable number of GIs in force for handicrafts in 2022. Only four jurisdictions - Brazil; China, Macao SAR; Serbia and the US - reported protecting GIs for services.

Foreign GIs accounted for almost all GIs in force in Bosnia and Herzegovina and Costa Rica

5.4. Distribution of geographical indications in force by source for selected national and regional authorities, 2022

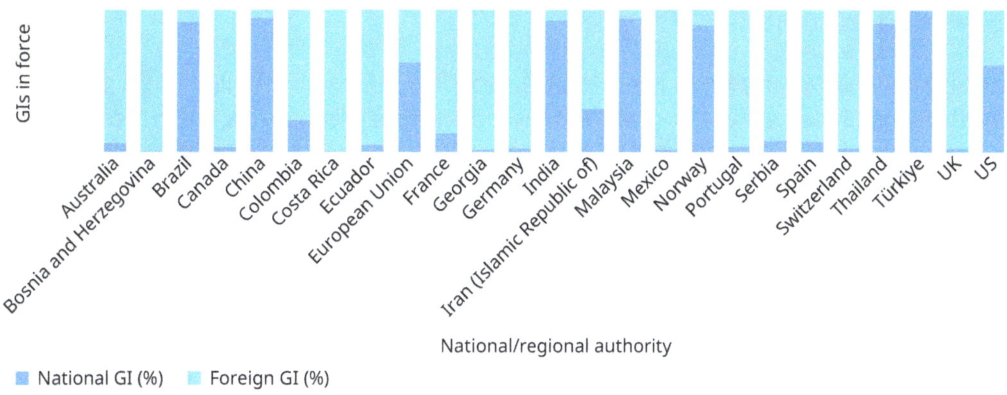

Source: WIPO Statistics Database, September 2023.

Wines and spirits accounted for half of GIs in force globally

5.5. Geographical indications in force by product category, 2022

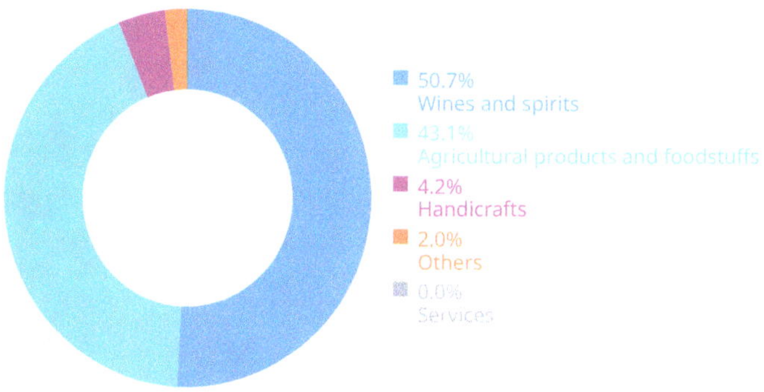

Note: The global total by product category is based on data from the 64 national jurisdictions plus the EU regional system for which 2022 data by product category are available. GIs in force through regional systems like the EU were counted once rather than multiple times, as they were in force in all the respective member states. This is in order to minimize double counting. For a number of countries, product category data for appellations of origin (AOs) and GIs protected via the Lisbon System are unavailable. China's product category data excludes GIs protected via the trademark system.
Source: WIPO Statistics Database, September 2023.

The GIs in force data reported here are partial and incomplete and therefore ought to be interpreted with caution. The questionnaire underlying the data collection requested information from respondents regarding GIs protected through *sui generis* systems, trademark systems, other national legal means, regional systems and international agreements (including GIs in force under the Lisbon System and the Madrid System). As table 5.7 indicates, many countries did not provide statistics on the number of GIs protected through the trademark system. This might be because the countries concerned do not use the trademark system to protect GIs or else some countries that do use it have difficulty separating GIs from other trademarks (most commonly, collective and certification trademarks). In addition, several countries could not provide data on how many GIs were protected through international agreements.

China (2,399) reported the highest number of GIs protected via the *sui generis* system, followed by Türkiye (1,300) and Canada (666).[4] The most GIs protected via the trademarks system were in China (7,076), followed by Viet Nam (1,756) and the US (389). Switzerland (4,156) and the UK (4,150) reported high volumes of GIs protected through international agreements.

4 Although the EU regional system is a *sui generis* system, GIs in force in the 27 EU member states via the EU are reported under the regional system category rather than the *sui generis* category.

In 2022, there were 1,039 appellations of origin and GIs in force via the Lisbon System

As of 2022, the Lisbon System consisted of 38 Contracting Parties. Cabo Verde and Ghana acceded to the Lisbon System in 2022.

In 2022, there were 1,039 appellations of origin (AOs) and geographical indications in force via the Lisbon System (figure 5.6). This is 14 fewer than in the previous year, which is due to cancellations of previous registered AOs originating from Czech Republic and Italy.

France remains the primary user of the Lisbon System. It accounted for two-fifths (40.9%) of the 2022 total, followed by Italy (16%), the European Union (13.7%), the Islamic Republic of Iran (6.6%) and the Czech Republic (3.8%). These five origins accounted for four-fifths of the 2022 total. The EU - a recent member of the Lisbon System - had 25 new registrations to take its tally to 142 AOs in 2022. The Islamic Republic of Iran (2 new registrations) and Switzerland (+3) also saw new registrations in 2022. The number of AOs in force via the Lisbon System decreased by 35 for the Czech Republic and 9 for Italy due to cancellations of previously registered AOs.

The EU registered 25 additional AOs through the Lisbon System in 2022

5.6. Appellations of origin in force by origin, 2022

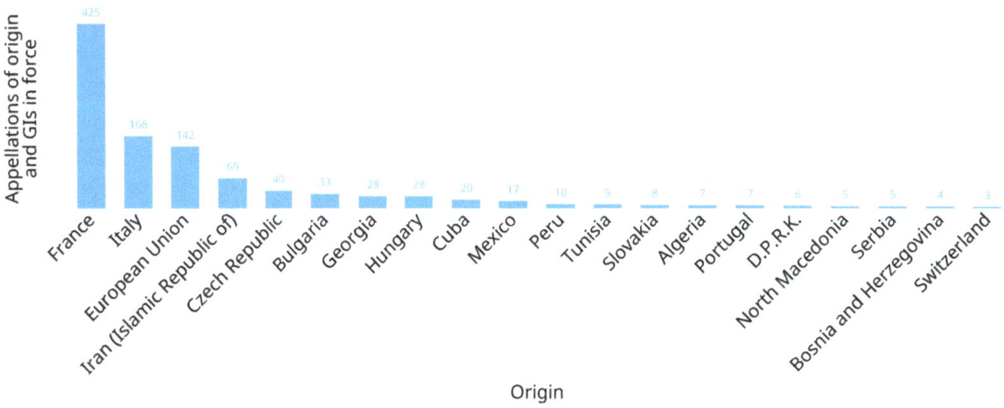

Note: D.P.R.K. is the Democratic People's Republic of Korea.
Source: WIPO Statistics Database, September 2023.

5.7. Geographical indications in force in 2022

Name	Total	*Sui generis*	Trademarks	Other national legal means	Regional system	Agreements	Lisbon System (a)
Albania	1,051	..	16	..	..	..	1,035
Argentina	120	120	..	..	..	..	..
Armenia	3,180	8	..	..	..	3,172	..
Australia	2,069	116	81	..	..	1,872	..
Austria	5,365	..	..	..	3,396	1,968	1
Azerbaijan	40	..	40	..	..	..	..
Bangladesh	10	10	..	..	..	..	..
Belgium	5,176	..	..	..	3,396	1,779	1
Bosnia and Herzegovina	4,534	16	..	..	..	3,513	1,005
Botswana	1	1	..	..	..	..	..
Brazil	109	109	..	..	..	..	..
Bulgaria	5,991	42	..	..	3,396	1,779	774
Burkina Faso	898	1	4	..	..	..	893
Cabo Verde	2	2	..	..	..	..	..
Cambodia	64	8	..	..	..	..	56
Canada	850	666	..	..	..	184	..
China	9,571	2,399	7,076	..	..	96	..
China, Hong Kong SAR	56	..	56	..	..	..	..
China, Macao SAR	23	3	20	..	..	..	..
Colombia	157	157	..	..	..	..	..
Costa Rica	1,064	..	33	..	..	..	1,031
Côte d'Ivoire	11	9	..	..	..	2	..
Croatia	5,179	3	..	..	3,396	1,779	1
Cyprus	5,176	..	..	..	3,396	1,779	1
Czech Republic	6,383	62	..	..	3,396	1,987	938
Denmark	5,176	..	..	..	3,396	1,779	1
Dominican Republic	978	..	10	..	..	14	954
Ecuador	145	7	..	..	..	138	..
El Salvador	29	29	..	..	..	..	..
Estonia	5,182	6	..	..	3,396	1,779	1
Ethiopia	21	..	21	..	..	..	..
European Union (b)	5,176	..	..	..	3,396	1,779	1
Finland	5,176	..	..	..	3,396	1,779	1
France	5,801	14	..	4	3,396	1,779	608
Georgia	4,437	64	..	..	..	3,471	902
Germany	7,386	..	2	..	3,396	3,987	1
Greece	5,208	16	..	16	3,396	1,779	1
Honduras	53	..	53	..	..	..	..
Hungary	7,843	10	..	..	3,396	3,420	1,017
India	429	429	..	..	..	..	..
Indonesia	121	121	..	..	..	..	..
Iran (Islamic Republic of)	590	179	..	..	..	..	411
Ireland	5,176	..	..	..	3,396	1,779	1
Israel	931	7	..	..	..	..	924
Italy	5,935	36	..	..	3,396	1,779	724
Jamaica	4	3	1	..	..	..	..
Jordan	6	..	6	..	..	..	..
Kazakhstan	36	36	..	..	..	..	..
Lao People's Democratic Republic	8	8	..	..	..	..	..
Latvia	5,176	..	..	..	3,396	1,779	1
Lithuania	5,176	..	..	..	3,396	1,779	1
Luxembourg	5,176	..	..	..	3,396	1,779	1
Malaysia	109	109	..	..	..	..	..
Mali	8	8	..	..	..	..	..
Malta	5,179	..	..	3	3,396	1,779	1
Mauritius	1	1	..	..	..	..	..
Mexico	1,304	24	..	..	..	382	898
Mongolia	46	46	..	..	..	..	..
Mozambique	4	..	..	4	..	..	..

Name	Total	*Sui generis*	Trademarks	Other national legal means	Regional system	Agreements	Lisbon System (a)
Netherlands (Kingdom of the)	5,176	..	..	..	3,396	1,779	1
New Zealand	24	24	..	..	..	..	..
Norway	38	30	..	..	..	8	..
Pakistan	6	6	..	..	..	..	..
Peru	1,112	10	..	..	..	115	987
Poland	5,177	1	..	..	3,396	1,779	1
Portugal	6,174	29	..	..	3,396	1,779	970
Republic of Moldova	4,602	25	..	..	..	3,648	929
Romania	5,194	18	..	..	3,396	1,779	1
Russian Federation	403	299	..	..	..	104	..
Serbia	1,115	87	..	..	..	..	1,028
Singapore	159	159	..	..	..	..	..
Slovakia	6,215	25	..	..	3,396	1,779	1,015
Slovenia	5,176	..	..	..	3,396	1,779	1
Spain	5,176	..	..	..	3,396	1,779	1
Sri Lanka	8	..	8	..	..	..	..
Sweden	5,176	..	..	..	3,396	1,779	1
Switzerland (c)	4,728	110	..	2	..	4,156	460
Thailand	195	195	..	..	..	..	..
Trinidad and Tobago	1	1	..	..	..	..	..
Türkiye	1,303	1,300	..	..	..	3	..
Ukraine	3,124	33	..	..	..	3,091	..
United Kingdom (d)	4,155	5	..	..	..	4,150	..
United States of America (e)	672	..	389	283	..	..	..
Venezuela (Bolivarian Republic of)	9	8	..	..	..	1	..
Viet Nam	2,055	130	1,756	..	..	169	..

Note: Identifying GIs protected via the trademark system (certification and collective marks) is extremely time consuming and requires extensive manual intervention. For this reason, a number of authorities like that of the United Kingdom were unable to report on GIs protected via the trademark system. Lisbon System data for Burkina Faso, France and Italy are based on WIPO estimates.
(a) Lisbon System data reported here refer to foreign GIs and AOs in force based on the Lisbon System.
(b) The EU's regional system for the protection of GIs covers agricultural products and foodstuffs, wines and spirits. Although the EU regional system is a *sui generis* system, GIs in force via the EU are reported under the regional system category rather than the *sui generis* category.
(c) There is no registration requirement for the *sui generis* protection of GIs in Switzerland. Only those denominations subject to registration or recognition on the basis of the instruments provided for in the Law on Agriculture and the Law on the Protection of Trademarks and Indications of Source, or of a court decision or special legislation, are counted under the national systems of protection.
(d) The United Kingdom created a new GI scheme after Brexit. This new scheme includes all GIs directly registered by the EU prior to December 31, 2022. The scheme covers England, Wales and Scotland.
(e) The United States of America protects geographical indications through its trademark system as certification marks, collective marks or trademarks. Complementary protection is provided under the Federal Alcohol Administration Act and its implementing regulations for wines and distilled spirits of both domestic and foreign origin.
.. indicates zero/not available.
Source: WIPO Statistics Database, September 2023.

Creative economy

Highlights

Introduction

Publishing industry data are not unified under a single authority. For this reason, data are drawn from three different surveys for an overview of the global publishing industry worldwide. This Creative economy section begins by presenting data from a publishing industry survey, followed by data from a legal deposits survey and data on International Standard Book Number (ISBN) registrations.[1]

Publishing survey data

This first subsection presents publishing industry data provided by the 30 countries that responded to the global publishing industry survey undertaken in 2023. In total, 28 national publishers' associations and copyright authorities agreed to share their 2022 data, while Mexico and the Republic of Korea provided the latest available 2021 data. Publishing industry revenue and the number of titles published are presented below.

Publishing industry revenue

The 2022 sales and licensing revenue data covering the trade and the educational sectors are available for 21 countries. In addition, Azerbaijan and Sweden provided revenue data for the trade sector only. The publishing industry revenue for these 23 countries combined was USD 57.3 billion in 2022. The United States of America (US) (USD 26.2 billion) reported the highest sales revenue, followed by Germany (USD 9.9 billion), the United Kingdom (UK) (USD 5 billion), Italy (USD 3.6 billion) and France (USD 2.9 billion) (figure 6.1). The 2022 revenue data for Japan and the Republic of Korea are unavailable; however, Japan's 2021 revenue covering both the trade and educational sectors was USD 11.3 billion, while the Republic of Korea's trade sector revenue amounted to USD 3.4 billion, enough to place them both among the top five countries according to sales revenue.

Trade sector revenue accounted for 50% or more of total revenue for 12 of the 20 countries for which 2022 data by sector are available – ranging from 55.5% in Italy and the UK up to 85.1% in Austria. Educational sector revenue accounted for around three-quarters of total revenue in Türkiye (73.5%). In Brazil (58.9%), Denmark (58.5%) and the Kingdom of the Netherlands (66%), the educational sector likewise generated a high share of total revenue (table F13).

1 The publishing industry survey was conducted by the World Intellectual Property Organization (WIPO), Centro Regional para el Fomento del Libro en América Latina y el Caribe (CERLALC) and the Federation of European Publishers (FEP). The legal deposits survey was conducted by WIPO and the ISBN data compiled by CERLALC and the International ISBN Agency.

6.1. Publishing industry revenue (USD million), 2022

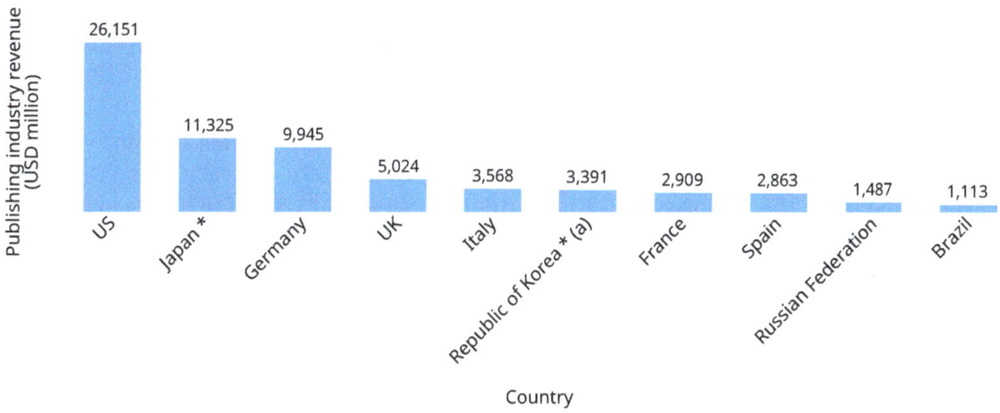

Note: Data for Germany, Italy and Spain are at market value calculated from retail prices.
(a) trade sector only.
* 2021 data.
Source: Table F13.

Publishing industry survey

The publishing industry survey was established in 2017 in a collaboration between the World Intellectual Property Organization (WIPO) and the International Publishers Association (IPA). WIPO has strengthened cooperation with Centro Regional para el Fomento del Libro en América Latina y el Caribe (CERLALC) and the Federation of European Publishers (FEP) in order to reduce the burden on respondents and extend the survey's geographical coverage. CERLALC provided data for several Latin America and the Caribbean (LAC) countries, while the FEP compiled and shared 2022 data relating to 16 European countries (all FEP members). WIPO is grateful to CERLALC and the FEP for sharing their data.

The scope of the publishing industry survey is limited to (a) the trade and educational sectors and (b) those published materials (i.e., books, monographs, and so on) issued with an ISBN, a Digital Object Identifier (DOI) or any other book identifier.

Every effort has been made to compile statistics based on the same definitions in order to facilitate international comparison. However, caution should be exercised when interpreting data, owing to some data points being incomplete or partial. For example, several countries provided only data on print format revenue and/or number of titles published, meaning that any digital components are missing. Similarly, a few countries reported revenue data at market value calculated from retail prices rather than net revenue. Furthermore, for most countries, respondents were national publishers associations (NPAs), with the overall publishing industry share represented by NPAs varying between countries.

The 2022 revenue by format – print, digital or audio – is available for 15 countries. The share for digital/audio formats ranged from 1.2% in Türkiye to 39.7% in Finland (figure F2). Digital/audio formats generated around one-third of total revenue in Denmark (37%), Finland (39.7%) and Sweden (36.1%). The 2022 digital/audio formats share for all three countries is considerably higher than it was in 2021. For example, Denmark's digital/audio formats share was 29.5%, in 2021, while Finland saw a similar increase of 6.5 percentage points over the same period.

Only 11 countries were able to provide publishing industry revenue by destination (domestic or foreign market) for 2022. Of these, Belgium (53.9%) generated more than half of total revenue from foreign markets, followed by the UK (44.1%) and Spain (11.4%). Foreign market share for Denmark (0.7%), Italy (1.5%), Türkiye (0.2%) and the US (4.1%) was below 5% (figure F3). Although only 4.1% of the US's total revenue was generated from foreign markets, in absolute terms this amounted to USD 1.1 billion in 2022.

Revenue data by sales channel – brick and mortar, online and others – are available for 16 countries for 2022. Online sales generated around two-thirds of total publishing industry revenue in Sweden (59.3%) and the UK (59.1%) in 2022 (figure F4). Italy (52.3%) generated more the half of total revenue through online sales. Belgium (44.6%), Finland (39.5%) and the Russian Federation (42.5%) also had a large proportion of total revenue generated through online sales. However, brick and mortar continued to generate the bulk of total revenue in France (69.3%), Japan (64.5%) and Spain (70.7%).

The total revenue generated from children's book sales is available for 19 countries and amounted to USD 9.1 billion in 2022. The US reported revenue of USD 4.9 billion from children's books in 2022, followed by Germany (USD 1.8 billion), the UK (USD 529 million), Spain (USD 495 million) and France (USD 398 million) (figure F5). Revenue from children's books represented more than one-third of trade sector revenue in Colombia (35.1%), Denmark (35.2%) and New Zealand (37.6%) (figure F6).

Number of titles published

Data on the total number of titles published in 2022 covering both the trade and educational sectors are available for 20 countries. Türkiye reported a combined total of 206,674 titles published in 2022. Brazil (146,575), France (111,503), Italy (121,127) and the UK (153,000) all reported more than 100,000 published titles in 2022 (figure 6.2).

The trade sector's share of titles published ranged from 25.1% in New Zealand up to 84% in Ireland. In every country where data was reported by sector, the trade sector accounted for more than half of all titles published, the exception being New Zealand (25.1%). Like in Ireland, the trade sector accounted for the vast bulk of titles published in Ecuador (79.5%), Italy (78.9%) and Norway (78.6%) (table F14).

6.2. Total number of titles published, 2022

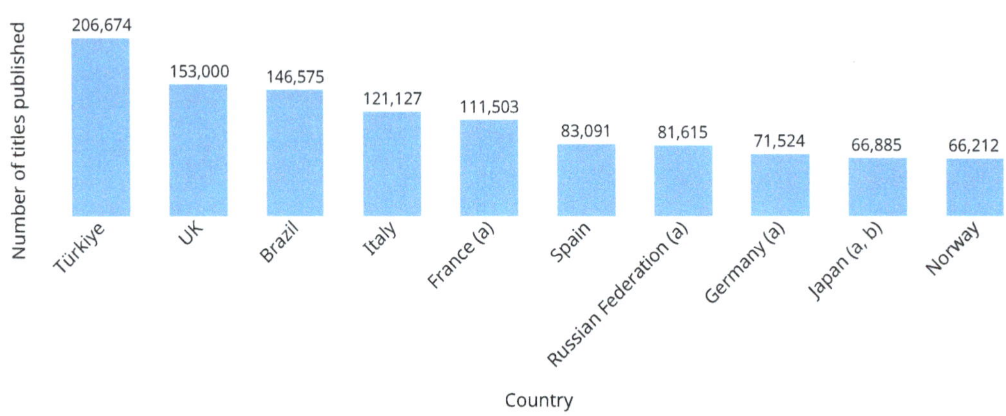

(a) print format only.
(b) trade sector only.
Source: Table F14.

In total, 15 countries reported data on the number of titles published by format (print, digital or audio) in 2022. The share of digital/audio formatted titles ranged from 12.5% in Türkiye up to 72.4% in Brazil (figure F8). Shares were largest in Brazil (72.4%), Finland (47.5%), Norway (47.5%) and Sweden (51.8%), where more than 47% of titles were in digital/audio formats. In contrast, less than 20% of titles published in Greece (13.3%) and Türkiye (12.5%) were in these formats.

Data on children's books published by the trade sector in 2022 is available for 14 countries. France (18,535) reported the highest number of children's books published in 2022, followed by Türkiye (17,238), the Russian Federation (13,857) and Italy (10,509) (figure F9). Children's books represented the largest share of trade sector published titles in New Zealand (38.6%), Greece (34.4%), the Russian Federation (30.7%) and Finland (30.1%) (figure F10).

Legal deposits in recognized repositories

This subsection presents data on legal deposits. In total, 82 national repositories shared their 2022 data with WIPO.[2] WIPO's legal deposits survey covers four categories of deposit, namely, (a) books, (b) music sheets and music audio files, (c) films and videos, and (d) periodicals (journals, e-series, etc.).

The highest number of books published and deposited in a national repository in 2022 was recorded by Germany (401,197), followed by the US (264,722), the UK (167,000), Japan (113,296) and Spain (98,289) (figure 6.3). China's 2022 data are unavailable, but in 2021 the National Library of China received 467,417 books, which is far above the number received by Germany. Where available, data for all countries are presented in table F15.

6.3. Number of books in legal repositories, 2022

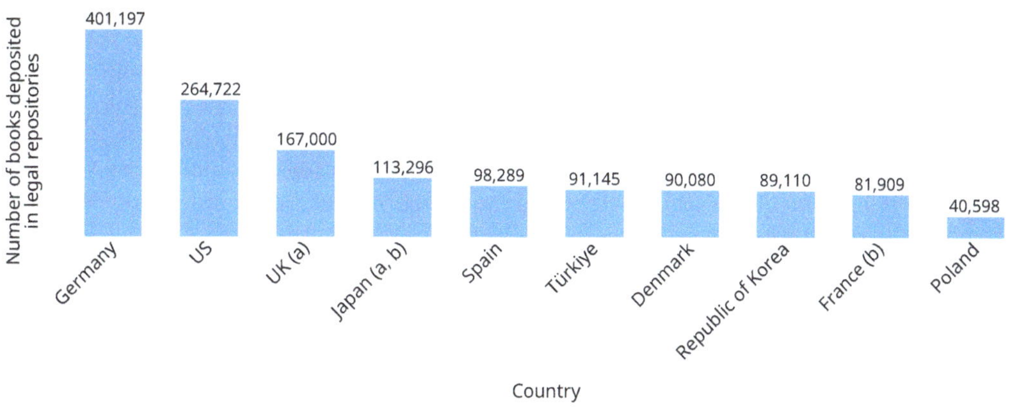

(a) 2020-2021 fiscal year.
(b) print format only.
Source: Table F15.

Of the top 10 national repositories, the US saw the biggest increase in deposits, which rose from 197,931 in 2021 up to 264,722 in 2022 (figure F11). Denmark (+49,700), Spain (+7,239) and the UK (+14,645) also received substantially more book deposits in 2022 compared to the year before. Germany (-11,961) and the Republic of Korea (-11,132) reported the steepest decreases over the same period. Of the 79 countries or territories for which data for 2021 and 2022 are available, 48 reported an increase in books deposited in 2022, whereas the remaining 31 saw a decrease.

Data on books deposited by format - print, digital or other - are available for 53 countries or territories. More than two-thirds of all books deposited in Denmark (82.4%), Germany (71.4%) and the US (91.7%) in 2022 were in a digital format (figure F12). In contrast, print format constituted almost all books deposited in Albania (99.9%), Azerbaijan (99.8%), Chile (99.8%) and Serbia (99.9%). The high shares reported for books in a print format could in part be because of the fact that data coverage for digital formats is not comprehensive in some countries.

Legal deposits

Legal deposit is a statutory obligation at the national level requiring publishers to deposit a certain number of copies of published documents at a repository, that is, a recognized place of legal deposit. Ordinarily, national legal provisions require at least two copies to be submitted, although this varies across countries and territories.

In some countries and territories, legal deposit is required only for printed books, whereas in others digital publications and other formats are also required. A number of countries reported items as having undergone a process of digitization recently, resulting in data coverage that is

2 In addition, China shared its 2021 data, while Zimbabwe replied saying it was unable to provide 2022 data. Colombia provided general aggregate 2022 data that is not comparable, and Italy provided partial 2022 data; hence, data for both countries are not included in the report.

more comprehensive, but also a significant increase in digital publications. In some countries, there is no legal obligation to deposit e-books, although this may be done on a voluntary basis. For this reason, care should be exercised when making cross-country comparisons.

International Standard Book Number (ISBN) data

This subsection presents data on ISBN registrations. An ISBN is a permanent international standard book identifier assigned to a publication and administered by the International ISBN Agency and national or regional ISBN agencies throughout the world. ISBN data gives a good indication as to the size of the publishing market in different countries and is a means of validating data from other sources. For 2022, the International ISBN Agency shared data for 50 countries provided by national ISBN agencies. In addition, CERLALC shared data for 15 countries covering the LAC region.

Table F16 presents data on (a) lifetime ISBNs registered and (b) number of ISBNs registered in 2022. The US, with 3.3 million registered ISBNs in 2022, was by far the biggest user of the ISBN identifier in 2022, followed by Japan (902,311), the Republic of Korea (338,237), India (281,091) and Germany (277,000). China's 2022 data - one of the top five users of the ISBN identifier - are unavailable. Registrations data for 2021 and 2022 are available for 48 countries, of which 23 reported an increase in ISBN registrations in 2022 compared to 2021. Japan (+717,326), the US (+394,608) and Brazil (+64,928) recorded the biggest increases. In contrast, Indonesia (-51,474), Ukraine (-16,031) and the UK (-15,793) reported considerably fewer ISBN registrations in 2022 compared to the year before.

Although ISBN data represents the number of publications, there will be some double counting. This is because alternative formats for the same publication (e.g., e-book, paperback and hardcover editions) will have been assigned a separate ISBN.

ISBN as an identifier

The International Standard Book Number (ISBN) is the most common publication identifier in use. The ISBN system has a three-tier administrative structure - the International ISBN Agency, the national and regional registration agencies, and publishers. The International ISBN Agency is the official registration authority appointed by the International Organization for Standardization (ISO) to supervise the global use of the ISBN Standard. There are around 150 registration agencies assigning unique registrant elements and ISBNs to publishers. Publishers are responsible for assigning unique ISBNs to individual publications from within the registrant elements they have been allocated.

However, publishers also use other identifiers, such as an Amazon Standard Identification Number (ASIN), a Digital Object Identifier (DOI), and others.

Creative economy statistics

Publishing industry sales revenue **174**

F1. Publishing industry revenue (USD million), 2022 174
F2. Distribution of publishing industry revenue by format, 2022 174
F3. Distribution of publishing industry revenue by destination, 2022 175
F4. Distribution of publishing industry revenue by sales channel, 2022 175
F5. Children's books revenue (USD million), 2022 176
F6. Share of children's books within trade sector revenue, 2022 176

Titles published **177**

F7. Number of titles published by the trade and educational sectors, 2022 177
F8. Distribution of titles published by the trade and educational sectors by format, 2022 177
F9. Number of children's books titles published by the trade sector, 2022 177
F10. Share of children's books in the number of titles published by the trade sector, 2022 178

Legal deposits in recognized repositories **178**

F11. Number of books deposited at the top 20 legal repositories, 2022 178
F12. Distribution of books deposited at selected legal repositories by format, 2022 179

Statistical tables **180**

F13. Total publishing industry revenue by sector (USD million), 2022 180
F14. Total number of titles published by sector, 2022 180
F15. Total number of books deposited at recognized repositories, 2022 181
F16. Total number of ISBN registrations, 2022 182

Publishing industry sales revenue

F1. Publishing industry revenue (USD million), 2022

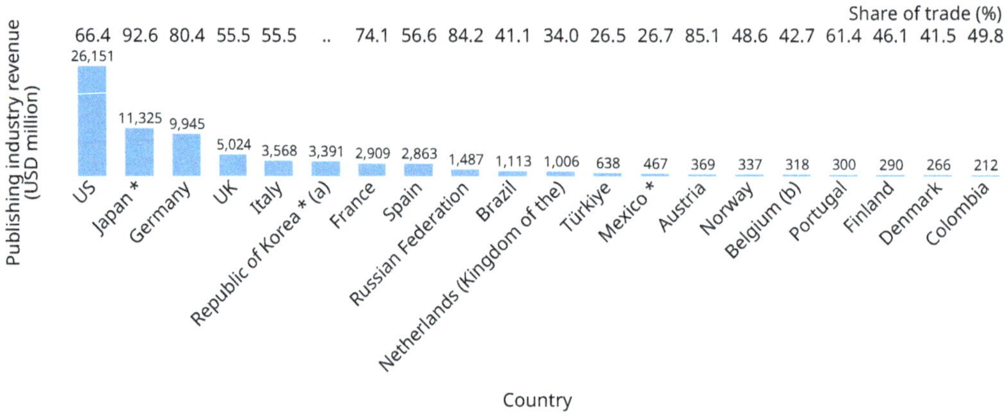

Note: Data for Austria, Germany, Italy, Portugal and Spain are at market value calculated from retail prices.
(a) trade sector only.
(b) French-speaking region.
* 2021 data.
.. indicates not available.
Source: WIPO Statistics Database and Federation of European Publishers (FEP), September 2023.

F2. Distribution of publishing industry revenue by format, 2022

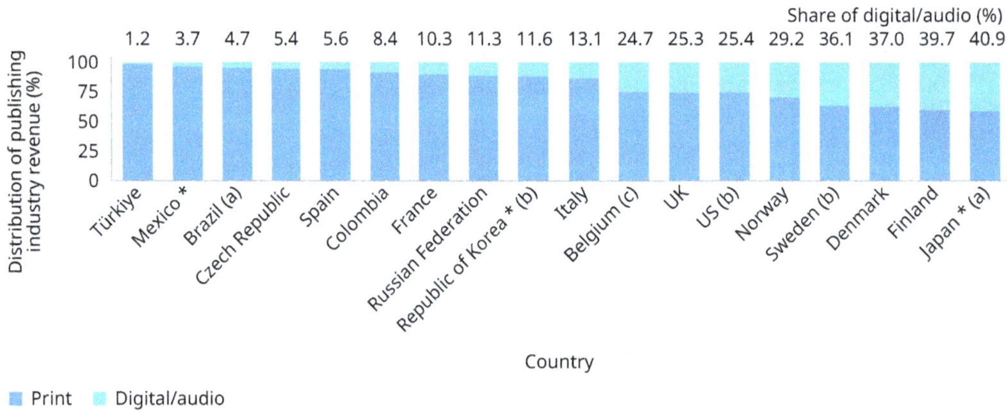

Note: Data for Italy and Spain are at market value calculated from retail prices.
(a) educational sector only.
(b) trade sector only.
(c) French-speaking region.
* 2021 data.
Source: WIPO Statistics Database and Federation of European Publishers (FEP), September 2023.

F3. Distribution of publishing industry revenue by destination, 2022

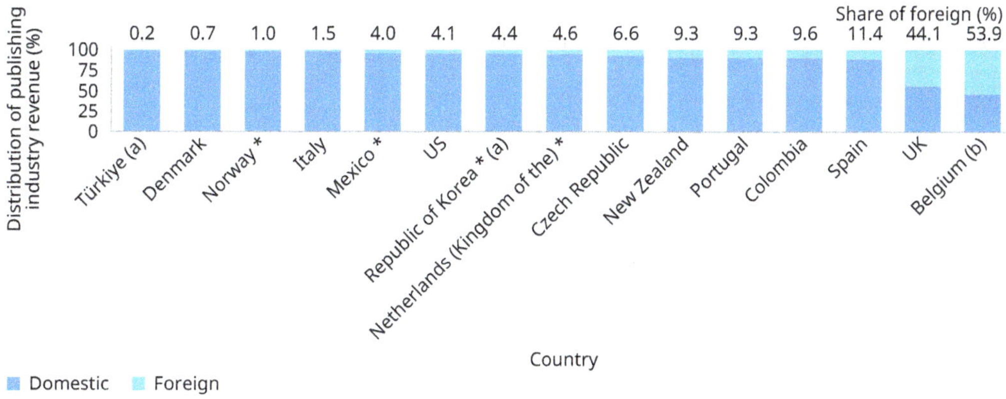

Note: Data for Italy, Portugal and Spain are at market value calculated from retail prices.
(a) trade sector only.
(b) French-speaking region.
* 2021 data.
Source: WIPO Statistics Database and Federation of European Publishers (FEP), September 2023.

F4. Distribution of publishing industry revenue by sales channel, 2022

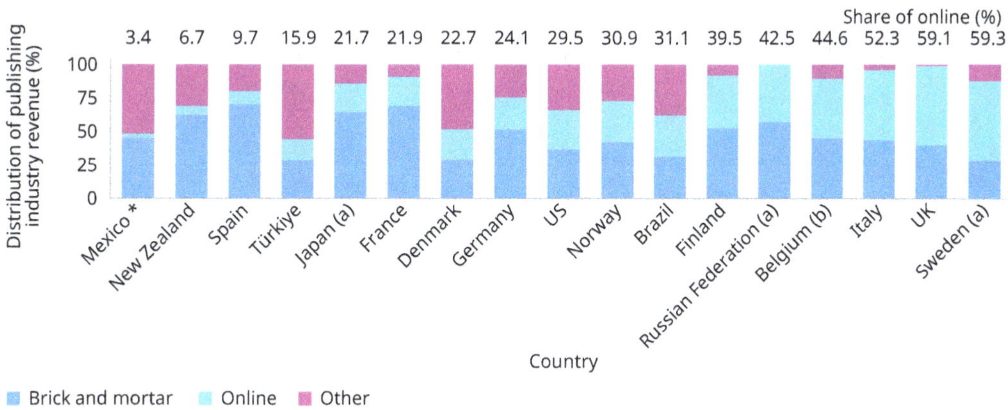

Note: Data for Germany, Italy and Spain are at market value calculated from retail prices. Online category includes digital sales.
(a) trade sector only.
(b) French-speaking region.
* 2021 data.
Source: WIPO Statistics Database and Federation of European Publishers (FEP), September 2023.

F5. Children's books revenue (USD million), 2022

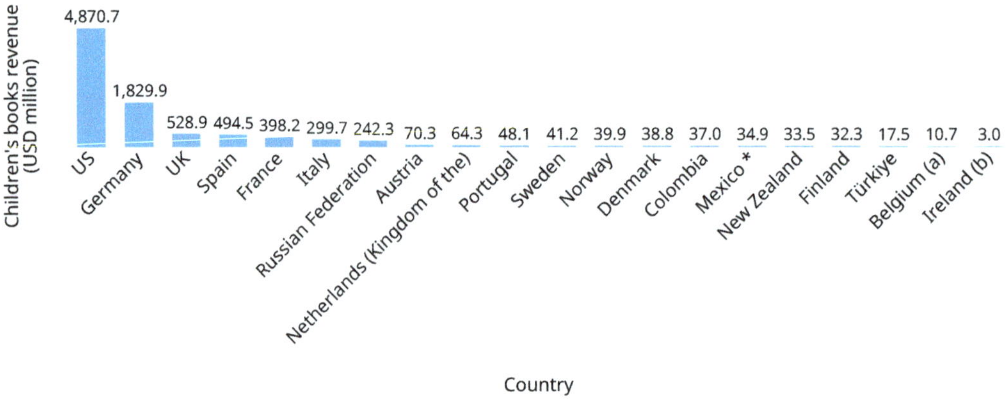

Note: Data for Austria, Germany, Ireland, Italy, Portugal and Spain are at market value calculated from retail prices.
(a) French-speaking region.
(b) print format only.
* 2021 data.
Source: WIPO Statistics Database and Federation of European Publishers (FEP), September 2023.

F6. Share of children's books within trade sector revenue, 2022

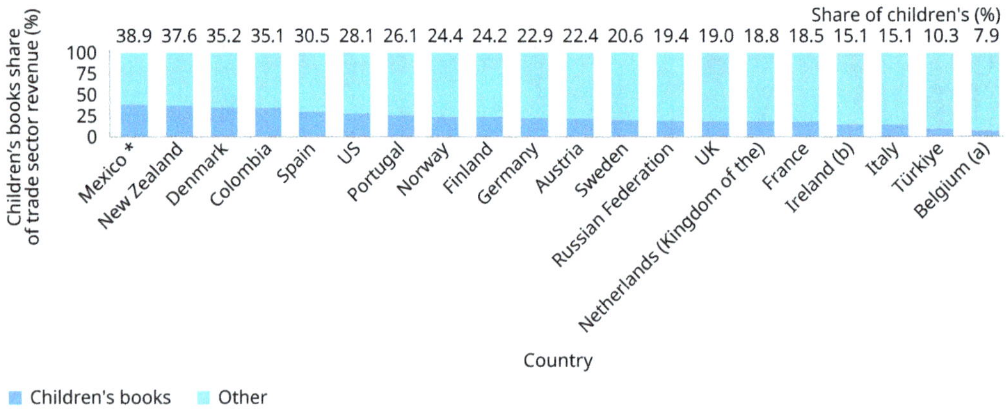

Note: Data for Austria, Germany, Ireland, Italy, Portugal and Spain are at market value calculated from retail prices.
(a) French-speaking region.
(b) print format only.
* 2021 data.
Source: WIPO Statistics Database and Federation of European Publishers (FEP), September 2023.

Titles published

F7. Number of titles published by the trade and educational sectors, 2022

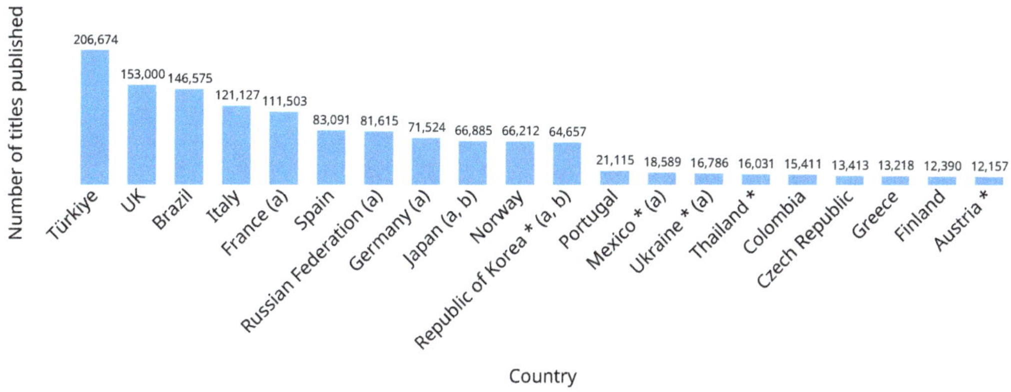

(a) print format only.
(b) trade sector only.
* 2021 data.
Source: WIPO Statistics Database and Federation of European Publishers (FEP), September 2023.

F8. Distribution of titles published by the trade and educational sectors by format, 2022

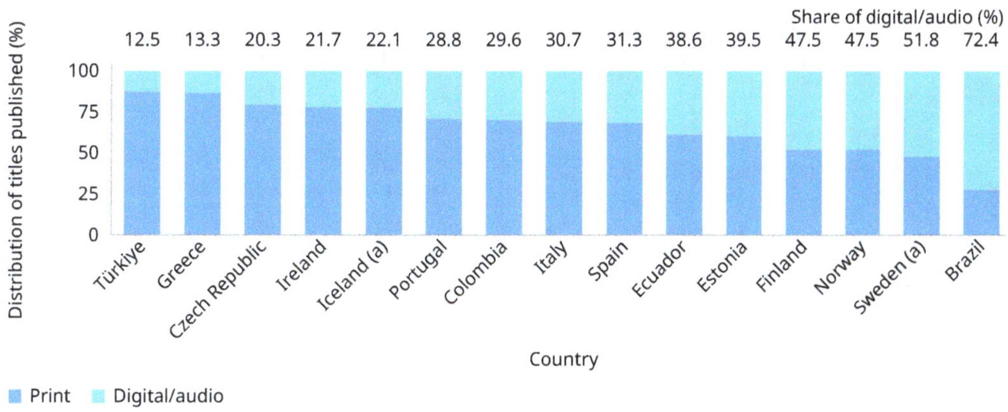

(a) trade sector only.
Source: WIPO Statistics Database and Federation of European Publishers (FEP), September 2023.

F9. Number of children's books titles published by the trade sector, 2022

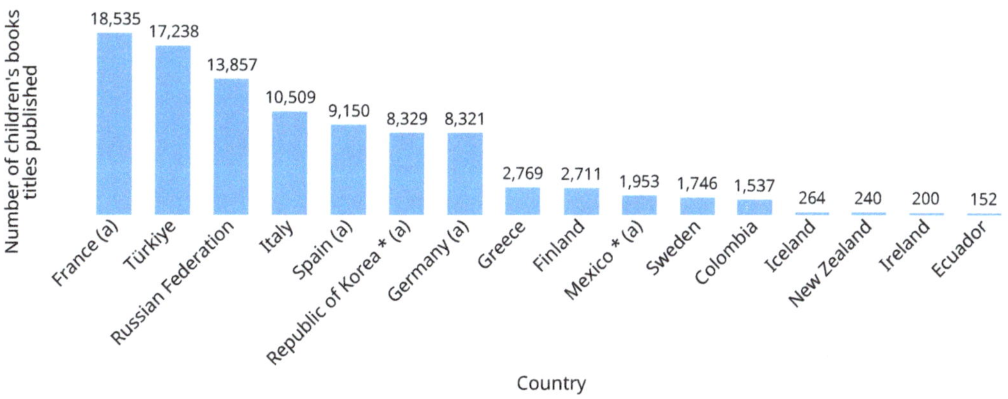

(a) print format only.
* 2021 data.
Source: WIPO Statistics Database and Federation of European Publishers (FEP), September 2023.

F10. Share of children's books in the number of titles published by the trade sector, 2022

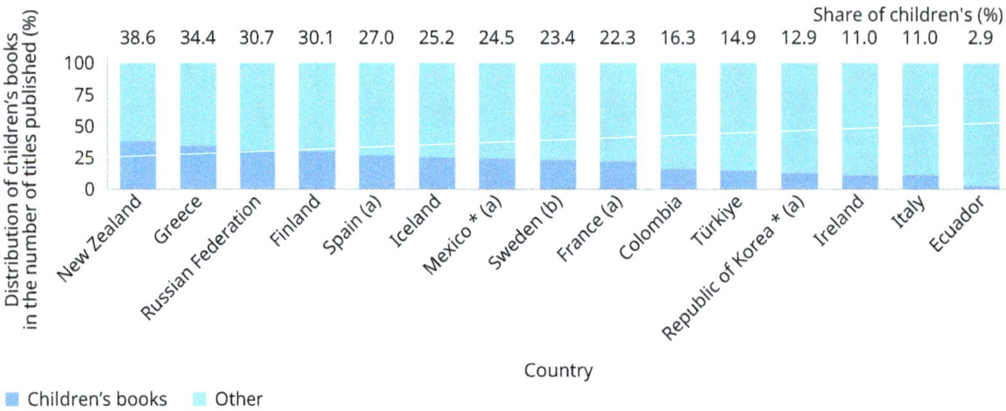

(a) print format only.
(b) trade sector only.
* 2021 data.
Source: WIPO Statistics Database and Federation of European Publishers (FEP), September 2023.

Legal deposits in recognized repositories

F11. Number of books deposited at the top 20 legal repositories, 2022

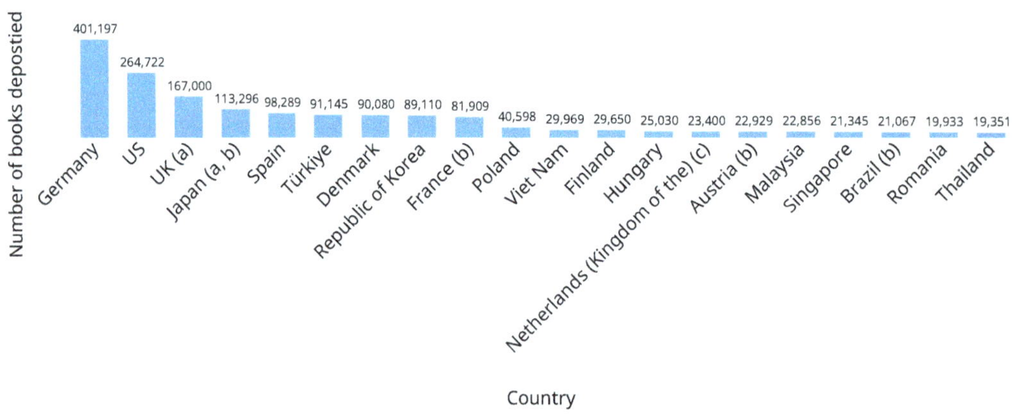

(a) 2020–2021 fiscal year.
(b) print format only.
(c) digital deposits collected on a voluntary basis.
Source: WIPO Statistics Database, September 2023.

F12. **Distribution of books deposited at selected legal repositories by format, 2022**

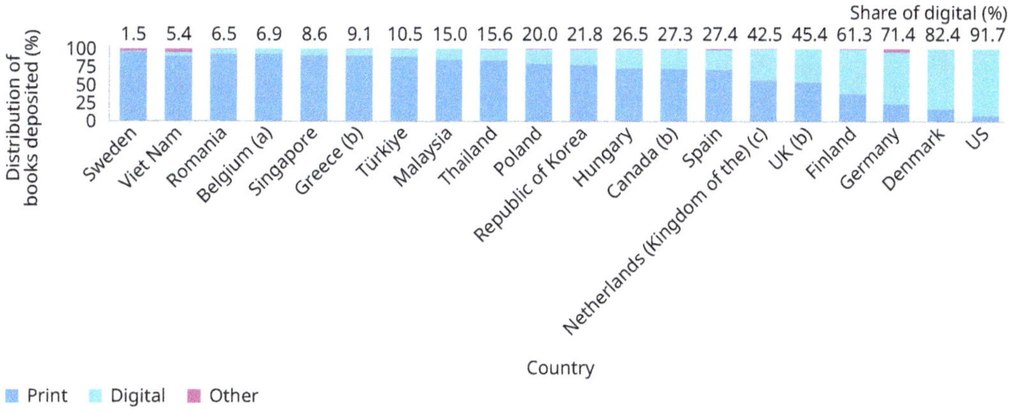

(a) digital deposits collected on a voluntary basis.
(b) 2020–2021 fiscal year.
(c) deposits are voluntary, as they are not covered by legislation.
Source: WIPO Statistics Database, September 2023.

Statistical tables

F13. Total publishing industry revenue by sector (USD million), 2022

				Share of total (%)	
Country	Total	Trade	Educational	Trade	Educational
Austria	369.1	314.2	54.9	85.1	14.9
Azerbaijan (a)	17.8	17.8	..	..	..
Belgium (b)	318.1	135.9	182.2	42.7	57.3
Brazil	1,113.4	458.0	655.4	41.1	58.9
Colombia	211.5	105.2	106.3	49.8	50.2
Czech Republic	153.0	119.0	34.1	77.7	22.3
Denmark	265.7	110.4	155.3	41.5	58.5
Finland	290.3	133.9	156.3	46.1	53.9
France	2,909.1	2,156.4	752.7	74.1	25.9
Germany	9,945.0	7,995.8	1,949.2	80.4	19.6
Iceland	33.5	..	..	..	..
Ireland (c)	30.7	20.1	10.6	65.6	34.4
Italy	3,567.8	1,980.0	1,587.8	55.5	44.5
Japan *	11,324.7	10,484.3	840.3	92.6	7.4
Malta *	4.3	2.9	1.4	68.1	31.9
Mexico *	467.0	124.5	342.4	26.7	73.3
Netherlands	1,006.0	341.9	664.1	34.0	66.0
New Zealand	111.7	89.0	22.7	79.7	20.3
Norway	337.1	163.8	173.2	48.6	51.4
Portugal	300.1	184.3	115.8	61.4	38.6
Republic of Korea * (a)	3,390.8	3,390.8	..	..	..
Russian Federation	1,486.8	1,251.7	235.1	84.2	15.8
Spain	2,862.7	1,619.8	1,242.9	56.6	43.4
Sweden (a)	199.9	199.9	..	..	..
Türkiye	638.3	169.1	469.2	26.5	73.5
United Kingdom	5,024.3	2,786.1	2,238.1	55.5	44.5
United States of America	26,150.9	17,360.8	8,790.1	66.4	33.6

Note: Data for Austria, Germany, Ireland, Italy, Portugal and Spain are at market value calculated from retail prices.
(a) trade sector only.
(b) French-speaking region.
(c) print format only.
* 2021 data.
.. indicates not available.
Source: WIPO Statistics Database and Federation of European Publishers (FEP), September 2023.

F14. Total number of titles published by sector, 2022

				Share of total (%)	
Country	Total	Trade	Educational	Trade	Educational
Austria *	12,157	..	..	..	..
Belarus * (a)	9,055	4,058	4,997	44.8	55.2
Belgium (b)	10,559	..	..	..	..
Brazil	146,575	85,555	61,020	58.4	41.6
Colombia	15,411	9,433	5,978	61.2	38.8
Cuba *	1,554	1,431	123	92.1	7.9
Czech Republic	13,413	6,896	6,517	51.4	48.6
Denmark *	11,859	..	..	..	..
Ecuador	6,600	5,246	1,354	79.5	20.5
Estonia	5,534	..	..	..	..
Finland	12,390	9,004	3,386	72.7	27.3
France (a)	111,503	83,116	28,387	74.5	25.5
Germany (a)	71,524	..	..	..	..
Greece	13,218	8,043	5,175	60.8	39.2
Iceland (c)	1,046	1,046	..	..	..
Ireland	2,162	1,815	347	84.0	16.0
Italy	121,127	95,583	25,544	78.9	21.1
Japan (a, c)	66,885	66,885	..	..	..
Kyrgyzstan * (a)	1,003	800	203	79.8	20.2
Lebanon	2,500	..	..	..	..

Country	Total	Trade	Educational	Share of total (%) Trade	Share of total (%) Educational
Malta *	530	436	94	82.3	17.7
Mexico * (a)	18,589	7,973	10,616	42.9	57.1
New Zealand	2,475	621	1,854	25.1	74.9
Norway	66,212	52,036	14,176	78.6	21.4
Portugal	21,115	..	..	..	..
Republic of Korea * (a, c)	64,657	64,657	..	..	..
Russian Federation (a)	81,615	45,151	36,464	55.3	44.7
Spain	83,091	..	..	..	..
Sweden (c)	7,475	7,475	..	..	..
Thailand *	16,031	13,805	2,226	86.1	13.9
Togo *	78	61	17	78.2	21.8
Türkiye	206,674	115,413	91,261	55.8	44.2
Ukraine * (a)	16,786	10,213	6,573	60.8	39.2
United Kingdom	153,000	..	..		

(a) print format only.
(b) French-speaking region.
(c) trade sector only.
* 2021 data.
.. indicates not available.
Source: WIPO Statistics Database and Federation of European Publishers (FEP), September 2023.

F15. Total number of books deposited at recognized repositories, 2022

Country/territory	Total	Print	Digital	Other formats
Albania	15,080	15,045	35	..
Algeria	5,375	5,305	70	..
Andorra	146	97	49	..
Argentina (a)	5,297	5,297	..	..
Armenia (a)	3,280	3,280	..	..
Austria (a)	22,929	22,929	..	..
Azerbaijan	5,433	5,410	23	..
Belgium (b)	17,422	16,223	1,199	..
Belize (a)	54	54	..	..
Brazil (a)	21,067	21,067	..	..
Burkina Faso (a)	222	222	..	..
Canada (c)	17,539	12,740	4,787	12
Chile	9,189	9,170	19	..
China, Hong Kong SAR (a)	11,123	11,123	..	..
China, Macao SAR	783	734	49	..
Costa Rica	4,713	2,496	2,217	..
Croatia	7,354	6,903	398	53
Cyprus (a)	35	35	..	..
Czech Republic	18,750	18,319	..	431
Denmark	90,080	15,830	74,250	..
Ecuador	1,707	1,667	40	..
Estonia	5,715	3,327	2,387	1
Finland	29,650	11,403	18,189	58
France (a)	81,909	81,909	..	..
Georgia	4,660	4,471	189	..
Germany	401,197	98,997	286,633	15,567
Ghana	1,389	1,137	252	..
Greece (c)	18,765	17,053	1,701	11
Hungary	25,030	18,384	6,625	21
Iceland	4,718	4,127	65	526
Ireland (a)	1,864	1,864	..	..
Israel	11,190	9,539	1,651	..
Jamaica	407	398	9	..
Japan (a, c)	113,296	113,296	..	..
Jordan	5,924	5,174	750	..
Kenya (a)	2,188	2,188	..	..
Latvia	3,777	2,876	822	79
Liechtenstein	509	381	100	28
Lithuania	9,443	8,447	996	..
Luxembourg	2,607	1,493	1,114	..

Country/territory	Total	Print	Digital	Other formats
Madagascar (a)	186	186	..	..
Malaysia	22,856	19,432	3,424	..
Maldives (a)	125	125	..	..
Malta (a)	471	471	..	..
Mauritius (a, c)	1,712	1,712	..	..
Mexico	6,692	5,512	1,180	..
Monaco (a)	160	160	..	..
Montenegro (a)	1,448	1,448	..	..
Mozambique (a)	81	81	..	..
Myanmar (a)	2,461	2,461	..	..
Namibia (a, c)	291	291	..	..
Netherlands (Kingdom of the) (d)	23,400	13,441	9,947	12
New Zealand (c)	6,400	2,523	3,876	1
North Macedonia (a)	1,359	1,359	..	..
Norway	14,735	8,060	6,648	27
Pakistan (a)	1,911	1,911	..	..
Panama	804	780	24	..
Paraguay (d)	1,109	750	302	57
Peru	9,645	7,644	2,001	..
Philippines	1,352	987	365	..
Poland	40,598	32,408	8,128	62
Portugal (a)	14,637	14,637	..	..
Republic of Korea	89,110	69,562	19,391	157
Republic of Moldova	3,044	2,800	244	..
Romania	19,933	18,620	1,294	19
Serbia	11,850	11,843	..	7
Seychelles (a)	101	101	..	..
Singapore	21,345	19,510	1,835	..
Slovakia	6,272	5,770	483	19
Slovenia	8,713	6,861	1,822	30
Spain	98,289	70,484	26,970	835
Sri Lanka (a)	3,082	3,082	..	..
Sweden	18,594	17,852	281	461
Thailand	19,351	16,288	3,020	43
Trinidad and Tobago (a)	53	53	..	..
Türkiye	91,145	81,550	9,525	70
Uganda (a)	1,523	1,523	..	..
United States of America	264,722	21,894	242,828	..
United Kingdom (c)	167,000	91,244	75,756	..
Uruguay (a)	2,593	2,593	..	..
Uzbekistan	1,387	1,338	48	1
Viet Nam	29,969	27,085	1,619	1,265

(a) print only.
(b) digital deposits collected on a voluntary basis.
(c) 2021-2022 fiscal year.
(d) deposits are voluntary basis, as they are not covered by legislation.
.. not available.
Source: WIPO Statistics Database, September 2023.

F16. Total number of ISBN registrations, 2022

Country	Lifetime ISBNs registered	ISBNs registered in 2022
Albania	57,118	3,174
Argentina (a)	668,592	35,500
Australia	732,071	31,708
Bangladesh	261,050	10,298
Belgium (b)	355,164	12,637
Bolivia (Plurinational State of)	26,053	1,718
Bosnia and Herzegovina	37,788	2,163
Brazil	1,903,440	179,042
Bulgaria	275,945	12,738
Canada (French) (c)	538,819	21,105
Chile	137,174	8,288
Colombia	376,778	20,840

Country	Lifetime ISBNs registered	ISBNs registered in 2022
Costa Rica	41,668	1,959
Croatia (a, d)	187,084	7,179
Cuba (a)	60,599	1,944
Cyprus (a)	35,669	2,193
Czech Republic	699,730	34,985
Dominican Republic	16,714	1,937
Ecuador	79,955	5,128
El Salvador	11,875	719
Estonia (c)	176,594	25,391
Germany (a)	6,208,861	277,000
Ghana (c)	104,000	2,000
Greece	379,108	22,622
Guatemala	20,065	1,291
Hungary	523,467	20,339
Iceland	24,568	1,470
India	..	281,091
Indonesia (a)	1,140,407	107,856
Italy	2,529,479	139,970
Japan	3,611,444	902,311
Jordan	139,634	4,785
Kenya	15,166	854
Latvia (c)	97,631	3,411
Lithuania	149,938	4,748
Malawi	15,909	395
Malta	16,730	1,229
Mexico	..	27,534
Mongolia	..	3,794
Netherlands	1,991,206	59,283
Nigeria	507,228	14,392
Norway	452,695	9,033
Panama	22,890	1,319
Paraguay	17,982	1,030
Peru	121,596	8,310
Philippines (a)	200,414	9,889
Poland	2,314,876	99,995
Portugal (c)	481,333	21,115
Republic of Korea	4,487,852	338,237
Singapore	..	25,980
Slovakia	314,456	14,603
Slovenia	173,966	9,656
Spain	2,775,121	95,811
Sri Lanka (c)	199,415	6,705
Sweden (a)	855,135	37,338
Switzerland	466,074	9,490
Syrian Arab Republic	31,737	2,540
Thailand	484,068	19,362
Tunisia	22,305	3,143
Turkey	1,093,743	83,653
UK (a)	8,218,167	153,167
Ukraine	486,910	9,691
Uruguay	25,527	2,786
US	46,098,130	3,279,217
Venezuela (Bolivarian Republic of)	54,892	2,855

Note: the starting year for lifetime data varies. For example, lifetime data for Costa Rica starts from 1998, while for Indonesia it is from 2012 onwards.
(a) the relevant ISBN Agency believes the statistics to be possibly underestimated, especially in terms of the lifetime figures, owing to a lack of or insufficient data.
(b) data are for Dutch-speaking Flanders only.
(c) data are estimates provided by the relevant ISBN Agency.
(d) ebooks that are chargeable or for which registration is required are not included.
.. not available.
Source: International ISBN Agency and Centro Regional para el Fomento del Libro en América Latina y el Caribe (CERLALC), September 2023.

Additional information

Data description

Data sources

Intellectual property (IP) data are taken from the WIPO Statistics Database and based primarily on WIPO's annual IP statistics surveys (see below) and on data compiled by WIPO in processing international applications/registrations through the Patent Cooperation Treaty (PCT) and the Madrid and Hague Systems. Data are available from WIPO's Statistics Data Center at www.wipo.int/ipstats.

Patent family and technology data are extracted from the WIPO Statistics Database and from the 2023 spring edition of the European Patent Office's PATSTAT database.

Gross domestic product and population data are from the World Bank's World Development Indicators database.

This report uses the World Bank's income classifications. Economies are classified according to 2022 gross national income per capita, calculated using the World Bank Atlas method. The classifications are low-income (USD 1,135 or less), lower middle-income (USD 1,136 to USD 4,465), upper middle-income (USD 4,466 to USD 13,845) and high-income (over USD 13,845).

This report uses United Nations (UN) definitions of regions and sub-regions, whereas the geographical terms used may differ slightly from the ones defined by the UN.

WIPO's annual IP statistics surveys

WIPO collects data from national and regional IP offices, other competent authorities and publishers' associations from around the world through annual surveys consisting of multiple questionnaires. These data are then entered into the WIPO Statistics Database.

Continuous efforts are being made to improve the quality and availability of IP statistics and to gather data from as many IP offices and countries as possible.

WIPO's long-established and regular IP survey covers patents, utility models, trademarks, industrial designs and plant varieties. It consists of 27 questionnaires, all of which are available in Arabic, Chinese, English, French, Russian and Spanish at www.wipo.int/ipstats/en/data_collection/questionnaire.

In 2017, WIPO started to collect data on geographical indications (GIs) through an annual survey. This simple questionnaire seeks to collect data on GIs in force broken down by legal means of protection (e.g., *sui generis* systems, trademarks, international agreements, and so on) and products types (e.g., wines and spirits, agricultural products, and so on). This 2023 edition reports data for 91 authorities – a considerable improvement upon the 54 responses that WIPO received in 2017.

Global publishing industry survey

WIPO's survey of the global publishing industry was established in collaboration with the International Publishers Association (IPA) in 2017. In addition, WIPO has strengthened its cooperation with Centro Regional para el Fomento del Libro en América Latina y el Caribe (CERLALC) and the Federation of European Publishers (FEP) in order to reduce the burden on respondents and extend the geographical coverage of the survey. This year, the FEP compiled and shared data with WIPO for 16 European countries (FEP members). In addition, CERLALC provided data for several Latin America and the Caribbean countries. WIPO is grateful to CERLALC and the FEP for sharing data. The scope of the publishing industry survey is limited to (a) the trade and educational sectors, and (b) published materials (i.e., books, monographs, and so on) issued with an International Standard Book Number (ISBN), a Digital Object Identifier (DOI) or any other book identifier (e.g., ASIN, and so on). This edition includes publishing industry data for the 30 associations and authorities who shared their latest data with WIPO.

To validate the data collected through the global publishing survey, WIPO has begun to collect data on legal deposit. Legal deposit is a statutory obligation at the national level requiring publishers to deposit a certain number of copies of published documents at a repository, that is, a recognized place of legal deposit. In 2019, WIPO conducted a pilot survey among national legal repositories, to which 51 countries responded. This 2023 edition reports data for 82 authorities.

IP office survey coverage

Intellectual property offices are requested to report data by the origin (country or territory) of applications, grants or registrations. Offices unable to provide this detailed breakdown instead report either an aggregate total or a simple breakdown by total resident and total non-resident counts. For this reason, the totals for each origin are underreported. However, shares of the 2022 totals where the origin is unknown are low – only 1.4% for patent applications, 0.8% for trademark application class counts and 0.2% for application design counts.

IP applications data coverage by IP type

IP type	Number of offices on which 2022 world totals are based	Number of offices for which 2022 data are available	Data coverage (%)
Patents	162	140	99.7
Utility models	82	72	99.9
Trademarks (a)	167	141	99.5
Industrial designs (b)	157	128	99.9
Plant varieties	72	68	99.3

(a) Refers to the number of trademark applications based on class count (i.e., the number of classes specified in applications).
(b) Refers to the number of industrial design applications based on design count (i.e., the number of designs contained in applications).

Estimating world totals

World totals of applications for, and grants/registrations of, patents, utility models, trademarks, industrial designs and plant varieties are WIPO estimates. Data are not available for every IP office each year. Missing data are estimated using methods such as linear extrapolation and averaging adjacent data points. The estimation method chosen depends on the year and the office in question. When an office provides data that is not broken down by origin, WIPO estimates the resident and non-resident counts using the historical shares recorded at that office. Data are available for most of the larger offices; only small shares of world totals are estimated. For example, the estimated total number of patent applications worldwide covers 162 offices, with data available for 140 of these, which together account for 99.7% of the estimated world total.

National and international data

Application and grant/registration data include data on both direct filings and filings made through WIPO-administered international systems (where applicable). For patents and utility models, data comprise direct filings at national patent offices, as well as PCT national phase entries. For trademarks, data comprise filings at national and regional offices and designations received by relevant offices through the Madrid System. For industrial designs, data comprise national and regional applications combined with designations received by relevant offices through the Hague System.

International comparability of indicators

Every effort has been made to compile IP statistics based on the same definitions in order to facilitate international comparison. Although data are collected from offices using questionnaires from WIPO's harmonized annual IP survey, national laws and regulations for filing IP applications or for issuing IP rights, as well as statistical reporting practices, may vary between jurisdictions. Because of the continual updating of data and the revision of historical statistics, data in this report may differ from data in previous editions and from data available on WIPO's website.

Change in method of counting IP applications by CNIPA in 2017

Because of a change in the method by which the National Intellectual Property Administration of the People's Republic of China (CNIPA) calculates how many patent, utility model and industrial design applications are filed, data on the number of such applications filed in China in 2017 and 2018 are not comparable with data for previous years. Prior to 2017, these data included all applications received; from 2017 onwards they include only those applications for which the necessary application fees were paid. As a result, it is not meaningful to report growth rates in the number of patent, utility model and industrial design applications filed in China in 2017 compared to 2016. Moreover, since China accounts for such a large proportion of IP applications globally, it is not meaningful to report growth rates in the numbers of such applications filed worldwide in 2017 compared to 2016. For reason of this break in the data series, figures A1 (page 24), A53 (page 52), C1 and C2 (page 119) do not report 2017 growth.

IP systems at a glance

The patent system

A patent is a set of exclusive rights granted in law to applicants for an invention that meets the standards of novelty, non-obviousness and industrial applicability. It is valid for a limited period (generally 20 years), during which time the patent holder may commercially exploit the invention on an exclusive basis. In return, applicants are obliged to disclose their inventions to the public, so that they may be replicated by others skilled in the art. The patent system is designed to encourage innovation by providing innovators with time-limited exclusive legal rights, thus enabling them to appropriate returns from their innovative activity.

The procedures for acquiring patent rights are governed by the rules and regulations of national and regional patent offices. These offices are responsible for issuing patents and rights limited to the jurisdiction of the issuing authority. To obtain patent rights, applicants must file an application describing the invention with a national or regional office.

Applicants can also file an international application through the Patent Cooperation Treaty (PCT) System, an international treaty administered by WIPO that facilitates the acquisition of patent rights in multiple jurisdictions. The PCT System simplifies the process of multiple national patent filings by delaying the requirement to file a separate application in every jurisdiction in which protection is sought. However, the decision on whether to grant a patent remains the prerogative of national or regional patent offices and patent rights limited to the jurisdiction of each patent granting authority.

The PCT application process begins with the international phase, during which an international search and optional preliminary examination and supplementary international search are performed. It concludes with the national phase, during which national (or regional) patent offices decide on the patentability of an invention according to national law. Further information about the PCT System is available at www.wipo.int/pct.

The utility model system

Like a patent, a utility model (UM) confers a set of rights to an invention for a limited period, during which time the UM rights holder can commercially exploit their invention on an exclusive basis. The terms and conditions for granting a UM differ from those for granting a traditional patent. For example, UMs are issued for a shorter period (6–10 years) and at most offices protection is granted without substantive examination. As with patents, procedures for granting UM rights are governed by the rules and regulations of national IP offices and rights limited to the jurisdiction of the issuing authority. In this report, the term "utility model" refers to UMs and other types of protection similar to UMs, such as short-term patents in Ireland.

Microorganisms under the Budapest Treaty

The Budapest Treaty on the International Recognition of the Deposit of Microorganisms for the Purposes of Patent Procedure plays an important role in relation to biotechnological inventions. Disclosing an invention is a generally recognized requirement for receiving a patent. When an invention involves microorganisms, national laws in most countries require the applicant to deposit a sample at a designated International Depositary Authority (IDA).

To eliminate the need to deposit a microorganism in every country where patent protection is sought, under the Budapest Treaty the deposit of a microorganism with any IDA is sufficient for the purposes of patent procedures at the national patent offices of all contracting states and at any regional patent office that recognizes the Treaty. An IDA is a scientific institution - typically a "culture collection" - capable of storing microorganisms. As of September 2023, there were 49 IDAs around the world. Further information about the Budapest Treaty is available at www.wipo.int/treaties/en/registration/budapest.

The trademark system

A trademark is a sign used to distinguish the goods or services of one enterprise from those of another and is protected as an intellectual property (IP) right. Trademarks can be registered for both goods and services. In the latter case, the term "service mark" is sometimes used. For simplicity, this report uses "trademark," regardless of whether the registration concerns goods or services. The holder of a registered trademark has the exclusive right to use the mark in relation to the goods or services for which it is registered and can block unauthorized use of the trademark, or a confusingly similar mark, to prevent consumers from being misled. Unlike patents, trademark registrations can be maintained indefinitely, provided that the trademark holder pays the required renewal fees.

The procedures for registering trademarks are governed by the legislation and procedures of national and regional IP offices. Therefore, trademark rights are limited to the jurisdiction of the authority that has registered the trademark. Trademark applicants can file an application with a relevant national or regional IP office or an international application through the Madrid System. However, when an applicant files internationally via the Madrid System, the decision to issue a trademark registration remains the prerogative of the national or regional IP office concerned and trademark rights remain limited to the jurisdiction of the authority issuing that registration.

Between December 1995 and October 2016, two treaties administered by the World Intellectual Property Organization (WIPO) governed the Madrid System for the International Registration of Marks - the Madrid Agreement Concerning the International Registration of Marks, adopted in 1891, and the Protocol Relating to the Madrid Agreement, adopted in 1989. As of October 11, 2016, following a decision by the Madrid Union Assembly that no country could accede only to the Agreement, the Protocol is now the sole governing treaty of the Madrid System. The Madrid System offers many advantages to trademark holders and IP offices compared with the alternative method of obtaining international protection for marks called the Paris route or the direct route. The Paris route involves filing separate applications directly at the IP office in the countries or regions where protection is sought (under the Paris Convention for the Protection of Industrial Property). In contrast, by paying a single set of fees in a single currency (Swiss francs), the Madrid System allows trademark holders to submit a single application in one language (English, French or Spanish) indicating the Madrid members where protection is sought (designations).

The Madrid System also simplifies managing the mark once it has been registered by making it possible to request centrally the recording of further changes or to renew the registration through a single procedural step. A registration recorded in the International Register has the same effect as a registration made directly with every designated Contracting Party (Madrid member), if the competent authority of that jurisdiction has not issued a refusal within a specified time period. Further information about the Madrid System is available at www.wipo.int/madrid.

The industrial design system

Industrial designs are applied to a wide variety of industrial products and handicrafts.[1] They refer to the ornamental or aesthetic aspects of a useful article, including compositions of lines or colors or three-dimensional forms that give a special appearance to a product or handicraft. The holder of a registered industrial design has exclusive rights over the design and can prevent unauthorized copying or imitation of the design by others.

The procedures for registering industrial designs are governed by national or regional laws. An industrial design can be protected if it is new or original and rights are limited to the jurisdiction of the issuing authority. Registrations can be obtained by filing an application with a relevant national or regional IP office or by filing an international application through the Hague System. Once a design is registered, the term of protection is generally five years and may be renewed for additional five-year periods up to a total of 15 years, in most cases. In some countries, industrial designs are protected through the delivery of a design patent rather than design registration.

The Hague System comprises two international treaties – the Hague Act and the Geneva Act. The System makes it possible for an applicant to register industrial designs in multiple territories by filing a single application with the International Bureau of WIPO, thus simplifying the multinational registration process. Moreover, by allowing the filing of up to 100 different designs per application, the System offers considerable opportunities for efficiency gains. It also streamlines the subsequent management of industrial design registration, since it is possible to record changes or renew a registration through a single procedure for all territories. Further information about the Hague System is available at www.wipo.int/hague.

Plant variety protection

To obtain protection, a plant breeder must file an individual application with every authority entrusted with granting breeders' rights. A breeder's right is granted only when a variety is new, distinct, uniform and stable, and has a suitable denomination.

In the United States of America (US), two legal frameworks protect new plant varieties: the Plant Patent Act (PPA) and the Plant Variety Protection Act (PVPA). Under the PPA, whoever invents or discovers and asexually reproduces any distinct and new variety of plant – including cultivated sports, mutants, hybrids and newly-found seedlings, other than a tuber-propagated plant (in practice, Irish potato and Jerusalem artichoke) or a plant found in an uncultivated state – may obtain a patent. Under the PVPA, the United States of America protects all sexually-reproduced plant varieties and tuber-propagated plant varieties, excluding fungi and bacteria.

The geographical indication system

A geographical indication (GI) is a sign identifying a good as originating in a specific geographical area and possessing a given quality, reputation or other characteristic essentially attributable to that geographical origin. Thus, the main function of a GI is to indicate a connection between the quality, characteristics or reputation of the good and its territory of origin.

World-renowned examples of GIs include "Café de Colombia" (Colombia), "Bordeaux" (France), "Kampot Pepper" (Cambodia), "Penja Pepper" (Cameroon) and "Scotch Whisky" (United Kingdom).

Geographical indications are mainly used for agricultural and food products, which typically tend to have a close natural link with their place of origin. However, there are many GIs for other kinds of products, whose specific characteristics may derive from traditional manufacturing skills or from a combination of local know-how and natural resources. Examples of GIs for

1 The products and handicrafts to which industrial designs are applied range from technical and medical instruments to watches, jewelry and other luxury items, and from homeware, electrical appliances, vehicles and construction materials to textile designs and leisure goods.

handicraft and manufactured goods include "Bohemia Crystal" (Czech Republic), "Solingen" for cutlery (Germany), "Isfahan Handmade Carpet" (Islamic Republic of Iran) and "Swiss Made" for watches (Switzerland).

Although GIs are commonly names of places, they may also consist of non-geographical terms with a traditional geographical connotation (traditional denominations); for example, "Argane" (Morocco) serves as a GI, although not a geographical name.

Geographical indications can only be used on goods that conform to the applicable requirements concerning the area of origin, processing method and typicity of the product. Goods from production sites located outside the area of origin and goods that do not meet the applicable requirements are prohibited from using the protected indication.

Appellations of origin

An appellation of origin is a special kind of geographical indication. It generally consists of a geographical name or a traditional denomination that serves to designate a product as originating in a defined geographical area, where the quality or characteristics of the product are due exclusively or essentially to that geographical environment, including natural and human factors, and which have given the good its reputation. The most important difference between appellations of origin and other GIs is that the link with the geographical area should be stronger in the case of an appellation of origin; in other words, appellations of origin are a more restrictive sub-category of GI.

Protection of GIs

At the national and regional levels, GIs are protected through a variety of legal means. These include *sui generis* systems – that is, laws specifically designed to protect geographical indications,[2] often based on a registration procedure. *Sui generis* systems generally provide protection against any direct and indirect commercial use of a GI, as well as against its imitation. *Sui generis* systems for GI protection are used in many countries and also by two regional intergovernmental organizations: namely, the African Intellectual Property Organization (OAPI) and the European Union (EU).

Geographical indications can also be protected on the basis of trademark law, commonly through the use of collective and certification marks. Because trademarks incorporating geographical terms are typically not recorded by IP offices as a separate category of trademark, and because not all trademarks incorporating geographical terms can be considered to be GIs, it may be difficult to determine the exact number of registered GIs within jurisdictions. It is also worth noting that GI protection via *sui generis* or trademark systems are not mutually exclusive, but often coexist under many legal frameworks and are available for the benefit of GI holders.

Finally, GIs are typically also protected under unfair competition regulations, consumer protection laws and administrative and judicial decisions, as well as under specific laws or decrees recognizing individual GIs.

As for other IP rights, the effects of a GI right obtained in a particular jurisdiction are limited to the territory of that jurisdiction. Thus, where a right over a GI is obtained in one jurisdiction, it is protected there but not abroad. In order to obtain protection in a foreign jurisdiction, GI holders must, in principle, seek protection under the relevant national or regional laws of the jurisdiction in question. However, international agreements can facilitate the acquisition of GI rights abroad. In particular, bilateral and regional agreements have incorporated lists of GIs that are to be protected within the jurisdiction of the relevant parties to the agreement. The listed

2 The terminology used at national and regional levels to refer to *sui generis* rights over GIs is not uniform. Different terms, such as appellations of origin, controlled appellations of origin, protected designations of origin, protected geographical indications, (qualified) indications of source, or simply geographical indications are used in different legislations. Despite the different terminology, however, the common denominator remains the link between the specific quality, characteristics or reputation of the product and its territory of origin. For simplicity, the present text generally uses "geographical indication (GI)," regardless of differences in national and regional terminology.

GIs may relate to existing or subsequent GI rights, but protection may also emanate from the trade agreements themselves.

Another way of obtaining protection for GIs abroad is through two international registration systems administered by WIPO: namely, the Lisbon System and the Madrid System.

The Lisbon System

The Lisbon System was established in 1958 to facilitate the international protection of appellations of origin through a single registration procedure.[3] Registration with the WIPO International Bureau ensures protection in all Lisbon contracting parties, without the need for renewal and for as long as the appellation of origin remains protected within its contracting party of origin. However, the decision as to whether to protect a newly registered appellation of origin at the national or regional level remains the prerogative of each contracting party and each Lisbon member can refuse protection based on any ground foreseen at national or regional level within one year of being notified of a new appellation of origin by the WIPO International Bureau.

Globally-renowned examples of appellations of origin protected under the Lisbon System include "Tequila" for spirits (Mexico), "Chianti" for wines (Italy), "Habanos" for cigars (Cuba) and handicrafts such as "Chulucanas" for ceramics (Peru) and "Herend" for porcelain (Hungary). The scope of the System extends to non-geographical traditional names, such as "Reblochon" for cheese (France) and "Vinho Verde" for wines (Portugal).

In 2015, with the adoption of the Geneva Act of the Lisbon Agreement on Appellations of Origin and Geographical Indications - which entered into force on February 26, 2020 - Lisbon contracting parties modernized the System in order to attract a wider membership, while preserving its principles and objectives. The Geneva Act formally extends the scope of the Lisbon System to the general category of GIs in addition to appellations of origin. The new Act also opened the Lisbon System to accession by intergovernmental organizations, such as the EU and OAPI. It also made the Lisbon System more flexible so as to secure a wider recognition for, and inclusion of, the various means by which countries may protect appellations of origin and GIs at a national or regional level (e.g., *sui generis* systems, trademark laws or specific ad hoc decrees, as well as judicial and administrative decisions).

Protection of GIs abroad through the Madrid System

Geographical indications can be protected in several countries as trademarks (most commonly collective and certification marks) through the Madrid System, an international registration system legally governed by the Madrid Agreement (1891) and the Madrid Protocol (1989) and administered by WIPO. A famous example of a collective/certification mark registered under the Madrid System is Napa Valley for wines from the United States of America.

3 The Lisbon System is administered by WIPO and comprises the Lisbon Agreement for the Protection of Appellations of Origin and their International Registration (1958), as revised at Stockholm in 1967 and amended in 1979, and the Geneva Act of the Lisbon Agreement on Appellations of Origin and Geographical Indications (2015), which entered into force on February 26, 2020.

Glossary

This glossary provides definitions of key technical terms and concepts. Many are defined generically (for example, "application"), but apply to several or all of the various forms of intellectual property (IP) covered by this report.

Applicant
An individual or other legal entity that files an application for a patent, utility model, trademark or industrial design. There may be more than one applicant in an application. For the statistics in this publication, the name of the first named applicant is used to determine the origin of the application.

Application
The procedure for requesting IP rights at an office, which then examines the application and decides whether to grant protection. Also refers to a set of documents submitted to an office by the applicant.

Application abroad
For statistical purposes, an application filed by a resident of a given state or jurisdiction with the IP office of another state or jurisdiction. For example, an application filed by an applicant domiciled in France with the Japan Patent Office (JPO) is considered an application abroad from the perspective of France. This differs from a "non-resident application," which describes an application filed by a resident of a foreign state or jurisdiction from the perspective of the office receiving the application: the example above would be a non-resident application from the JPO's point of view.

Application date
The date on which an IP office receives an application that meets the minimum requirements.
Also referred to as the filing date.

Book
A book represents informational content in the form of many pages of text or images published in print and/or digital format in all manifestations.

Budapest Treaty
Disclosure of an invention is a requirement for granting a patent. Normally, an invention is disclosed by means of a written description. Where an invention involves a microorganism or the use of a microorganism, disclosure is not always possible in writing and can sometimes only be effected by depositing a sample of the microorganism with a specialized institution. To eliminate the need to deposit a microorganism in every country where patent protection is sought, under the Budapest Treaty the deposit of a microorganism with any International Depositary Authority (IDA) is sufficient for the purposes of patent procedure at the national patent offices of all contracting states and at any regional patent office that recognizes the Treaty.

Certification trademark
Certification marks are usually awarded for compliance with defined standards, but are not confined to any membership. They may instead be used by anyone able to certify that the products involved meet certain established standards. In many countries, the main difference between collective marks and certification marks is that collective marks may only be used by a specific group of enterprises – for example, members of an association – while certification marks may be used by anybody who complies with the standards defined by the owner of the certification mark.

Class
May refer to the classes defined in either the Locarno Classification or the Nice Classification. Classes indicate the categories of goods and services (where applicable) for which industrial design or trademark protection is requested. See "Locarno Classification" and "Nice Classification."

Class count
The number of classes specified in a trademark application or registration. In the international trademark system, and at certain national and regional offices, an applicant can file a trademark application specifying one or more of the 45 goods and services classes of the Nice Classification. Offices use either a multi-class or a single filing system. For example, the offices of Japan, the Republic of Korea and the United States of America (US), as well as many European IP offices, have multi-class filing systems. On the other hand, the offices of Brazil, Mexico and South Africa follow a single-class filing system, requiring a separate application for each class in which an applicant seeks trademark protection. To capture the differences in application and registration numbers across offices, it is useful to compare their respective application and registration class counts.

Collective trademark
Collective marks are usually defined as signs that distinguish the geographical origin, material, mode of manufacture or other common characteristics of goods or services of different enterprises using the collective mark. The owner may be either an association of which those enterprises are members or any other entity, including a public institution or a cooperative.

Community Plant Variety Office (CPVO) of the European Union (EU)
An EU agency that manages a system of plant variety rights covering all EU member states.

Design count
The number of designs contained in an industrial design application or registration. Under the Hague System for the International Registration of Industrial Designs, it is possible for an applicant to obtain protection for up to 100 industrial designs for products belonging to one and the same class by filing a single application. Some national or regional IP offices allow applications to contain more than one design for the same product or within the same class, while others allow only one design per application. In order to capture the differences in application and registration numbers across offices, it is useful to compare their respective application and registration design counts.

Designation
A request made in an international application or registration by which the applicant/international registration holder specifies the jurisdiction(s) in which they seek to protect their industrial designs (Hague System) or trademarks (Madrid System).

Direct filing
See "National route."

Educational publishing
Educational publishing refers to books intended for teaching in schools and educational institutions. This includes the following two sub-sectors: (a) school textbooks (K-12) are books for schools and (b) higher education publishing are books for colleges, universities, and other higher education institutions. Educational books should include books sold to educational institutions, governments or through specialist academic vendors and outlets, and so on.

Equivalent application
Applications at regional offices are equivalent to multiple applications, one in each of the member states of those offices. To calculate the number of equivalent applications for the Benelux Office for Intellectual Property (BOIP), the Eurasian Patent Organization (EAPO), the African Intellectual Property Organization (OAPI), the Patent Office of the Cooperation Council for the Arab States of the Gulf (GCC Patent Office) and the European Union Intellectual Property Office (EUIPO), each application is multiplied by the corresponding number of member states. For European Patent Office (EPO) and African Regional Intellectual Property Organization (ARIPO) data, each application is counted as one application abroad, if the applicant does not reside in a member state, or as one resident application and one application abroad, if the applicant resides in a member state. The equivalent application concept is used for reporting data by origin.

Equivalent grant (registration)
Grants (registrations) at regional offices are equivalent to multiple grants (registrations), one in each of the member states of those offices. To calculate the number of equivalent grants (registrations) for BOIP, EAPO, the EUIPO, the GCC Patent Office or OAPI, each grant (registration) is multiplied by the corresponding number of member states. For EPO and ARIPO data, each grant is counted as one grant abroad, if the applicant does not reside in a member state, or as one resident grant and one grant abroad, if the applicant resides in a member state. The equivalent grant (registration) concept is used for reporting data by origin.

European Patent Office (EPO)
The EPO is the regional patent office created under the European Patent Convention (EPC), in charge of granting European patents for EPC member states. Under Patent Cooperation Treaty (PCT) procedures, the EPO acts as a receiving office, an International Searching Authority and an International Preliminary Examining Authority.

European Union Intellectual Property Office (EUIPO)
The EUIPO is the office responsible for managing the EU trademark and the registered community design. The validity of these two IP rights extends across the jurisdictions of the 27 EU member states.

Filing
See "Application."

Foreign-oriented patent families
A special subset of patent families that comprises foreign-oriented patent families, this includes only those patent families with at least one filing office that differs from the office of the applicant's country of origin. Some foreign-oriented patent families include only one filing office, because applicants may choose to file directly with a foreign office. For example, if a Canadian applicant files a patent application directly with the United States Patent and Trademark Office (USPTO) without having first filed at the patent office of Canada, that application will form a foreign-oriented patent family.

Geographical indication
A geographical indication (GI) is a sign identifying a good as originating in a specific geographical area and possessing a given quality, reputation or other characteristic essentially attributable to that geographical origin. The main function of a GI is to identify goods while informing about a connection between the quality, characteristic or reputation of the good and its territory of origin.

Grant
A set of exclusive rights legally accorded to the applicant when a patent or utility model is granted or issued.

Gross domestic product (GDP)
The total unduplicated output of economic goods and services produced within a country as measured in monetary terms.

Hague System
The abbreviated form of the Hague System for the International Registration of Industrial Designs. The System comprises two international treaties: the Hague Act of 1960 and the Geneva Act of 1999. The Hague System makes it possible for an applicant to register up to 100 industrial designs in multiple jurisdictions by filing a single application with the International Bureau of WIPO. It simplifies multinational registration by reducing the requirement to file separate applications at each IP office. The System also simplifies the subsequent management of the industrial design, since it is possible to record changes or renew a registration through a single procedural step for all designated Hague members.

Industrial design
Industrial designs are applied to a wide variety of industrial products and handicrafts. They refer to the ornamental or aesthetic aspects of a useful article, including compositions of lines or colors or any three-dimensional forms that give a special appearance to a product or handicraft. The holder of a registered industrial design has exclusive rights against unauthorized copying or imitation of the design by third parties. Industrial design registrations are valid for a limited period. The term of protection is usually 15 years in most jurisdictions. However, differences in legislation exist, notably in China (which provides for a 10-year term from the application date).

In force
Refers to IP rights that are currently valid or, in the case of trademarks, active. To remain in force, IP protection must be maintained.

Intellectual property (IP)
Refers to creations of the mind: inventions, literary and artistic works, and symbols, names, images and designs used in commerce. IP is divided into two categories: industrial property – which includes patents, utility models, trademarks, industrial designs and geographical indications of source – and copyright, which includes literary and artistic works (such as novels, poems, plays, films), musical works, artistic works (such as drawings, paintings, photographs and sculptures) and architectural designs. Rights related to copyright include those of performing artists in their performances, those of producers of sound recordings in their recordings and those of broadcasters in their radio and television programs.

International Depositary Authority (IDA)
A scientific institution – typically a culture collection – capable of storing microorganisms that has acquired the status of an International Depositary Authority under the Budapest Treaty and provides for the receipt, acceptance and storage of microorganisms and the furnishing of samples thereof. As of September 2023, 49 such authorities were in existence around the world.

International Patent Classification (IPC)
An internationally recognized patent classification system, the IPC has a hierarchical structure of language-independent symbols and is divided into sections, classes, sub-classes and groups. IPC symbols are assigned according to the technical features in patent applications. A patent application that relates to multiple technical features can be assigned several IPC symbols.

International Union for the Protection of New Varieties of Plants (UPOV)
An intergovernmental organization established by the International Convention for the Protection of New Varieties of Plants (the UPOV Convention) that was adopted on December 2, 1961. UPOV provides and promotes an effective system of plant variety protection aimed at encouraging the development of new varieties of plants for the benefit of society.

Invention
A new solution to a technical problem. To qualify for patent protection, the invention must be novel, involve an inventive step and be industrially applicable, as judged by a person skilled in the art.

Lisbon System
The Lisbon System was established in 1958 and revised first in 1967 and then again in 2015 in order to facilitate the international protection of appellations of origin and geographical indications through a single registration procedure. Registration with the WIPO International Bureau ensures protection in all Lisbon contracting parties, without the need for renewal and

for as long as the appellation of origin or the GI remains protected in its contracting party of origin. However, the decision on whether to protect a newly registered appellation of origin or GI at the national or regional level remains the prerogative of each contracting party, and each Lisbon member can refuse protection based on any ground foreseen at national or regional level within one year of being notified of a new appellation of origin or GI by the WIPO International Bureau. The Lisbon System is flexible with regard to the means by which countries may provide protection at national or regional level for their appellations of origin or GIs (e.g., *sui generis* systems, trademark laws or specific ad hoc decrees, as well as judicial and administrative decisions).

Locarno Classification
The abbreviated form of the International Classification for Industrial Designs under the Locarno Agreement used for registering industrial designs. The Locarno Classification consists of 32 classes and their respective subclasses with explanatory notes, plus an alphabetical list of the goods in which industrial designs are incorporated and an indication of the classes and subclasses into which they fall.

Madrid System
An abbreviation describing the system for the international registration of trademarks, originally established by the Madrid Agreement Concerning the International Registration of Marks and later also governed by the Protocol Relating to the Madrid Agreement. Following a decision by the Madrid Union Assembly in October 2016, the Protocol is now the sole governing treaty of the Madrid System. The Madrid System is administered by the International Bureau of WIPO.

Maintenance
An act by the applicant to keep an IP grant/registration valid (in force), primarily by paying the required fee to the IP office of the state or jurisdiction providing protection. That fee is also known as a "maintenance fee." A trademark can be maintained indefinitely by paying renewal fees; however, patents, utility models and industrial designs can be maintained for only a limited number of years.

Microorganism deposit
The transmittal of a microorganism to an International Depositary Authority (IDA), which receives and accepts it, the storage of such a microorganism by the IDA, or both transmittal and storage.

National phase under the PCT
The phase that follows the international phase of the PCT procedure and which consists of the entry and processing of the international application in the individual countries or regions in which the applicant seeks protection for an invention.

National route
Applications for IP protection filed directly with the national office of, or acting for, the relevant state or jurisdiction (see also "Hague route," "Madrid route" and "PCT route"). The national route is also called the direct route or Paris route.

Nice Classification
The abbreviated form of the International Classification of Goods and Services for the Purposes of Registering Marks, an international classification established under the Nice Agreement. The Nice Classification consists of 45 classes, which are divided into 34 classes for goods and 11 for services. (See "Class.")

Non-resident
For statistical purposes, a "non-resident" application refers to an application filed with the IP office of, or acting for, a state or jurisdiction in which the first named applicant in the application is not domiciled. For example, an application filed with the Japan Patent Office (JPO) by an applicant residing in France is considered to be a non-resident application from the perspective of the JPO. Non-resident applications are sometimes referred to as foreign applications. A non-resident grant or registration is an IP right issued on the basis of a non-resident application.

Origin (country or region)
For statistical purposes, the origin of an application means the country or territory of residence of the first named applicant in the application. In some cases (notably in the United States of America), the country of origin is determined by the residence of the assignee rather than that of the applicant.

Paris Convention
The Paris Convention for the Protection of Industrial Property, signed on March 20, 1883, is one of the most important treaties, as it establishes general principles applicable to all IP rights. It establishes the "right of priority" enabling an IP applicant, when filing an application in countries other than the original country of filing, to claim priority of an earlier application filed up to 12 months previously for patents and utility models, and up to six months previously for trademarks and industrial designs.

Paris route
An alternative to the Hague, Madrid or PCT routes, the Paris route (also called the direct route or national route) enables individual IP applications to be filed directly with an IP office of a country/territory that is a signatory to the Paris Convention.

Patent
A set of exclusive rights granted by law to applicants for inventions that are new, non-obvious and commercially applicable. A patent is valid for a limited period (generally 20 years), during which time patent holders can commercially exploit their inventions on an exclusive basis. In return, applicants are obliged to disclose their inventions to the public in a manner that enables others skilled in the art to replicate the invention. The patent system is designed to encourage innovation by providing innovators with time-limited exclusive legal rights, thus enabling them to appropriate returns from their innovative activity.

Patent family
Applicants often file patent applications in multiple jurisdictions, meaning some inventions are recorded more than once. To take this into account, WIPO has indicators related to patent families, defined as patent applications interlinked by one or more of: priority claim, Patent Cooperation Treaty national phase entry, continuation, continuation-in-part, internal priority, and addition or division. WIPO's patent family definition includes only those patent families associated with patent applications for inventions and excludes those associated with utility model applications.

PCT System
The PCT, an international treaty administered by WIPO, facilitates the acquisition of patent rights in a large number of jurisdictions. The PCT System simplifies the process of multiple national patent filings by reducing the requirement to file a separate application in each jurisdiction. However, the decision on whether to grant patent rights remains the prerogative of national and regional patent offices, and patent rights remain limited to the jurisdiction of the patent granting authority. The PCT application process starts with the international phase, during which an international search and, possibly, a preliminary examination are performed, and concludes with the national phase, during which a national or regional patent office decides on the patentability of an invention according to national law.

Pending patent application
In general, this refers to a patent application filed with a patent office for which a patent has yet to be either granted or refused, and for which the application has not been withdrawn. In jurisdictions where a request for examination is required in order to begin the examination process, a pending application may refer to an application for which a request for examination has been received or one for which a patent has neither been granted nor refused, and for which the application has not been withdrawn.

Plant Patent Act (PPA) of the United States of America
Under the law commonly known as the "Plant Patent Act," whoever invents or discovers and asexually reproduces any distinct and new variety of plant, including cultivated sports, mutants, hybrids and newly-found seedlings, other than a tuber-propagated plant or a plant found in an uncultivated state, may obtain a patent therefor.

Plant variety
According to the UPOV Convention, plant variety means a plant grouping within a single botanical taxon of the lowest known rank which, regardless of whether the conditions for the granting of a breeder's right are fully met, can be defined by the expression of the characteristics resulting from a given genotype or combination of genotypes, distinguished from any other plant grouping by the expression of at least one of the said characteristics and considered as a unit with regard to its suitability for being propagated unchanged.

Plant variety title
Under the UPOV Convention, the breeder's right is granted (title of protection is issued) only when the variety is new, distinct, uniform, stable and has a suitable denomination.

Plant Variety Protection Act (PVPA) of the United States of America
Under the PVPA, the United States of America protects all sexually reproduced plant varieties and tuber-propagated plant varieties, excluding fungi and bacteria.

Prior art
All information disclosed to the public about an invention, in any form, before a given date. Information on prior art can assist in determining whether the claimed invention is new and involves an inventive step (i.e., is non-obvious) for the purposes of international searches and international preliminary examination.

Priority date
The filing date of the application on the basis of which priority is claimed. (See "Paris Convention.")

Publication date
The date on which an IP application is disclosed to the public. On that date, the subject matter of the application becomes prior art.

Publishing industry revenue
Total revenue refers to net revenue generated by sales and licenses excluding value-added and/or local sales tax. The net revenue calculation should exclude discounts offered to retailers and distributors. Whereas, revenue at market value is calculated from retail prices, including deductions for discounts, value-added tax, and so on.

Regional application/grant (registration)
An application filed with or granted (registered) by an IP office having regional jurisdiction over more than one country. There are currently seven regional offices: the African Intellectual Property Organization (OAPI), the African Regional Intellectual Property Organization (ARIPO), the Benelux Office for Intellectual Property (BOIP), the Eurasian Patent Organization (EAPO), the European Patent Office (EPO), the European Union Intellectual Property Office (EUIPO) and the Patent Office of the Cooperation Council for the Arab States of the Gulf (GCC Patent Office).

Registered Community Design
A registration issued by the EUIPO based on a single application filed directly with the office by an applicant seeking protection within the EU as a whole.

Registration
An exclusive set of rights legally accorded to the applicant when an industrial design or trademark is registered or issued. See "Industrial design" or "Trademark." Registrations are issued to applicants allowing them to make use of and exploit their industrial designs or trademarks for a limited period of time and can, in some cases (particularly in the case of trademarks), be renewed indefinitely.

Renewal
The process by which the protection of an IP right is maintained (kept in force). This usually consists of paying renewal fees to an IP office at regular intervals. If renewal fees are not paid, the registration may lapse. See also "Maintenance."

Resident
For statistical purposes, a resident application refers to an application filed with the IP office of, or acting for, the state or jurisdiction in which the first named applicant in the application is resident. For example, an application filed with the Japan Patent Office (JPO) by a resident of Japan is considered a resident application from the perspective of the JPO. Resident applications are sometimes referred to as "domestic applications." A resident grant/registration is an IP right issued on the basis of a resident application.

Trademark
A sign used to distinguish the goods or services of one undertaking from those of another. A trademark may consist of words and combinations of words (for instance, names or slogans), logos, figures and images, letters, numbers, sounds, or, in rare instances, smells or moving images, or a combination thereof. The procedures for registering trademarks are governed by the legislation and procedures of national and regional IP offices and WIPO. Trademark rights are limited to the jurisdiction of the IP office that registers the trademark. Trademarks can be registered by filing an application at the relevant national or regional office(s), or by filing an international application through the Madrid System.

Trade publishing
Trade publishing refers to books intended for the consumer market and distributed through various channels. It includes a wide variety of genres in fiction, non-fiction, children's and young adult books.

Utility model
A special form of patent right granted by a state or jurisdiction to an inventor or the inventor's assignee for a fixed period of time. The terms and conditions for granting a utility model are slightly different from those for normal patents (including a shorter term of protection and less stringent patentability requirements). The term "utility model" can also describe what are known in certain countries as "petty patents," "short-term patents" or "innovation patents."

World Intellectual Property Organization (WIPO)
A United Nations specialized agency dedicated to the promotion of innovation and creativity for the economic, social and cultural development of all countries through a balanced and effective international IP system. WIPO was established in 1967 with a mandate to promote the protection of IP throughout the world through cooperation between states and in collaboration with other international organizations.

Abbreviations

ARIPO	African Regional Intellectual Property Organization
BOIP	Benelux Office for Intellectual Property
CNIPA	National Intellectual Property Administration of the People's Republic of China
CPVO	Community Plant Variety Office of the European Union
EAPO	Eurasian Patent Organization
EPO	European Patent Office
EU	European Union
EUIPO	European Union Intellectual Property Office
GCC	Patent Office Patent Office of the Cooperation Council for the Arab States of the Gulf
GDP	gross domestic product
GERD	gross domestic expenditure of research and development
GI	geographical indication
IDA	International Depositary Authority
IP	intellectual property
IPA	International Publishers Association
IPC	International Patent Classification
JPO	Japan Patent Office
KIPO	Korean Intellectual Property Office
LAC	Latin America and the Caribbean
NPA	national publishers' association
OAPI	African Intellectual Property Organization
PPA	Plant Patent Act of the United States of America
PRO	public research organization
PVPA	Plant Variety Protection Act of the United States of America
UK	United Kingdom
UM	utility model
UN	United Nations
UPOV	International Union for the Protection of New Varieties of Plants
US	United States of America
USPTO	United States Patent and Trademark Office
WIPO	World Intellectual Property Organization

Annexes

Annex A. Definitions for selected energy-related technology fields

Energy-related technologies	International patent classification (IPC) symbols
Solar energy technology	E04D 1/30, E04D 13/18, F03G 6/06, F24J 2/00, F24J 2/02, F24J 2/04, F24J 2/05, F24J 2/06, F24J 2/07, F24J 2/08, F24J 2/10, F24J 2/12, F24J 2/13, F24J 2/14, F24J 2/15, F24J 2/16, F24J 2/18, F24J 2/23, F24J 2/24, F24J 2/36, F24J 2/38, F24J 2/42, F24J 2/46, F24S%, G02B 5/10, G02F 1/136, G05F 1/67, H01L 25/00, H01L 31/00, H01L 31/04, H01L 31/042, H01L 31/048, H01L 31/052, H01L 31/18, H01L 33/00, H02J 7/35, H02N 6/00, H02S
Fuel cell technology	H01M 4/00, H01M 4/86, H01M 4/88, H01M 4/90, H01M 8/00, H01M 8/02, H01M 8/04, H01M 8/06, H01M 8/08, H01M 8/10, H01M 8/12, H01M 8/14, H01M 8/16, H01M 8/18, H01M 8/20, H01M 8/22, H01M 8/24
Wind energy	B60L 8/00, F03D
Geothermal energy	F03G 4/00, F03G 7/05, F24J 3/08, F24T
Hydro	B63H 19/02, B63H 19/04, E02B 9/00, E02B 9/02, E02B 9/04, E02B 9/06, F03B, F03C

Note: For definitions of IPC symbols, see www.wipo.int/classifications/ipc. The correspondence between IPC symbols and technology fields is not always clear-cut, therefore it is difficult to capture all patents in a specific technology field. Nonetheless, the IPC-based definitions of the four technologies presented above are likely to capture the vast majority of related patents.
Source: WIPO.

Annex B. Composition of industry sectors by Nice goods and services classes

Industry sector	Abbreviation (where applicable)	Nice classes
Agricultural products and services	Agriculture	29, 30, 31, 32, 33, 43
Management, communications, real estate and financial services	Business services	35, 36
Chemicals	..	1, 2, 4
Textiles – clothing and accessories	Clothing and accessories	14, 18, 22, 23, 24, 25, 26, 27, 34
Construction, infrastructure	Construction	6, 17, 19, 37, 40
Pharmaceuticals, health, cosmetics	Health	3, 5, 10, 44
Household equipment	..	8, 11, 20, 21
Leisure, education, training	Leisure & Education	13, 15, 16, 28, 41
Scientific research, information and communication technology	Research & Technology	9, 38, 42, 45
Transportation and logistics	Transportation	7, 12, 39

Source: Edital®.

Annex C. Industry sectors by Locarno classes

Sector	Locarno classes
Advertising	20, 32
Agricultural products and food preparation	1, 27, 31
Construction	23, 25, 29
Electricity and lighting	13, 26
Furniture and household goods	6, 7, 30
Health, pharma and cosmetics	24, 28
ICT and audiovisual	14, 16, 18
Leisure and education	17, 19, 21, 22
Packaging	9
Textiles and accessories	2, 3, 5, 11
Tools and machines	4, 8, 10, 15
Transport	12

Source: Organisation for Economic Co-operation and Development (OECD).

www.ingramcontent.com/pod-product-compliance
Lightning Source LLC
Chambersburg PA
CBHW080539240926
51846CB00005BA/945
9789280535464